Beer

FOR

DUMMIES®

2ND EDITION

by **Marty Nachel**
with **Steve Ettlinger**

Foreword by Jim Koch
Brewer, Samuel Adams Boston Lager

WILEY

John Wiley & Sons, Inc.

Beer For Dummies® 2nd Edition

Published by
John Wiley & Sons, Inc.
111 River St.
Hoboken, NJ 07030-5774
www.wiley.com

WILEY

About the Authors

The course of **Marty Nachel's** life took a portentous turn in 1982, when a spontaneous road trip to Toronto led to an even more spontaneous tour of the Molson Brewery. Never before had Marty tasted beer so fresh and so diverse. With that new and wonderful sensory experience, the die was cast. Life had changed for the better.

Marty went on to visit many more breweries — somewhere in the neighborhood of 250 — in North America and Europe. More importantly, he started brewing his own beer at home (1985). Not satisfied with just tasting his own brew, he chose to become a Certified Beer Judge so he could taste others' beer as well (1986).

All the while Marty was brewing beer, judging beer, and touring breweries, he also furthered his career as a freelance writer on these topics. After his first article was published in *All About Beer* magazine (1987), there was no looking back. Marty's articles began appearing in many beer and food publications — in print and online.

By 1995, Marty had scored his first book contract, writing *Beer Across America,* which was based on the newsletters he wrote for the Beer of the Month club of the same name. The following year he authored the first edition of *Beer For Dummies,* followed immediately by *Homebrewing For Dummies.* Due to the ever-growing popularity of homebrewing, the second edition of *Homebrewing For Dummies* was written in 2008.

Never one to let his taste buds sit idle, Marty kept them busy by serving as a beer evaluator at the Beverage Testing Institute in Chicago from 1995 to 1998. That same year, Marty got the call from Denver — he was invited to judge beer at the Great American Beer Festival and is now a regular there.

For several years now, Marty has been hosting beer tastings and leading beer appreciation classes as well as beer sensory classes for homebrewing groups in the Chicago area.

Always looking for new opportunities to promote good beer, Marty recently launched the Ale-Conner Beer Certification program, which allows beer enthusiasts to prove their knowledge, passion, and appreciation of craft beer. Check out www.beerexam.com.

Steve Ettlinger is the book producer/editor/agent/co-writer of more than 40 consumer-oriented books and the author of 7, most of which are food- and drink-related (he produced the best-selling *Wine For Dummies*). His first book, *The Complete Illustrated Guide to Everything Sold in Hardware Stores,* has been in print since 1988. His most recent book is *Twinkie, Deconstructed.* You can find more information on Steve at www.steveettlinger.com.

Dedication

Marty Nachel: Dedicating this book to my wife, Patti, is but one miniscule way of acknowledging her endless patience and forbearance as I've rabidly pursued my avocation these past 20-some odd years (some odder than others). For all the times she listened to me babble on about a great beer I tasted or brewery I visited or watched me jet off to another beer festival or beer junket, I owe her so, so much more.

I also want to dedicate this book to my children, Drew and Jill, both now in college. They've visited more breweries in their young lives than most people do in an entire lifetime. Mostly in the course of family vacations, I'd schedule brewery stops in between visits to national parks and theme parks. They patiently endured my mania so I might continue to pursue my love of writing about beer. I hope that someday they'll recognize snippets of their youth in the pages of my books.

Authors' Acknowledgments

Marty Nachel: Acknowledgements are the least I can extend to a team of dedicated people at John Wiley & Sons, Inc., who have given their unwavering support and enthusiasm to this project. That team includes Tracy Boggier; David Lutton; my very patient and focused project editor, Georgette Beatty; copy editor Jennette ElNaggar; and Carrie Sherrill in the marketing department, who saw that my requests for publicity materials were promptly taken care of. Last but not least is technical reviewer Clay Robinson of the phenomenal Sun King Brewery in Indianapolis (I'm a fan!).

I consider myself fortunate to be one of the *For Dummies* authors. I'm indebted to book producer and co-writer Steve Ettlinger for opening the door to this opportunity way back in 1996, when we wrote the first edition of *Beer For Dummies*. Steve's focus and attention to detail helped make the book complete, but his wry wit added humor when and where it was needed most.

Grateful acknowledgments also go out to Candy Lesher, beer gourmand *par excellence*. Candy's contribution of original recipes in Chapter 14 of this book is invaluable. A huge thanks to her for lending her considerable talents and credentials to this effort. Also contributing to the success of this chapter on cooking with beer are recipe tester Emily Nolan and nutritional analyst Patty Santelli. They sure must enjoy their jobs.

Thanks also to the folks who provided permissions to use photos and artwork in this book, including Sarah Warman (on behalf of BrewDog), Eric Olson (PedalPub, LLC), Alastair Macnaught (Cask Marque), Steve Krajczynski and Mali Welch (Kona Brewing Co.), and Paul Virant and Jimmy McFarland (Vie Restaurant). Also, many thanks for the fantastic illustrations created by Liz Kurtzman.

Finally, the road that led to this book was long and enjoyable, and I had lots of company along the way. I'd like to acknowledge those individuals and organizations that have inspired, supported, or otherwise contributed to my passion for beer. They include the Bard of Beer Michael Jackson; Charlie Papazian; Randy Mosher, Ray Daniels, and many other long-time members of the Chicago Beer Society; Steve Kamp, Dick Van Dyke, and the Brewers of South Suburbia (BOSS); Robin Wilson; and all the neighbors, friends, and relatives who ever shared time with me in the pursuit and praise of good beer.

Steve Ettlinger: First of all, I'm eternally grateful to Marty Nachel for becoming my personal beer trainer, patiently explaining over and over again the intricate differences between the various beer styles. He taught me all I know about beer (my father taught me to appreciate it). I'm also in awe of Marty's sublime homebrewed beer.

Thanks to all those brewers and beverage salespeople who took time to answer my endless questions; to my sister, Betsy, and her pals for advice on beer appreciation; to my mother, Marge, for her editing as well as her testing of the beer-food recipes.

Special thanks go to CAMRA, in England, for research assistance, and to Tim Smith, my managing editor, for constant, patient revisions and fact-checking.

Thanks also to freelance editor Ted Scheffler as well as the knowledgeable Hercules Dimitratos of Fancy Grocery in New York City — my retail beer supplier.

Above all, I'm grateful to Dylan and Gusty (Chelsea, too) for their support and enthusiasm, especially when it came to extended deadlines and my having to burn so much midnight oil away from home.

Beer may be fun, but it took a lot of work to get here. I won't forget your help, all of you.

Publisher's Acknowledgments

We're proud of this book; please send us your comments at http://dummies.custhelp.com. For other comments, please contact our Customer Care Department within the U.S. at 877-762-2974, outside the U.S. at 317-572-3993, or fax 317-572-4002.

Some of the people who helped bring this book to market include the following:

Acquisitions, Editorial, and Vertical Websites

Senior Project Editor: Georgette Beatty

(Previous Edition: Melba Hopper)

Acquisitions Editor: Tracy Boggier

Copy Editor: Jennette ElNaggar

(Previous Edition: Diane L. Giangrossi)

Assistant Editor: David Lutton

Editorial Program Coordinator: Joe Niesen

Technical Editor: Clay Robinson

Editorial Manager: Michelle Hacker

Editorial Assistants: Alexa Koschier, Rachelle S. Amick

Art Coordinator: Alicia B. South

Cover Photo: © iStockphoto.com / Jill Chen

Cartoons: Rich Tennant (www.the5thwave.com)

Composition Services

Project Coordinator: Kristie Rees

Layout and Graphics: Claudia Bell, Carl Byers

Proofreaders: Lauren Mandelbaum, Toni Settle

Indexer: Valerie Haynes Perry

Illustrator: Elizabeth Kurtzman

Special Help
Elizabeth Rea, Jessica Smith, Jennifer Tebbe

Publishing and Editorial for Consumer Dummies

Kathleen Nebenhaus, Vice President and Executive Publisher

Kristin Ferguson-Wagstaffe, Product Development Director

Ensley Eikenburg, Associate Publisher, Travel

Kelly Regan, Editorial Director, Travel

Publishing for Technology Dummies

Andy Cummings, Vice President and Publisher

Composition Services

Debbie Stailey, Director of Composition Services

Contents at a Glance

Table of Contents

Foreword

I love beer. My dad was a brewmaster, so I grew up in breweries and came to appreciate the kettles, the tanks, and the smell of a brewery. As a kid, I read the family beer recipes, which had been handed down over six generations.

In 1984, when I brewed my first batch of Samuel Adams beer, there was no need for a basic guide book like *Beer For Dummies,* especially in the U.S. Mass-produced beers had undergone 40 years of becoming lighter and blander. And beers from abroad, then the only widely available alternative, were often stale because of their long, transoceanic crossing and lengthy warehousing.

But today, beer lovers are in heaven. We are in the midst of a genuine renaissance in what's known as craft brewing. Literally hundreds of new brands and styles are crowding the shelves and the bar backs — pretty intimidating for the uninitiated unless they have a copy of *Beer For Dummies* with them. Personally, I love walking into a bar and seeing a dozen tap handles for great, interesting beer styles.

I grew up knowing that beer can have all the nobility and complexity of a fine wine, and it's fun to see more and more people acknowledging that today.

I think it has to do with education. The more you know about beer — its ingredients, its history, its brewing — the more respect you have for it. That's why I applaud Marty Nachel and Steve Ettlinger for writing *Beer For Dummies.*

In this book, Marty and Steve tell you what good beer is and how to find and enjoy it. I appreciate the opportunity to endorse *Beer For Dummies* and am sure it will entertain you, educate you, and make you thirsty for a really great beer.

Cheers,

Jim Koch

Brewer, Samuel Adams Boston Lager

Jim Koch is credited by many as the leader in the current craft-brewing renaissance. As a brewmaster, he continues a family tradition — six first-born sons in his family have become brewmasters. Jim's own experience with brewing started at the age of four, when he tasted his first beer. He loved it.

In 1984, armed with his great-great-grandfather's original recipe for Samuel Adams beer, Jim started the highly successful Boston Beer Company. At the time, he didn't dream that there'd be a market for more than one style of Samuel Adams. Today, the Samuel Adams family of beers comprises over 30 different brews.

Introduction

··

*T*here once was a man named Stu —

About beer, he hadn't a clue.

At the behest of his chummies,

He read Beer For Dummies,

And now he's the Master of Brew!

Like many people, I first discovered beer while sitting on my father's knee. My earliest recollections of the beer that Dad drank were that it was always ice cold and foamed like soapsuds — probably an accurate taste descriptor as well. Too bad Dad bought the cheap stuff.

After years of unconsciously buying the cheapest beer, like my father did, I found that my regular beer started to become regularly boring and much less appealing. By chance, a tour of a famous brewery — Molson's, in Toronto — that made fresh, tasty beer in a number of traditional styles, opened my eyes to an undiscovered world of beery possibilities unavailable in the United States at that time. Beer drinking for me would never be the same again because I had discovered the secrets to true beer happiness: freshness and variety. From that point on, I went in search of good beer and got an education in the difference between it and mediocre beer (and worse).

Learning this difference wasn't only easy but also fun — so much fun, in fact, that I now make a living doing it! But even for the casual beer drinker, a little beer knowledge can turn a possibly daunting experience into an enjoyable one. Good beer, unlike fine wine, is widely available and relatively inexpensive, but choosing among all the various styles can be a little confusing without some help. If you've fallen in love with beer, you have plenty of ways to increase your beer appreciation. This book should be of help to neophyte and serious beer enthusiast alike. And the best news is that in the United States, good beer is being offered by more brewers every day.

And that's something to drink to!

About This Book

Beer For Dummies, 2nd Edition, is a reference tool above all. You don't have to read it from cover to cover (although I won't mind if you do); you can turn to any part, chapter, or section that gives you the information you need when you need it. If you decide to read the book in order, you'll find that the information is presented in a logical progression.

Conventions Used in This Book

I include the following conventions to help you navigate this book:

- **Boldface** highlights key words in bulleted lists and action steps to follow in a specific order.
- New terms and emphasized words are in *italics.*
- Web addresses appear in monofont.

When this book was printed, some of the web addresses I mention may have broken across two lines of text. If that happened, rest assured that I didn't include any extra characters (such as hyphens) to indicate the break. If you want to visit a website whose web address has been broken, just type exactly what you see in this book, as though the line break didn't exist.

One more note: You may notice that two names are on the cover of this book, yet the text is written in first person. Much of what is written in this book is anecdotal, opinionated, and based on personal experiences. Expressing these passages in a singular voice is much easier than attributing them individually to Steve or Marty.

What You're Not to Read

If you're in a hurry, feel free to skip any text that's marked with a Technical Stuff icon or featured in a sidebar (a shaded gray box). This information is interesting and sometimes entertaining, but not critical to gaining a deeper understanding of beer (unless you thrive on trivia and minutia).

Foolish Assumptions

When I was writing this book, I assumed only one thing about you, dear reader: You're looking for a resource to aid your understanding, purchasing, drinking, and all-around enjoyment of beer, whether you're new to beer and don't know much about it, or whether you're a beer enthusiast who wants to know more. You've come to the right place!

How This Book Is Organized

The first parts of this book are for people who have just discovered the world of quality beer and who may want to get a little background or check out some specific information about beer — or carry on an intelligent conversation with someone who happens to be a beer nut. The latter parts are more oriented toward those of you who have caught the beer bug or have gone completely nuts about beer. Ultimately, this book is a guide to increasing your beer drinking pleasure, from broadening your choices among the many styles of beer to opening your eyes to beer-related fun, like homebrewing or beer travel.

Part 1: Getting a Taste of Beer

These three chapters are meant to answer the first questions that most people who are new to the world of beer tend to ask.

- Chapter 1 lays the groundwork for understanding and appreciating beer in its many forms. You should probably take the time to read this chapter.

- Chapter 2 is all about the ingredients needed to brew great beer — and odd beer as well. You'd probably never expect the ingredients in some beer.

- Chapter 3 aims to answer the basic questions about how beer is made. Many drinkers are just plain curious, but you may want to know this stuff because beer labels and menus often mention the brewing process.

Part II: Taking a Look at Beer Styles — Old, New, and Revived, Too

For anyone who's just starting to learn about beer, this part is pretty important. Not only are all the old beer styles explained in detail, but also all the hot new beer styles and trends are given ample attention.

- Chapter 4 describes the most popular beer styles and defines the basic terms you see or hear used around beer. This chapter should help you make your first choices without being intimidated. It's really essential reading.

✔ Chapter 5 goes to great depths to demystify *real ale,* which is an old and traditional British form of serving beer that's rapidly gaining in popularity in the United States and elsewhere in the world.

✔ Chapter 6 points out that aging in wood is no longer the sole province of wineries and distilleries. This chapter is all about beer aged with wood.

✔ Chapter 7 attempts to describe and explain the nature of extreme beer. Curious about what qualifies as *extreme* beer? Read this chapter.

✔ Chapter 8 makes the lives of beer drinkers easier who, for various reasons, can't drink the same regular beer as most of us; you find out about organic, gluten-free, and kosher beer in this chapter.

Part III: Buying and Enjoying Beer

This part is where I make sure you get what you pay for. Beer is a perishable food and has to be shipped, stored, and sold as such. Often it isn't, making your life as a beer consumer fraught with perils — until you find the answers in this part.

Some beer lovers come dangerously close to being snobby about beer, almost like (shudder!) wine snobs, but this part helps you sort out the really important stuff to know about the enjoyment of beer (which is actually a very complex subject).

✔ Chapter 9 gives you the tools you need to shop for beer with confidence.

✔ Chapter 10 gets into the specifics of labeling laws and mysterious label lingo, while cutting through marketing department guff and bluster.

✔ Chapter 11 explains that there's a lot more to serving beer than you think.

✔ Chapter 12 is probably the most serious because tasting jargon is serious. Tasting beer isn't serious business, though. The bottom line: If you like it, it's good.

✔ Chapter 13 opens your eyes to the world of beer and food, a world that's easily enjoyed. Beer and wine comparisons and substitutions are covered in detail here.

✔ Chapter 14 shows that cooking with beer is not only easy but often more satisfying than cooking with wine. Recipes are included.

Part IV: Exploring Beer around the World and at Home

This part is for people who like to move around a bit. Your own local bars and homes aren't the only places to enjoy beer — this part gives you plenty of ideas for places around the world to explore and enjoy. But if you do like to hang around your home, consider brewing your own beer there.

- ✔ Chapter 15 covers the best places to find beer in North America, including beer bars, brewpubs, gastropubs, beer dinners, and festivals.
- ✔ Chapter 16 takes you on a trip to experience beer in far-flung places, such as Europe and Asia.
- ✔ Chapter 17 shows how easy it is to take a beer vacation — just leave the planning to others.
- ✔ Chapter 18 leads you by the hand as you brew your very first batch of beer, made from a just-add-water kit. As it happens, the same steps form the basis for brewing on the intermediate level with more ingredients and directions — covered in step-by-step fashion.

Part V: The Part of Tens

The Part of Tens is a *For Dummies* series tradition, and this part is where you can find new and different ways to increase your appreciation of beer, useful information about great beer cities around the world, as well as insider information on some of the biggest and best beer festivals that beer lovers can (and maybe should) attend.

Part VI: Appendixes

This part is the basic resource for all that is beer. Appendix A is loaded with information about beer styles, beer alcohol contents, and examples of commercial beers for each style. Appendix B provides a somewhat brief history of beer — from the hypothetical explanation of its discovery to the renaissance we're currently enjoying.

Icons Used in This Book

Icons are the pictures you see in the margins of this book. Here are descriptions of all the icons:

Text marked with this icon tells funny, intriguing, or just plain interesting beer trivia or lore. It's entertaining but also may be educational. This stuff is excellent material for beer-bar banter, if you're into that kind of thing.

This icon signals really important facts that are essential to know if you want to be sure you understand beer.

This icon shows pointers, suggestions, recommendations, and things to do yourself.

As you may guess, this icon means "Don't do this!" or "Pay attention and do this right the first time!" You'll harm your beer or beer experience if you blow it.

Text marked with this icon explains technical subjects that are important only if you're really getting into beer or you're really into technical stuff. The rest of you can easily skip these tidbits.

Where to Go from Here

Where to go from here? How about straight to your fridge to grab a beer before sitting down to leaf through this book.

Now, if you're new to beer, you may want start with basics about how beer is made in Chapters 2 and 3. If you're already into beer but not quite up on all the beer styles, check out Chapter 4. Do you consider yourself a foodie or a gourmand? If so, you're certain to find something of interest in Chapters 13 and 14. Are you a traveler looking for some beer-soaked adventures? Then you'll want to peruse Chapters 15, 16, 17, 20, and 21. But if you're already on your way to beer geekdom, head directly to Chapter 19 to seal the deal.

Note: Partly because beer is so widely available and partly because so many different people make beer, beer styles aren't always consistent from brand to brand. Artisanal brewers are notorious for putting their own little spin on beer styles, sometimes individualizing them to the point where they barely fit a style at all. What I've tried to do in this book is define the most important styles in everyday language, but you'll no doubt find other descriptions elsewhere that are stated differently. Descriptions mostly reflect an individual writer's perception, as a good many of the style descriptions aren't really definitive. I've followed the Beer Judge Certification Program (BJCP) guidelines as a base and added my own twist to make them more easily understood by the average reader.

If you're confused, don't worry. It's just beer, after all. Please go have one now!

Part I
Getting a Taste of Beer

In this part . . .

They say you have to learn to walk before you can run, so before you run to your local beer retailer, it may be a good idea if you walked through this part. This part is where the mysteries of beer are unraveled: what beer is made of and how it's made. These chapters lay out the basics you need to be comfortable as you pursue your new hobby — that is, beer drinking.

Chapter 1

Drink Up! Beginning with Beer Basics

In This Chapter

▶ Building beer from the ground up

▶ Checking out a variety of beer styles

▶ Buying and enjoying beer in different ways

▶ Taking a worldwide tour of beer

▶ Making your own brews

*T*o most people, beer is a simple, one-dimensional product that serves two primary purposes: as an antidote for thirst and as an inexpensive, easy-to-obtain intoxicant. (One's viewpoint is often determined by one's age.) In American culture, beer has generally been considered a blue-collar beverage, undeserving of respect or a rightful place on your dinner table.

From a more worldly perspective, particularly in those countries known for their brewing expertise, beer is an unpretentious — but respected — socially accepted libation meant to be enjoyed on any occasion or at any time of day. It's also produced in various flavors and regional styles that make it more conducive to comparative tasting and even (gasp!) enlightened discussion.

Historically speaking, beer was for the longest time a staple in the human diet, as well as the respected handicraft of the local brewer. Beer was not only a means of refreshment but also an important source of vitamins and nutrients in a form that was happily ingested and easily digested. Looking far beyond written history, beer has also been theoretically linked with the civilization and socialization of mankind. Impressive, no?

In this chapter, I give you an introductory tour of the wonderful world of beer: its ingredients, its styles, its uses, and much more. Enjoy!

One of the side benefits of the current beer craze is the profusion of websites you can visit in search of good information about beer. Notice that I said *good information;* plenty of bad information is out there, too. To make sure you get lots of the good and none of the bad, here are just a few sites you can rely on for trustworthy and timely beer info:

✔ www.beerinfo.com

✔ www.beerme.com

✔ www.brewersassociation.org

✔ www.craftbeer.com

✔ www.realbeer.com

Introducing Beer's Building Blocks

So what is beer exactly? By excruciatingly simple definition, *beer* is any fermented beverage made with a cereal grain. Specifically, beer is made from these four primary ingredients:

✔ Grain (mostly malted barley but also other grains)

✔ Hops (grown in many different varieties)

✔ Yeast (responsible for fermentation; based on style-specific strains)

✔ Water (accounts for up to 95 percent of beer's content)

Grain provides five things to beer:

✔ **Color:** The color of the grains used to make a beer directly affects the color of the beer itself.

✔ **Flavor:** The flavor of the beer is primarily that of malted barley, although hops and yeast characteristics play a secondary role.

✔ **Maltose:** *Maltose* is the term for the fermentable sugars derived from malted grain. Yeast converts these sugars into alcohol and carbon dioxide.

✔ **Proteins:** Proteins in the grain help form and hold the *head* (foam) on the beer.

✔ **Dextrins:** *Dextrins* are the grain components that help create *mouthfeel* (the feeling of fullness or viscosity) in the beer.

 Archaeologists and anthropologists have helped shed some light on the development of beer around the world. Evidence of beer making throughout the millennia has been found on six of the seven continents on earth (no harvest in Antarctica). Wherever grains grew wildly, the indigenous people made a beer-like beverage with them. Here are some examples:

✔ Asians used rice.

✔ Mesopotamians used barley.

✔ Northern Europeans used wheat.

- ✔ Americans used corn.
- ✔ Africans used millet and sorghum.

Over time, beer makers discovered that barley lent itself best to beer making, with the other grains playing a lesser role.

Hops provide beer with four attributes:

- ✔ **Bitterness:** Bitterness is essential to the flavor balance of the beer; it off-sets the sweetness of the malt.
- ✔ **Flavor:** Hops have flavor that's distinctly different from bitterness, and it adds to the overall complexity of the beer.
- ✔ **Aroma:** The piquant aroma of hops, which mirrors their flavor, is derived from essential oils in the hops.
- ✔ **Stability:** Hops help provide the beer with stability and shelf life; their beta acids stave off bacterial contamination.

Brewers choose yeast strains based on which style of beer is being made (see the next section for an introduction to beer styles). The two main classifications of beer yeast are

- ✔ Ale yeast *(Saccharomyces cerevisiae):* Top-fermenting
- ✔ Lager yeast *(Saccharomyces uvarum):* Bottom-fermenting

The quality of brewing water is extremely important because beer is about 90 to 95 percent water. The mineral content of water can be manipulated and adjusted according to the requirements of the beer style being brewed.

For additional information on beer ingredients, check out Chapter 2. See Chapter 3 to find out how these ingredients are magically turned into beer during the brewing process.

Surveying Different Styles of Beer

As a generic word, *beer* includes every style of fermented malt beverage, including ales and lagers and all the individual and hybrid styles that fall under this heading. I provide a quick introduction to major beer styles in the following sections; for greater detail, check out Chapter 4 and Appendix A.

Within the realm of major beer categories, you find some truly special brews, such as real ale, barrel-aged and wood-aged beer, extreme beer, organic beer, gluten-free beer, and kosher beer. These kinds of beers don't represent new or different beer styles, per se. Rather, they represent different ways of making and presenting beer. Chapters 5 through 8 provide insight into these beers.

Ales versus lagers

The two major classifications of beer types are ale and lager. Every beer enthusiast should know some basic facts about these classifications:

- ✔ Ales are the ancient types of beer that date back into antiquity; lager beers are relatively new (only several hundred years old).

- ✔ Ales are fermented at relatively warm temperatures for short periods of time, while lagers are cold fermented for longer periods of time.

- ✔ Ales are fermented with *top-fermenting yeasts* (the yeasts float on top of the beer during fermentation), while lagers are fermented with *bottom-fermenting yeasts* (the yeasts sink to the bottom of the beer during fermentation).

Painless so far, right? Now to delve a little deeper: Within the ale and lager classifications, major beer style categories include Pale Ales and Brown Ales (in the ale family) and Pilsners and Dark Lagers (in the lager family). And the majority of major beer style categories include several different beer sub-styles. Here are just two examples of how this beer hierarchy plays out; many others are similar to these.

Stout (a type of ale)
Irish Dry Style Stout
London Sweet Style Stout
Foreign Style Stout
Oatmeal Stout
Russian Imperial Stout

Bock (a type of lager)
Traditional Bock
Helles Bock
Maibock
Doppelbock
Eisbock

Hybrid and specialty beers

In addition to the two major beer classifications (ales and lagers), a third beer classification that's an amalgam (more or less) of the first two is *hybrid beers.* Hybrid beers cross over ale and lager style guidelines. A beer fermented at cold temperatures, using an ale yeast, is an example of a hybrid, likewise for a beer that's warm fermented, using lager yeast.

Specialty beers, on the other hand, are practically limitless. This unofficial style of beer covers a very wide range of brews that are hard to define, much less regulate. Typically, specialty beers are brewed to a classic style (such as Porter or Weizenbier) but with some new flavor added; some are made from unusual foods that are fermented. Guidelines are useless, and brewing anarchy rules the brewhouse. The rules-be-damned attitude is what makes specialty beers so fun to brew and drink.

Shopping for and Savoring Beer

With the ever-increasing number of flavorful beers being made at craft breweries, along with the growing bounty of beers imported from elsewhere, today's beer consumers face monumental decisions every time they have to make a beer choice. The following sections provide pointers for buying, serving, tasting, dining with, and cooking with beer.

Buying beer

Beer is food. And like most foods, especially bread, beer is perishable and becomes stale over time, so the fresher the beer, the better it is. Therefore, beer consumers on the way to enlightenment want to consume beer that's freshly made and has been handled properly to maintain freshness — particularly if it has no preservatives, as is the case with most good beers.

Beer freshness has three enemies: time, heat, and light. Anything you can do to avoid buying beer that's been mistreated (and to avoid mistreating it yourself) is done in the name of fresh, tasty beer. Check out Chapter 9 for the full scoop on buying beer wisely.

As with all beverages that contain alcohol, governments maintain strict control over the labeling of those beverages. Unfortunately, when it comes to beer, the labels don't always help consumers understand what they're really buying. Similarly, breweries take liberties when they market their beers; these marketing liberties also lead to confusion on the part of the consumer. Chapter 10 walks you through this minefield of label laws and liberties to help you make good beer-buying choices.

Serving and tasting beer

Serving and tasting beer don't seem to be activities that require diligence, but, as a matter of fact, they do. Failing to properly serve a beer can have a measurable effect on your beer drinking pleasure.

Here are some pointers for proper beer enjoyment:

- **Make sure the beer is properly chilled or warmed, depending on the beer style.** Most beers should be served around 42 degrees Fahrenheit. (Make sure the beer isn't so cold that it numbs your tongue.) But some beers should be served lightly chilled or at room temperature.

> ✔ **Always pour your beer into a drinking vessel.** In other words, never drink straight from the can or bottle. Pouring your beer into a glass releases carbonation, which creates a head (and reduces its gassy "bite") and brings out more of the beer's aroma.
>
> ✔ **Always make sure your beer glasses are properly cleaned and stored.** Dirty, smelly glasses can ruin your beer and be a bad reflection on you.

For more tips on serving and tasting beer, have a look at Chapters 11 and 12.

Dining with beer

Where wine was once the preeminent beverage on dinner tables, it's now being boldly challenged by the formerly blue-collar beverage called beer. People everywhere are discovering just how versatile and interesting beer is when you pair it with appropriate food choices.

Here are a couple of simple rules to get you started:

✔ Think of the lager beer category as the white wine equivalent. When compared to ales, lagers have the following characteristics:

- Generally lighter in body and color

- Narrower flavor profile and a high degree of drinkability (that is, tend to appeal to a wider audience)

✔ Think of the ale category as the red wine equivalent. When compared to lagers, ales have these qualities:

- Typically darker

- Rounder, more robust, and more expressive

- Wider flavor profile and thus a lower drinkability (that is, tend to appeal to those with a more experienced beer palate)

Just to keep you on your toes, keep in mind that these guidelines are really general — full-bodied Dark Lagers exist just as surely as do light Mild Ales.

Still curious about dining with beer? Turn to Chapter 13 to learn more about successful beer and food pairings.

Cooking with beer

Sure, cooking with beer has been a kitchen standard for eons — if you consider dumping a can of Olde Foamy into a pot of chili "cooking with beer." With all the new and interesting beers in the market these days, chefs and gourmands have a newfound interest in beer, and they're flexing their fun muscles in the kitchen.

Intimidated by the thought of cooking with beer? Consider the following factors when choosing a beer for cooking purposes:

✔ **Color:** Beers brewed with a lot of dark grain, such as Stout and Porter, are likely to transpose their color to your meal — not an appetizing hue for fettuccine Alfredo or scrambled eggs.

✔ **Level of sweetness (maltiness) versus level of bitterness (hoppiness):** Malt is by far the predominant beer flavor in a recipe, but beer's bitterness increases with *reduction* (that is, the decrease in volume caused by boiling). In general, go with a mild beer rather than a bold one and avoid highly hopped beers, such as some Pale Ales. Reserve the sweeter, heavier beers (such as Belgian Tripels or Scotch Ales) for dessert mixes and glazes. *Note:* As water and alcohol boil off, both the sweet and bitter flavors of the beer intensify.

✔ **Other flavors:** Beers are available in a wide variety of styles, many with flavors that aren't traditionally associated with beer. You may encounter Fruit Beers, Chocolate Beers, Sour Beers, and Smoked Beers, among others. These flavored beers present many culinary possibilities in their own right, but they're just not meant for use in the average recipe.

Undaunted? Chapter 14 has good info on this topic (and some great recipes!).

Taking a Tour of Beers around the Globe

Craft and artisanal beer has gotten so popular in the past several years that people are even organizing vacations and launching spontaneous jaunts in search of good beer. In the following sections, I introduce you to the beer scenes in North America, Europe, and other spots around the world. Make your way to Chapters 15, 16, and 17 for more about beer travel.

North America

Despite beer's decidedly European roots, North American beer explorers don't have to travel very far to find good beer. People can find lots to celebrate and explore in North American breweries, beer festivals, and brewery museums. With more than 2,000 craft brewers or brewpubs now plying their trade in the United States and Canada (more than 1,700 in the U.S. alone), you can find good beer just about everywhere. The majority of these craft brewers are brewpubs where you can sample the local brew while enjoying a good meal. The same can be said for the growing number of beer bars and gastropubs that continue to spring up in urban areas.

Europe, Asia, and beyond

Although beer wasn't born in Europe, it grew up there and became the world's most popular beverage because of European brewers. Commercial brewing has been serious business in Europe since the 12th century. Since then, it's been a major European export to the rest of the world. Not just the beverage itself, but also European technology and expertise to make good beer have helped build the brewing industries in Asia and elsewhere.

 You can drink well in almost all European countries, but the crown jewels of beerdom are Germany (especially Munich and Bavaria as a whole), the United Kingdom, Ireland, Belgium, and the Czech Republic. The pub culture in most of the major brewing nations is mostly intact, and a visit to practically any local bar is likely to yield a good beer discovery. In Germany, you can become overwhelmed by the sheer number of breweries that exist (Bavaria alone has more than 600), while beer trekkers in Belgium may get thoroughly bewildered by the variety of unusual beer styles served at any given bar.

Australia gets an honorable mention as a beer-drinking country, especially because it's not in Europe. Despite the deep Anglo influence on the Australian brewing industry and an occasional well-made ale, it's primarily a lager beer country-continent.

Japan, China, and Thailand owe their brewing successes to the Germans, who greatly influenced beer production and consumption in these Asian countries. In more recent years, however, the American craft-brewing industry has begun to attract interest in these Asiatic countries — especially Japan.

Brewing Your Own Beer

The world's first beer producers (around 8,000 BC) made beer at home for personal (or communal) consumption; hence, homebrewing has been around since the beginning. This practice continued well into the Middle Ages, when beer making became more of a business, although homebrewing never stopped completely. In fact, brewing beer at home is what got thousands of Americans through 13 years of prohibition, when production of alcoholic beverages was against the law.

Homebrewing is also credited with sowing the seeds of the current craft beer renaissance. Many of today's artisan brewers started brewing beer in their own homes before going pro. (It's no coincidence that homebrewing became legal in 1979, and the craft beer movement began in the early 1980s.)

Ever dream about making your own beer at home? Well you may be surprised by how easy the process is — and how great the reward. All you need is access to a good equipment and ingredient supplier, good instruction (see Chapter 18), and some patience.

Chapter 2

From the Sublime to the Ridiculous: Beer Ingredients

*B*eer is made almost entirely of water. Expensive water. Water that's been steeped, boiled, cooled, flavored, aged, pumped into a bunch of places, sealed inside a container, and finally shipped to you. But although water is the dominant ingredient, there's a whole lot more to beer than just water. The taste and style of beer are profoundly affected by the individual ingredients used in the beer-making process, even though only four ingredients are absolutely necessary to make good beer. The fab four are:

- ✔ Barley
- ✔ Hops
- ✔ Yeast
- ✔ Water

These four ingredients form the basic foundation of beer (most fine beers are made *only* from these ingredients). This chapter explores the four main ingredients of beer and their contributions to that delicious brew. However, beer making isn't without experimentation, and new and unique ingredients are now being used in brewing to explore different flavor possibilities. I also introduce you to some of those nontraditional ingredients that are used for better or worse by some brewmasters.

Barley: Cereal for Beer, Not for Breakfast

What comes to mind when you think of cereal grains? Rice Krispies, Corn Flakes, Wheat Chex, Quaker Oatmeal? You may be surprised to know that cereal grains (not the flakes, the grains) and many other grains can be used to make different kinds of beer. But the cereal grain that lends itself best to beer making is barley (shown in Figure 2-1).

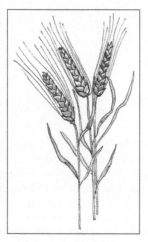

Figure 2-1: Barley, a cereal grain, has natural starches that brewers convert into sugars that feed the yeast during the fermentation of beer.

Before barley grain can be used to make beer, it must undergo a process known as *malting*, in which moisture stimulates the natural germination process inside the grain (see Chapter 3 for more about beer processes).

Malted barley gives beer its color, malty sweet flavor, dextrins to give the beer body, protein to form a good head, and perhaps most important, the natural sugars needed for fermentation. Barley's role in beer making is equivalent to grapes' role in winemaking: fundamental. Malted barley comes in a variety of colors, flavors, and degrees of roastiness that profoundly affect the color and taste of the beer.

Although barley is the most commonly used grain in beer making, many brewers use additional grains, such as wheat, oats, or rye, to imbue their beer with different flavors. These *specialty grains* all serve the purpose of creating different flavors and levels of complexity in the beer (and perplexity in the beer critic). The principal difference between these grains and cheaper, adjunct grains, like rice or corn (see the later section "Wing of Bat, Eye of Newt: Adjuncts You May Love or Hate") is that specialty grains enhance the barley, not replace it.

Hops: Flowers for Flavor and Aroma

Hops are the pinecone-like flowers of a female climbing plant in the cannabis family of plants (see Figure 2-2). They're grown on enormous trellises as tall as 18 feet (5.5 meters). Traditionally, hops were hand-picked because they're so delicate, but that's a rarity these days.

Figure 2-2:
Hops are vining plants with cone-like flowers that give beer its bitterness and unique aroma and flavor.

Hops contain pinhead-sized glands of *lupulin,* a sticky substance that's secreted when boiled. Lupulin contains the essential oils, bitter acids, and resins that do the following four big jobs in beer making — a lot of work for a tiny flower:

- Contribute bitterness that counterbalances the sweetness of the barley
- Add flavor
- Provide aroma
- Help preserve the beer

Hops' unmistakably pungent aromatics (sometimes described as spicy, herbal, floral, piney, and citrusy) are unique; however, prior to the common use of hops in the Middle Ages, bitter herbs and spices, like juniper berries (which are now used to make gin), were used. Beers with strong hop aroma and flavor are said to be *hoppy,* and beer fans who crave this kind of beer are said to be *hopheads.* To them, hoppy = happy!

Hops' fourth benefit to beer — natural preservation — was realized several centuries after the advent of regular hop usage. While the alpha acids in the hops are responsible for bittering the beer, the beta acids have been found to counteract and delay the inevitable effects of bacterial spoilage, thereby giving beer a longer shelf life.

Hops history

In ninth-century central Europe, hops were cultivated for the first time instead of being picked in the wild. Records show that hop growing flourished in Bohemia in 859. Prior to hop usage in beer making, brewers bittered their beer with flowers, leaves, berries, spices, and a host of odd and unpalatable ingredients, many of which failed miserably. By the 16th century, hops had become the most widely accepted spice for beer.

In the following sections, I talk about hop varieties and their bittering potential, aromatic properties, and flavor qualities. I also touch on what types of hops brewers use during different stages of the brewing process.

Nothing that occurs naturally in the beer-making process is pathogenic, or virally harmful to your health. (Note the use of the word *naturally*. . . .)

Getting to know top hops

Scores of hop varieties are grown in five major hop-growing regions throughout the world. You'll often see these varietal names on labels and beer menus. Many of the various hop varieties have been dubbed with names that hint at their origins in these regions; here's just a small sampling:

- ✔ East Kent Goldings (England)
- ✔ Saaz (Bohemia, Czech Republic)
- ✔ Hallertau (Germany)
- ✔ Pride of Ringwood (Tasmania)
- ✔ Cascades (U.S. Pacific Northwest)

Most of the North American hops are grown in the Pacific Northwest. North American hops are pretty assertive, meaning that they leave no doubt about their presence in the beer. *Centennial,* primarily a bittering hop, and *Cascade,* an aroma hop, are among the best known (see the section "Hopping for bitterness, aroma, and more" for more on bittering and aroma hops).

The vast majority of the hop varieties (or *cultivars*) are hybrids of original varieties, cross-bred to capitalize on specific genetic qualities, such as high yields and resistance to disease. An amazing amount of effort has gone into cultivating hops, considering that they're used so sparingly in the beer-making process, almost like herbs in cooking.

Hopping for bitterness, aroma, and more

Each kind of hop is distinctive in its bittering, aroma, and flavor profile. The differences between them are sometimes so subtle that even experienced beer judges are hard put to recognize the use of different hops in a given brew.

Each hop variety is more or less bitter, just like rejected lovers. Only instead of being measured in the number of forlorn letters and pleading phone calls, hop bitterness is measured scientifically and expressed in terms of alpha acid content, from a low of about 2.5 percent to a high of about 15 percent.

Brewers learn these bitterness numbers so they can determine what they call the *bittering potential* of each hop variety, which allows them to substitute different types of hops (because of availability or price) and to determine the exact quantity of hops needed for a particular brew recipe. They also learn each variety's unique aromatic and flavor properties, which helps them decide how the hops should be used. And, in case you're wondering, the brewers generally aren't bitter with their lovers (or so I'm told), though they may love their British Bitters.

The distinctive aroma of each type of hop comes from the essential oils that dissipate during the boiling part of brewing, so some hops are added after that stage in order to get their aroma into the beer, in a step known as *late kettle hopping*. If the brewer wants even more hop aroma in the beer, he'll add hops directly to the beer in the fermenter or aging tanks in a process known as *dry hopping*.

Brewers take into account all these variables — bitterness, flavor, and aroma — when designing a beer recipe. That's why you see hops mentioned on some beer menus. People actually know and appreciate this stuff!

Yeast: A Fungus Is Among Us

Yeast works hard but really enjoys itself (like me, most of the time). This little, single-cell organism, one of the simplest forms of plant life, is responsible for carrying out the fermentation process in beer making, thereby providing one of life's simplest forms of pleasure (and its production of carbon dioxide is what causes bread dough to rise).

Many brewers consider their yeast to be their most secret ingredient and often guard its identity jealously, calling it a *proprietary* ingredient.

Yeast is in the fungus family and, because of its cell-splitting capabilities, is self-reproducing. Yeast has a voracious appetite for sweet liquids and produces abundant quantities of alcohol (ethanol) and carbon dioxide in exchange for a good meal (which means that yeast is also responsible for producing brain-splitting headaches if you drink too much).

The vast majority of beer contains between 4 and 6 percent alcohol, but occasionally, brewers make beer with higher alcohol contents. In these beers, after reaching a level of 8 or 10 percent alcohol by volume, the beer yeast falls into a stupor, and fermentation is effectively over. When the brewmaster wants higher alcohol levels, he uses hardy champagne yeast to do the job.

Ale yeast has a lineage that reaches into antiquity — wild, airborne strains did the trick. Yeast wasn't even considered an ingredient in beer until its role in fermentation was discovered and understood. (This discovery began with the invention of the microscope in the early 1700s and was furthered by Louis Pasteur nearly a century later when Pasteur proved that a rapid heating process would kill bacteria and other microorganisms. Pasteur was more interested in beer than milk, by the way, as am I.) The genetically engineered lager yeast variety was perfected only in the mid-1800s. This factoid isn't all that important, except that before this discovery, brewers couldn't make what's now called a lager by plan. They had to brew ale, ferment and store it at cold temperatures, and hope for the best.

In the early days, knowing only that the frothy, sludgy substance that accumulated on the top of a vat of fermenting beer was somehow responsible for turning raw, sweet stuff into finished beer, English-speaking brewers spoke from the heart when they christened it *Godisgood,* and when warm-weather fermentations went sour, they blamed it on beer witches.

Nowadays, brewers can order yeast strains from a catalog, by number: *Internetcommerceisgood.* (If it doesn't arrive, blame it on e-mail witches.)

Since the late 1800s, numerous pure yeast strains — more than 500 different types — have been isolated, identified, and cultured. Commercial yeast banks inventory these strains in the form of sterile *slants* (test tubes), and some individual breweries keep their own sterile cultures on hand for future brews.

Yeast can also take credit for the classification of the beer style. Brewmasters pick a yeast according to the recipe or the style of beer they want to make. As I mention in Chapter 1, yeast is identified as either an ale yeast *(top-fermenting)* or a lager yeast *(bottom-fermenting)* strain (whether it's *top* or *bottom* depends on where it feeds in the unfermented beer).

- ✔ Ale yeast, which is a top-fermenting strain, works best in warm temperatures (60 to 75 degrees Fahrenheit, 15 to 24 degrees Celsius).

- ✔ Lager yeast, which is a bottom-fermenting strain, performs best in cooler temperatures (38 to 52 degrees Fahrenheit, 3 to 11 degrees Celsius).

Because of the temperature differential, each yeast strain produces the vastly different flavor and aroma characteristics that, in turn, create the different beer styles you know and love (and drink). Yeast, in combination with different fermentation processes, can also contribute fruitiness and other flavor characteristics to the beer. Brewmasters try to keep these flavors in check, depending on which beer style they're brewing.

Yeast genus and genius

For all you biology fans out there, here's the scoop on yeast. I'm talking about two different species of the genus *Saccharomyces*: ale yeast *(S. cerevisiae)* and lager yeast (*S. uvarum,* sometimes called *S. carlsbergensis*). And bread (or baker) yeast is part of the same genus, in case you wondered.

Do you recognize a familiar root word in the ale yeast strain's Latin name? *Cerevisiae* is based on Ceres, the Roman goddess of agriculture. It's also the root of the Spanish word for beer: *cerveza.*

Do you recognize a familiar root word in the lager yeast strain's Latin name? *Carlsbergensis* is named for the giant Danish brewery, Carlsberg. The founder's son, Jacob Christian Jacobsen, who counted Louis Pasteur among his friends and colleagues, set up a company laboratory in 1875. In this lab in 1883, the first single-cell yeast culture was definitively isolated. Emil Hansen set the stage for modern lager brewing by giving the brewmaster the ability to choose a specific strain of yeast that produced good beer and thereby establish brand consistency.

Another member of this order, but of a different genus, is *Brettanomyces* (the term *Brettanomyces* comes from Greek for British fungus). Known informally as *Brett,* this yeast is even more voracious than its *Saccharomyces* relatives and can eat sugars not normally consumed by regular beer yeast. Oddly enough, Brett is becoming quite popular in certain circles within the beer community even though beers fermented or aged with Brett have a very distinct barnyard aroma and acidic tinge in the flavor (see Chapter 6 for more info). Like its lager yeast cousin, Brett was also discovered at the Carlsberg Brewery in 1904.

Water: A Big Influence on Beer

Considering that it constitutes up to 95 percent of a beer's total ingredient content, water can certainly have a tremendous influence on the finished product. Today's brewers are fortunate to have the ability to alter and adjust the mineral profile of a given water source to suit their brewing needs by adding calcium carbonate, magnesium, gypsum, and the like.

Some of the classic world styles of beer became classics because of the water used to make the brew. The famed Pilsner beers of Bohemia, such as Pilsner Urquell, are considered premier examples. These crisp, hoppy lagers are made with extremely soft water pumped from the aquifers below the brewery. By contrast, the legendary British Ales of Burton-upon-Trent, such as Bass Ale, are made with particularly hard water. Brewers attempting to emulate these British beers simply add minerals called *Burton salts* to the brewing water in a process named *Burtonizing.*

You've heard ads for beer "from the land of sky-blue waters" or "brewed with Rocky Mountain spring water." Breweries like to gloat about the purity of the local water used in their beer. But any given water source can be, and usually is, chemically manipulated to match another source — some of the traditional sources are treated anyway.

Wing of Bat, Eye of Newt: Adjuncts You May Love or Hate

Although the four ingredients of barley, hops, yeast, and water are all you need to make beer, they're by no means the only ingredients used. Additional grains, natural sugars, and flavorings are often added to create unique flavors or to cut costs. These little additions are referred to as *adjuncts*.

Brewing artistes like to use a wide variety of nontraditional ingredients, including spices, fruits, and grains, to give their beers unique and unusual flavors. Big beer factories, on the other hand, tend to use adjunct grains to cut costs rather than to create different or innovative brews.

Many industrial brewers use adjunct grains that include unmalted cereal grains, such as corn and rice, to save money because barley is a relatively expensive grain. Using corn and rice as adjuncts also produces lighter and less malty beers. While some European brewers use between 10 and 20 percent adjunct grains in their beers, some large U.S. brewers are notorious for using as much as 30 to 40 percent adjunct grains (which is why some people call these *add-junk* beers!). In Germany, the use of adjuncts — or anything other than malt, hops, yeast, or water — in lagers is prohibited by the famed German Purity Law (see Chapter 10 for info on this law).

Non-grain adjuncts may include the following:

- ✔ Brown sugar
- ✔ Honey
- ✔ Lactose
- ✔ Maple syrup
- ✔ Molasses
- ✔ Treacle

Then you have the chemical additives and preservatives, including more than 50 antioxidants, foam enhancers, and miscellaneous enzymes. All these ingredients are permitted under U.S. law, but most small brewers, especially those in the U.S. craft beer movement, pride themselves on their voluntary exclusion of these additives and preservatives.

That some brewers put rather odd ingredients into their beers is no longer unusual. These days, adventurous beer lovers can find beers with fruits and fruit flavorings, licorice, herbs and spices, even whole jalapeño peppers right in the bottle! And as long as the market can stand it, brewers will continue to introduce beers with new and unique ingredients.

Chapter 3

A Little Brew Magic: Understanding How Beer Is Made

*B*rewing beer is fairly complex and involves a lot of equipment, especially when compared to winemaking. The ingredients are roasted, ground, heated, cooled, boiled, stirred, and so on. Brewmasters have plenty of room to assert their taste and demonstrate their talent, but brewing takes a lot of work and skill. The brewmaster's symbol is the same as the alchemist's symbol, a six-pointed star. Small wonder.

After you read this chapter, you can appreciate how hard a brewmaster must work to achieve a balance of all the flavors, aromas, and textures that the various ingredients and processes contribute to this complex beverage. The struggle to balance the final aroma, palate, and finish of the beer and to take into account all the variables is well worth the price of a pint when it works. (Just so you can recognize when it works, check out Chapter 12 for the nuances of appreciating beer, Chapter 2 for a rundown on beer ingredients, and Chapter 4 for a look at the styles of beer.)

A visit to any brewery will show you that although all breweries are in the business of brewing beer, no two breweries are exactly alike in terms of the equipment they use and the processes they follow. Brewpub owners usually like to show off their breweries. *Brewpubs* — restaurants/taverns with small breweries attached — are less automated than the big breweries, and everything is on a smaller scale.

Kettles, Tuns, and Tanks: Brewing Equipment

Although the equipment needed to brew beer traditionally was fairly simple, large commercial breweries today use equipment that does everything from crack the grain to seal the cases and a multitude of chores in between. The following list gives you the basics (see Figure 3-1 for a schematic of the brewing equipment and process used in most breweries):

✔ Most folks visiting a brewery immediately recognize the large, round brew kettle that usually dominates the brewhouse. Somewhere nearby is usually a second, sometimes smaller, similar-looking vessel called a *mash tun,* and if the place is big and brews lagers, it has yet another one, called a *lauter tun.* These vessels are vented through stacks that carry the steam out of the brewhouse, consequently treating the whole neighborhood to the intoxicating, malty-sweet aroma of beer in the making.

Traditionally, these vessels were made of copper and were often referred to simply as the *coppers* (which always reminds me of Dick Tracy in his black fedora, but he was no brewer). Nowadays, the term has fallen out of use, mostly because modern brewing equipment is fabricated from the relatively cheaper and easier-to-obtain stainless steel.

✔ After the first three vessels are used, the beer is pumped (and cooled at the same time) into a big tank called a *fermenter.* For sanitation purposes, fermenters are usually airtight vessels that allow only for the escape of the carbon dioxide pressure built up inside. However, some traditionalists in the industry, particularly in Britain and Belgium, still allow their beer to ferment in open vessels, and some even encourage spontaneous fermentations caused by wild, airborne yeast (Belgian Lambic brewers, for example).

✔ At this point, each brewery uses different kinds of tanks and does different things to its beer. For example:

  • Most breweries allow beer to go through a short aging process after the initial fermentation, using additional vessels cleverly named *aging tanks* for this purpose.

  • Next, breweries transfer the aged beer from aging tanks into *finishing tanks* to prepare them for their introduction into society (sounds a lot like finishing school, right?).

In case you're actually taking this stuff seriously and walking around a brewery with this book as a guide, please note (before you bang your head against the stainless steel in confusion) that brewers tend to use these tank terms loosely and interchangeably. Aging tanks are often called *secondary fermentation tanks* (because the primary fermentation took place in the previous tank); finishing tanks are alternatively called *conditioning tanks* by packaging breweries or *serving, holding,* or *bright beer* tanks by brewpubs (*bright* because the beer has clarified by this point). Is that clear?

✔ Because the beer must be regularly transferred from one vessel to another throughout the brewing and aging processes and because everything has to be super-clean, various pumps and hoses are scattered throughout the brewery, making some setups look like a Rube Goldberg device. Watch your step!

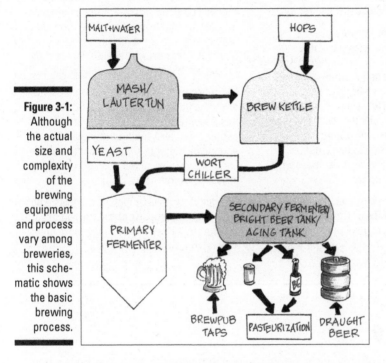

Figure 3-1: Although the actual size and complexity of the brewing equipment and process vary among breweries, this schematic shows the basic brewing process.

Note: After the brewery tour, a simple "Tanks a lot" will do.

So if you're itching to start your own brewery, you'll only need, oh, about a million dollars to get all the basic equipment.

Ale Alchemy: The Brewing Process

Explaining the usual sequential steps to making beer on the commercial level gets a bit technical — you have my permission to skip this section and move on. If you're sticking around, grab a brew and get comfortable; refer to Figure 3-1 to help you figure out what happens when.

Mega, micro, and more

It takes all kinds to make the world work, especially in the world of beer. Brewers tend to fall into categories by size, with some correlation to styles brewed. You often hear these terms:

✔ **Megabrewers:** These brewers are the biggest of the bunch. For example, Anheuser-Busch (now a part of the international brewing conglomeration AB/InBev) makes hundreds of millions of barrels of beer each year. European giants Heineken and Guinness brew somewhat less, and the relatively new partnership of Miller and Coors (cleverly called MillerCoors) also produces millions of barrels of beer on an annual basis. That's why they're called megabrewers.

✔ **Regional brewers:** These guys fall between the big and the small. They distribute mostly on the regional level and may produce either gourmet or mass-market beer under their own or other labels.

✔ **Contract brewers:** Anyone with a good recipe and a ton of cash for marketing can have a commercial brewery (usually a regional one) make beer for them, perhaps at several locations. Only one contract brewer ever broke the million-barrel-a-year mark (and that brewer eventually went on to operate two of its own brewing facilities).

✔ **Microbrewers:** Small entrepreneurs with breweries that make less than 60,000 barrels a year are called microbrewers. Some people disregard the quantity qualifier — and the dictionary — and simply associate microbrews (also called *micros*) with good, artisanal, flavorful beer.

✔ **Brewpubs:** Brewpubs include the folks who brew on the premises of their own bar (or restaurant). They rarely brew more than several thousand barrels a year.

Malting

The first step of brewing is *malting,* in which raw barley (or sometimes wheat) is converted to malted barley (also known as *barley malt* or just plain *malt*). If you want to get technical, the malting process involves preparing the starchy insides of the kernel (the *endosperm*) for conversion into soluble sugars called *maltose* by stimulating the natural germination process with moisture.

Most often, professional *maltsters* (the companies that malt the grain) with large malting plants handle the whole process and sell the malt to the breweries. The megabrewers, on the other hand, often do their own malting in an effort to control the process as well as the financial expenditure.

Thinking that it's in a moist springtime meadow and not on the floor of some enormous factory, the barley seedling begins to grow. When this little shoot (called the *acrospire*) reaches a certain length, the maltster blows hot air through the bed of grain, stopping the germination cold (sorry — hot!) and turning the grain into malted barley. Who said it's not nice to fool Mother Nature?

After the malt is dry, the maltster takes some of the malt and roasts it further in a kiln to bring out various colors and roasty or toasty flavors that create different colors and flavors in the beer, much as with coffee beans and coffee. The maltster also heats some malt to the point of becoming crystallized, charred, or deeply browned, slyly called *crystal malt, black malt,* or *chocolate malt,* respectively. Crystal malt is a bit crunchy and fun to eat at this stage (ask a brewer for a handful), and it may also be used to make other products, like malted milk (which isn't as much fun as beer).

Milling

Before brewers can put the grain (which may include malted and unmalted grain) into the mash tun and begin brewing (see the next section for details), they have to mill it. *Milling* is a relative term here; the intent isn't to make flour — just to crack open the husk of the barley kernel to expose the starches inside.

The brewer then transfers the cracked grain, now called *grist,* into the mash tun. If the grain has to be moved up or around, it must be moved by an auger or conveyor (in the old days, everything was moved by gravity, from one floor to the one below).

Mashing

After the grist is in the mash tun, the brewer infuses it with hot water, just like making a couple thousand pots of tea. Quite often, a brewer blends several different kinds of malt or specialty grains (like those mentioned in Chapter 2) to achieve unique colors and flavors. He then measures the water's pH (measure of its acidity and alkalinity) and adjusts as necessary. Together, the grist and the water create a thick porridge called the *mash.* Strict time and temperature controls help to effectively convert the starches to natural sugars within the kernels of grain.

Brewing through the ages

A team of Yale archaeologists excavated the remains of a 4,500-year-old bakery and brewery outside Cairo, Egypt. They believe that the remains are from a village that housed pyramid laborers on the Giza Plateau. In addition to earthenware pots and petrified grain stores, they discovered tombs and clay tablets with hieroglyphics. One of these tablets describes the brewing processes and sings the praises of a Sumerian beer goddess. The "Hymn to Ninkasi" has been studied not only by students of ancient history but also by brewers who want to learn more about brewing in the past.

Malt whisky: A beer without hops

The Scotch whisky–making process starts somewhat similarly to that of beer, its barley malt–family cousin. Malt whisky is made from malted barley (which gets its smoky character from being kilned with peat), which is also milled and mashed. Malt whisky is also fermented with yeast, but the similarity stops there: Malt whisky doesn't use hops. Whisky makers sometimes call the result of this fermentation the *beer!*

Beer (the regular kind) and whisky (especially unblended, single-malt whisky) share a scent of malt and, as you can expect, many fans. In fact, at least one magazine, *The Whisky Advocate*, covers both beer and whisky, along with some coverage of cigars. However, at last report, cigars weren't known to be distilled or hopped, but like whisky malt, they *are* smoked. (You had to see that one coming.)

When the brewer determines that the mash is complete, he transfers the thick, sweet, sticky *wort* (as the malt juice is now called) over to the brew kettle for the boil (see the next section for details on this part of the process). Depending on the mashing method, the brewer either drains the liquid through a false bottom that keeps the grain in the mash tun or, if the beer is a lager, transfers it first to a lauter tun, which is built like a giant kitchen colander.

The grain, now called *spent grain,* is no longer of use to the brewer after mashing, so the brewer often sells or donates it to local farmers to be used as hog slop. Some brewpubs use the spent grain to bake a high-fiber bread. (I wonder whether it's sold to go.)

Boiling

After the mashing process, the wort is boiled in the brew kettle — usually for an hour or so. The boil accomplishes many things, not the least of which is the complete sterilization of the liquid and any other ingredients added to it.

The brew kettle is also where the brewer goes about balancing the sweet wort with the pleasant bittering effects of the hops. By choosing a measured amount of a certain hop variety or a blend of several varieties and adding them at prescribed times (*bittering hops* at the start, *flavoring hops* late in the boil, and *aroma hops* at the very end), the brewer gives the beer its indelible hop signature. When added skillfully and evenhandedly, the hops' bittering, flavoring, and aromatic attributes are in perfect contrast and balance to the flavor and complexity of the malt. That's the brewer's art.

The brewer can infuse additional aromatic hop character through a process called *dry hopping,* where the brewer puts aromatic hops directly into the secondary fermenter along with the beer after it's undergone primary fermentation. The next section has more details about fermenting.

After an hour or two of boiling time, the brewer shuts off the heat and pre-pares the beer, now called *bitter* or *hopped wort,* for transfer to the fermenta-tion tank. Next, it's time to remove the hops. The hops can be removed by a *hop extractor,* which functions much like the false bottom of a mash tun, or by a *whirlpool,* in which centrifugal force forces all solid matter to the center of the vessel, and the now-clarified wort draws off from the side.

The brewer pumps the wort from the kettle through a *wort chiller,* or heat exchanger, which works like the radiator in your car and utilizes cold water or a food grade coolant to quickly drop the temperature of the wort. Now rid of unwanted solids, the hot wort needs to cool down quickly for two reasons:

- Warm, sweet liquid is the perfect medium for bacterial growth.
- The wort has to be made ready for yeast, which can be negatively affected by any temperatures over 100 degrees Fahrenheit or 38 degrees Celsius.

Fermenting

After boiling the wort and letting it cool, the brewer pumps the wort into the fermentation tank, and *pitches,* or adds, a slurry of fresh, aerated yeast to the tank. Commercial brewers use about a liter of yeast for each barrel (approxi-mately 31 gallons) of beer. That little bit of yeast packs a wallop.

At this point, the brewer either seals or leaves the fermenter open to nature's way, depending on the beer style being made, for the *primary fermentation.* During the primary fermentation, the yeast consumes the liquefied maltose sugars created during the mashing process. In return, the yeast produces carbon dioxide and alcohol. Within 24 hours of the yeast pitching, vigorous fermentation takes place, and a thick layer of dense foam appears on top of the turbid liquid. This process goes on for five to ten days, depending on the yeast strain as well as the fermentation temperature — determined, again, by the recipe. (The cooler the fermentation temperature, the slower the action of the yeast.)

Aging

Beer ages quickly, compared to wine and people (especially people who drink beer, of course). As I mention earlier in this chapter, after primary fermenta-tion is complete, the brewer transfers the beer to an aging tank called a *sec-ondary fermentation vessel* for — guess what — secondary fermentation and a period of aging and maturation that ranges from a couple of weeks (for ales) to a couple of months (for lagers), depending on the beer style. A small brewpub may curtail aging and send the beer straight to the bright beer tank for the final stage and sale as draught beer (see the next section for more information).

The pros and cons of extract brewing

Some brewers, mostly very small brewpubs, are able to circumvent the mashing procedures by using a dehydrated wort called *malt extract*. *Extract brewers,* as people who use this stuff are called, need only to pour these extracts into their brew kettle and rehydrate them with boiling water. Malt extract can also be used to increase the gravity and, thus, the alcohol level, of a regular beer made from grain.

Although this shortcut may sound like a tremendous time, money, and energy saver, malt extracts are considerably more expensive than raw grain, and extract beers are often inferior to *all-grain beers* (beers made with freshly milled grain). There's no such thing as a free lunch, or even a free beer, for that matter.

Packaging

After the beer has been given the appropriate amount of aging (also known as *conditioning*), it's ready to be packaged for you to drink.

In brewpubs, where the beer is meant to be served on the premises, the pubkeeper transfers the finished beer to the finishing tank, which, in this case, is often called the *serving, holding,* or *bright beer tank.* The tank, which acts like a giant keg, is usually connected directly to the tap standards at the bar where the beer is drawn.

In most packaging breweries, where the beer is packaged and shipped, the brewer draws the beer from the tank, after the appropriate amount of conditioning, to be filtered and kegged (under pressure) or bottled or canned. Bottled or canned beer may be pasteurized to kill any rogue yeast cells or bacteria that may have slipped through the system. However, kegged beer that isn't being shipped abroad is rarely pasteurized, a big distinction to some drinkers. Why? The downside to pasteurization is that although it creates a more stable product, it also damages the product to some extent, killing off as much of the beer's taste as bad microorganisms.

The pasteurizing process stabilizes the beer by heating it up to relatively high temperatures. *Tunnel pasteurization,* favored by megabrewers, sprays hot water over the bottles and cans for up to an hour. A gentler method, favored by some microbrewers, is called *flash pasteurization,* which may use extremely hot water or even steam, but for no more than a minute or so.

In Germany, only draught beer that's scheduled for export is pasteurized. In other parts of the world, the chances are 50-50 that draught beer for export has been pasteurized. Keep in mind that unpasteurized beer usually tastes better, but only if it's fresh; unpasteurized beer is likely to go bad faster.

Cleaning

Brewers say that more water ends up on the floor of the brewery than in the brew kettle because of all the cleaning and rinsing that must take place before and after each brew (be sure to wear your galoshes when you visit). Sanitizing the brewing equipment is as critical to making good beer as cleaning the kitchen is to cooking good food (most gourmet kitchens are spotless). So cleaning is an integral part of the brewing process.

Part II

Taking a Look at Beer Styles — Old, New, and Revived, Too

The 5th Wave   By Rich Tennant

In this part . . .

So much has taken place in the brewing industry over the past two decades that it's taken me almost this entire part of the book to sort it out. Thanks to the beer renaissance we're experiencing, the industry is very fluid (if you'll pardon the pun) and dynamic; beer styles are being revived and invented with regularity.

As if that wasn't enough, I thought it may also be a good idea to shine a spotlight on certain niche beers that address the needs or preferences of certain segments of the population. So dive right in!

Chapter 4

Getting to Know the Mother Beer Categories: Ales, Lagers, and More

In This Chapter

▶ Figuring out how beer is classified

▶ Understanding how to differentiate various beer traits

▶ Appreciating the many beer styles out there

*W*hat had been missing from the beer landscape for many years is now back in style: style itself (beer style, to be more accurate). Beer is now being brewed in a great profusion of styles, so much so, that new styles are actually being invented. But it wasn't always this way.

Looking back through beer history, ales are considered the beer of antiquity. Eventually, in the mid-19th century, lager beer took hold. And somewhere along the way, the concept of hybrid beer was introduced.

In this chapter, I sift through the main differences among ales, lagers, and hybrid beers. I also note a few important beer traits that you can use to describe various beer styles.

Two Big Branches on the Beer Family Tree: Distinguishing Ales and Lagers

If you're new to the world beyond Budweiser, you may be asking, "What's an ale?" and "What's a lager?" — as well as the obvious sequel, "What's the difference?"

All beers are made as ales or lagers; *ale* and *lager* are the two main branches (classifications) of the beer family tree and are closely related branches at that. Ales are the older, distinguished, traditional brews of the world, predating lagers by thousands of years, whereas lagers are a relatively modern creation, less than 200 years old.

In the following sections, I explain how brewers use different types of yeast to create ales and lagers, and I note the differences in taste that you may find in ales and lagers.

Yeast makes the beer

The branch of the beer family tree — ale or lager — corresponds to the type of yeast used to ferment the beer. You have ale yeast and lager yeast, and these types of yeast, in turn, typically dictate the temperature at which the beer is fermented. Ales are traditionally fermented at warmer temperatures (55 to 70 degrees Fahrenheit, 12 to 21 degrees Celsius), while lagers are typically fermented at cooler temperatures (38 to 50 degrees Fahrenheit, 3 to 10 degrees Celsius).

The cooler fermentation and aging temperatures used with lager yeast slow down the yeast activity and require a longer maturation time. The cold environment inhibits the production of fruity aromas (called *esters*) and other fermentation byproducts common in ales. This process creates the lager's cleaner taste. Long aging (or *lagering*) also acts to mellow the beer.

You can taste the difference, sometimes

Taste — ah, yes. Every beginner wants to know how ales taste different than lagers. If only it were that easy! This question is sort of like asking how red wines taste different than white wines. (Shameless plug: See the latest edition of the wonderful sister book from Wiley, *Wine For Dummies,* by Ed McCarthy and Mary Ewing-Mulligan.)

Ironically, you can find beer styles called *red beer* and *white beer,* but that's another story altogether, and you can be sure that it doesn't involve grape skins. (See the nearby sidebar "Red and Amber Beer: Neither is clear" for more information.)

Ales share many common characteristics, and so do lagers, but the two groups overlap so much that any absolutes about either class are usually wrong. This overlap creates some confusion and the need for experts to explain the different characteristics, but it also creates the need for beer exploration. Didn't you always want to be an explorer? Now's your chance.

Gimme a beer — no, an ale!

When the lager beer style was fully commercialized in the late 1800s, it was an instant hit in Germany and most of Europe, but lagers never really caught on in Belgium, Britain, and Ireland. Even today, if you ask for a beer in those countries, you'll likely be served an ale, unless you specifically ask for a lager.

Lagers quickly became *the* beer in North America, where the brewers were mostly German. Until recently, if you asked for a beer in North America, you were likely served a lager. (Beware the occasional beer menu that categorizes the brews as *Beers* and *Ales* — the correct division is ales and lagers, because both are beers.)

But the beer renaissance is changing that. Even in the remote villages of the hinterlands, beer drinkers can choose from among most, if not all, the world's beer types and styles — ales, lagers, and hybrids of every hue, strength, and flavor.

You can say that *ales* generally

- ✔ Include more robust-tasting beers
- ✔ Tend to be fruity and aromatic
- ✔ Include more bitter beers
- ✔ Have a pronounced, complex taste and aroma
- ✔ Are enjoyed warmer (45 to 55 degrees Fahrenheit, 7 to 12 degrees Celsius)

And you can say that *lagers* generally

- ✔ Include lighter-tasting beers
- ✔ Tend to be highly carbonated or crisp
- ✔ Tend to be smooth and mellow
- ✔ Have a subtle, clean, balanced taste and aroma
- ✔ Are served fairly cool (38 to 45 degrees Fahrenheit, 3 to 7 degrees Celsius)

If someone says, "I don't like ales," or "lagers give me headaches," respond by saying that simply too much variety exists for that kind of distinction to hold water (or beer, for that matter). Beer exploration is called for!

Red and Amber Beer: Neither is clear

One consequence of the craft-brewing renaissance has been the creation of newer, nontraditional styles, such as Red Beer and Amber Beer.

✔ In my opinion, *Red Beer* exists only because of marketing creativity — and you can thank the folks at Coors for introducing America to Killian's Irish Red. Before the profusion of Red Ales and Lagers (mostly brewed by megabrewers or their subsidiaries) hit the store shelves, no such style existed. The only true Red Beer was Belgian Flanders Red — but that's a different animal altogether (Belgian Flanders Red is a complex, sour, wine-like ale).

The parameters for Red Beer are hard to outline; Red Beers are pretty much whatever the brewer or marketing genius wants them to be, though these beers tend to be light- to medium-bodied, fairly well malted, with a distinct caramel, nutty or toasty flavor directly attributable to the grain used to infuse the beer with a reddish-brown color.

✔ Because of the profusion of Amber Beers in the marketplace, Amber Ale and Amber Lager were designated true styles. Because this designation is based primarily on beer color, though, distinguishing between Pale Ales and Amber Ales is often difficult as many Pale Ales tend to appear amber in color.

Old-School Beer: Understanding Ales

As I note at the start of this chapter, ale is the beer classification that predates written history. Presumably, the very first beers brewed by our hominid forebears were a crude form of ale spontaneously fermented by wild airborne yeasts. These yeasts became known as top-fermenting yeasts for their propensity to float on top of the beer as it's fermenting. Hence, ales are, likewise, considered top-fermented beers.

Actually, until the invention of the microscope in the 18th century, brewers didn't know exactly what yeast was or how it fueled fermentation, they just knew it did — and they were grateful. They even called it *Godisgood!*

Dating back into antiquity, most ales were thick and gruel-like, often containing bits of the grain that was used to make the beer and opaque from the yeast that fermented it. (Archaeologists and anthropologists have determined that people used straws to drink the beer from huge communal bowls.) Ales were also fairly dark and often smoky due to the process of drying the grain over a fire. In Scotland, where grain was dried over peat fires, the local ale took on the character of its sister swill, whisky.

The basic premise of brewing ales is to ferment them at fairly warm temperatures (55 to 70 degrees Fahrenheit, 12 to 21 degrees Celsius). At these temperatures, the yeast tends to remain quite active, thus completing the fermentation process in rather short order — in about a week or so. Ale yeast likes to float on top of the beer as it ferments it, so ale yeast has come to be known as *top-fermenting yeast.*

Pretty much any beer style introduced prior to the advent of artificial refrigeration in the 1800s qualifies as an Old World ale style; however, those ale styles that are on the lighter end of the color spectrum, as well as those styles that are served crystal clear, have certainly benefitted from the technologies of our modern era. Beers are no longer all dark and smoky and cloudy, thanks to state-of-the-art grain drying apparatus and filtration systems.

Not unlike the wild-fermented potions brewed by our Neolithic ancestors, some commercial brewers still produce their unique ales in a very antiquated and somewhat risky method. After brewing their beer, they pour it into large, shallow, open-topped vessels and allow Mother Nature to take over. Resident microflora find their way to the unprotected beer and have their way with it, producing some of the most odd and esoteric — not to mention, sour — beers on the planet. Aging and blending soften some of these ales' acidic sting, but they still qualify as an acquired taste.

Very few brewers produce spontaneously fermented beers in the world, and the one thing they all share is the importance of their breweries' location. (I did say *resident* yeasts.)

The "New" Beer on the Block: Getting Familiar with Lagers

The key to understanding lager beer is in the word *lager* itself. The German word *lagern* means to store. Lagers are aged, or stored, for long periods of time at temperatures ranging from 38 to 50 degrees Fahrenheit, 3 to 10 degrees Celsius. This long-term aging is what gives lager beers a mellowness and drinkability that's rarely found among ales.

Long-term aging alone can't make lagers' mellowness possible; lower aging temperatures are also an imperative to achieving lagers' finesse. Early brewers of lager beers often located their brewing facilities on or near mountainous terrain so they could dig beer cellaring caves to store their beer. Flatlander brewers who had to forego Alpine caves, cut huge blocks of ice out of local lakes and rivers in the winter to store in an icehouse in order to achieve the same lagering effect in their beer. With the advent of compressed-gas refrigeration in the late 1800s, brewers who could afford this newfangled technology were able to set up shop anywhere they wanted — with nary a hilltop or frozen pond in sight.

The nature of the long and cold lagering process stunts the yeast activity. Due to the cold fermentation and aging temperatures, the yeasts' fermentation ability slows down, and brewers find it necessary to *pitch,* or add, a greater quantity of yeast to the beer than is typical for fermenting ales.

The yeast also drops out of suspension, settles on the bottom of the fermenter very early in the process, and continues to do its work there. Therefore, lager yeast is also known as *bottom-fermenting yeast,* and lager beer is considered bottom-fermented beer.

By any measure, the introduction of artificial refrigeration is the dividing line between Old World ales and New World lagers — even though lagers were already being produced without that technology. But their lager quality was immeasurably enhanced by the total control brewers now had over the fermentation and aging process. The length of the lagering process also had a secondary effect on the beer: It was more crystal clear at packaging time.

Mixed Up: Taking Note of Hybrid Beers

As in many families, beers can have mixed parentage. These types of beers have been dubbed *hybrid* beers. As you find out in the following sections, hybrid beers exist due to brewers' flaunting of conventions by fermenting a beer with lager yeast at ale (warm) temperatures and fermenting a beer with ale yeast at lager (cool) temperatures. Kooky, huh?

Warm fermentations with lager yeast

The exact temperatures used to produce hybrid beers and how long the beer is fermented and aged isn't an exact science. The processes vary from one brewer to the next, as do the beers they create.

Not a lot of beer styles represent this type of hybrid. The most famous style is known as Steam Beer, but because the San Francisco brewery that popularized the style also trademarked the name *Steam Beer,* the style is now generically referred to as *California Common Beer.* (The Steam Beer style is also recognized as *Dampfbier* in Germany. See the later section "Hybrid beers" for more information.)

Though it can no longer be confirmed, one theory suggests that the origination of the steam label had to do with the vigorous warm fermentation that caused the vessel to hiss, or steam, while venting the increasing carbon dioxide inside it.

Cold fermentations with ale yeast

Ale yeasts, when fermented at warm temperatures (the usual process), tend to produce fruity flavors and fruity or floral *esters* (aromas). When beers are fermented with ale yeast at colder temperatures, however, the yeasts' production of esters is reduced, thereby producing a beer with a more subdued aroma and refined flavor that mimics lager beers.

Because brewers tend to have individual ways of doing things, pinning down the exact fermentation temperatures or lengths of fermentation of these beers is difficult. Thus, you can expect individualistic beers from these guys as well.

The three most common beer styles in this hybrid category are Altbier, Kölsch, and Cream Ale (see the later section "Hybrid beers" for full details on these three). The first two styles are of German origin, and the last one is uniquely American.

Baltic Porter is kind of in a class all its own. Typically, Porter is considered an ale and is warm fermented. Many brewers who make Porters in the Baltic States like to cold ferment their beer, though — most often with lager yeast but occasionally with ale yeast, too. Go figure.

Everything but the Kitchen Sink: Looking at Specialty Beers

Specialty beers are one of the most fun and popular beer categories in the world. This category is fun for the brewers and popular for the consumers because it really has no clearly defined boundaries or guidelines. It's kind of an anything-goes and rules-be-damned category.

So how did specialty beers come to be? Well, most craft brewers approach their profession with the same passion as an artist; they love the creative aspect of their job. Although beer style guidelines are fundamental to their creations, they're also occasionally seen as confining. Craft brewers are often at their best when they're allowed to cut loose in their brewhouse. When they shed the constraints of conformity, they prove themselves to be impressively gifted artisans capable of producing nothing less than nectar of the gods.

Goose Island Brewery in Chicago, or *The Goose,* is already known far and wide for its phenomenal Bourbon County Stout (BCS), but the brewers there weren't content to rest on their laurels. They decided to add strawberries and vanilla bean to a batch of BCS and voilà! They had concocted a creamy chocolate-strawberry-vanilla libation they dubbed Neopolitan — it was sublime!

Part of brewers' creative drive is constantly searching for new and unique ingredients to add to their beers. This search is done mostly to push the envelope and expand horizons, but it's also done in the name of marketing. In other words, the more out there the ingredients, the better.

Here's just a partial list of oddball ingredients that have recently gone into commercial beers around the world:

- Bog myrtle
- Cedar tips
- Coconut
- Heather tips
- Hemp
- Hibiscus flowers
- Hot peppers (ancho, jalapeño, ghost)
- Juniper berries
- Kopi Luwak coffee

> The beans used to produce Kopi Luwak coffee are collected from the scat of the feline Asian Palm Civet. The civets first eat whole coffee cherries for their pulp, after which the inner beans ferment inside their stomachs. After defecated, the beans — still whole — are collected, cleaned, and roasted. The result is a remarkably complex, full-bodied coffee. At least three brewers are known to have made a beer with Kopi Luwak coffee as an ingredient.

- Peppercorns
- Rose hips
- Seaweed (Kelp)

The Anatomy of Beer Styles: Examining the Traits of Different Beers

In order to fully understand and appreciate the various beer styles that exist in the world, knowing how beer styles differ from one another and how those differences are measured is helpful. In the following sections, I explore three ways to differentiate beer styles, define several terms used to describe the flavor of beer, and introduce the concept of craft beer.

Defining beer styles with three parameters

All beer styles can be easily identified and differentiated by three simple measurements:

- ✔ **Color:** All beers have color, whether it's light, dark, or somewhere in between. The color of beer is determined primarily by the grain used to make the beer. Light-colored grain results in a pale-colored beer; conversely, darker-roasted grains produce darker beers.

  The spectrum of beer color ranges from straw to black, and this color range is measurable on the Standard Reference Method (SRM) scale (0 to 50). An American Light Lager may have a color of between 2 to 4 SRM while an Imperial Stout may have a color of 44 SRM. (You don't necessarily need to know the details behind the Standard Reference Method, just that the numbers on this scale correlate to color; low numbers represent paler beer, high numbers represent darker beer.)

- ✔ **Bitterness:** All beers have some level of bitterness, whether it's a lot or a little. Bitterness in beer is primarily the result of extracting alpha acids from *hops* (which I talk about in Chapter 2) during the boiling process. Numerous hop varieties are grown in various locations throughout the world, resulting in varying alpha acid contents (more alpha acid = more bitterness). Brewers know all about these varieties and use the hops accordingly.

  Hop bitterness is measured in International Bittering Units (IBUs). An American Light Lager may have 5 to 8 IBUs, while an Imperial India Pale Ale (IPA) may have 100 or more IBUs.

- ✔ **Gravity:** All beers have some level of viscosity, whether it's dense or watery. The term *gravity* refers to the density of beer. Gravity is measured on the day the beer is brewed and is determined by the amount of soluble sugars — known as *maltose* — dissolved in the beer. Maltose is derived from malted grain, and beer gravity can be raised or lowered simply by increasing or decreasing the amount of malted grain used to brew the beer.

  Gravity can be measured on the specific (or original) gravity scale (1.000 to 1.150) or the Balling Scale (0 to 40); these scales are like the Fahrenheit and Celsius scales of the beer world. An American Light Lager may have an original gravity of 1.024 to 1.040 (6 to 10 Balling), while a Barleywine may have an original gravity of 1.080 to 1.120 (21 to 28 Balling).

  Because maltose is consumed by yeast during fermentation, the gravity of the beer lowers to about 20 to 25 percent of its original level by the time it's ready for packaging.

Keep in mind, all these numbers can tell you a lot about how the beer looks and tastes, but the yeast still determines whether the beer's an ale or a lager (see the earlier section "Yeast makes the beer" for details).

Using a few tasting terms

I examine many tasting terms in Chapter 12, but you need to know at least the following ones to understand the beer styles I list later in this chapter. Knowing these terms may also encourage you to explore and experiment (and also give you something to talk about with any hophead you may encounter at the bar):

- **Aggressive:** As you may expect, an aggressive beer has a boldly assertive aroma and/or taste.

- **Balanced:** Balanced simply means that the malt and hops are in similar proportions, and the flavor has an equal representation of malt sweetness and hop bitterness — especially at the finish.

- **Body:** The body is the sensation of fullness, or viscosity, of a beer on the palate, ranging from watery to creamy. Beer is generally described as thin-, light-, medium-, or full-bodied (*strong* simply refers to alcohol content).

- **Complex:** Complex means the beer is multidimensional, involving many flavors and sensations on the palate (the opposite of simple).

- **Crisp:** Crisp means the beer is highly carbonated or effervescent. Beers regarded as crisp are typically on the drier side as well.

- **Diacetyl:** This term describes a buttery or butterscotchy aroma or flavor.

- **Estery:** Estery is full of aromas that are reminiscent of fruits.

- **Floral:** Floral is full of aromas that are reminiscent of flowers.

- **Fruity:** Fruity means the beer has flavors reminiscent of various fruits.

- **Hoppy:** Hoppy means the hops have earthy, herbal, spicy, or citrusy aromas and flavors.

- **Malty:** Malty describes flavors derived from malted grain. Malty beers have a more pronounced malt richness and sweetness.

- **Mouthfeel:** Mouthfeel is the tactile sensations of alcoholic warmth, carbonation, dryness, and the like. Body is also part of mouthfeel.

- **Roasty/toasty:** Roasty/toasty describes the malt (roasted grain) flavors.

- **Robust:** Robust describes a rich and full-bodied beer.

Crafting great beers

Taste, style, and variety: These words aren't abstract concepts, like quality, but a combination of straightforward, measurable, easily described aspects of color, flavor, aroma, and body (as I describe in the preceding sections).

To use another food analogy, the craft brewer is like a great chef. Just as gourmet bakers turn out bread in astonishing but now familiar varieties, from breadsticks to bagels (with pumpernickel, jalapeño rye, and hot dog buns in between), brewers can come up with an almost infinite number of variations on the classic, traditional styles noted later in this chapter. Craft brewers tend to use more expensive ingredients (all malted grains and lots more of them per barrel) than the big commercial brewers.

Craft brewers are artisanal brewers who all together brewed just under 10 million barrels in the United States in 2010 (about 5 percent of all U.S. beer sales). Although artisanal beer isn't inherently better than mass-market beer, it generally has more taste and comes in a much wider range of styles. The well-known, heavily advertised mass-market brands brewed by the world's largest brewers are generally top-quality products that represent a fairly narrow range of taste and style to appeal to the largest number of consumers. They're famed for an excellent quality control and consistency not always found in gourmet beers.

So while the megabrewers, such as Heineken and Anheuser-Busch, are producing the beer equivalent to Wonder bread, smaller craft brewers are making a wide range of beer styles, and you can taste the difference. Same basic ingredients, vastly different approach — that's the difference.

Style Is Everything: Listing Common Beer Styles

If you were to use fruits as a metaphor for all the beer styles in the world, the beer styles would be kind of like apples, bananas, grapefruits, pineapples, or kiwis: all with quite different colors, textures, flavors, aromas, and prices. In that case, the U.S. national-brand beers may be apples. Sure, you have some variety, what with (to name a few) Golden Delicious, Jonathan, Granny Smith, and McIntosh. They're all good, but they're just apples. Now imagine never tasting anything but apples; your concept of fruit would be rather narrow, wouldn't it? Many beer consumers have this same concept of beer! (And if beer grew on trees, I guarantee there'd be a lot more farmers.)

If you ask a bartender to suggest a good beer, he or she will probably ask in reply, "What do you like? Dark, light? Strong, mild? Malty, hoppy?" The information in the following sections about the more common beer styles should help you make sense of a friend's or bartender's queries and recommendations; the beers themselves can, no doubt, help you answer life's most vexing questions.

The beer lists and descriptions that follow are based on classic bottled brands; the fun thing about beer exploring is that your local brewpubs (and friendly local homebrewers) usually offer their own versions of these standard styles. They've also been culled from beer style guidelines compiled by the Brewers Association and the Beer Judge Certification Program (BJCP). This list is by no means complete.

Note: Beer nuts can have heated arguments over the subject of beer styles. I've stuck to traditional, historically accepted styles in the following sections (and in this book, for that matter), as well as some newer styles that have been introduced in recent years.

Though the following beer styles are referred to as international or world styles, they're all originally from Europe and North America. Please don't think of me as being thoughtlessly Eurocentric — that's just the way the beer world is. Although other, lesser-known styles exist elsewhere, they're typically not available outside their local areas.

Ales

Ales come in a very wide range of flavors and styles. The following list covers some of the best known (Figure 4-1 shows the ale family tree).

- **Barleywine:** A hefty ale with fruity and caramel-like aromas, complex malt flavors, and as much alcohol as some wine, Barleywine is one of the few beer styles that's noticeably stronger than other beers. Barleywine is often served in a wine glass or brandy snifter. (After all, it's often called the beer version of cognac; it ages well, too.) It's usually produced in limited quantities for winter's holiday celebrations. It can be found in English and American substyles; the English leans toward malty, the American leans toward hoppy.

- **Belgian Dubbel:** Originated at monasteries in the Middle Ages and revived after the Napoleonic era, Belgian Dubbel is a deep reddish, moderately strong, malty, and complex ale. Traditionally this beer is *bottle conditioned* (it undergoes a subtle secondary fermentation in the bottle, which means it contains yeast).

- **Belgian Pale Ale:** Belgian Pale Ale is a fruity, malty, somewhat spicy, copper-colored ale commonly found in the Belgian provinces of Antwerp and Brabant. It's considered a *session beer,* which means it contains a moderate alcohol content and is easy to drink.

- **Belgian Tripel:** Belgian Tripel is a yellow-gold brew that's effervescent with bleached white head. It has spicy and fruity malt character with citric notes. This style was originally popularized by the Trappist brewery at Westmalle in Belgium.

    Note: Only religious brewers — Trappist monks — can use the term *Trappist,* so secular brewers market Trappist-style beer as *Abbey* beer (also *Abby, Abt, Abdij*).

ALES

Porter	Stout	Brown Ales	Amber/Red Ales	Pale Ales	
Brown	Dry	Mild	Irish Red	American Pale Ale	Ordinary Bitter
Robust	Sweet	English Brown	Amber Ale	India Pale Ale (IPA)	Special/Best Bitter
Baltic	Oatmeal	American Brown	Scottish Ale		
	Foreign			Double/Imperial India Pale Ale	Extra Special Bitter (ESB)
	Russian Imperial				

Strong Ales	Belgian Trappist/Abbey	Belgian Ales	Belgian Sour Beers
American Barleywine	Dubbel	Golden/Blonde	Flanders Red
English Barleywine	Tripel	Saison	Flanders Brown/Oud Bruin
Scotch Ale	Quadrupel	Biere De Garde	
Old Ale			

Wheat Beers	Spontaneously Fermented Beer	Specialty Ales
Hefeweizen	Lambic	Herb & Spice
Dunkelweizen	Gueuze	Fruit
American Wheat Ale	Fruit Lambic	Winter Warmers/Holiday Beers
Berliner Weisse		
Witbier		Smoke

Figure 4-1:
The ale
family tree.

✔ **Berliner Weisse:** Berliner Weisse is a very pale, refreshingly sour, wheat-based ale from Berlin. To cut the sourness, a dollop of raspberry or woodruff is often added to the glass before drinking.

In 1809, Napolean referred to Berliner Weisse as the Champagne of the North for its elegant and lively character.

✔ **Bière de Garde:** A traditional farmhouse ale from Northern France, Bière de Garde is fairly strong and malt-accented. Like Saison, Bière de Garde is also produced in the spring for summer consumption.

✔ **Bitters:** This style isn't really that bitter — it's betrayed by the name given it centuries ago when hops were first used by English brewers. A very common, popular beer in British pubs, Bitters come in a range of substyles, including Ordinary Bitter, Special/Best Bitter and Extra Special/Strong Bitter (ESB).

Out in the colonies: The story of India Pale Ale

India Pale Ale, or *IPA*, gets its name from Britain's colonial presence in India during the 1800s. Along with other creature comforts from home, British royal subjects living in India demanded to have their favorite ales shipped to them, but the months-long journey on the open sea devastated the average cask of beer.

It's widely believed (but unproven) that a British brewer named George Hodgson recognized this problem and decided to brew an ale of greater alcoholic strength that could more easily withstand the rigors of oceanic transit. The antiseptic properties of the increased alcohol volume, coupled with a high concentration of hop acids,

assured the colonialists of a palatable, if slightly more potent, product at journey's end.

For a long time, people believed that the gentle rocking motion of the ship on water caused the beer within the casks to pick up some of the oaky character, much like barrel-aged wine. But that myth has been debunked as beer barrels were typically lined with pine pitch, which would act as a liner to shield the beer from contact with the wood. Nevertheless, some brewers today press on and maintain that hypothetical link with the past by employing unlined oak barrels or using oak chips for the aging process of IPA.

- ✔ **Blonde Ale:** Brilliant light yellow to golden with a bleached white head, Blonde Ale is similar to a Pale Ale in terms of flavor but its hop character is less assertive. Blonde Ale is a relatively new staple beer at many American breweries and brewpubs and is produced as a good entry-level transitional beer.

- ✔ **Brown Ales:** Brown Ales have both English and American versions. Brown Ales are good beginner beers for timid beer drinkers who are looking to try something beyond the ordinary (not bad for old-timers, either). Not too malty, not too thin, with subdued fruity and caramel-like flavors, Brown Ales are mellow but flavorful. American versions tend to be more aggressively hopped.

- ✔ **Dry (Irish) Stout:** Dry (Irish) Stout is a very dark, roasty beer with creamy mouthfeel. It's more roasty-flavored and coffee-like than porter. Dry (Irish) Stout is great for nursing (beers, not babies, though in the past, it was often recommended for nursing mothers!).

- ✔ **Dunkelweizen:** Brownish in color with spicy aromatics, Dunkelweizen is the dark version of the very popular Bavarian-style Weizenbier (or Weissbier). Its unique aromatic profile includes clove, banana, and occasionally bubblegum.

- ✔ **Flanders Brown/Oud Bruin:** This ale is a well-aged, fruity, and sour Brown Ale from Flanders (Belgium). Dark reddish-brown in color, this malty beer exhibits fruity complexity, often reminiscent of raisins, plums, figs, dates, and prunes.

- **Flanders Red:** A complex, sour, wine-like ale from Flanders in Belgium, the Flanders Red is traditionally aged in oak tuns for up to two years. The more refined versions are blended with young beer.

- **Foreign Style Stout:** The Foreign Style Stout is a very dark, moderately strong, roasty ale. Foreign Style Stouts are a rather broad class of Stouts and can be fruity and sweet or dry and bitter. They have a higher gravity and alcohol content than Dry or Sweet Stouts but less than the Russian Imperial Stout.

- **Gueuze:** The Gueuze is a spontaneously fermented ale from the region near Brussels, Belgium. It's a complex, pleasantly sour beer, resulting from the blending of 1-, 2-, and 3-year-old Lambic Beer.

- **India Black Ale:** One of the newest beer styles introduced to the world, the India Black Ale is a dark version of India Pale Ale. Caramel malt character and dark roasted malt flavor join to support aggressive hop presence. The India Black Ale is also known colloquially as *Cascadian Dark Ale.*

- **India Pale Ale (IPA):** The India Pale Ale is a hoppy, moderately strong ale of golden-to-copper color. British versions accentuate English malts, hops, and yeast; the resulting beer is malty and fruity with a corresponding earthy hop bitterness. American versions accentuate North American malts, hops, and yeast strains; the resulting beer is drier, cleaner (less fruity), and rather citrusy from American hop varieties.

- **Irish Red Ale:** The Irish Red Ale is an easy-drinking, malt-focused beer with generous caramel malt notes. Buttery or toffee flavors may also be experienced. The use of small quantities of roast malt provide for the reddish tinge in the beer.

- **Lambic:** A complex, sour, wheat-based ale from the area surrounding Brussels, Belgium, Lambic Beer is spontaneously fermented by the airborne yeast around the Senne River Valley. Lambic Beers are also blended to create Gueuze and have various fruits added to them for further complexity and flavoring.

- **Mild Ale:** A decidedly British beer, Mild Ale (or Mild) was once one of the most widely produced beer styles in the United Kingdom. Most Milds are low-gravity session beers intended for extended drinking. Generally malty, Milds often exhibit caramel, toffee, nutty, and toasty aromas and flavors. A substyle of Brown Ale, Mild isn't widely brewed in or imported to the United States.

- **Old Ale:** Old Ales are fruity and malty with a variety of buttery, nutty, and toasty flavors. These heavyweight sippers are great for casual after-dinner or late-night imbibing. Well-aged versions may display hints of souring.

✔ **Pale Ales:** Pale Ales are rather fruity beers with light malt flavors and a pleasantly dry and often bitter aftertaste. Despite their name, they're generally golden to amber in color. English versions are more balanced and have more of an earthy hop character. See also India Pale Ale.

✔ **Porter:** A dark but not imposing ale, the Porter has light malt sweetness and pleasant dark grain flavors and makes for a wonderful sipping beer. Porters may range from medium-bodied and mild to big-bodied and robust. Look for British Brown Porter and American Robust Porter. Porter and its cousin *Stout* are quite distinct from other beers. See also Baltic Porter in the later section on hybrid beers.

✔ **Porter (Baltic):** Baltic Porter is a very dark brew from countries that border the Baltic Sea and is influenced by Russian Imperial Stouts. Dark, roasty flavors evoke flavors of bittersweet chocolate, toffee, molasses, and licorice notes. Polish versions tend to be more malty sweet. Baltic Porter is typically cold fermented, but it may be fermented with either ale or lager yeast.

✔ **Oatmeal Stout:** Oatmeal Stout is a very dark, full-bodied, roasty, malty ale with a complementary oatmeal flavor. Oats are added for body and complexity.

✔ **Roggenbier:** Roggenbier is a specialty beer brewed in Bavaria as a more distinct variant of Dunkelweizen, using rye in place of wheat. These beers have a moderately spicy rye flavor, reminiscent of rye or pumpernickel bread.

Some American brewers add caraway seed to their rye beer to further accentuate the rye experience.

✔ **Russian Imperial Stout:** A rich, intense, complex, and roasty dark ale, the Russian Imperial Stout has dark grain flavors that evoke bittersweet chocolate, cocoa, or strong coffee. It's traditionally brewed to a high gravity and alcohol content by British brewers for export to the Baltic States and Russia and is said to be a favorite of the Czar's Imperial Court in St. Petersburg.

✔ **Saison:** Saison is a refreshing, fruity ale that's quite effervescent and has a dry, quenching acidity. Saisons were traditionally brewed in Wallonia (the French speaking part of Belgium) in late spring to be consumed throughout the summer months.

✔ **Scotch Ale:** Scotch Ales are malt accented with a variety of caramel, nutty, and toasty flavors. These heavyweight sippers are great for casual after-dinner or late-night imbibing. Scotch Ale is the maltier Scottish counterpart to the English Old Ale.

✔ **Scottish Ale:** This beer style is relatively unknown, and thus, underappreciated in most of the world. Scottish Ales are more commonly found on draught rather than in bottles or cans. They possess a soft and chewy malt character that may be perceived as caramel or toffee and can range from golden amber to deep brown in color.

Two Entire-ly new beers

In the mid-to-late 1870s, working-class men in London gathered at their local pub to relax and solve the world's troubles over a pint of their favorite ale. At one pub in particular, it became a habit of mixing two or three different draught beers into a single pint. One especially tasty mixture came to be known as *Entire,* and word of this beery concoction traveled to other pubs.

When London brewer Ralph Harwood caught wind of this practice, he decided to create a beer that closely approximated the pub blend.

He dubbed it *Porter* after the porters and other manual laborers who favored this beer.

After Harwood found success with his new Porter beer, many other London brewers immediately imitated it. The key to gaining attention for each new Porter that was introduced was to make it darker, richer, and bolder tasting. In a bit of one-upmanship, another brewer decided to call his new brew *Stout Porter.* Eventually, the blacker, more intensely flavored beer became known simply as *Stout* — and the rest is history.

Scottish Ales are identified by an antiquated shilling system based on their alcohol content. The lightest Scottish Ale is designated 60 shilling, the middle is 70 shilling, and the heaviest/strongest (which is hardly heavy or strong at all) is designated 80 shilling. For comparison, the bigger and bolder Scotch Ale is designated 120 shilling — twice the gravity and alcohol of the 60 shilling.

- **Sweet (London) Stout:** The Sweet (London) Stout is a very dark, sweet, full-bodied, roasty ale. It's historically known as Milk Stout or Cream Stout due to the use of unfermentable milk sugar (lactose).

- **Weizenbier/Weissbier:** This traditional refreshing wheat-based beer of Bavaria is golden-colored and spritzy. Unique aromas include cloves, fruity esters — especially banana — and bubblegum. Hefeweizen (*hefe* = yeast) is simply a Weizenbier that still has yeast in the bottle.

- **Weizenbock:** Weizenbock is a dark, medium-full bodied wheat based beer of Bock strength (find out more about Bock Beer in the next section). This style was created in Munich in 1907, a top-fermented creative response to the profusion of bottom-fermented Doppelbocks produced by local brewers.

- **Witbier:** This light, refreshing, citrusy wheat ale originated in the city of Hoegaarden more than 400 years ago. *Wit* — white in Flemish — refers to the beer's pale cast. Its citrusy, perfumy character is a result of the brewers' use of coriander and the bitter rind of the Curacao orange. Another spice supposedly used is called Grains of Paradise. It sounds lovely but tastes even better!

✔ **Wheat Beers:** Wheat Beers are the ultimate summer quenchers. Their fruity-perfumy aromas, citrusy tanginess, and spritzy effervescence make these ales especially easy to enjoy when the weather is hot. Generic Wheat Beers are rarely as wheaty as traditional German Weizenbiers, nor do they exhibit the full range of yeast-derived aromatics (clove, banana, bubblegum, and so on).

Lagers

The name *lager* is taken from the German word *lagern,* meaning to store. Most of the mass-produced beers of the world are lagers, but a wider range of styles exists than what those commercial brands may lead you to believe (Figure 4-2 shows the lager family tree).

✔ **American Pale Lagers:** Although these beers differ greatly from brand to brand in the mind of the unknowing consumer (thanks to advertising campaigns), they're, for the most part, identical in taste and strength (about 4 to 5 percent alcohol by volume). All the *light, standard,* and *premium* brands were originally based on the classic Pilsner style that I describe later in this section, but they're now much different from that style. They're light-colored, gassy, and watery, with a delicate sweetness and an *adjunct* (corn or rice is the adjunct grain mixed with the barley) aroma and flavor (light versions have almost no taste or aroma). Primarily thirst quenchers, they're designed to be served very cold.

Despite the resurgence of the worldwide brewing industry and the reintroduction of many traditional beer styles, more than 80 percent of all the beer made in the world is still the Pale Lager style.

✔ **American Dark Lagers:** Like their lighter counterparts, these lagers are timid versions of European exemplars. They lack the fullness and rich, malty flavor of the German Dark Lager style and have more bark than bite — which is why they can easily be man's best friend. However, they're not widely available.

✔ **Bock Beer:** Traditional Bock Beers are generally dark, somewhat strong, and pretty intensely malty. This style originated in the Northern German brewing city of Einbeck and was later introduced to Bavaria where it became even more popular.

The name is believed to be a corruption of the Einbeck name in the Bavarian accent. *Bock* also means billy goat in German, thus, the association between Bock Beer and goats.

✔ **Doppelbock:** A dark and dangerously delicious malty brew of rich body and high alcohol, Doppelbock was first brewed in the Italian Alps by the monks in the monastery of St. Francis of Paula for sustenance throughout the Lenten season. Often referred to as *liquid bread,* Doppelbocks are easily spotted on beer menus because of the *-ator* suffix (Celebrator, Salvator, Maximator, Triumphator, and so forth).

✔ **Dortmunder Export:** This bright golden lager hails from the industrial region of Dortmund in Germany. It offers the maltiness of a Munich Helles and the hoppiness of a Pilsner, and it's slightly stronger than both. The term *export* refers to the beer's alcoholic strength and can be applied to other beer styles as well. This style is in decline and isn't always easy to find outside of Germany.

✔ **Eisbock:** An anomaly in the brewing world, Eisbock (ice bock) doesn't come by its full body and high alcohol content naturally. By subjecting the already fermented beer to subfreezing temperatures, brewers can then sieve out the water crystals that form in the beer. The beer that's left behind is a much more concentrated version of itself (7 to 33 percent concentration).

The process of partially freezing beer to extract ice crystals and concentrate the beer is called *ice distillation*. Because this process is a form of distillation, some brewers may be required to get a special license.

✔ **Helles Bock:** This beer is a pale version of traditional Bock Beer (*Helles* means pale).

✔ **Maibock:** Maibock is a nod to the month it's brewed in (*Mai* is May). These paler, hoppier versions of Bock Beer are a fairly recent development in comparison to other members of the Bock Beer family.

✔ **Märzenbier/Oktoberfest Beers:** Märzenbier was Bavaria's answer to Austria's Vienna Lager. It's malt-forward, amber in color, and very easy to drink. It was traditionally brewed in the month of March (*Marz*) at the end of the brewing season, stored in caves over the summer, and served in autumn amidst harvest celebrations. Märzenbier eventually became the official beer of Oktoberfest.

✔ **Munich Dunkel:** This classic brown lager of Munich was developed as a darker, maltier counterpart to Munich Helles. It became very popular throughout Bavaria, especially Franconia.

✔ **Munich Helles:** A pale (*Helles* means pale) lager, Munich Helles is malty-sweet and clean on the palate. The creation of this beer style can be traced back to Munich in 1895, when the Spaten Brewery introduced a maltier Bavarian beer to compete with the famous Pilsner style beers.

✔ **Pilsner (also spelled Pils, Pilsener, and in the Czech Republic, Plzensky):** Pilsner is the authentic beer from the Czech Republic that many American brand-name beers aspire to be: an aromatic, subtly malty, crisp, and refreshingly bitter (hoppy) lager. It's a real classic, brewed since 1842 by the folks who originated it (Pilsner Urquell was the first golden, clear beer) and the most imitated style throughout the world.

✔ **Rauchbier (Smoked Beer):** The Rauchbier can range from a friendly campfire-like smokiness to an intense and acrid pungency. It's definitely an acquired taste, but you haven't lived until you've tasted one with smoked ham or sausage and some sharp cheddar cheese. This beer is for sipping, not inhaling!

The traditional wood used to smoke the malts for making Rauchbier is beechwood — the same type of wood used to age Budweiser.

✔ **Schwarzbier:** The Schwarzbier is a regional specialty beer from northern Bavaria. It's believed to be a variant of the Munich Dunkel style but darker and drier (less sweet) on the palate. Some people liken Schwarzbier to a black Pilsner.

✔ **Vienna Lager:** The Vienna Lager is the malty, amber-colored, medium-bodied cousin of Märzenbier. Vienna Lager is actually more abundant and visible in Mexico than its home country of Austria, due to Emperor Maximilian's rule there back in the 1800s.

LAGERS

Pale Lager	Amber Lager	Bock	Dark Lager	Specialty Lager
American Light Lager	Marzen/Oktoberfest	Traditional Bock	Munich Dunkel	Herb & Spice
Pilsner	Vienna Lager	Helles Bock	Schwarzbier	Fruit
Dortmunder	Rauchbier	Maibock		Smoke
Munich Helles		Doppelbock		Winter Warmers/Holiday Beers
		Eisbock		

Figure 4-2: The lager family tree.

Hybrid beers

Some beer styles don't fit perfectly into the ale and lager categories because brewers mix the ingredients and processes of both categories into one beer (as I explain earlier in this chapter). For example, a brewer may use an ale yeast but a lager fermentation temperature.

Where do hybrids, like the following, fit into the beer family tree? Think of an exotic, mysterious, well-traveled uncle: a bit off the chart, not to everyone's liking, but with a definite appeal for some of us.

✔ **Altbier:** Altbier is a German Ale (a rare bird, indeed). *Alt* means old, referring to the fact that the beer is fermented the old way — with top-fermenting ale yeast strains (see the earlier section "Old-School Beer: Understanding Ales" for details). Modern Altbiers are fermented warm like ales but aged cold like lagers. The typical Altbier is malty with an assertive palate and a fair amount of hop bitterness, though the hop blend (because it's complex) tends to differ from one brewery to the next. Dusseldorf, Germany, is considered the center of Altbier production.

✔ **California Common Beer (formerly known as Steam Beer):** Like its Steam predecessor, this beer features a medium body, a toasty and malty palate, and a fairly aggressive hop presence in aroma, flavor, and bitterness. The California Common Beer is warm fermented with lager yeast.

✔ **Cream Ale:** Cream Ale is a light-bodied, thoroughly American invention. As American brewers continued to produce light-bodied ales, they tried making them with longer and colder fermentations, as was being done with lager beer (these ales weren't spared the introduction of adjunct grains, either). The resulting beer is similar to American lagers and is often noted for its obvious corny aroma and flavor, along with a mild, perfumy-sweet grain palate. Cream Ale is pale in color and highly carbonated.

✔ **Kölsch (roughly pronounced *kelsh*):** Being named after the city of Köln (Cologne), Germany, indicates that the beer was brewed in the traditional style of that city. Kölsch is brewed as an ale with top-fermenting yeast strains but undergoes a cold fermentation process. It's noticeably pale and hazy, partly due to the addition of wheat, but mostly the result of being unfiltered. Kölsch is clean on the palate with a slight lactic (milky) sourness, relatively thin-bodied, and not very strong. Its medium hop bitterness has a drying effect. Overall, Kölsch is a refreshing, summery type of beer.

Because Kölsch is a protected appellation, only members of the Köln Brewer's Union may call their beer a Kölsch.

Specialty beers

The *specialty beers* category is more or less a catch-all for the beer styles that don't fit elsewhere. When it comes to specialty beers' place on the beer family tree, the wild artiste cousin is the model: bold, loud, experimental, often goofy, usually quite memorable, and lovable despite having flouted convention.

As I explain earlier in this chapter, specialty beers are typically regular beers brewed to a classic style (such as Porter, Stout, or Pale Ale) but with some new flavor added. Others beers in this category are made from unusual fermented foods. The addition of fruits, herbs and spices, miscellaneous flavorings (such as licorice, smoke, and hot pepper), and odd fermentables (such as honey, maple syrup, and molasses) turn an ordinary beer into a specialty beer. In many ways, specialty beers are the most fun to try.

People who are new to beer drinking or perhaps claim not to be beer fans seem especially surprised and pleased when they try these exotic brews for the first time, especially fruit-flavored beers. This fact isn't lost on brewers, who now make creating new beers with broad appeal a high priority. Urge them on!

Brewmasters take a great deal of pleasure and artistic liberties when creating specialty beers. Everything but the kitchen sink can be added to a beer, and I'm sure it won't be long until someone tries the sink, too. After all, people have tried garlic beer (very, very bad idea) and even hot chili pepper beer (which is sort of like drinking liquid heartburn). *Caveat emptor.* Some of the more subtle blends are often the most outstanding — a Blackberry Porter comes to mind.

- **Fruit Beers:** Fruit Beers are generally light- to medium-bodied lagers or ales that have been given a fruity flavor by way of real fruit or fruit extract. They tend to have a sweeter finish than other beers. The popular fruit flavors are cherry, raspberry, and blueberry, but finding a beer that tastes of apricot, peach, or merionberry isn't unusual.

  Note: Belgian Lambic Beers are also fruited, but they're in a class by themselves (see the ale descriptions earlier in this chapter).

- **Herb and Spice Beers:** These herbs and spices may include anything from cinnamon to tarragon; any beer style can be made with any herbs or spices. Summer and winter seasonal brews are typical.

  Although Pumpkin Beers have been made with real pumpkin, the big-name commercial versions are generally just laced with the spices that are reminiscent of pumpkin pie (cinnamon, ginger, nutmeg, and allspice).

- **Smoked Beer:** A Smoked Beer is any beer style that's been given a smoky character, though one style in particular lends itself well to a smoky aroma and taste: Porter. The flavor profile of the underlying beer should always show through the smoke.

- **Wassail:** Wassail isn't a specific beer style, *per se,* but a very traditional style of spiced beer that's brewed for Christmas and the holiday season. Wassail is often called by other names, like *holiday beer, yule ale, winter warmer,* and if it contains fruit, *mulled ale.* (Wassail can be grouped with the fruit or the spice beers — it's hard to plug neatly into a slot — but as an old standard, it merits its own listing.)

  The word *wassail* (rhymes with *fossil*) comes from the Old English *waes hael* — be hale or be whole, both of which meant be of good health. This term was considered the proper toast when presenting someone with a libation. The drink of choice back then was usually *mulled ale,* a warmed-up strong ale laden with spices like nutmeg and ginger and sweetened with sugar or pieces of fruit, usually roasted crab apple.

Chapter 5

Investigating "Real" Ale

*O*ne of the options beer drinkers may encounter on their beer excursions is to order a pint of *real* ale. Not that fake ale ever really existed, but some ale is more real than others. Curious? Confused? Read this chapter for the full scoop on real ale, how it's made, and how it's served.

Understanding What Makes Ale "Real"

Real ale refers to beer that's served the old-fashioned way. Real ale is brewed from traditional ingredients (the ones I describe in Chapter 2) and is allowed to mature and age naturally. Maturing and aging naturally means the beer is unfiltered and unpasteurized, which means it still has live yeast in it and continues to condition and develop flavor and character even after it leaves the brewery. (When a beer is *conditioning,* it's still fermenting a little bit, thus creating a gentle, natural carbonation within its container.) So, real ale is considered living ale.

Real ale is always served without any extraneous carbon dioxide, nitrogen, or any other gas pushing it from its container — commonly referred to as *head pressure.* Real ale is traditionally pulled manually with a hand pump or by gravity dispense (see the later section "Dispensing Real Ale" for more about these methods).

Most real ales are packaged in casks (as you find out in the following section). But by these very clear parameters of what constitutes real ale, *bottle-conditioned beer* also qualifies as real ale. Bottle-conditioned beer still has live yeast in the bottle that can cause the beer to continue to change over time. Hooray for homebrewers (and a handful of commercial brewers)!

Despite persistent rumors to the contrary, real ale isn't warm and flat. Well, okay, when compared to near frozen American mass-market lagers, real ale is warmer and flatter. But when judged on its own merits, real ale is very fresh and delicate. The aromas and flavors are more alive in your nose and on your palate, and your tongue isn't attacked by aggressive carbonation but rather tickled by a soft and gentle spritziness.

In England, Scotland, and Ireland, a voluntary accreditation scheme allows *publicans*, or pub owners, to display a special symbol in the pub that indicates the real ale served there is of good quality. Look for the Cask Marque, which is "the sign of a great pint," if you want to be assured of a good, fresh pint of real ale (see Figure 5-1).

Figure 5-1:
The Cask Marque — the sign of a great pint.

Courtesy of Cask Marque

Oh, and although Britain is the only country in the world that commonly serves real ale, finding real ale in the United States and other countries, where beer culture is evolving and progressing, is rapidly becoming popular.

Starting the Real Ale Journey in Casks

Real ale that's conditioned and served as described in the preceding section is also known as *cask ale* or *cask beer.* The terms *cask ale* or *cask beer* are used to differentiate from keg beer. Both cask beer and keg beer are brewed the exact same way — same ingredients, same processes. The only difference is how the beer is treated after primary fermentation is complete.

In the following sections, I describe the parts of a cask and I list different cask sizes used for real ale.

So how exactly is keg beer different from cask beer? *Keg beer* is packaged in and served from a pressurized keg. After active fermentation, keg beer is filtered and sometimes pasteurized — depending on its destination — to kill off and remove the yeast from the beer. (Keg beer that's brewed and sold in the United States is rarely pasteurized, but beer that's imported to the United States is almost always pasteurized due to the long period of time — often months — that it takes a shipment of beer to reach its destination.)

Filtering and pasteurizing the beer is an effective way to increase the stability and shelf life of the beer, but it also kills some of the flavor and character. Filtering not only removes the yeast, but it also filters out body-building dextrins, which can make the beer seem thinner and lighter bodied, as well as proteins that would otherwise aid in head retention. (Flip to Chapter 9 for more information about kegs.)

A barrel of fun: Checking out the parts of a cask

Casks resemble typical barrels in that they have a larger circumference at their middle than they do at their ends. They're designed to rest on their sides, or horizontally, when filled with beer that's ready for dispensing. (Old-fashioned kegs used to have this barrel shape, but today, most are straight-sided and are designed to sit upright as the beer is dispensed.)

Casks also have parts that are unlike those on a standard keg — and that are key to serving real ale. Casks have *shives* and *keystones,* and they're meant to rest in a *stillage* (see Figure 5-2). I describe each of these parts in the following list:

- **Shive:** The shive, which is used like a stopper to close the hole in the cask, is found on the side of the cask at its widest circumference. The shive is where the *landlord* (a British term for pub owner) or *cellarman* (the person in charge of ensuring that the real ale is cared for in the cellar) places the soft *spile,* or peg, that allows the ale to breathe as it conditions (see the later section "From the spile file: Letting real ale breathe" for details).

✔ **Keystone:** The *keystone,* which closes a hole found on the head of the cask (one of the flat ends of the cask), is where the landlord or cellarman inserts the spigot (tap) or draught line if the cask is tapped via a beer engine (see the later section "Pulling real ale through a beer engine" for more information).

✔ **Stillage:** The stillage is a cradle of sorts that holds the cask in place on its side while the beer is conditioning and being dispensed from it. A stillage may hold a single cask, or it may hold several casks, depending on its size.

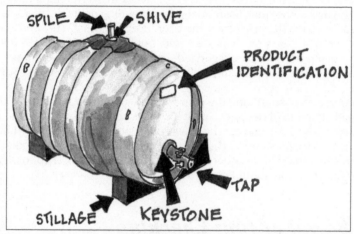

Figure 5-2:
The parts of
a cask.

Sizing up the situation: Pins, firkins, kilderkins, and beyond

From a historical perspective, all vessels designed to hold large amounts of beer, wine, or distilled spirits were originally made of wood. Nowadays, these vessels can also be made out of stainless steel, aluminum, and even food-grade plastics. You can find casks (and kegs, for that matter) in all these types of materials, but stainless steel is the most common today.

Despite their transition from wood to more modern materials, casks still go by nomenclature that's both odd and interesting — and may even make you snicker. But understanding the different types of casks is really all about size and liquid volume. Table 5-1 provides a list of various casks, their names, and their liquid volumes (note that according to tradition, these casks are listed in Imperial gallons; to convert Imperial gallons to standard U.S. gallons, multiply by 0.83257).

Table 5-1	What's in a Name — or Cask, That Is	
Cask Name	*Liquid Volume*	*Other Cask Equivalents*
Pin	4.5 gallons	
Firkin	9 gallons	= 2 pins
Kilderkin	18 gallons	= 2 firkins / 4 pins
Barrel	36 gallons	= 2 kilderkins / 4 firkins / 8 pins
Hogshead	54 gallons	= 3 kilderkins / 6 firkins / 12 pins
Puncheon	72 gallons	= 2 barrels / 4 kilderkins / 16 pins
Butt	108 gallons	= 2 hogsheads / 3 barrels / 10 kilderkins / 12 firkins
Tun	216 gallons	= 2 butts / 3 puncheons / 4 hogsheads / 6 barrels

The names for the barrels in Table 5-1 were believed to have been designated way back in the 15th century, and they've remained unchanged ever since.

Because of the nature of real ale — poor stability, limited shelf life, and so on — most brewers prefer to package their beer in smaller vessels to help ensure product freshness. The smaller the vessel, the quicker its contents are emptied. Therefore, real ale is typically found only in pins, firkins, and kilderkins.

Refining and Conditioning Real Ale

For the vast majority of breweries around the world, after their beer is packaged and leaves the premises, all that really matters is that the beer is kept cold as much as possible and is consumed as soon and as fresh as possible. Not so with real ale. In the following sections, I talk about adding clarifiers to real ale during packaging and letting it breathe after it arrives at its destination.

Most old-fashioned pubs have cellars below the public space. The cellar is the perfect place for keeping a large stillage where many casks may condition simultaneously. Most cellars also keep a consistent optimum temperature for cask ales; 55 degrees Fahrenheit (12 degrees Celsius) is considered perfect cellar temperature.

Let me make this perfectly clear: Clarifying with finings

Beer that's unfiltered and unpasteurized (like real ale) still contains millions of live yeast cells in liquid suspension. With the help of gravity, and in due time, beer clarifies all by itself. But to clear the beer of all this yeast in an expeditious manner, brewers use what are called *finings*. A brewer adds finings to real ale when he *racks* or transfers the ale in its natural, unfiltered, and unpasteurized state into a cask. These finings basically clot yeast cells and other organic matter and drag them to the bottom of the cask where they settle and form a jelly-like mass of sediment. When this happens, the beer is said to have *dropped bright*.

What finings do is fairly uncomplicated; what finings are is a bit more interesting. Here are two of the most common finings:

- **Carrageen:** Also known as Irish moss, *carrageen* is a species of red algae found in abundance along the rocky shores of the Atlantic coasts of Europe and North America. In addition to its abundance, carrageen is also a prized clarifier due to its ability to hold 20 to 100 times its weight in water when hydrated, forming a thick jelly-like substance.

- **Isinglass:** *Isinglass* is a form of collagen derived from the swim bladders of certain fish. After the bladders are removed from the fish, they're processed and dried. Isinglass was originally made exclusively from sturgeon, but now it may also be a cheaper substitute made from cod. Isinglass may occasionally be used along with another fining agent to further accelerate the process of sedimentation.

  Not to gross you out, but prior to the introduction of the less expensive gelatin, isinglass was used in confectionary and desserts, such as fruit jelly and marmalade.

Other less-commonly used beer clarifiers include the following:

- **Albumen:** Albumen is derived from egg whites. Dried albumen is rehydrated with water and added to the beer. Similar to gelatin, albumen is also positively charged so it attracts negatively charged proteins and yeast.

- **Bentonite:** Bentonite is a non-organic material combined with a form of fine powdered clay. When mixed with water, bentonite is very effective at clarifying liquids.

- **Gelatin:** Gelatin is derived from the ground hooves of cows and horses. It's a colorless, tasteless, and odorless water soluble protein that attracts negatively charged proteins and yeast.

✔ **Pectinase:** Pectinase is a general term for the various pectic enzymes that break down pectin, a jelly-like substance found in the cell walls of plants. Pectinase breaks down the pectin haze that can form in beer — especially those that contain fruit.

✔ **PVPP (polyvinylpolypyrrolidone):** Say that five times fast! Also known by its commercial name, *Polyclar* is made up of minute plastic beads that are statically charged, thereby attracting particulate matter to themselves like electrostatic glue. (Pharmaceutical companies also use this product to produce capsule-type drugs.)

When a brewer adds finings to a cask of real ale, he may also add more hops and priming sugar. The extra dose of hops provides the beer with more hop aroma — not bitterness — and the priming sugar gives the yeast a little something to eat in order to create carbon dioxide within the cask. The cask is then sealed and shipped off to the pub.

From the spile file: Letting real ale breathe

When the cask arrives at its destination, the landlord or cellarman is now in charge of seeing that the cask is properly cared for before serving that beer to the public. Doing so requires much more than simply putting the beer on tap. Suffice it to say that the cellarman's role in the quality of real ale is just as crucial as the brewer's.

When the cellarman determines that the beer has dropped bright and is about ready for serving, he knocks a soft spile into the shive, which is located on the side of the cask. (I talk about shives in the earlier section "A barrel of fun: Checking out the parts of a cask.") The soft spile — sometimes called a *peg* — is made of porous material that allows air to pass through it, thus allowing the cask to breathe.

Because CO_2 gas is allowed to vent off through the soft spile, the cellarman can gauge conditioning activity by the bubbles that form around the spile. After wiping the spile clean, the cellarman can watch how fast the bubbles reform. If the bubbles reform slowly, it means the yeast is settling down, and the ale carbonating is near completion. If the bubbles reform quickly, it means the yeast is still active, and the ale isn't yet fully carbonated.

When the beer has reached the desired clarity and carbonation level, the cellarman replaces the soft spile with a hard spile, which doesn't allow gases in or out of the cask. The beer is then allowed to settle for about 24 hours before serving.

The cask has to be open and breathing (with a soft spile in place) while drawing a beer, or you'll create a vacuum in the beer line (and cask), which is why casks have such a short shelf life (about three days). You not only draw air in to the cask with each pour — which hastens the staling process — but you also have a vessel that isn't under any pressure, so the beer will eventually lose all its carbonation.

Real ale should be consumed within three days of drawing the first beer from the cask, because it begins deteriorating immediately thereafter. With this in mind, some landlords insist on using a *cask breather,* which allows a small amount of carbon dioxide to replace the oxygen in the cask. Cask breathers don't release enough carbon dioxide to carbonate the beer or push the beer through the beer lines but just enough to blanket the beer to keep it fresher tasting for longer. (Because using a cask breather is considered adding extraneous carbon dioxide, this method isn't endorsed by CAMRA, a group that I talk about later in this chapter.)

Dispensing Real Ale

When the time comes to serve real ale, the cask has to be fitted with a dispensing device. Depending on where the cask is kept at the pub, it may be fitted with a simple tap or a beer line to draw the beer through a beer engine. I discuss both options in the following sections.

Pulling real ale through a beer engine

A *beer engine* is a manual device used to siphon beer from a cask. Because it requires a bartender to literally pull the beer through the beer line, beer engines are also referred to as *handpulls.* In the following sections, I explain how a beer engine works and describe how to pour real ale from a beer engine.

The first beer engine was invented by Joseph Bramah in 1797. Bramah is one of the two founders of hydraulic engineering who first gained fame by improving the functionality of water closets (toilets) in London. Am I the only one who sees a connection here?

The workings of a beer engine

The mechanics of a beer engine are quite simple (see Figure 5-3). The airtight piston chamber is at the heart of it all. When the bartender pulls the beer engine handle, beer is drawn from the cask into the piston (it may take several pulls, depending on how long the beer line is). A one-way valve holds the beer within the piston. When the bartender pulls the handle again, the beer in the piston flows out through another one-way valve and to the beer engine's tap as more beer is drawn to fill the void in the piston chamber.

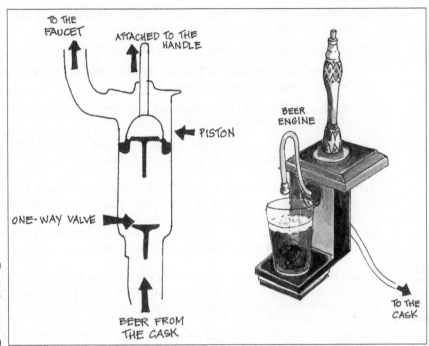

Figure 5-3:
How a beer
engine
works.

The typical beer engine can draw about half a pint of beer with each pull of
the handle, so a good, strong, and efficient bartender should be able to fill
your pint glass with two full draws. Cheers!

Though some beer engines may have short spouts and a small flip tap, the fan-
cier ones have elongated spouts that travel first upward then downward in an
elegant 180 degree curve. This type of spout is called a *swan neck.* Some pubs
also attach an adjustable *sparkler* (which functions like a small shower head)
to the end of the swan neck, which regulates the flow of beer into the glass.
When the sparkler is tight, the beer is agitated as it flows through and results
in a large head and less carbonation in the beer. When the sparkler is wide
open, less head is created, but the beer has more spritz to it.

The "proper" pour from a beer engine

Some patrons can be downright persnickety about how their pint of real ale
is drawn and served, so bartenders had better be on their toes. Knowing how
to pull a pint may be more of a science than an art, but it can still be done
with a flourish; just follow these steps:

1. Make sure the glassware is *beer clean* — the highest degree of glassware cleanliness. (See Chapter 11 for details.)

2. Make a smooth and even draw on the handle.

3. Wait several seconds to allow the head to rise and begin to fall a bit before starting the second draw.

4. Make sure the customer gets a *full measure* of beer — that is, fill the glass up to the top with minimal head.

   The well-poured pint has a head that rises just above the rim of the glass, which is referred to as *just proud* of the rim.

Some controversy exists about whether the pint glass should be held up to the beer engine so the swan neck is immersed in the beer as it's drawn. Some people say this method keeps the foaming to a minimum as the beer is being poured, and others say the swan neck can become a breeding ground for bacteria if not rinsed after each pour. The debate rages on.

What's known as *draft beer* to millions of people is really *draught beer.* The word *draught* means to pull, as you would a beer engine's handle. Wagon-pulling equines are called draught horses for the same reason.

Presentation, for all its pleasant visuals, is all for naught if the beer itself isn't in palatable condition. The beer line and the piston chamber in the beer engine continue to hold beer between draws. This beer goes stale when left overnight, so it's of utmost importance that the bartender pours the first pint or two drawn the next day down the drain and not serve stale beer to an unsuspecting customer.

Using a tap for gravity dispense

Having a classic pub setup for your real ale just isn't feasible for some times, locations, and events, such as when you don't have a downstairs cellar or a bar top to affix the beer engine to. Or maybe you have only a single cask of a special, one-time-only guest beer available to serve. For these situations, simple gravity dispense works best.

Gravity dispense, or *gravity pour,* is all about letting Mother Nature do the work for you. By simply fitting the cask with a spigot and a soft spile, you can draw beer rather quickly and easily. No pushing, no pulling, no gas — of the inert type, anyway.

Because gravity dispense requires very little setup or take-down, most beer festivals that feature real ale favor this method of pouring.

Pump it up: The use of tall fonts

Northern England and Scotland have a tradition of using electric pumps — or air pressure *tall fonts,* as they're called — to push beer out of a cask. Air is forced into the headspace of the cask, thus forcing the beer to the tap. For all its convenience, this method contravenes the standards for real ale.

CAMRA: Campaign for Real Ale

Mirroring the downsizing of the American brewing industry and the homogenization of American beers, the British brewing industry was suffering a similar fate. The land of the venerable English Ale was succumbing to a lager invasion from both the United States and Europe.

Similarly, the friendly, local, independent, neighborhood pubs were disappearing from the scene — or were being taken over by corporate brewing concerns that were attracting a younger, hipper, rowdier, lager- and cider-drinking crowd.

Real ale, it seemed, had seen better days.

That was until 1971. It was then that four, dedicated British beer drinkers decided to oppose what they saw as the ruination of their heritage, their favorite tipple, and their beloved local pub. Graham Lees, Bill Mellor, Michael Hardman, and Jim Makin formed the Campaign for the Revitalization of Ale. Perhaps no other group has been more influential in the world of beer and brewing — especially in Britain. The group, known simply as *CAMRA,* eventually decided to make its title easier to remember and say by shortening it to *Campaign for Real Ale.*

Today, CAMRA is an independent, voluntary, consumer organization whose main aims are promoting real ale, real cider, and the traditional British pub. CAMRA is the largest single-issue consumer group in the United Kingdom and is a founding member of the European Beer Consumer's Union (EBCU). CAMRA reached the 100,000 member mark in 2009 and since surpassed 120,000 members.

CAMRA is very involved in issues that affect the British brewing industry, including

- Promoting less common styles of beer and traditionally brewed beverages
- Promoting small brewing and pub businesses

- Reducing consolidation among local British brewers
- Reducing taxes on beer
- Reforming licensing laws

CAMRA is also very active in consumer issues as well, such as the following:

- Promoting quality, choice, and value for money
- Protecting and improving consumer rights
- Seeking improvements in all licensed premises and throughout the brewing industry
- Supporting the public house as a focus of community life

CAMRA gets its message out in a variety of ways, starting with publishing. In addition to its monthly newsletter, *What's Brewing,* and its very cleverly titled quarterly magazine, *Beer,* CAMRA also publishes the *Good Beer Guide,* which is an annually compiled directory of its recommended pubs and brewers. Anyone planning on doing a little beer trekking in the United Kingdom would be well served by using this guide. For information on this and anything else about CAMRA, go to www.camra.org.uk/.

CAMRA also maintains a Pub Heritage Group, which was established to identify, record, and protect Public House interiors of historic and/or architectural importance. The group maintains two inventories of Heritage Pubs:

- The National Inventory for pubs that have maintained their original condition for at least 30 years. As of 2009, the National Inventory contained 289 pubs.
- The larger Regional Inventory of pubs that aren't eligible for the National Inventory.

And finally, CAMRA supports and promotes numerous beer (and cider) festivals around Britain each year, but none is as large or as prestigious as the Great British Beer Festival (see Chapter 21 for the scoop). This annual event, which takes place each August in London, is where CAMRA doles out its most coveted award: Champion Beer of Britain.

Chapter 6

Exploring Barrel-Aged and Wood-Aged Beer

In This Chapter

▶ Distinguishing barrel-aged beer from wood-aged beer

▶ Determining which wood is best for aging beer

▶ Discovering some milestones in the aging process

*P*erhaps you've heard, sung, or even danced the old beer-drinking song "Roll Out the Barrel." That harkens back to a day when beer used to be stored in wooden barrels. Well, the song is still as popular as ever — and it's a good thing, too, because wooden barrels are once again being used to store beer. If that doesn't get you up dancing the polka, nothing will.

In this chapter, you discover the difference between barrel-aged and wood-aged beer, get the scoop on the best types of barrels to use in aging beer, and explore a few milestones in the aging process.

Differentiating Between "Barrel-Aged" and "Wood-Aged"

At first glance, the terms *barrel-aged* and *wood-aged* may seem a bit redundant. After all, the barrels I'm talking about are made out of wood, so what gives?

You can argue that beer can be aged *in* wood or beer can be aged *on* wood. The simple difference is this:

✔ Beer aged *in* wood is beer aged inside a wooden barrel. In other words, it's barrel-aged (of course).

✔ Beer aged *on* wood is beer that's had wood added to the vessel in which the beer is aging — which isn't necessarily made of wood. In other words, it's wood-aged.

The irony of barrel-aged beer's comeback

Perhaps you've heard the saying "What's old is new." This phrase couldn't be more relevant than it is on the topic of beer being aged in wooden barrels these days.

About a century and a half ago, all beer was aged in wooden barrels. In fact, beer was fermented, aged, transported, and served in wooden vats and barrels. The worldwide brewing industry primarily used wooden barrels for hundreds and hundreds of years, having replaced earthenware jugs and amphorae several millennia ago. It wasn't until aluminum and stainless steel became the materials of choice that wooden beer barrels were made somewhat obsolete — at least to brewers.

Ironically, as the brewing industry left the wood world behind, favoring much cleaner, safer, and more durable metal containers, the wine and spirits industries continued to use wooden barrels to age their products unabated. Today, barrel-aged beer is the hottest ticket in the market.

American megabrewer Anheuser-Busch touts the fact that Budweiser is beechwood aged. What this means is that small, rough planks of beechwood are added to the aging vessel, which "enhances fermentation creating a crisper, more sparkling carbonation while imparting smoothness to the characteristic taste of Budweiser." Note that this method doesn't leave any residual wood flavor in the beer.

Flavoring wood — overwhelmingly of the oak variety — is sold in different forms: rough chips, smooth and uniform cubes, and long spirals (spirals are 1½- to 2-inch diameter spindles cut in spirals to create maximum contact with the beer, and they're typically 1 to 4 feet in length). Toast levels refer to how richly toasted the wood is. Brewers can order light, medium, or heavy toast, depending on the flavors he wants to imbue in his beer.

Figuring Out Which Wood Is Best

The whole point of having beer in contact with wood is for the beer to pick up some of the aroma and flavor characteristics of the wood. Additionally, if the beer is aging in a barrel that previously held another fermented beverage, such as wine or whiskey, the beer will also pick up the character of that beverage.

So what type of wood is best to use? I describe some considerations for brewers in the following sections.

Choosing new or used barrels

Buy new or used? People have asked this question millions of times when it comes to big-ticket items like houses and cars, but you'd think it'd be a moot point when it comes to beer barrels. Why wouldn't a brewer want all new barrels for his beers?

- ✔ Brewers don't want all new barrels because of the cost. Whether brewers have their own cooperage or buy their barrels from others, brand-new barrels represent a considerable expense for the brewery.

  In the days before aluminum and stainless steel beer barrels, most breweries had their own on-premise cooperages, which is where the wooden barrels were constructed. The Samuel Smith brewery in Yorkshire, England, is one of the few breweries in the world that still has its own cooperage.

- ✔ New barrels (especially oak) can impart a very raw, woody flavor in beer that's sharp and astringent. *Tannin,* the bitter component that's leached from grape skins to give red wine more backbone, is also leached out of wood. Tannins can make beer bitter and unpleasant. In order to avoid high tannin levels in their cask beer, brewers coat the interior of their barrels with pine *pitch* to minimize contact with the wood (pitch is a gooey, sticky liquid derived from resin collected from coniferous trees).

The whole point of utilizing previously used barrels for aging beer is to saturate the beer with the flavor enhancements from whatever beverage was last in that barrel. That unique flavor is something you can't get from a brand-new barrel. (See the later section "Creating new beer flavors with old barrel flavors" for more information.)

The advantages to using new barrels are that when they're newly constructed, they're as sturdy and water tight as they'll ever be, and a well-made barrel can last many years. Old barrels can dry out, leak, and fall apart at inopportune times.

Opting for oak

You can choose from a fair variety of different wood species for making barrels, each with its own wood character. Oak is the species of preference for barrel-making for these reasons:

- ✔ Oak is a durable wood.
- ✔ Oak isn't a porous wood.
- ✔ Oak imbues beer (and wine and whiskey) with pleasant and desirable flavors.

✔ Oak is abundant in Europe and North America (where most of the world's wines, whiskies, and beers happen to be made).

American white oak is more robust than European white oak, which isn't necessarily a good thing — unless you're a bourbon maker. For many beverage producers, subtlety and refinement are better than coarse and unbalanced flavors.

Creating new beer flavors with old barrel flavors

Today's brewers realize that much can be gained by aging their beers in barrels that once held other fermented beverages. They also realize that barrel aging isn't an exact science; in fact, it's much closer to an art form. And many brewers are learning as they go.

Barrel aging beer isn't simply a matter of brewing a beer, fermenting it, and then letting it sit in a barrel for a few weeks or months and then packaging it. A handful of variables come into play when barrel aging beer (as you discover in the later section "Marking Some Milestones in the Aging Process"). When it comes to choosing barrels for their beer, brewers have to consider the following, as I explain in this section:

✔ What kind of barrel will be used (wine, cognac, whiskey, and so on)?

✔ What's the base beer style (Porter, Stout, Barleywine, and so on)? (Flip to Chapter 4 for an introduction to beer styles.)

✔ Will the finished beer be *straight* (unblended) or blended with another beer?

Picking your poison: Bourbon barrels and beyond

Brewers have the following barrel choices for barrel aging.

✔ **Bourbon barrels:** Right now, American bourbon barrels are the hottest ticket for barrel aging. One reason is their easy availability. Another reason is their intense flavor characteristics.

By law, bourbon must be aged for two years in new American oak barrels, and the barrels can be used only once, which means bourbon distillers must rid themselves of thousands of almost-new casks every year. Soaked with the potent flavor of bourbon, these barrels have new roles to play in the aging of rum, tequila, sherry, and, now, beer.

Bourbon barrels are charred on the inside, according to the distiller's specifications; they can be lightly charred or they can be heavily charred. This char, along with the oak character, can permeate the beer, creating an incredible blend of vanilla, caramel, toffee, toast, and/or smoke aromas and flavors.

✔ **Wine and sherry barrels:** Wine and sherry barrels (and to a lesser extent, cognac barrels) are also used with great success. Chardonnay wine barrels, for instance, which aren't charred, infuse the beer with warm oak toastiness and coconut and vanilla aromas and flavors.

One American craft brewer — Dogfish Head — even ages his beer in the exotic Paraguayan Palo Santo wood. *Palo Santo* means holy tree, and its wood has been used in South American wine-making communities.

✔ **Whiskey barrels:** Whiskey barrels give beer flavors similar to those gained by aging beer in bourbon barrels, but whiskey barrels aren't as plentiful.

Choosing an old barrel flavor in the type of beer wanted

In this new age of beer enlightenment, brewers who are making that foray into barrel-aged beer are discovering that a lot of choices exist when it comes to choosing what type of barrel should be used to age their beer. Each barrel has its own personality and character and presents a different possibility.

Choosing between wine and whiskey barrels isn't always a simple choice, but choosing between different types of wines (red or white), fortified wines (port and Madeira), and distilled wines (brandy and cognac) makes the decision even harder. The choices also extend beyond bourbon to other distilled spirits, such as scotch, rum, and tequila.

Generally speaking, bourbon and whiskey barrels are perfect for dark and rich beers, like Imperial Stout, because the dark grain flavors of the beer meld wonderfully with the charred, smoky character of the wood. Wine barrels are for more delicate flavoring. Paler beer styles, such as India Pale Ale, may work better with wine barrels that lend their fruity character to the beer without imbuing any smokiness or color.

Whenever sherry or cognac barrels are used to age beer, it's usually at the whims of the brewer. No hard, fast rules exist about mixing and matching beer styles and barrel types in the brewhouse.

The Boston Beer Company ages its Barrel Room Collection of beers in used brandy barrels. The oak itself, along with the residual brandy character, imparts unique flavors to the beers it houses. The process of aging in this wood helps soften the beers' character and mellows out some of their ethanol (alcohol) harshness.

What's even more impressive is that brewers are making concerted efforts to pair specific beer styles with specific types of barrels. Different types of barrels have general characteristics that make them especially suitable for certain beers.

Barrel-aged beers by the numbers

At the 2011 edition of the Great American Beer Festival in Denver, Colorado, wood- and barrel-aged beer had 307 entries, broken down in the following categories:

✔ Wood and Barrel Aged Beer: 40 entries

✔ Wood and Barrel Aged Strong Beer: 118 entries

✔ Wood and Barrel Aged Strong Stout: 74 entries

✔ Wood and Barrel Aged Sour Beer: 75 entries

Considering these beer styles didn't even exist a few years ago speaks volumes about the interest in these categories.

The Russian River Brewing Company in California goes so far as aging individual beers in barrels of their own specific wine type. Temptation, a Belgian Blonde Ale, is aged in Chardonnay barrels. Supplication, a Belgian Brown Ale, is aged in Pinot Noir barrels, and Consecration, a dark Belgian Ale, is aged in American Cabernet Sauvignon barrels.

Much of what's taking place in the craft-brewing industry these days as it pertains to aging beer *in* and *on* wood is completely experimental. To what extent a brewer can foresee the outcome of any beer that's aged long-term in a wooden barrel is questionable — especially those brews that are blended. Only repeated experimentation yields predictable results. See the "Blending beers from two or more barrels" section later in this chapter.

Marking Some Milestones in the Aging Process

Brewers can't always set a packaging date on the calendar ahead of time for barrel-aged and wood-aged beer. More often than not, the beer decides when it's ready. Barrel-aged and wood-aged beers need to be tasted periodically to assess their flavor progression. This process can take months or even years.

In the following sections, I describe several important milestones in the barrel-aging and wood-aging process (check out Chapter 3 for general information on brewing beer).

Checking the beer's oxidation

As if choosing barrel types and pairing beer styles (as I explain earlier in this chapter) wasn't enough for brewers to think about, they also have to take into consideration the level of oxidation that occurs while the beer is aging.

As beer ages in wooden barrels, the *staves* — long slats that make up the barrel (see Figure 6-1) — absorb a portion of the beer, and an additional amount may evaporate over time, which can leave a void. At this point, brewers have a few options:

✔ Top off their barrels with more beer to fill that void in order to avoid oxidation in the beer and the aromas and flavors that result from oxidation.

✔ Fill the void with CO_2 (carbon dioxide) gas. Because carbon dioxide gas is heavier than oxygen — and ambient air — it will effectively flush oxygen out of the barrel and leave an invisible protective blanket on top of the beer. That blanket protects the beer from oxidation and its effects.

✔ Allow their beer to age and develop naturally and not do anything about the void in the barrel. The process of allowing minute amounts of air to seep through the wood is a very slow, controlled oxidation that leads to a depth of flavor that can't be gained any other way.

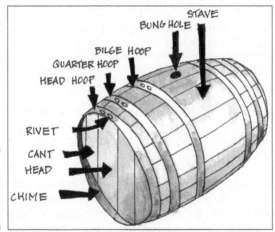

Figure 6-1: The parts of a wooden barrel.

Deciding whether to let the beer sour

In addition to considering oxidative qualities of the aging beer, brewers also have the option of allowing their beer to sour during maturation and aging. Yes, I said *sour!*

Sour Beers have been a part of brewing reality throughout the millennia, but sour flavor in beer was typically considered a negative. In days of yore (whenever yore was), brewers did what they could to avoid letting their beer go sour, but now it's considered a viable option. Many see Sour Beers as a sort of sociable middle ground between adventurous beer drinkers and adventurous wine drinkers. Tart and tangy beers can be either subtle or intense, but they're always brisk and refreshing.

Following are the three different levels of Sour Beer:

- ✔ **Unintentional Sour Beer:** Unintentional Sour Beer comes about just like it sounds — unintentionally — and is basically beer that went bad as the result of a mistake at the brewery, including poor handling or poorly maintained equipment.

- ✔ **Intentional Sour Beer:** This beer is made according to style — in other words, brewers design the recipe to produce a sour-tasting beer (like Berliner Weisse; see Chapter 4).

- ✔ **Anticipated Sour Beer:** The sourness of this beer is a matter of barrel aging's predicted influence on the finished beer, due to wild yeasts and bacteria present in the wood. This process can result in unanticipated flavors in the finished beer — some desirable, some not so much.

Note: For the purpose of this chapter, I'm discussing only level three. And on an important related note, not all barrel-aged beers are sour, and not all Sour Beers are barrel-aged.

In the following sections, I note the risks required in letting beer sour, the types of yeast and bacteria that lead to Sour Beer, and a few great Sour Beers you may want to try.

The risks required

Because barrel aging is more an art than a science, it's not as controllable as standard brewing practices. Producing barrel-aged Sour Beer is taking a leap of faith that involves some risks and requires plenty of patience for the following reasons:

- ✔ **Barrel aging is an expensive wait.** Brewers may have to wait a year or two (or more) to see whether the hazy, yeasty brew resting in dusty, seeping barrels develops into the delectable tangy nectar that was anticipated, or whether it's been rendered undrinkable, ravaged by aggressive yeast and ravenous bacteria.

- ✔ **Barrel aging is a strange dynamic.** Even if the beer turns out to be a majestic example of the brewer's art, brewers may still have to persuade consumers to drink it. One craft brewer reports that he still gets phone calls from customers telling him that a bottle of his barrel-aged beer must have gone bad because it tasted sour!

The microbes that lead to souring (and the beers that result)

Beers that are soured during barrel aging typically come in contact with these wild yeast or bacteria harbored in the barrel wood:

- **Brettanomyces:** *Brettanomyces,* also lovingly referred to as *Brett,* is a wild yeast that many brewers consider to be the evil twin of common beer yeast *(Saccharomyces)*. When Brett sours beer, it leaves a tell-tale barnyard character and sweaty horse blanket aroma.

  If you want to check this souring microbe out — and who wouldn't — sample what many beer connoisseurs consider a classic Brett beer: Orval Trappist Ale from Belgium.

  Barrel oxidation (which I discuss earlier in this chapter) isn't as much of a problem with Brettanomyces. Brett forms a *pellicle* (a lumpy, slimy white film) on the surface of the beer that guards against oxidation from the air-filled void in the barrel.

- **Lactobacillus:** *Lactobacillus* is a beer-souring microbe that creates lactic acid (lactobacillus also sours milk, thus the *lacto* part of the name).

  One of the all-time classic Sour Beers in the world is the highly esteemed Rodenbach Grand Cru from Belgium. What makes this Grand Cru so intriguing is its blend of a young beer (33 percent) with an older beer (67 percent) that's been matured in oak vats for two years. The high percentage of the older aged-in-oak beer gives the Grand Cru the complex and intense bouquet and its lengthy finish. Both are fermented with the same multi-strain yeast, which includes lactobacillus and Brettanomyces.

- **Pediococcus:** *Pediococcus* is also a beer-souring bacteria that's *anaerobic* (meaning it lives without oxygen) and is, therefore, a major potential spoiling bacteria in any beer. One of the major flavor developments as a result of Pediococcus in beer is the production of *diacetyl* — a buttery aroma and flavor.

- **Acetobacter:** *Acetobacter* is a bacteria that produces acetic acid. When beer gets infected with acetobacter, it's on its way to becoming malt vinegar. And you *don't* want to drink that!

Before anyone goes running out in search of a barrel-aged-and-soured beer in her favorite beer style, I need to point out that only a handful of beer styles are designed to be soured during the barrel-aging process. If you're a fan of Czech Pilsner, Dortmunder Export, or Bavarian Bock beer, I'm afraid you're out of luck. As a matter of fact, no lager styles are intentionally soured. Note the word *intentionally.* Some lager styles are barrel aged but only with the intention of deriving the flavor of the wood, not to take on the beer-souring microbes. And even un-soured barrel-aged lagers are few and far between.

If you're interested in tasting the finest examples of old-world barrel-aged beers, check out the Flanders Red Ale style from the Belgian province of West Flanders near the town of Roeselare. Prepare to be amazed and impressed. Prepare to spend a little money, too; they don't crank these beers out in assembly line fashion.

Blending beers from two or more barrels

One of the unsung talents among today's barrel-aging brewers is the ability to assess the progression of the beers' aging in the cask (including the tasks in the preceding sections). Furthermore, very often these brewers must skillfully and artfully blend the contents of two or more barrels to achieve the perfect balance of flavor and beer intensity before packaging it. Blending is one of the greatest challenges brewers face, but it may also be one of their greatest accomplishments when they get it right. Becoming a master blender takes more than skill; it usually takes years of experience, too.

Blending of beer is done all the time in the brewing industry at the corporate level. Big brand-name beers are routinely blended to ensure consistency from batch to batch. Blending beer at the artisanal level is done to develop unique and complementary flavors between two or more barrels of beer, as well as to smooth over a rough edge or two.

Here's a short list of blended beers to get you started:

- ✔ Cuvée Du Jongleur, brewed by Cascade Brewing Company
- ✔ Vlad the Imp Aler, brewed by Cascade Brewing Company
- ✔ Burton Baton, by Dogfish Head Brewing Company
- ✔ Jim, brewed by Hair of the Dog Brewing Company

Over a barrel: The cost of barrel-aged and wood-aged beer

When questioned about the price of their barrel-aged products, most brewers emphasize that these beers aren't created overnight. These brews take time to reach maturity and the height of their magnificence. Most brewers are committed to aging their beers for a minimum of one year. Some brewers believe that their beers may continue to improve for as long as five years in the barrel, but few have the time or financial resources to prove it.

One thing the budding beer buff will notice as he embarks upon the trail of barrel-aged beer discovery is that finding and buying these beers isn't an inexpensive or trivial pursuit. Barrel-aged beer has reached the pinnacle in the beer market, commanding ever higher prices at the cash register. At least two economic factors are at work here:

- ✔ The time it takes to properly age these beers — measured in years, not months.
- ✔ The demand for these beers on the open market is exceeding the supply.

Until someone invents a way to speed up the beer-aging process or until a brewery finds a way to economically produce millions of barrels of barrel-aged beer, this scenario is unlikely to change any time soon. If you like it and you want it, you're going to pay for it. That, my friends, is what they call "being over a barrel!"

Chapter 7

Diving In to Extreme Beer

. . . .

In This Chapter

▶ Defining extreme beer

▶ Discovering the origins of extreme beer

▶ Taking extreme beer to even higher levels

. . . .

*I*f you asked a dozen craft brewers to design an extreme beer, you'd probably get a dozen different recipes based on the brewers' notion of that word. However, one thing is guaranteed: All the beers would be over the top in terms of aroma, flavor, mouthfeel, and potency. Subtlety just left the building.

Making extreme beer is about pushing the boundaries any which way you can. The bigger, bolder, and badder your beer is, the more likely it's going to find avid fans. Now, not everyone finds extreme beers easy to drink and enjoy, but plenty of people on the fanatical fringe just can't seem to get enough of them.

This chapter gets you acquainted with the characteristics of extreme beers and some of the original versions. It also gets you up-to-speed on one of the most common types of modern extreme brews and the various ways the makers of extreme beers try to outdo one another.

What Makes a Beer "Extreme"?

As part of the brewing process, which I walk you through in Chapter 3, malted barley undergoes a mashing process that leeches out the grain's fermentable sugar, or *maltose*. Maltose is then converted to alcohol by the yeast during fermentation. That same grain also transposes its color in the beer and provides the beer with body, mouthfeel, and flavor. These three effects of the brewing process can be used to make a beer extreme by creating bigger body, bolder flavor, and a higher alcohol content.

I think it's safe to say that when it comes to extreme beers, thirst-quenching quaffability isn't part of the program. These beers are really meant for sipping, not chugging.

Bigger body

That extreme beers have bigger body than normal beers is just part-and-parcel of the brewing process. In order to get more flavor and more alcohol in the beer, bigger-bodied beer is the result. The process of creating a bigger-bodied beer is simple, really. If you want to brew a beer with more flavor and body, just use more malt. Adding more malt to the brew means more of everything that malt provides: color, flavor, texture, and fermentable malt sugars.

Even though most of the malt sugars are consumed by the yeast during fermentation, the average yeast doesn't consume more than 75 to 80 percent of the available sugars. This means that, on average, 20 to 25 percent of the malt sugars remain in solution after fermentation. These leftover sugars translate to sweetness and body.

Dextrins are another important component derived from malt. Though they can't be tasted, dextrins give the beer a sense of fullness and thickness on the palate. A beer with lots of dextrins in it feels more like motor oil on your palate than it does water.

Bolder flavor

Extreme beers are all about bold flavor. Table 7-1 introduces you to some of the ingredients used to take a regular ol' beer and turn it into an extreme brew. It also clues you in to why brewers add these ingredients and the effects these ingredients have on a beer's flavor.

Table 7-1 Packing a Flavorful Punch with Various Ingredients

Ingredient(s)	Examples	Why Added	Effect
Dark-roasted grains	Roasted barley, black malt, chocolate malt	Increased flavor intensity	Roasty, burnt, or dark chocolate flavors
Different malts	Crystal malt, wood-smoked malt, peat-smoked malt	Added malt sweetness, additional complexity	Complexity and depth of flavor
Different hop varieties (or increased quantities)	Cascade, Centennial, Simcoe	Increased hop aroma and flavor, increased bitterness	More intense overall hop character

Ingredient(s)	Examples	Why Added	Effect
Sugar sources and syrups	Fruit and fruit extracts, brown sugar, honey, maple syrup, treacle, and molasses	More flavor, unusual flavors, increased alcohol content	Complexity and flavor intensity
Herbs, spices, and unfermentable flavorings	Vanilla bean, licorice, coffee, tea, ginger root, pumpkin, heather, chamomile, and hot peppers	More flavor, unusual flavors	Complexity and flavor intensity
Yeast	Champagne strains of wild yeasts and bacteria	Greater degree of fermentation, unusual flavors	More alcohol, drier beer, flavors such as banana, bubblegum, and clove. Wild yeasts can create Sour Beers (more on these in Chapter 6).

Brewers also have the option of aging their beer for extended periods of time in oak barrels. Barrel-aging a beer results in a wide range of woody, oaky, cedary characteristics that aren't unlike those you may encounter in some wines or whiskies. For more on barrel-aged beers, flip to Chapter 6.

Higher alcohol content

Not all brewers who set out to create an extreme beer have high alcohol content on their minds — literally or figuratively. In many cases, elevated ethanol levels in beer are just a happy byproduct of the recipe. When brewers brew a big-bodied beer for the purpose of flavor and mouthfeel intensity, the alcohol that results from all that malt almost can't be helped. A brewer would have to go out of his way to keep the yeast from doing what it does naturally.

On the other hand, some brewers specifically set out to make high-octane brews. Some may do it for experimentation ("how strong can I make this beer?"), some as part of a game of one-upmanship, and some with the express intent of marketing big buzz beers. (For examples of all the above, see the nearby sidebar "Battling it out for the highest alcohol content.")

Battling it out for the highest alcohol content

Back when I first started getting into fine beer in the mid-1980s, the two strongest beers in the world at that time were Hürlimann's Christmas seasonal Samichlaus Bier (Switzerland), and EKU's Kulminator Urtyp Hell 28 (Germany), both at 14 percent alcohol by volume. When the Boston Brewing Company (BBC) introduced its Triple Bock in 1995, the limit had been incrementally raised to 17 percent. Several years later, BBC released Sam Adams Utopias, with an impressive 27 percent alcohol content (and an equally impressive price per bottle: $150).

Just since 2009, the alcohol content of beer raised to twice that limit — and then some. First, BrewDog Brewery in Scotland created Tactical Nuclear Penguin at 27 percent. Not to be outdone, the Schorschbräu Brewery in Germany countered with Schorschbock at 31 percent. BrewDog's return salvo was

dubbed Sink the Bismarck, and weighed in at 41 percent — which just happened to coincide with the year the British sunk the Bismarck. Schorschbräu quickly responded with another Schorschbock, this one at 43 percent. BrewDog had no choice but to up the ante, this time with what was thought to be the knockout punch: The End of History (at 55 percent, only 12 bottles of this beer were produced and were sold for $780 apiece!).

Nothing but silence was heard from the Germans, but out of nowhere a Dutch brewer by the name of Brouerwij t'Koelschip (The Coolship) joined the beer feud. Start the Future, with an astonishing 60 percent alcohol content, hit the market in July 2010. Strength-wise, drinking just one bottle of this beer would be like consuming an entire 12-pack of Heineken. War over. For now.

For even the hardiest of beer yeasts to ferment a beer beyond 12 or 14 percent alcohol without falling into a stupor from alcohol toxicity isn't normal. In order for yeasts to get to that level and beyond requires a little help from the brewer. Some tricks of the trade include

- Raising the fermentation temperature
- Adding newer, fresher yeast to the brew
- Agitating the fermentation vessel to keep the yeast in liquid suspension
- Using hardier strains of yeast normally used to ferment sherry or champagne

And then there's the cheater's method, known as *ice distillation*. The idea is that by cooling the beer down well below the freezing point, the water content in the beer begins to form ice crystals. These ice crystals are then sieved out of the beer, leaving behind a much more concentrated liquid — and related alcohol content. Each time this process is done, the beer gets thicker and thicker, and the alcohol content goes higher and higher.

Monastic Brews: The Original Extreme Beers

Religious orders have been brewing beer in Europe since the Middle Ages. These *monastic brews* are always widely praised and prized but often misunderstood — mostly due to their origins. Many people believe that monastic brews are both rare and of high potency. Though some are, indeed, rare and many can pack a punch, the exquisite brews made by the Cistercian, Benedictine, and Trappist orders can't be so easily defined.

Most of the monastic beer styles are very old, and, thus, are ales, but at least one is born of lager parentage. Irrespective of their classification on the beer family tree, monastic brews are older examples of how beer gets to be extreme. The next sections introduce you to two types of monastic brews.

The origins of Dubbels, Tripels, and Quadrupels

Historically, monks throughout Europe produced only a beer of modest alcohol level, also known as *table beer,* that was regularly consumed with their meals. In preparation for special events or holidays, they'd also brew a beer, or beers, of greater strength — a Dubbel or Tripel or whatever they had in mind (for more info on these beer styles, see Chapter 4). Eventually, these bigger beers were sold to the public, while the least potent was still reserved for in-house consumption.

The simple and easy way to distinguish between the beers was to call the table beer a *Single,* with the beers of increasing gravity and strength becoming *Dubbel* and *Tripel* respectively. It was just a matter of time before a *Quadrupel* was added to the monks' brewing repertoire.

Craft brewers today have taken a page out of the monastic brewers' playbook by creating beer styles of increasing strength and flavor intensity. They have, likewise, borrowed the monks' simple and unambiguous terminology used to distinguish between them. Peruse some beer lists, and I guarantee it won't take you long to stumble upon a beer that claims to be "double this" or "triple that." You may not immediately know what that designation means, but there's just something intuitive about it. Obviously, a beer that's a double or a triple something suggests that it's bigger, better, or more impressive than the single version of itself (kind of like how doubles and triples are bigger, better versions of singles in baseball).

The creation of Doppelbock

Italian monks from the order of Saint Francis of Paula and living in Bavaria took Bock Beer a step further by creating a whole new style of beer known as *Doppelbock* (double bock). Doppelbock wasn't brewed for the sake of ego or greed but out of need. The brothers of Saint Francis wanted to brew a beer that not only quenched their thirst but also sated their hunger during the long Lenten period of fasting that precedes the Easter holiday. Due to its grain base and high carbohydrate content, Doppelbock is referred to as *liquid bread* for a good reason.

In 2011, Iowan J. Wilson decided to live out an experiment based on the original purpose of Doppelbock. He vowed to go an entire 46 days consuming nothing but Doppelbock and water. Allowing himself up to four servings of beer each weekday and five beers a day on weekends, the Doppelbock was his only source of nutrition (the beer he drank was 288 calories per 12-ounce serving). He survived his self-induced dietary ordeal no worse for wear, but he won't be joining a monastery anytime soon.

The monks at Saint Francis of Paula were given permission to sell their beers to the public in 1780. After word of their malty and spirituous brews spread, the monks and their beer became famous. Denizens of Munich are credited with calling the beer style Doppelbock, but the monks named it *Salvator* in reverence to The Saviour. Eventually, the monastery and its brewery were sold to a private brewing company that to this day goes by the name Paulaner.

As more and more Bavarian breweries produced Doppelbock, they each named their particular beer with a word that ended with the suffix *-ator,* out of reverence to the original Doppelbock. Be on the lookout for these German brands of Doppelbock:

- Augustiner Bräu Maximator
- Ayinger Celebrator
- Hacker-Pschorr Animator
- Hofbräu Delicator
- Löwenbräu Triumphator
- Spaten Optimator

Munich's Starkbierfest (strong beer fest) is a springtime festival based on Doppelbock that's said to be even better than that city's Oktoberfest. Starkbierfest takes place when the weather is cooler and the tourists are scarce. If you're into beer and Bavarian culture, this is the time to be in

Munich. Because it's tied to the church calendar, the dates of Starkbierfest vary from year to year. The season begins on the third Friday after Ash Wednesday and runs three weeks — three of the best weeks in beerdom.

If It's Imperial, It Rules: Intensifying Beer Styles for a Bigger Punch

Anywhere you turn, you're bound to find some option on a beer list that happens to be Imperial, whether it's an Imperial Pale Ale, an Imperial Brown Ale, an Imperial Red Ale, and the list goes on and on. To *imperialize* a beer is to take a base beer style and turbo-charge it. In other words, you intensify whatever it was about the base beer that made it worth drinking in the first place. (Technically, the term *imperializing* isn't currently part of the brewing lexicon, but it probably should be.)

The earliest known Imperial beer was found in Russia but arrived there from Britain. In order for their beers to survive shipment abroad, British brewers used the time-honored trick of making a beer of high gravity and higher resulting alcohol. These extreme British ales, Porters, and Stouts arrived at many ports in Northern Europe, including the Baltic States. From there, these esteemed beers found their way to points inland, including Russia. Catherine the Great is said to have developed a fondness for the strong British Stout as did the Czars and many members of the Imperial Russian Court. Brewery records of Imperial Russian Stout being shipped to Russia date back to the late 1780s.

Imperializing beer is also all about giving the beer industry's most passionate and enthusiastic fans what they crave — more! More malt, more hops, and, of course, more alcohol. I can only imagine (and salivate at) what the world's first Imperial Belgian Quadrupel is going to taste like. Trust me; it's coming.

Then again, not every Imperial brew is worth drinking (or even imagining). In their zeal, craft brewers have gone so far as to imperialize beer styles that are traditionally meant to be light bodied and low-alcohol content, with results that are mixed at best. Case in point: Imperial Witbier. The base beer (Belgian Witbier) is a delicate, very pale-colored, light-bodied brew. Its tangy, citrusy flavor and spritzy carbonation combine to make it the ultimate summer thirst quencher. The spicing of the Imperial version, along with the 10 percent alcohol content, created an offensive medicinal and solvent character that's unpleasant to smell or drink.

Although I haven't encountered the following styles — yet — I hope brewers take a pass on making an Imperial British Mild, an Imperial Berliner Weisse, an Imperial Kölsch, or an Imperial Cream Ale. Sometimes it's best to just leave well enough alone.

Getting more buck for the extreme brew bang

For all their knowledge, passion, and artisanal skill, when it comes to the bottom line, brewers are businessmen (and women), first and foremost. Being able to increase brewery sales and revenue is part of their job description, and producing extreme beer appears to give brewers a means to that end (not to mention that it's also more fun to make).

For all their popularity, extreme beers often lack one key component of beer drinking enjoyment: quaffability. Extreme beers aren't designed to be consumed one after the other or in any quantity at one time. Coupled with the increased retail price of the average extreme beer, consumers are less likely to drop $15 or $20 for a six-pack. As a result, brewers have come up with packaging and pricing that makes extreme beer easier to swallow — in a manner of speaking.

More and more of these high-end brews are appearing on store shelves in 22-ounce bottles — or similarly sized liter equivalents. Although the total volume of beer being purchased is reduced by half or more, the unit price isn't reduced by the same percentage.

Here's a true case in point: A well-known brewery produced a highly regarded extreme beer that was initially sold in four-packs of 12-ounce bottles for $18.99. When the brewer switched over to 22-ounce bottles and sold them for $10.99, the brewer increased his sales from 39.6 cents per ounce of beer to 50 cents per ounce. (Not only did the brewer increase his sales, but he also decreased his expenditures; fewer bottles, caps, and labels, and no cardboard packaging were used). The consumer also sees this new packaging as a savings because he's spending only $11 instead of $19.

Beer Wars: My Beer Is More Extreme than Yours

As if being an extreme beer in and of itself wasn't enough to draw consumers' attention, inventive brewers have found other ways to get noticed. Consider this section your personal crash course into Extreme Beer Marketing 101.

Stealing attention away from other brews with zanier names

When it comes to extreme beers, the brand names seem to follow the pattern of bigger, badder, and bolder. So much so that, in some cases, governmental agencies have to step in to enforce regulations regarding profanity and the like (see the nearby "Dirty dog" sidebar for a good example). Some brand names even seem desperate in their attempt to grab your attention.

Like 'em or not, here's a list of authentic and unadulterated beer names for your entertainment and reading pleasure (proof that tasting good and good taste aren't always one and the same):

- ✔ Arrogant Bastard
- ✔ Bitches Brew
- ✔ Camel Toe
- ✔ Dead Guy Ale
- ✔ Dirty Bastard
- ✔ Fornicator
- ✔ Golden Shower
- ✔ Gorch Fock

- ✔ Hairy Eyeball
- ✔ Hop Stoopid
- ✔ Moose Drool
- ✔ Raging Bitch
- ✔ Santa's Butt
- ✔ Sheep Shagger
- ✔ Sticky Zipper
- ✔ Yellow Snow

One-upping the competition with wackier packaging

For the most part, beer packaging hasn't been particularly noteworthy — until more and more beers began tip-toeing to the extreme. The higher octane extreme beers in particular were bottled in 22-ounce bomber bottles, not only for their potency but also for their ever-increasing retail price (see the earlier sidebar "Getting more buck for the extreme brew bang"). It quickly became in vogue to dip the bottles in colored sealing wax. The always creative folks at the Three Floyds Brewing Company in Munster, Indiana, even use the colored wax to differentiate between vintages of their Dark Lord Imperial Stout.

Dirty dog

In 1990, when the Flying Dog Brewery opened in Aspen, Colorado, artist and "demented genius" Ralph Steadman (introduced to brewery owner George Stranahan by writer Hunter S. Thompson) was commissioned to produce the brewery's label art.

Ralph's first work for the brewery was for the Road Dog Porter label. He blessed the art with the simple phrase, "Good Beer, No S**t" — only without the asterisks. "We liked where he was going with that," said Stranahan, "so we let it be."

As soon as the beer hit the shelves, the Colorado liquor board deemed it profane and removed all Road Dog beer from the market. Temporarily replacing it with "Good Beer, No Censorship," Flying Dog Brewery fought along with the American Civil Liberties Union for four years to get the original text reinstated. In 2000, it was decided that art should not be censored. From then on "Good Beer, No S**t" (without the asterisks) proudly adorns all labels for Road Dog Porter.

Even the sometimes staid Anheuser-Busch (A-B) Brewery couldn't resist the opportunity to show off a bit. In 2005, A-B introduced its Brew Masters Special Reserve (8.5 percent alcohol by volume, which for A-B was definitely extreme). This holiday brew was packaged in a stately, though unusually sized, 1 quart, 14.5-ounce bottle, replete with a self-sealing swing-top cap.

When the Boston Beer Company later launched its highly intoxicating Utopias, nothing less than a 24-ounce gold decanter would suffice. This unusual bottle was designed to look like a brew kettle in all its shiny copper glory.

Taking the wacky packaging concept to an obscene extreme, Scotland's BrewDog Brewery pushed the limits of sanity. Each bottle of its The End of History (only 12 bottles total) was decked out in its finest road kill. With the help of creative taxidermy, each bottle came complete *inside* a squirrel that also happened to be decked out in its finest black tuxedo and top hat! (Don't believe me? Check out Figure 7-1 for proof!)

Figure 7-1: BrewDog Brewery's squirrel-bedecked The End of History.

Courtesy of Manifest London Ltd

The Future of Extreme Beers

For all their guff and bluster, extreme beers don't always live up to their hype, nor do they always deliver on their promises. Often, they're created simply to help breweries gain shelf space and tap space, as well as attention and market share. Extreme beers have been born of a whatever-it-takes attitude in the brewing industry. Many have what it takes, and some don't.

Even as this niche continues to grow, build, and find thirsty converts to big beers, a backlash is already forming. In this go-for-broke competition to see whose brews can scream the loudest, some are quietly calling for calm in the industry and the marketplace. They pine for beers with subtlety and nuance. They long for the return to easy-drinking brews with low alcohol contents and moderately hopped beers that don't scour the enamel off your teeth. I'll drink to that!

Chapter 8

Checking Out Organic, Gluten-Free, and Kosher Beer

*F*or one reason or another, certain people aren't able to drink what the rest of us consider "regular" beer. For some, it's a personal choice; for others, it's a matter of health or religious practice. If you fall into either of these groups, you've come to the right place. This chapter seeks to provide you with the information you need to continue enjoying beer (of the organic, gluten-free, and kosher varieties) without compromising your health, conscience, or religious convictions.

Natural Selection: Organic Beer

In this day and age, an organic movement is in place toward all things, well, organic. Organic coffee, organic fruits and vegetables, organic juices — and following organic wine, organic beer seemed to be in the natural progression of things. In the following sections, I cover the origins of organic beer, organic beer certification and labeling, some reasons to consider drinking organic beer, and different organic beers you can try.

In the beginning: The rise of organic beer

The modern organic beer movement traces its roots to Brauerei Pinkus-Müller in Münster, Germany, where the first all-organic beer was brewed in 1979. It came as the result of Pinkus-Müller's disappointment in the declining quality of conventional malt at the time. He found organic malt to be a superior substitute, and his brewery switched to all-organic brewing a little more than a decade later. Germany now boasts about 30 organic breweries, and Pinkus-Müller's organic beer eventually influenced brewmasters abroad. In 1997, the U.S. Department of Agriculture (USDA) established the National Organic Program, which opened the door for Morgan Wolaver to found the first all-organic brewing company, Wolaver's Organic Ales, in Santa Cruz, California.

U.S. sales of organic food and drink grew from $1 billion in 1990 to $14 billion in 2006, according to the USDA. Naturally, beer would also follow the trend — and it has. By 2005, organic beer ranked with coffee as the fastest-growing organic beverage. As of 2006, organic beer still represented less than 1 percent of U.S. beer sales, but those sales doubled to $19 million between 2003 and 2005, according to the Organic Trade Association. In 2009, the organic beer sector more than doubled the sales numbers reported just four years prior, to just over $41 million.

Sorting through organic beer certifications

The worldwide brewing industry is making huge strides in the organic beer sector, but U.S. commercial brewers are lagging a bit behind. Perhaps more brewers in the United States would make organic beer if it weren't for the many challenges they face. For example, the organic certification process can be expensive and burdensome, and some of the raw ingredients can be difficult to secure in bulk. It can also be expensive to maintain separate equipment for organic brewing (using the same equipment to handle organic and nonorganic ingredients can cause cross-contamination).

Simply put, the USDA standards for organic beer are the same as those for organic foods: Ingredients must be grown without toxic pesticides or synthetic fertilizers in soil free from chemicals for at least three years, and genetically modified ingredients (or GMOs) are a no-no.

A GMO is a *genetically modified organism.* GMOs are common in food production, and they include genetically modified corn, which may appear in the brewing industry. The certified-organic label is a guarantee that the product doesn't contain GMOs.

Organic certification for beer is broken down to two primary levels:

- ✔ **100 percent organic:** This certification is the highest level and requires that the beer be brewed entirely from organically produced ingredients (absolutely no chemicals or pesticides) and nothing else.

- ✔ **Organic:** The next level, *organic,* comprises the largest number of beers. Organic beers must be brewed from 95 percent organically produced ingredients. The remaining 5 percent of ingredients must not be available in organic form in the quality and quantity needed. Furthermore, the remaining 5 percent of ingredients must be included in the USDA's National List of Allowed and Prohibited Substances. This list consists of cornstarch, water-extracted gums, kelp, unbleached lecithin, and pectin.

Keep in mind that this organic certification process is kind of a work in progress; USDA regulations are likely to continue changing in the future. I should also add that this description of what's organic is oversimplified. Although it may all sound pretty straightforward, the specifics regarding how organically grown ingredients affect brewing processes and exactly how to define organic ingredients make this topic anything but simple. Check out the nearby sidebar "It's not organic until the USDA says so" for all the details.

Unless you've memorized the entire list of the USDA's organic certifications, what you read on product labels ranges from vague at best to outright confusing at worst.

Why go organic? Help the environment — drink a beer!

So why drink organic beer? You won't find any real financial incentive for drinking organic beer because it's usually every bit as pricey as craft beers. The real incentive to drink organically is rooted in the deep satisfaction of knowing that you're not placing an added burden on the environment. A commitment to sustainable agriculture and the environment is what drinking organic beer is really all about, as I outline in the following list:

✔ Drinking organic beer can contribute to your overall health and well-being. By consuming organic beers, you can avoid consuming the chemicals used in agriculture and food processing —many of which are known to be toxic.

✔ Drinking organically brewed beer contributes to a better environment. Organic farming reduces erosion, soil nutrient depletion, water shortages, and pollution by not using chemicals to fertilize crops or to fight pests and diseases.

✔ Drinking organic beer supports the organic farming industry, which contributes to the amount of land that's farmed in a chemical-free and sustainable way. Organic farming also provides more agricultural jobs per acre than conventional farming.

Beware of the urban myth that organic beers are less likely to produce hangovers due to their lack of chemicals — not true! Now where did I put the aspirin?

It's not organic until the USDA says so

For a beer to carry the "USDA Organic" label, according to federal law, it must contain 95 percent organic ingredients, with the other 5 percent being nonorganic ingredients on the USDA National List, provided that organic equivalents aren't commercially available in sufficient quantity. (Are you still with me?) Currently, the National List contains only five items: cornstarch, water-extracted gums, kelp, unbleached lecithin, and pectin. Besides hops, an additional 38 ingredients are currently under consideration for inclusion on the National List.

The USDA breaks down its organic certifications according to product composition:

✔ A raw or processed agricultural product sold, labeled, or represented as *100 percent organic* must contain, by weight or fluid volume, 100 percent organically produced ingredients.

✔ A raw or processed agricultural product sold, labeled, or represented as *organic* must contain, by weight or fluid volume, not less than 95 percent organically produced raw or processed agricultural products. Any remaining product ingredients must be organically produced, unless not commercially available in organic form, or must be nonagricultural substances or nonorganically produced agricultural products produced consistent with the National List.

✔ Multi-ingredient agricultural products sold, labeled, or represented as *made with organic (specified ingredients or food groups)* must contain, by weight or fluid volume, at least 70 percent organically produced ingredients produced and handled in accordance with USDA organic specifications.

Thirsty yet? Read your labels carefully!

Organic movement: A list of organic beers

If you're interested in trying some organic brews, you're in luck; Table 8-1 gives you a list of beers to start with.

Table 8-1	A Sampling of Organic Beers	
Beer	*Brewery*	*Country*
Foret	DuPont	Belgium
Jade	Bénifontaine	France
Pinkus Organic Münster Alt	Pinkus-Müller	Germany
Golden Promise	Caldonian	U.K.
Organic Best Ale	Samuel Smith	U.K.
Chocolate Stout	Bison	U.S.

Beer	Brewery	Country
Cru D'Or	North Coast	U.S.
Elliott Bay (10 varieties)	Elliott Bay	U.S.
Fish Tale Amber Ale	Fish	U.S.
Green Lakes	Deschutes	U.S.
Laurelwood Free Range Red Ale	Hopworks	U.S.
Mothership Wit	New Belgium	U.S.
Mud Puddle PNW Red Ale	Oakshire	U.S.
Naughty Nellie's Golden Ale	Pike	U.S.
Oceanic Organic Saison	Kailua Kona	U.S.
Organic Barley Wine	Lakefront	U.S.
Organic ESB	Lakefront	U.S.
Organic Zwickel Bier Pale Ale	Redrock	U.S.
Squatters Organic Amber Ale	Utah Brewers Cooperative	U.S.
Stone Mill	Anheuser-Busch	U.S.
Wild Hop	Anheuser-Busch	U.S.
Woody Organic IPA	Roots Organic	U.S.

Celebrating organic beer

Started several years ago by the owner of Roots Organic Brewing in Oregon, the North American Organic Brewers Festival (NOABF) is a three-day celebration of certified-organic beer and sustainable living practices.

Like the organic movement itself, the NOABF continues to grow. The weekend festival, which showcases more than 50 certified-organic beers, typically attracts in excess of 20,000 attendees who are greeted by a festival staff of more than 600.

Aware that large events create large environmental footprints, festival promoters minimize the event's impact in a number of ways: by endorsing the use of public transportation, by promoting an extensive composting and recycling program, and by utilizing an on-site solar array that provides much of the electricity for the festival.

Check out www.naobf.org for more information about the festival.

Organic hop crop flop

Hops represent the largest percentage of non-organic brewing ingredients in organic beer, but their certification, status, and viability are currently in a state of flux (I think that's near Rhode Island). Yes, organically grown hops are out there, but not in great quantities; hops are subject to a variety of diseases and other growth-related problems (see Chapter 2 for more about hops). This fact is why no large-scale commercial hop grower in the United States has taken the risky leap to organic hop production. Currently, most of the few organic hop varieties available in the United States are imported from New Zealand, Germany, and the United Kingdom. Of course, this scarcity affects the brewers' bottom lines as well; imported organic hops are 20 to 30 percent more expensive than conventional domestic hops.

Quite a bit of confusion also surrounds the need for organic hops in the first place. Most small organic brewers insist on using them to make their products 100 percent organic, or at least to make their beers USDA organic certified (95 percent organic ingredients). Larger breweries argue that because hops constitute less than 5 percent of the total ingredient profile of their beers, beers brewed with nonorganic hops still qualify for organic certification.

Members of the American Organic Hop Grower Association (AOHGA) argue that the National Organic Standards Board (NOSB) has created an economic disincentive to grow organic hops by allowing the use of nonorganic hops in organic beer. Likewise, many brewers who produce beers with organic hops have argued that their costs are higher and that a difference exists between their products and those produced without organic hops. This situation, created by the NOSB, has slowed the growth of U.S. organic hop production by preventing the development of a viable organic hops market in America.

As a result of a subsequent AOHGA petition to the USDA, all beers labeled *organic* must be brewed with organic hops by 2013. The two-year window is to allow brewers and growers time to secure enough organic hop stocks to satisfy their needs.

Some Hope for People with Celiac Disease: Gluten-Free Beer

As I mention in Chapter 2, many different grains have been used to brew beer over the millennia. Of course, barley is best, followed by wheat and then rye. The problem with these grains — at least for people who suffer from celiac disease — is that they all contain *gluten*. Gluten is responsible for triggering an autoimmune reaction in the small intestines of those people with this particular affliction. That reaction can be debilitating, causing great discomfort and possibly long-term disruption to the function of the small intestine. This means that people with celiac disease don't get the nutrients they need out of their food and may experience a range of other health issues. (See the nearby sidebar "A few facts about celiac disease" for more info.)

Gluten helps make bread dough very elastic so yeast can make it rise, and gluten gives bread a characteristic chewiness. As a component of barley, wheat, and rye, gluten gives beer a thickness and chewiness as well.

The only treatment available for people with celiac disease is a life-long avoidance of products that contain gluten, which means no regular beer in their diet. Ouch! Imagine going the rest of your life without beer. What a depressing thought that is. Fortunately, there's hope; it comes in the form of beer that's made without products that contain gluten.

In response to the growing demand for gluten-free beers in the commercial market, several breweries around the world are introducing new products each year. In the following sections, I note grains and starches that are safe for folks with celiac disease to consume in beer, and I provide a starter list of gluten-free beers to try.

The gluten-free gang: Grains and starches used in gluten-free beer

Here's a list of the prohibited grains and their derivatives that people with celiac disease should avoid:

- Barley and barley malt
- Malt, malt extract, malt flavoring, and malt vinegar
- Rye
- Wheat — including durum, semolina, kamut, and spelt

A few facts about celiac disease

Celiac disease (CD) is also referred to as *gluten sensitive enteropathy, gluten intolerance,* or *celiac sprue.* It's the most under-diagnosed common disease today, potentially affecting 1 in every 133 people in the United States. Celiac disease is a chronic, inherited disease, and, if untreated, can ultimately lead to malnutrition. It's the result of an immune-mediated response to the ingestion of gluten that damages the small intestine. Nutrients are then quickly passed through the small intestine instead of being absorbed.

The disease is permanent. Damage to the small intestine occurs every time you consume gluten, regardless of whether symptoms are present.

I'll be honest here — beer made from gluten-free grains isn't likely to match regular beer for taste and quality, but to someone facing a lifetime restriction from drinking beer, gluten-free beer is like manna from heaven — made without gluten, of course!

Sorghum, millet, and buckwheat are the three most common substitutions for glutenous grains used to brew beer, but here's a more complete list of the grains and starches that are safe to consume:

- ✔ Beans
- ✔ Buckwheat

Buckwheat is an herb of the Buckwheat family *Polygonaceae,* and it has origins in central and western China. Its small beechnuts are milled, which separates the edible groats from their hulls. These groats are then roasted and used as a grain product.

- ✔ Corn
- ✔ Millet

Millet is a family of grasses and represents some of the oldest cultivated crops known to man. Millet seeds are harvested and used for food or feed; in this case, that food is beer! Millet has regularly been used for making beer in Africa, and it's now one of the most widely used grains for brewing commercially made gluten-free beer.

- ✔ Potato
- ✔ Quinoa
- ✔ Rice
- ✔ Sorghum

Sorghum is native to northeast Africa. As a valuable food source, it followed the trade routes through India and China and eventually made its way to America. Sorghum is a vigorous grass that tolerates dry weather and is commonly used as one of the ingredients in African beer.

- ✔ Soybean
- ✔ Tapioca

Free of gluten but full of flavor: A list of gluten-free beers

Are you in the market for a gluten-free brew? Table 8-2 features a sampling of commercially produced gluten-free beers that you can try.

Most brewers of gluten-free beer have formulated their products with 100 percent gluten-free ingredients and processes that ensure purity of product. But some filtering processes used by brewing companies render gluten undetectable in low-gluten beer; so unless a beer is totally gluten-free, people with celiac disease have no assurance that it's completely safe. And because *gluten-free* is a health claim, current U.S. beer label regulations don't allow the term *gluten-free* to appear on any beer sold in the United States. Buyer and imbiber beware!

Table 8-2	Commercially Produced Gluten-Free Beers	
Beer	*Brewery*	*Country*
Australia Pale Ale	Billabong	Australia
O'Brien Premium Lager	O'Brien	Australia
Green's Discovery Amber Ale	De Proef	Belgium
Green's Endeavor Dubbel	De Proef	Belgium
Green's Quest Tripel	De Proef	Belgium
La Messagère	New France	Canada
Kukko Pils	Laitilan	Finland
Beer Up Glutenfrei Pale Ale	Brauerei Grieskirchen	Germany
Birra 76	Bi-Aglut (food products)	Italy
Mongozo Palmnut	Mongozo Beers	The Netherlands
Mongozo Quinua	Mongozo Beers	The Netherlands
Celia Saison	The Alchemist	U.S.
Dragon's Gold	Bard's Tale	U.S.
New Grist	Lakefront	U.S.
Mbege	Sprecher	U.S.
Passover Honey Beer	Ramapo Valley	U.S.
Redbridge	Anheuser-Busch	U.S.
Shakparo Ale	Sprecher	U.S.
Tread Lightly Ale	New Planet	U.S.

Following the Law: Kosher Beer

For millions of observant Jews around the world, following the *kashrut,* or Jewish dietary laws, is a very important part of everyday life. Food and drink that are in accord with *halakha* (Jewish law) are termed *kosher* in English. Kosher simply means fit for consumption by Jews according to traditional Jewish law. In the following sections, I explain exactly what makes a beer kosher and provide a list of kosher beers you can try.

In order for food or drink to be kosher, it must first be inspected and certified by one of the many certifying bodies around the world. One of the largest certifying agencies in North America, Star-K, is responsible for certifying most of the beers made in, and imported to, the United States.

Figuring out what qualifies as kosher

Based on the kashrut, most beers produced by typical methods don't violate dietary law. In other words, beer is generically kosher; none of the raw ingredients and additives used to brew regular beer present kashrut concerns.

The rules change, however, when atypical ingredients, additives, and flavorings — fruit, fruit syrups, spices, and so on — are added. In these cases, the beer requires certification. Likewise, if beers with higher alcohol contents require fermentation with yeasts other than typical beer yeast, the beers require certification.

Here are a few safe generalizations:

- ✔ All unflavored beers with no additives listed on the ingredient label, are acceptable, even without a kosher certification. This generalization applies to both U.S.-produced and imported beers, including nonalcoholic and dark beers.

- ✔ All unflavored beers, including dark or malt beer, from the following countries are kosher: Belgium, Canada, England, Germany, Mexico, Norway, and the Netherlands.

- ✔ Although the safest route is to purchase beer with kosher certification, in circumstances where facts of evidence overwhelmingly prove no kashrut concerns exist, the Torah yields to whatever the evidence shows.

Any beer that contains *lactose* (milk sugar) is non-kosher due to its inclusion of dairy ingredients. Lactose is typically used to make Sweet Stout, which may also be marketed as Milk Stout or Cream Stout.

Products that have been certified as kosher are labeled with a mark called a *hekhsher* that ordinarily identifies the rabbi or organization that certified the product. The kashrut status of a product changes with changes in production methods or kashrut supervision. Always look for the kosher mark on the beer label or packaging.

He'Brew: The Chosen Beer

In the beginning, there was an idea, and it was good: a microbrew to complement the Jewish American experience. In the year 5757 (1996), Jeremy Cowan started the Shmaltz Brewing Company to create beer meant to accompany the rites and rituals of life, both sacred and secular. Genesis Ale became the first world-class microbrew certified under the highest standards of the Orthodox kosher community.

The Shmaltz Brewing Company went on to brew Jewbelation Ale, Rejewvenator Doppelbock,

R.I.P.A. or Rye India Pale Ale, Origin Pomegranate Ale, and Bittersweet Lenny's Rye I.P.A. — a tribute to comedian Lenny Bruce.

The Chosen Beer, according to a company press release, is the perfect libation for weddings, bar mitzvahs (ID required), Beastie Boys concerts, Supreme Court sessions, or anywhere people are kibbitzing or cavorting. *L'Chaim!*

Everything's kosher: A list of kosher beers

For a selection of beers that can help keep you kosher, check out Table 8-3.

Table 8-3	A Sampling of Kosher Beers	
Beer*	*Brewery*	*Country*
Best Extra Stout	Coopers	Australia
Extra Strong Vintage Ale	Coopers	Australia
Original Pale Ale	Coopers	Australia
Premium Lager	Coopers	Australia
Special Old Stout	Coopers	Australia
Amber Dry	Brick	Canada
Anniversary Bock	Brick	Canada
Brick Premium	Brick	Canada
Blue Moon	Coors	U.S.
Bohemian Black Lager	Spoetzl	U.S.
Boston Ale	Sam Adams	U.S.
Boston Lager	Sam Adams	U.S.
Brooklyn (all products brewed in Utica)	Brooklyn	U.S.
Cherry Wheat	Sam Adams	U.S.

(continued)

Table 8-3 *(continued)*

Beer*	Brewery	Country
Chocolate Bock	Sam Adams	U.S.
Copperhook Spring Ale	Redhook	U.S.
Cranberry Lambic	Sam Adams	U.S.
Cream City Pale Ale	Lakefront	U.S.
Double Bock	Sam Adams	U.S.
Eastside Dark	Lakefront	U.S.
Fuel Cafe Stout	Lakefront	U.S.
FX Matt (all products)	FX Matt	U.S.
Hefeweizen	Sam Adams	U.S.
Honey Porter	Sam Adams	U.S.
Imperial Stout	Sam Adams	U.S.
Imperial White Ale	Sam Adams	U.S.
Klisch Pilsner	Lakefront	U.S.
Longhammer IPA	Redhook	U.S.
Oktoberfest	Sam Adams	U.S.
Old Fezziwig	Sam Adams	U.S.
Pale Ale	Sam Adams	U.S.
Redbridge Gluten-free	Anheuser-Busch	U.S.
Redhook Blonde	Redhook	U.S.
Redhook ESB	Redhook	U.S.
Riverwest Stein Beer	Lakefront	U.S.
Saranac (all products)	Saranac/FX Matt	U.S.
Shiner Blonde	Spoetzl	U.S.
Shiner Bock	Spoetzl	U.S.
Shiner Hefeweizen	Spoetzl	U.S.
Shiner Kosmos Reserve	Spoetzl	U.S.
Shiner Smokehaus	Spoetzl	U.S.
Summer Ale	Sam Adams	U.S.
Winter Lager	Sam Adams	U.S.
Winterhook Winter Ale	Redhook	U.S.
White Ale	Sam Adams	U.S.

*Included in this list are all unflavored Heineken, Guinness, and Corona products.

Part III

Buying and Enjoying Beer

"Cook with beer? I've been doing it for years.
Add it to the food? I'll have to try it
someday."

In this part . . .

Beer drinkers, in general, don't give much thought to the process of buying beer, except maybe grabbing whatever's on sale. In this part, I aim to rectify this situation by making you an informed beer consumer.

Though it comes as a surprise to some folks, beer merits as much attention in terms of serving and tasting as does wine. Beer even substitutes very nicely for wine in the kitchen and at the table. Like wine, beer has a vocabulary and set of techniques that can really increase your understanding and enjoyment of beer. You find out what you need to know in this part.

Of course, if you're merely thirsty, just go pop a cold one!

Chapter 9

The Better Way to Buy Beer

. . . .

. . . .

Beer is food. Sometimes you hear Europeans refer to beer as *liquid bread* (although making a sandwich with beer is kind of difficult). Like most foods, especially bread, beer is perishable and becomes stale over time, so the fresher the beer, the better it is. Therefore, beer consumers on the way to enlightenment want to consume freshly made beer that's been handled properly to maintain freshness — particularly if it has no preservatives (most good beers don't have preservatives in them).

Beer freshness has four enemies: time, heat, light, and oxidation. In this chapter, I tell you how to deal with these problems and become a more informed consumer in the process.

Cans, Bottles, Growlers, and Kegs: Deciding on Your Container of Choice

Beer drinkers have argued endlessly over whether beer is better bottled or canned. Rather than make an authoritative pronouncement and give you my opinion (which, of course, is the right one), this section presents the facts and lets you arrive at your own conclusions about beer cans, bottles, growlers, and kegs.

(On second thought, let me give my opinion straightaway: The beer can offers the most convenience, but you can't argue against the aesthetics of the old brown bottle — call me old-fashioned. Besides, where would great bottle-neck slide guitarists, like Eric Clapton and Bonnie Raitt, be without glass beer bottles? Have you ever heard of an aluminum-can slide guitarist?)

From flat top to ring top: A brief history of the beer can

Collectors, take note! Since the beer can was first introduced to the brewing industry, it has become very popular and has undergone a number of changes:

- Released on January 24, 1935, Krueger Cream Ale (Gottfried Krueger Brewing Company) was the first beer ever sold in a can. It was so successful that 37 American breweries — including Pabst and Schlitz — were canning their beer by the end of the year.

- The Felinfoel Brewery in Wales became the first brewery outside of the United States to can its beer in 1935. At the time, brewers could choose from two can sizes — 10 ounces for the domestic market and 12 ounces for the export market.

- Early on, two types of beer cans existed: the flat top (which had to be punctured with a can opener) and the cone top (which was sealed with a crown cap, just like a bottle).

- In 1936, several breweries simultaneously introduced 32-ounce quart cans to the market.

- The Coors Brewing Company was the first brewery to package its beer in aluminum cans (back in the early 1950s).

- In 1954, the Schlitz Brewing Company was the first to introduce the 16-ounce beer can.

- In 1962, the Pittsburgh Brewing Company was the first to introduce the lift-tab aluminum can.

- Ring top cans, also known as *pull tabs*, first appeared in 1965.

- In 1969, canned beer outsold bottled beer for the first time.

- Push button cans were introduced in 1974 but only lasted a few years due to customers having difficulty pressing down on the buttons to open them.

Doing the cancan

The bottle predates the can by, oh, about 4,000 years. People went from drinking fresh, draught beer at a neighborhood tavern (or carrying it home in a bucket) to buying it in stores, in bottles. Beer cans, first introduced in 1935, revolutionized the brewing industry. When canned-beer packages (six-packs) were introduced, they were much lighter, quicker to chill, and more convenient than bottles all around (which holds true today). Sadly, the beer all too often tasted like the can it came in.

Eventually, a synthetic liner that shielded the beer from contact with metal was invented, and the can became more popular than ever. Somewhere along the line, the old tin can was replaced by the newer, lighter, aluminum can, and partly due to the rise of mass marketing, the beer industry hasn't looked back. But even today's aluminum cans are lined with a food-grade liner to keep any beer from coming in contact with the can.

One of the many advantages cans have over bottles is the complete elimination of light damage and a considerable reduction in oxidation damage (*oxidized beer* is beer that's been exposed to oxygen). Heat, however, can still be a problem as it accelerates the oxidation process.

Whether bottled or canned, the beer should taste the same. However, craft brewers have traditionally used bottles almost exclusively because canning equipment is more expensive than bottling equipment. But the tide is turning. Aluminum cans are once again becoming the package of choice, even within the craft-brewing industry. This trend became particularly evident in Colorado where, in 2002, the Oskar Blues Brewery took the bold step of having its Dale's Pale Ale be one of the first craft beers to be canned instead of bottled. This choice wasn't just a marketing move, either; outdoorsy Coloradans find that cans are much more environmentally friendly than bottles and much easier to pack for hiking, biking, rafting, and camping trips.

Opting for bottles

In spite of the beer can's popularity, the beer bottle never really faded away. The only notable changes were in the realm of convenience. The old, heavy, returnable bottle was replaced in most markets by a lighter, throwaway version and a twin with a twist-off top.

The most common reasons for buying beer in bottles rather than cans are

- Bottles keep the beer colder than cans after you remove them from the refrigerator or cooler.
- More brands are available in bottles than in cans.
- Bottles seem to be more aesthetically pleasing than cans.

Not only do devotees of beer in glass argue in favor of bottles, but they also argue over the bottle size and shape that most enhance the beer, such as longnecks versus stubbies. (I've yet to hear an argument convincing enough to convert me to any particular bottle style.) Today, breweries around the world use dozens of beer-bottle shapes; some of the more curious (Mickey's Big Mouth and Orval Trappist Ale, for example) are made according to individual brewer specifications. Don't even get me started on the Vortex bottle!

Going for growlers

These days, one of the most interesting aspects of retail craft beer sales is actually a throwback to pre-Prohibition days. *Growlers* are becoming quite popular for carry-out sales of beer at brewpubs and microbreweries. Growlers are typically ½-gallon glass jugs filled on demand from the brewery's taps and sold to go. Most often, breweries charge a set price for a filled growler (depending on the beer of choice), with a reduction in price when you bring your growler back for a refill. Some breweries even give you a free fill after so many paid refills.

The growler's connection to the past makes an interesting anecdote. Drinking beer on lunch breaks used to be an acceptable practice for manual laborers. These workers paid local kids a nickel to run to the local brewery to fill a small bucket with beer. This bucket was referred to as a *growler* — named for the growling in your stomach — and the act of filling the bucket hurriedly was called *rushing the growler*.

Buying a growler from a brewpub is often the only way to enjoy that brewery's beer away from the brewery. Very few brewpubs bottle their beer, so growlers serve as their only form of packaging.

Kicking it with kegs

You may not need to buy a keg of beer very often, but you'll probably get one at least once for a picnic, a softball tournament, a 30th birthday party (or a 40th or 50th), or a burn-the-mortgage bash. And at least some of you belonged to the popular fraternity Tappa Kegga Bru in college. Besides, the only way to have fresh, unpasteurized draught beer is to buy a keg. In the following sections, I describe different keg sizes and parts, and I provide a few handy pointers for using a keg.

Buying a keg is easy; transporting it is the hard part. The big ones are really, really heavy — like 150 pounds. Don't lift one yourself! Have someone big and strong pick it up, or have it delivered straight to your party.

Keg sizes

You need to figure out how many people are attending the festivity and their level of participation in order to determine what size keg to order. See Table 9-1 for the breakdown of keg sizes. Keep in mind that in beer parlance, a *barrel* — 31 gallons — doesn't really exist except for accounting and brewery-capacity purposes.

Table 9-1	U.S. Kegged-Beer Serving Table	
Size of Keg	*Number of 12-Ounce Servings*	*Number of 8-Ounce Servings*
Sixth barrel "mini" keg (5.16 gallons)	55	82
Quarter barrel/Pony keg (7.75 gallons)	82	124
Half barrel (15.5 gallons)	165	248

One for the ditch

Talk about being sure to drink your beer before it goes stale — back when England still held public hangings, the tradition was to give the condemned a complimentary cup of ale on the way to his execution. (Dare one say, "Down the hatch"?)

In the United States, beer from other countries usually comes in 50-liter (13.2-gallon) and 30-liter (7.9-gallon) kegs. To further complicate matters, vendors sometimes use different names for these items, confusing brand names with sizes and nicknames. Solution: Always focus on the liquid volume figure (gallons or liters).

Another keg option becoming more prevalent in the craft beer industry is the availability of 5-gallon *Cornelius kegs* (also referred to as *Corny kegs*). These slim, cylindrical vessels are the same things that soft drink producers have been using for years to dispense draught soda pop. Some craft brewers are now selling their beer in these mini kegs both for the wholesale and retail markets.

Be aware of the two styles of Corny kegs: *ball lock* and *pin lock,* which refer to the different ways the CO_2 hoses and beer hoses attach to the keg. Make sure you get the appropriate connection equipment when you pick up your Corny keg.

The parts of a keg

Figure 9-1 shows an example of a popular keg, called the *Sankey beer keg.* The parts of this particular keg include the tap pump and the tap head. The *tap pump* is what increases the pressure inside the keg to force the beer out. The *tap head* (or spigot) is where the beer is dispensed.

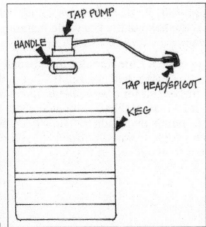

Figure 9-1:
A 15.5-gallon Sankey beer keg is one of the most common and easy-to-use kegs.

Don't let "draught" cans and bottles fool you

Don't be fooled by bottled and canned products that are called *draft* or *draught* anything. Draught means "drawn fresh from a tap" — period! Having draught beer in a can or bottle is literally impossible, despite the artfully worded labels.

Brewers in the United Kingdom have devised a can (labeled *Pub Draught*) containing its own miniature nitrogen canister (called a *widget*) that releases nitrogen into the beer when the can is opened, thus creating the fine-bead carbonation and creamy mouthfeel of a freshly pulled pint of ale. Is it just like the beer from hand-pumped taps of London pubs? It's good and close — but only *close* — to the real thing.

Guidelines for using a keg

Although you may think that buying a keg, making it easily accessible, and letting your guests do the rest is enough, follow these tips to make your keg party even better:

- **Make sure to get the right tap for your keg when you pick up the keg or accept the delivery.** You're charged a refundable deposit for the tap equipment, so treat it with care.

- **Understand the keg system you're using.** The two most common keg systems in the market are the straight-sided, easy-to-use Sankey kegs — used by Anheuser-Busch, Miller, and most microbreweries (refer to Figure 9-1) — and the outdated Hoff-Stevens kegs, with their bulging sides and obvious *bung hole* (the corked opening where the keg is filled).

    The Hoff-Stevens system must be screwed carefully onto the keg (watch out for spray!). Make sure the taps are clean and properly seated on the openings, or else the keg won't pressurize properly. If the keg doesn't pressurize, you don't drink! Such pain that causes! Pain and, shall I say, disappointment.

- **Keep the beer as cold as possible.** If you don't have a huge refrigerator, place ice on top and around the base of the keg while it stands in a large bucket or plastic garbage can.

- **Expect the first gallon or so to be a little foamier than usual.** After all, it's probably been jostled a bit during delivery, but the beer eventually comes out normal. Letting the keg sit for a while helps, as does filling a pitcher and serving from it instead of filling individual cups. Fooling around with the air-pressure pump also leads to foamy beer; serving from a pitcher prevents that problem as well. Always open the tap completely when dispensing beer to avoid excess foaming.

✔ **Be prepared for leftovers.** Some people may say that you can never have too much beer, and no good host wants to run out. That means possible leftover beer. If you don't want to return that precious nectar along with the keg after the party, plan ahead: Thoroughly clean some plastic milk jugs — or growlers, if you have them — and empty the contents of the keg into them. Refrigerate immediately and drink within a day or two. I'm serious. Unpasteurized keg beer goes stale very quickly.

Purchase or Perish: Looking for the Freshest Beer

Most people aren't the least bit self-conscious about squeezing tomatoes, thumping melons, sniffing ground beef, or reading the freshness date on bread wrappers at the supermarket. And don't wine enthusiasts pay great attention to the harvest (vintage) year? Why, then, should beer drinkers be willing to dash in to a store, grab any old six-pack off the shelf, and assume that the beer is fresh?

In the following sections, I provide pointers on seeking the freshest beer out there. Bottom line: Don't expect beer to be any more resistant to time, heat, and direct sunlight than other fresh foods. If your retailer stacks exposed six-packs in the front windows of the store where they're allowed to sunbathe for several hours a day, file a report with the beer police at once! To summarize: time = bad, heat = bad, light = bad, refrigeration = good.

Knowing that time isn't on your side

As I mention earlier in this chapter, beer gets stale over time. Three months is the average window of freshness (the shelf life) for pasteurized bottled or canned beer. Some beers have a longer shelf life than others. Fully pasteurized beers (heated for up to one hour, as are most megabrews) are more stable than flash-pasteurized beers (heated for only one minute, as are some craft brews). Also, hops and alcohol serve as natural preservatives, so well-hopped and stronger beers have a longer shelf life.

Conscientious brewers demand that their beer be pulled from the shelves if it doesn't sell within the appropriate time. Unfortunately, many of the small stores in the United States that are just beginning to carry craft and imported beers may unwittingly keep old stock on sale long after it should be returned. The lesson for you is this: Always check the dates before buying; never buy old beer!

Calling it close

There's a saying, "Beer should be drunk as close to the brewery as possible."

Fans say that Guinness (an Irish Stout) doesn't travel well. One fan tested this theory out, with an amusing result. He made a pilgrimage to the famed Dublin brewery in order to have the ultimate, freshest possible, perfect pint of his favorite brew. But before his first sip, a local wag managed to put him off a bit with classic Irish wit by saying, "Oh, I don't know. It's pretty far from here to the vat. It doesn't travel well, you know."

Aging beer like fine wine — but only in a few special cases

With the following handful of styles, not only can you keep the beer for a long time, but you can actually improve its character with short-term aging of about six months to a year. The following complex, strong beers tend to mellow over time, much as whiskey and wine do:

- ✔ High-gravity Barleywines

- ✔ Old Ales

- ✔ Barrel-aged beers (see Chapter 6 for details about this type)

- ✔ Some of the higher-gravity Belgian Trappist Beers (Dubbels and Tripels)

Although some beers, like Thomas Hardy's Ale (an Old Ale), are still good after a decade (developing some almond and sherry-like tastes), even the hardiest beer is likely to wither beyond a year or two because oxidation take its toll and the beer goes stale.

Many people collect beer bottles and cans, but no one in his or her right mind (and surely that doesn't disqualify any of you) collects vintage beer without planning to drink it. Besides, only a few brewers (of the styles noted previously) date their beers by vintage — although the number continues to increase. Wine is vintage-dated and is subject to good and bad years; certain vintages keep well for many years and are prized possessions in the cellars of those who own them. For the wine collector, owning these wines is often more important than drinking them. No such aspirations exist among beer drinkers, because no beers inspire such pretensions. Besides, I'm lucky if a good bottle of beer lasts a weekend around my house, never mind years!

Beer is really much more democratic than wine and generally less expensive. Anyone can have a cellar full of the best beer.

Staying away from beer left out of the cold

Heat makes beer go stale really fast. Refrigeration is, therefore, the ideal way to extend the shelf life of beer. However, lack of proper refrigeration is a major problem for beer retailers and distributors. Beer retailers often have limited cooler space, and most tend to reserve refrigeration space for big-name beers. Distributors often store vast amounts of other beers in cavernous, unrefrigerated warehouses that may subject the beer to extreme temperature fluctuations. Not to mention beer imported from other countries that spend months in the cargo holds of ships.

Life's not fair: Go have a beer and ponder this.

So what beer gets the dreaded warm reception? Beer that isn't supported with at least one mainstream form of advertising, beer distributed by a company with shallow pockets (*read:* no freebies for the retailer, no neon signs, no plastic clocks), or any Johnny-come-lately beer that has yet to find an audience. These beers are usually left to languish on warm store shelves or in sunny window displays that look enticing but are terrible for the beer. And these beers may be among the best-tasting ones!

Avoiding the light

Any form of light is potentially harmful to beer. Light produces chemical reactions in the hop compounds. These reactions create a mild *skunky* (*catty* in the United Kingdom) odor. Incandescent lighting is bad enough, but fluorescent lighting — found in most stores — is even worse. (No, the light in your fridge isn't going to destroy your brew.) Beer's worst enemy is sunlight, however, because it's both light *and* heat.

A beer that smells skunky is said to be *lightstruck.* Lightstruck beer is beer that's been exposed to ultraviolet and visible light. This exposure causes a reaction that breaks down *isohumulone,* a molecule derived from hops. Another molecule that results from this reaction is *3-methylbut-2-ene-1-thiol,* which shares an odorous similarity to the skunk's musky natural defense.

One form of protection against light damage is colored glass. The more opaque the glass, the better: Green is good, but amber (brown) is best.

So why don't certain beers in clear bottles, like Miller High Life, get skunky? It has to do with that particular brewery using a chemically altered hop extract that doesn't contain isohumulones. No isohumulones, no reaction to light, no skunkiness!

Checking out the store scene before buying

How can you, the customer, know when a particular beer arrived in the store? Unfortunately, you can't, but you can find clues in the beer or on the packaging that help you figure out which beers are fresh stock and which ones are on a long-term lease. Here are some general buying tips:

- Whether you buy beer in cans or bottles, always reach for refrigerated stock first.

- Check for a readable date stamp — if there is one (see the nearby sidebar "Breaking the code"). Look at the tops of the cans or the shoulders of the bottles; be wary of any that wear a mantle of dust.

- When buying bottled beer, consider the color of the bottle. Keep in mind that green glass allows more light to penetrate than brown glass does and clear glass allows the most light.

- Hold a bottle up to the light and assess the beer's clarity. Except for beers purposely bottled in the unfiltered state, a fresh filtered beer should be crystal clear. Look for sediment. Unless the beer in your hand is a Hefeweizen or a bottle-conditioned beer (see Chapter 4), sediment suggests that the beer has been sitting around a while.

- Give the bottle a gentle shake. Any little chunks of stuff swirling around are probably protein flakes that have settled out of the liquid — a definite sign that the beer is eligible for social security.

- Check the airspace (the *ullage*) at the top of the bottle. The proper ullage should be no more than 1 inch from the top of the liquid to the cap. A larger-than-normal ullage may promote oxidation, especially with unrefrigerated beer. Don't buy that bottle!

Breaking the code

All major American brewers date-stamp their products so distributors can keep track of their stock. Distributors are generally expected to remove and return an outdated product to the brewer, but occasionally a distributor and retailer agree to sell outdated beer at a drastically reduced price — without informing the consumer how old it is. Checking the date stamps before buying seems like the common-sense thing for a customer to do; however, some brewers use encrypted date stamps, so only those who know the code (and probably certain CIA operatives) can understand the information.

Most craft brewers, who live and die by freshness of product, date-stamp their products with uncoded, easy-to-read freshness dates. Kudos to them.

Certain megabrewers' date-stamping indicates not only at which brewery the beer was brewed but also on which production line it was packaged — accurate down to the 15-minute period of production! But when written in 12-figure alphanumeric code, the information may as well be in hieroglyphics. A prize of one fresh beer to anyone who can break it.

Making friends with your local beer retailers

Get to know your local beer retailers. If they carry a varied beer selection, make your face well known. Let them know you're a beer geek. Don't be afraid to ask questions. After establishing a relationship, you may want to approach your local beer retailers about their storage and stock-rotation practices. You'll probably get straight answers, especially if the proprietor is a dedicated beer lover. In time, you may even suggest additions or deletions to the stock. Who knows — before you're through, they may just make you a business partner.

Another way to ensure a supply of quality beer, especially if you don't live in a major urban area, is to join a beer-of-the-month club. You can find several online, and most send you 12 bottles, along with a newsletter, for about $25 to $35 per month. This kind of connection serves the dual purpose of bringing you fresh beer as well as exposing you to a variety of microbrewed beers that aren't normally distributed nationally.

Did You Get Burnt? Checking Your Beer at Home

After you've plunked down your money and taken your carefully scrutinized brew home, the post-purchase evaluation begins; I explain what to do in the following sections.

Popping your top

Your evaluation of your newly purchased beer starts with the removal of the bottle cap. Did the bottle give a quick, healthy hiss? Did it gush like Mt. Vesuvius or fail to release any carbonation at all? Unless the bottle was allowed to get very warm or you did the hokey-pokey with it just before opening, a gusher indicates a potential wild fermentation in the bottle — not a good thing, but not anything that'll kill you, either. If a quick sniff doesn't verify this possibility, a follow-up taste will. Vinegary tastes and aromas are usually good indications of a fermentation gone wild, but proper pasteurization makes this occurrence infrequent. And keep in mind that certain beer styles are meant to have a sour taste, and some are just naturally more highly carbonated than others. Don't be too quick to judge.

If you didn't get the usual *fizzzt* from the bottle, either the beer was improperly carbonated at the brewery (very unlikely) or the cap's seal had a leak that allowed the carbonation to escape. These types of problems are virtually unheard of in well-known, brand-name beers and are usually limited to products from small, technologically challenged breweries.

There's rain in your beer!

Ever notice the cloud that appears in the neck of a beer bottle when the cap is removed? It's a real cloud, just like outside!

The airspace in the unopened bottleneck contains carbon dioxide and water vapor. Because the inside pressure is approximately twice the air pressure at sea level, when the cap is removed, the gases and vapors expand rapidly. This decompression causes a precipitous drop in temperature (remember your high school science?) within the neck of the bottle — estimated to be approximately –30 degrees Fahrenheit (–34 degrees Celsius). That's cold, man!

This instantaneous drop in temperature causes the water molecules to become so sluggish that they become *nucleation sites* for water droplets (condensation) — the same way clouds form in the sky.

Battling the oxidation blues

Any beer that's been laying around too long, regardless of whether it was pasteurized, reaches a point when it goes stale (becomes *oxidized*). The result is a beer that smells and tastes papery in the early stages and cardboardy in the advanced stages. Refrigerated beer is far less likely to become oxidized, but it can still happen over time.

Because the only ways to detect oxidation in beer are by smelling it and tasting it, you're not likely to discover this flaw until you've already purchased the beer. This is another good reason to check freshness dates on the label or packaging before you buy.

Chapter 10

Looking at Label Lunacy and Marketing Mayhem

In This Chapter

▶ Making sense of beer labels

▶ Understanding beer advertizing and marketing

▶ Discovering the health benefits of beer

M aking an informed choice when buying packaged beer can be a small challenge. Sometimes weird government regulations and, let's face it, brewer's poetic license combine to make beer labeling and advertising less than helpful. Determining what you're buying, or paying extra for, is sometimes hard to do.

The brewer's poetry is usually obvious (a rundown on the taste, which is helpful, and ingredients and brewing processes, which are mostly irrelevant to the average consumer). The words *malty* and *hoppy* can give you a good idea of the taste, but a list of the specific malts or hops doesn't mean much to most people, though it is appetizing and fun, even educational. Other information, like *finest grains,* is sometimes confusing. Do these things make the beer better? Should a beer fan understand the terms and make a choice based on that information? Mostly, the answer is no.

What's *not* listed on the label is of more concern and raises even more questions in the mind of the informed consumer. This chapter gives you some background on what's what in the world of beer labeling and marketing so you can consume with confidence.

Understanding Labeling Laws

In the United States, the American brewing industry (along with American wine and spirits industries) is overseen by both the Bureau of Alcohol, Tobacco, and Firearms (ATF) and the Alcohol and Tobacco Tax and Trade

Bureau (TTB). As far as the production of beer goes, the ATF is more concerned with illegal diversion of alcohol for criminal purposes, whereas the TTB is now the governing body behind all the do's and don'ts that control beer labeling and marketing.

As you can imagine, over the years, the American brewing industry has been beset by some very archaic laws, some predating Prohibition (which was in effect from 1920 to 1933). The situation is similar in the United Kingdom and Europe. The bottom line is that despite their best intentions, governments may have managed to prevent useful information — like nutritional content and strength — from reaching you. A bizarre paradox. With the craft beer renaissance in full swing, many changes have taken place and continue to do so at a dizzying pace.

Label must-haves

U.S. rules say that very little is required on beer labels. In fact, U.S. rules require only the basics, and they can be both incomplete and incorrect from a beer enthusiast's point of view.

- ✔ For domestic beers, the name and address of the bottler or packer, but not necessarily the actual brewer of the beer (or the actual street address), must appear on the label.

- ✔ For imported beers, the label must include the words *imported by* followed by the name of the importer, or exclusive agent, or sole distributor responsible for the importation, together with its principal place of business in the United States.

- ✔ The class (ale or lager) *must* be stated, and the type (style — Porter, Bock, and so on) *may* be stated. Unfortunately for consumers, the type is the more important distinction of the two.

The law spells out — often inaccurately — which beers can and can't be called *Ale, Porter,* or *Stout.* At least one brewer has actually resorted to deliberately mislabeling an ale as a lager or as a nonexistent style in order to conform. Big bummer.

In the European Union (E.U.), laws are similar, with a few important additions: Brewers exporting within the E.U. need to list the country of manufacture, alcohol content by volume (not done in the United States), and a *best before* date, something that some of the leading U.S. brewers do by choice in an effort to impress discerning fans.

By U.S. law, plenty of other statements and representations may not be used on container labels, including any statement or representation relating to nutritional analysis, ingredients, standards, or tests.

Impure but good

The belief that today's German brewers aren't allowed to make beer with anything other than the four basic ingredients is somewhat misleading. Brewers are allowed to use fruits and spices in their beer (and even sauerkraut, if they choose); the stipulation is that they can't call that beer a lager if it's being marketed in Germany — even though it may be one. Weird, no?

As a result, the distinction between ales and lagers is twisted, in what must be one of the first and most bizarre loopholes in a consumer protection law. Regardless, the Reinheitsgebot is still a universally recognized standard.

Of course, rules can be interpreted, not followed to the letter, and still be honored. For a brewer who breaks the confines of the Reinheitsgebot to develop an unusual taste — using unmalted barley, extra sugar for prolonging fermentation, or adding some fruit for flavor (see Chapter 2 for more on beer ingredients) — there should be no shame. That the brewer continues to use high-quality ingredients and doesn't rely on additives and preservatives to artificially enhance a product is what's most important.

The weak, the strong, and the unintelligible: Alcohol content

Even though *all* other alcoholic beverages are *required* to clearly list alcohol content on their labels, listing any indication of strength, including percentage of alcohol (unless the beer has no alcohol at all), was prohibited for beer labels until 1996. For years, the government had been afraid that people might sell or buy beer based on strength alone. (Why didn't the same reasoning apply to wine or spirits?)

The vast majority of beers from around the world have alcohol contents of 4 to 6 percent alcohol by volume (for example, Budweiser has 5 percent). Many beers may contain as much as 7 or 8 percent, and a select few contain alcohol levels equivalent to quality wines, which are about 12 to 14 percent. I address the alcohol content of specific beer styles in Appendix A.

The more common method of listing alcohol content in beer is by actual percentage of volume, which is the law in the United Kingdom and Europe. In the United States, it had been the big brewers' custom to note alcohol by weight. Of these two methods, alcohol by volume is easier to understand because you buy beer by volume, and today, the vast majority of brewers list alcohol contents by volume.

Why is the weight method used? Because alcohol weighs less than water, beer, and many other liquids and, therefore, appears to be lower when comparative measurements are made. In English measure, a pint of water, for example, weighs 1 pound (actually, a fraction of an ounce over). A pint of alcohol, on the other hand, weighs only 0.79 pound. So a beer with an alcohol content of 3.2 percent by weight is actually 4 percent by volume. A beer that is 4 percent by weight is actually 5 percent by volume. To figure it out yourself, convert an alcohol-by-weight reading to its alcohol-by-volume equivalent by multiplying by 1.25. To convert an alcohol-by-volume reading to its alcohol-by-weight equivalent, multiply by 0.80. Fun, huh?

Some internationally published beer writers give both measurements in their beer reviews. Read labels and menus carefully and remember that figures for weight are *lower* than those for volume. You may be consuming much more (or less) alcohol than you think.

Europeans are accustomed to seeing some indication of the alcohol content in their beers, whether or not it's accompanied by a figure:

- In Germany, beer bottle labels are likely to contain one of the following three legal strength designations: *schankbier* (light), *vollbier* (medium), or *starkbier* (strong).

- Belgium has four categories of beer strength, ranging from *Catégorie III* (weakest) and moving up through *Catégories II* and *I*, ending with *Catégorie S*, for strong.

- The French have to be different, of course. They invented their own strength measure, called *degrees Régie*, which they use to measure beers ranging from *bière petite* (the lightest) through *bière de table*, *bière bock*, *bière de luxe*, *bière de choix*, and *bière spéciale* (the strongest).

If you want to know the strength and brewing details about a particular beer, you can check out good reviews on the Internet (see Chapter 19 for some suggested websites), or check out Appendix A for info on the alcohol content of various beers.

Know-nothing labels: Additives and preservatives

The U.S. brewing industry is one of the few consumable-producing industries not required by the government to list ingredients on product labels. Surprisingly, consumers haven't demanded that brewers do so, either.

Among the many allowable additives and preservatives are more than 50 antioxidants, foam enhancers, colorings, flavorings, and miscellaneous enzymes, such as aspergillus oryzae, propylene glycol, sodium bisulfite, benzaldehyde, ethyl acetate, and food coloring. And you thought beer was just nicely flavored water!

The first consumer protection law

Written in 1516 by Duke Wilhelm IV of Bavaria, the Reinheitsgebot guaranteed that a true Bavarian beer was made with nothing other than malted barley or wheat, hops, and water. This purity law was updated (to include yeast, for example, which people didn't know about in 1516) and became part of modern laws over time.

Actually, the question of allowable ingredients constituted only half of the subject matter of the original decree. At that time, the more important issue dealt with the pricing structure of beer.

The cost was to be preset according to measure (quart and ½ quart) and the time of year. (Apparently, 16th-century Bavarian beer was more expensive in the summer months when demand was greater — a concept not lost on my electric company.) The Duke realized that the well-regarded Bavarian brewing industry could be developed into a taxable powerhouse, and history proved him right.

The Reinheitsgebot has defined the basic building blocks of quality beer. It cast these guidelines in stone and has been honored and respected for some 480 years by the German brewing industry. In 1919, all German breweries reaffirmed their informal allegiance to the law — something that loyal German consumers hold dear.

As recently as spring 1986, a brewer named Helmut Keininger was arrested for putting chemicals in his beer. The infraction was considered so professionally devastating that he ended up committing suicide in his Munich jail cell.

Purist beer nuts planning a pilgrimage should know that the original copy of the Reinheitsgebot is on display at the Bavarian State Library in Munich.

One of the hallmarks of craft-brewed beers is that they're made without chemical additives and preservatives. My opinion is that the large corporate brewers are infamous for using cheaper ingredients (adjunct grains, such as corn and rice — see Chapter 2 for ingredients most often used in beer) to make beer, but to good-beer fans like me, far worse than their frugality is their use of additives and preservatives.

The Reinheitsgebot: The German beer purity law

Many beer labels boast some phrasing of the following: *Brewed in strict accordance with the German beer purity law of 1516.* That's saying a lot; that means that the beer has no adjuncts (sugar, rice, corn), additives, or preservatives and is brewed using only malted barley or wheat, hops, yeast, and water. The absence of such a claim doesn't necessarily mean the beer has adjuncts, although a weak equivalent is *all malt,* meaning no adjunct grains were used (only barley and wheat are malted).

Originally, the *Reinheitsgebot* (pronounced rine-*hites*-ga-boat) was known as the Bavarian beer purity law because Bavaria was a Protectorate ruled by a king back in 1516 — not quite yet a part of modern-day Germany. *Freistaadt Bayern* (the free state of Bavaria) didn't join the other German states of the Weimar Republic until 1919, at which time other German brewers adopted the Bavarian beer purity law as their own.

Even though the Reinheitsgebot is rooted in German political history, it has become synonymous with U.S. craft brews. Why? Because the Reinheitsgebot stands for beer purity, and U.S. craft brewers have wholeheartedly embraced that idea; some even advertise the fact.

The Reinheitsgebot isn't applied to beer being exported from Germany. Some of the most popular German beers imported to the United States aren't brewed according to the Reinheitsgebot; the recipes have been legally altered with adjuncts and preservatives both for U.S. tastes and for added shelf life. That may be why many U.S. travelers to Germany say that German beers never taste as good back home as they do in Germany.

Beer Advertising and Marketing

Oddly, most of the emphasis in U.S. beer promotion is on name recognition, so ads feature humor or social situations unrelated to the taste, ingredients, or general quality of the beer. In other words, while advertising should extol the virtues and the various features of a product, megabrewed beer advertising tends to ignore the beer itself (don't get me started as to why). For examples, try a Swedish bikini team, an ugly dog named Spuds, animated frogs, and beer labels that tell you when your beer is cold (do we really need this?). Get the idea? They may be creative and effective methods of advertising, but they say little about beer. Same with the labels.

In the following sections, I explore the nonessential details often included in beer advertising and also introduce some marketing schemes, like stealth micros and contract brewing.

Touting nonessential details

Some of the buzzwords peculiar to the brewing industry include *unique blends, select grains, premium hops,* and *pure spring water.* The two most overused terms (despite the fact that they say very little about the taste of the beer) are *smooth* and *mellow.* In too many cases, *insipid* and *lifeless* would be more apt.

Watchdogs through the ages

Throughout history, people have made sporadic attempts to patrol the brewing industry and perform the equivalent of quality-control analysis, purity law or no purity law. We beer lovers take this stuff seriously!

- ✔ The first watchdog was an Egyptian fellow, in the time of the Pharaohs, who held the title of Chief Beer Inspector, or something to that effect. It was his responsibility to maintain the level of quality of the beer being produced for the Pharaoh's household. No mention is made of penalties for failure.

- ✔ One of the oldest public offices in England is that of the *ale-conner,* or taster, a post created by William the Conqueror in the 11th century in order to keep ale prices and quality in line. Not only was the ale-conner an expert judge of beer, but he had the power to condemn a batch of beer or order its sale at a reduced price if it didn't meet his high standards. This token civil position still exists in England, paying a small annual allowance with free beer thrown in for good measure. (William Shakespeare's father, John, was an ale-conner, an appointment of considerable significance in Elizabethan England. The young bard obviously learned to appreciate a good beer: "Blessing of your heart, you brew good ale," from *Two Gentlemen of Verona.*)

According to British lore, besides tasting the liquid wares, the resourceful ale-conner evaluated the new brews in a most peculiar way. Garbed in leather breeches, he'd pour a measure of ale on a wooden bench and dutifully sit in the puddle of beer for no less than half an hour. If his breeches stuck to the bench, the ale was deemed young and imperfect — with too much sugar — and the ale-conner could levy a penalty against the brewer. (Brewers may have felt that they were getting the short end of the stick when, in fact, they were getting the sticky end of the shorts.) (Find out more about the ale-conner in Chapter 19.)

- ✔ In 18th-century Alsace, sworn beer assayers were called *bierkiesers.* In the neighboring regions of Artois and Flanders, their equivalents were called *coueriers, egards,* or *eswarts.* Their job was to taste freshly tapped beer in order to ensure that it met local standards, which closely mirrored the Reinheitsgebot. The addition of any unauthorized ingredient was a punishable offense.

Megabrewers aren't alone in advertising and label latitude: Many labels on craft brews tout the variety of hops or water used. (Can you imagine being told which kind of corn was used in your corn flakes?) That kind of detail matters to brewers, but for the rest of us, it's largely hype. What really matters is how all the ingredients are put together and how the beer turns out. It's the beer, folks. You can ignore the rest.

And all our bottles are made from the finest carbon

Try not to be taken in by flowery language and fancy packaging. The following is copied verbatim from the bottleneck label of a popular and excellent craft-brewed beer (with good ingredients) whose marketers simply got carried away:

Ajax Traditional Pale Ale [name changed to protect the guilty] *is brewed with six specially blended malts, hopped with English*

East Kent Goldings and American Cascades to give this traditional ale a distinctive yet drinkable quality.

Especially impressive is the ability of the beer to retain a *drinkable quality* after all those malts and hops. What else should it be? Paintable? Wearable? Come on — *drinkable?*

Invading craft brew territory with stealth micros from megabrewers

Shortly after the craft beer revolution got underway, the lion (megabrewers) noticed the thorn (craft brewers) in its paw, leading to some clever marketing and business strategizing. Megabrewers liked the craft brewer's cachet of quality — and premium prices.

In an illustration of the maxim that imitation is the sincerest form of flattery, some of the big U.S. megabrewers have either bought or become partners with a number of successful regional craft brewers; some of the big guys have also started making their own craft-like brands disguised as microbrews through clever marketing (one wag dubbed them *stealth micros*). Here are a couple of megabrewers who have put out craft-like brews:

- **The Miller Brewing Company:** Miller merged with Molson a few years back and introduced Blue Moon white beer under the auspices of the Blue Moon Brewing Company. Blue Moon continues to be very popular despite the fact that it's brewed by a megabrewery corporation. Together, they've produced several variations on the moon theme.

- **The Anheuser-Busch (A-B) Brewing Company:** Tinkering with macro-made microbrews for quite a while now, A-B's most recent introductions to the world of pseudo craft beers are Shock Top Wheat, Stone Mill Pale Ale, and Land Shark Lager, the latter of which is brewed specially for Jimmy Buffett's Margaritaville restaurant chain.

Although some of the stealth brews are terrific, quality, and award-winning traditional brews, many are the plain old, same old bland stuff masquerading as good stuff. *Caveat emptor.*

In the United Kingdom, the big brewers are pushing *nitrokeg* beer (filtered and pasteurized keg beer artificially carbonated and pressurized with a nitrogen/carbon dioxide blend) disguised as the more costly and appreciated naturally carbonated, unfiltered, unpasteurized, and hand-pumped cask-conditioned ales. The brewers even supply fake hand pumps. Traditionalists are in an uproar.

Getting the lowdown on contract brewing

Microbreweries (brewers who make fewer than 60,000 barrels a year) have sort of cornered the image market on gourmet beer: Most of these beers sell for more because consumers consider them superior, largely due to the freshness that comes from being made locally and in small batches. Consumers are also willing to pay more for beer with the cachet of being small and hand-crafted, like artisanal bread or handcrafted furniture.

A lot of the best and best-known *craft brews* (gourmet beers made in a wide range of classic styles, using quality ingredients) aren't microbrewed but are *contract brewed* in larger volumes than a microbrewery can handle. Contract brewers hire underutilized but well-equipped regional breweries to produce a recipe with the contract brewer's own ingredients and formulas. The giveaway label lingo, if you can find the small print along the edges, is something like, "Brewed by XX Brewing Co. under special agreement, xyz Brewing Co., ABC State." The only other way to learn what's contract brewed is to follow beer blogs, do Google searches, or consult the online beer-rating sites (see Chapter 19).

The very popular Boston Beer Company (Samuel Adams Boston Lager and so on) started as a contract-brewed beer, but now the company owns and operates two separate brewing facilities to keep up with demand for its products. The first of the Boston Beer Company's breweries set up shop in the former Haffenreffer Brewery in Jamaica Plain, Massachusetts (near Boston). The second is set up in the old Hudepohl-Schoenling Brewery in Cincinnati, Ohio.

You'll see a definite trend as certain brands become successful enough to build up national demand that can be met only by regional brewing, which is better than having to resort to adjuncts and preservatives. Nothing wrong with that — the quality is the same. Still, you may find it disconcerting.

Your full-of-character beer with its artsy label and catchy name reeking of homemade goodness and local freshness may not be made nearby by some wonderfully talented beer nuts slaving away on homemade equipment; it may actually be produced at an industrial site hundreds of miles away, perhaps financed by venture capital and moved by top-notch marketing muscle. For example, Chicagoans with a fondness for the hometown State Street Beer were surely surprised to find that it's produced in Evansville, Indiana.

However, if the beer tastes good, don't worry! The taste — and your satisfaction — is all that really matters.

The label as an art form

One of the nicest aspects of the American craft-brewing renaissance is the artwork on the labels. Some labels are downright inspired and splendid works of art, while others, like the following label from Flying Dog Ales, are wacky and irreverent. Appreciating them brings a whole new dimension to beer drinking. And the brand names! They're creative and humorous, making the spirit of beer live inside and outside the bottle.

Used with permission from Flying Dog Brewery; artwork by Ralph Steadman

"Guinness Is Good for You": Nutritional Content

In the United States, the TTB doesn't allow the Food and Drug Administration's (FDA) Nutrition Facts chart to appear on a beer bottle or can. And in the European Union, proposals to mandate the listing of ingredients have fallen by the wayside. Governments fear that consumers may infer suggestions of "curative and therapeutic claims" stemming from the fact that well-made craft-brewed beer can have more protein than a dry bowl of corn flakes, with half the carbohydrates and twice the potassium and without the additives or preservatives so often found in prepared foods, as well as in some megabrewed beers.

In a February 1993 article in *Seattle Weekly,* Jack Killorin, an ATF spokesman, is cited as saying that listing a beer's nutrients would suggest that beer is a food. According to the article, Killorin said that beer isn't a food because alcohol is bad, and the FDA doesn't allow bad food. (Now, I ask, does this same rule of thought apply to TV dinners and marshmallows?) Regardless of this statement, strong indications show that this attitude is changing and that nutrition labels will eventually be listed on beer products.

In fact, in the United States, the government guidelines on which these things are based are reviewed every five years. The 2010 revised Dietary Guidelines for Americans, released by a joint committee of the U.S. Department of Agriculture and the Department of Health and Human Services, actually contradict the ages-old government line. These guidelines state that accumulating evidence suggests that moderate drinking (*read:* no more than one drink per day for women or two drinks per day for men) is associated with lower risk of cardiovascular disease and that moderate alcohol consumption "also is associated with lower risk of all-cause mortality among middle aged and older adults and may help to keep cognitive function intact with age." A drink is defined as 12 fluid ounces of regular beer (5 percent alcohol by volume) or 5 fluid ounces of wine (12 percent alcohol by volume) or 1.5 fluid ounces of distilled alcohol (40 percent alcohol by volume/80 proof).

This modest statement is downright revolutionary for the U.S. government. After all, the 1990 guidelines said that drinking had *no* net health benefit. However, they're not exactly inviting you to a big party. *Moderation* is key, as is a well-balanced, low-fat diet combined with exercise. The guidelines rightly go on to warn that higher levels of alcohol intake are risky in terms of raising blood pressure and incidents of stroke, heart disease, and some forms of cancer, as well as being the less direct cause of birth defects, suicide, and accidents. The guidelines continue to remind us of the dangers of drinking and driving as well as irresponsible overconsumption in general. The government warning on beer labels remains in effect.

Cholesterol and fat free

For years, the great Irish Stout, Guinness, has been advertised with the slogan "Guinness Is Good for You." Americans take that kind of statement too seriously, so it wasn't used in Guinness advertising in the United States. But it was partially correct: Beer is actually nutritious, though you should consume it only for pleasure and thirst-quenching purposes.

Beer is free of cholesterol and fat. More good news: 12 ounces of a typical American Pale Lager actually have fewer calories than 12 ounces of 2 percent milk or even apple juice (a bit less than wine, too)! And some lower-alcohol styles, such as Dry Stouts, have even fewer calories. Beer may not be diet delite, but I'll bet you're happy to know that it has good dietary qualities.

Those Germans sure know a good thing when they see it

In mid-19th-century Munich, some nursing mothers and wet nurses went out of their way to drink up to seven (sic) pints of beer a day, thinking that amount was required to adequately breast-feed a child. In 1876, the Munich city health department tried to break this habit, stating that only two pints a day were necessary. Of course, today we know that any alcohol consumed by nursing women can be passed on to their children; therefore, it's unwise and unsafe to drink any amount of beer while breast-feeding.

Things are a bit different for men, though: In 1987, a German federal petition to the European court on a related matter stated that as much as 25 percent of the average German man's daily nutrients came from beer. That's serious consumption.

If the government *did* allow the listing of nutritional content on beer labels, here's what the content of a standard Nutrition Facts chart may look like for a 12-ounce (355-milliliter) bottle of a typical megabrewed U.S. lager:

- 151 calories (⅔ from alcohol)
- 0 grams fat
- 0 milligrams cholesterol
- 25 milligrams sodium
- 13.7 grams carbohydrate
- 1.1 grams protein
- Trace amounts of calcium, potassium, and phosphorus and many of the B vitamins

For comparison's sake, here are the numbers on a high-quality, microbrewed beer, such as Stone's Arrogant Bastard Ale, produced in the state of California. A 12-ounce serving has 190 calories, 0 fat, 0 cholesterol, and 12 grams of total carbohydrates. It contains no dietary fiber, 12 grams of sugars, 0.5 grams of protein, and 20 grams of alcohol. And you won't find any additives or preservatives. (Most light beers check in at about 95 calories, with the lightest one in the world — Budweiser Select — checking in at just 55 calories.)

Drink beer, live longer

One of the greatest little tidbits of news that beer drinkers ever heard was the spring 1996 report that dark beer can help prevent heart disease.

This welcome news came from John Folts, the director of the Coronary Thrombosis Research and Prevention Laboratory at the University of Wisconsin, the man who discovered that aspirin helps prevent heart disease. The key to dark beer's role, along with red wine and black tea, is that it contains vitamin-like compounds called *flavenoids* that inhibit platelet activity in blood, making it less likely to clog arteries. And other studies show that moderate consumption of any alcohol may increase HDL (good cholesterol) levels, as well as help your longevity.

I'm not suggesting that you should go out and drink beer for medicinal reasons. On the contrary, increased consumption of tea, grape juice, or fruits and vegetables is the better way to go. But still, this information gives you a great excuse (if you need one) to drink beer.

Chapter 11

Serving Beer

The simple act of serving someone a beer needn't be done with a flourish, but it should go a bit beyond sliding an ice-cold can of Yahoo Brew across the bar or kitchen table.

If you're into good beer, you're into tasting it right, and to taste it right, you have to pay attention to which glass you use, how you pour the beer, and how you clean and store the glass when you're done using it. You discover all these aspects of serving beer in this chapter. Ensuring that the beer you serve tastes as good as it can to you and your guests takes only a little effort. I know the brewers appreciate it and so will you.

Choosing a Glass with Class

You should always pour beer from its bottle or can before serving. Period. Any *clean* vessel will suffice, but transparent glass has a clear advantage over opaque cups and steins because it allows you to appreciate the color and head of the beer. After all, as the saying goes, "We drink first with our eyes." A bright, bubbly beer capped by a dense and rocky head of foam is a sight for thirsty eyes.

Besides looking good, however, the various shapes and sizes of beer glassware play a meaningful role in your enjoyment. Glassware that's deep or that curves inward toward the top is very effective in capturing and concentrating the beer's aromas. In the following sections, I describe a number of basic glass styles and a few types that are out of the ordinary. I also give you some pointers on determining which glasses are right for your needs.

Mug and thistle, clean as a whistle: A short history of beer glassware

The ancient Sumerians were known to drink their beer directly from a communal bowl into which they dipped straws, or hollow reeds. Some later civilizations learned how to fashion rough earthenware vessels to hold their liquids, while others sewed animal hides together to create a *bottel* — much like the bota bag of today. As civilization progressed, wood, glass, and bronze were used to great effect.

That wooden bowls, clay steins, and pewter chalices were opaque mattered little to these people, whose ales were dark and murky. These turbid brews scored low on the scale of visual appeal and were just as well drunk from nontransparent vessels.

Glassware's fullest potential wasn't realized until the mid–19th century, when Czechoslovakian Pilsners and Pale Lagers from Germany first appeared. These brilliant golden beers were shown to their best advantage in tall, thin, footed glasses. The invention of the glass-pressing machine just prior to these beers' entry into the world made possible the production of glasses in a variety of shapes and sizes. As the popularity of these beers spread, so did the use of style-specific glassware.

With modern society's heathenish return to drinking beer directly from its container, civilized beer drinking was set back several centuries.

Nowadays, a quiet revival of style-specific glassware is going on, likely an outgrowth of the microbrewing revolution, wherein brewpubs or beer bars may feature a range of glassware styles as extensive as the number of beer styles being served.

The concept of brew-specific glassware may be new to Americans, but it's old hat in many European nations. Beer-producing countries are generally more observant of this unwritten code of beer protocol — the Germans and the Belgians can be downright finicky about it. In some instances, Belgian and German brewers have commissioned world-famous glassmakers to design unique glasses for their brews.

One story tells of a foreign visitor to a Belgian beer bar who, upon placing his order, was told that all the glasses for that particular beer were in use and that he was welcome to order a second choice or wait until a glass for his first choice became available!

The glass lineup: Basic types of glassware

Traditionally, certain beers have a specific glass style associated with them. (I describe these glass styles in the following sections.) Using these glasses is a sign of your high regard for great beer. The nice thing about beer glassware, though, is that it doesn't involve hard-and-fast rules. Not using these styles is a sign of being a normal person without really cool glassware, so don't freak out if you lack a certain glass. If you don't have the perfect glass, don't worry; that Flintstones iced-tea glass in the cupboard has been known to serve the purpose.

Matching glass style to beer style

Simple beers can be served in simple glasses; well-aged and expensive beers should get the regal treatment. Table 11-1 describes which basic glass to use for which kind of beer.

Table 11-1	The Right Glasses for Select Beer Styles
Glass Description	*Beer*
Deep, tulip-shaped glasses	Strong beers, such as Belgian Ales
Simple pint glasses	Mild Ales and Brown Ales, Porters, Stouts
Small, brandy snifter–type glasses or even cordials	Rich and spirituous Barleywines, Old Ales, and Imperial Stouts
Thin, stemmed flutes	Some aromatic Trappist and Abbey Ales and Belgian Fruit Beers
Tall, narrow glasses	Light, spritzy, and aromatic beers, such as Pilsners and Witbiers
Tall, thick glasses	Wheat Beers
Wide-bowled goblets	Aromatic beers, such as Berliner Weisse

Surveying specific types of glasses

You may run across some of the following glass styles in your beery journeys. (Check out some of the most popular kinds in Figure 11-1 and see Chapter 14 for a basic metric-conversion table.)

- **Altbier glass:** The Altbier glass is a short, slim, cylindrical glass similar to a Tom Collins glass. This glass is a shorter and fatter version of a Kölsch beer glass.

- **Beer flute:** Rather thin and dainty with a stem and a base, the beer flute is used for Pilsners and similar beers but is meant for beers that emulate wines, such as Belgian Fruit Beers. This glass emphasizes tart and vinous qualities.

- **Dimpled pint mug:** The dimpled pint mug was used at one time as the standard drinking vessel in British pubs. This glass was slowly and quietly replaced by the straight-sided pint glass, which was easier to store on crowded pub shelves. The dimpled pint mug is well suited to English Ales and Bitters.

- **Goblet:** The goblet is used almost exclusively for Berliner Weisse and some Trappist and Abbey Ales. Chalice-like in appearance, with a wide and shallow bowl and a heavy stem and foot, the goblet discourages excessive head formation and allows the drinker's nose inside the opening of the glass.

Figure 11-1:
A wide
range of
beer
glasses
allows you
to choose
the right
one for a
particular
beer style.

- ✔ **Halbe:** Meaning "half" in German, for half-liter, a halbe is a simple glass mug preferred by many Germans for everyday Helles. The halbe is similar to a British pint glass with a handle.

- ✔ **Kölsch beer glass:** The Kölsch beer glass is a tall, slim, cylindrical glass, similar to a Tom Collins glass. It's a taller version of the Altbier glass.

- ✔ **Krug:** Krug literally means mug or tankard (it may also refer to a jug or pitcher). The krug is rather large and usually made of sturdy glass, making it safe for ceremonial clinking following a toast.

- ✔ **Mass:** Mass, pronounced *mahss*, means measure in German. This glass is also called a Bavarian *masskrug*. The mass is a large and heavy dimpled glass mug with a liquid capacity of 1 liter (34 ounces, or the equivalent of 2⅔ bottles of beer). The mass glass allows for 2 inches of head space, stands about 8 inches tall, and weighs about 2½ pounds when empty. This glass is the standard serving size at Munich's Oktoberfest.

German quaffers say that when the large mass glass mug is in use, each sip (gulp?) of beer should lower the liquid level to the next dimple in the glass. The glass has only four vertical dimples, so each sip is equivalent to about 8 ounces of beer! *Ein, zwei, G'suffa!*

- ✔ **Middy:** Of Australian origin, the middy size depends on where you're drinking: In Sydney, a middy holds 10 ounces, but in Perth, it holds only 7.

- **Pilsner:** The Pilsner glass comes in a variety of styles. The more elegant ones are tall and footed and made of wafer-thin glass; they hold 10 or 12 ounces. The more ordinary versions are usually hourglass-shaped or slightly flared tumblers, holding between 8 and 12 ounces.

- **Pint glass:** Probably the most pedestrian and interchangeable of beer glasses, the standard — or shaker — pint glass is made of thick glass, tapers slowly outward toward the top, and holds 16 ounces of beer (before you say, "duh," read on). The *imperial pint* glass holds 20 ounces of beer (not too common in the United States). The *nonic* (pronounced *no knick*) pint glass has a bulge near the top of the glass that protects the lip from nicks should the glass be tipped over (these bulges also allow the glasses to be stacked one inside the other without becoming stuck). Another variation is a slightly curvaceous version of the standard pint, simply called a *pub glass.*

Many bars and pubs in the United States serve beer in pint glasses that aren't legitimately pint-sized (16 ounces); they're often only 14 ounces in volume. Whether bars do this to intentionally rip off the consumer may never be known. So, drinker, beware!

- **Pony:** The pony is an Australian liquid measure of ⅕ pint. The actual glass may hold 4 or 5 ounces of beer, depending on whether you're in Victoria or New South Wales (no one knows why, though these territories were once quite independent of one another).

- **Schooner:** The schooner is typically a tall glass similar to a tumbler, measuring 15 ounces. Drinking from a schooner in Australia gets you anywhere from 9 to 15 ounces, depending on the bar. Laid-back types, those Aussies.

- **Schnelle:** The schnelle is a tall, slender, tapered earthenware tankard with a hinged lid.

- **Sham:** The sham is generally of small proportions, ranging from 5 to 10 ounces, regardless of shape. The exact origin and definition of this beer glass is dubious (after all, the word *sham* is defined as an impostor).

- **Stein:** The stein, or *stone* in German, is made of clay or ceramic and often features a hinged lid (usually made of pewter). A *glass stein* is a contradiction in terms.

- **Thistle:** The silhouette of the thistle glass is exactly as the name implies. The thistle is a uniquely shaped glass, almost exclusively used for strong Scottish Ales (the thistle is the emblem of the Scottish Crown). However, the glass itself is attributed to the Belgians, who developed a fondness for this style when Scottish soldiers who were stationed in Belgium during World War I brought their strong ale with them. Thistle glasses help intensify the beer's aroma.

- **Tulip:** The tulip glass shape closely resembles its name and is effective in capturing the aromatic qualities of beer. The flared opening allows the drinker to sip the beer and the foam at the same time, creating a creamy mouthfeel. The tulip glass is favored for Belgian Strong Ales.

What style of beer goes best in *that* glass?

This explanation of the word *skull* in the English language may not be etymologically correct, but it's a story worth repeating: The fierce Norse warriors, forever drunk on ale, had a particularly barbaric way of celebrating their conquests. They would drink strong ale from the boiled craniums of their foes, toasting their victory with the word *Skol* (skull)!

- **Tumbler:** The tumbler can be rather pedestrian, but beveled edges add some panache. The tumbler is used for a wide variety of beer styles.
- **Weizen beer glass:** Tall, shapely, wide-rimmed, with a capacity usually exceeding 18 ounces, the Weizen beer glass is designed to hold a half-liter of Wheat Beer and its towering head.

To the next level: Sport drinking tools

Some non-style–specific glassware can provide the unsuspecting drinker with a challenging and often surprising outcome. Please don't try drinking from these glasses at home!

- **Yard glass (or yard-of-ale or aleyard):** The yard glass holds about 2½ pints of beer. The yard class is, well, a yard (3 feet) tall with a bell-shaped top, a ball-shaped bottom, and a long, skinny body (picture a coach horn or see Figure 11-2). The yard glass also comes in a half-yard size.

  The world record for emptying a yard glass is a scant 5 seconds; the previous record of 12 seconds was held by former Australian Prime Minister Bob Hawke, achieved while he was a student at Oxford.

- **Stiefel (or boot):** The Stiefel is literally a glass in the shape of a boot (see Figure 11-3). It can vary in size but commonly holds 4 to 5 pints of beer. The Stiefel is popular among young fraternal groups, because it's meant for communal drinking (and whoever takes the last gulp buys the next round). Drinking from a boot filled with beer presents a problem similar to that of a yard glass. The solution? Drink with the toe pointed horizontally.

- **Kwak glass:** Another glassware oddity, the Kwak glass, is a drinking receptacle made specially for a single brand. The Belgian brewer of the dark and richly herbal Kwak Bier encourages bar owners to serve this beer in the famous Kwak glass. This glass stands about 1 foot high and is part Weizen beer glass, part yard glass (see Figure 11-4). Because of its shape and size, the Kwak glass can't stand up without its own supportive wooden frame. Together, glass and frame represent a fair investment on the part of the brewer.

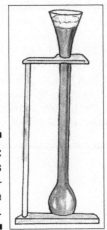

Figure 11-2:
Yard glass
and stand —
not for the
faint of heart.

Figure 11-3:
The Stiefel
glass is in
the shape of
a boot.

Drinking by the yard can create quite a splash

The problem (the challenge? the sport?) with drinking out of a yard glass is that when the rising air bubble reaches the bulbous bottom of the glass, the remaining beer is released in a sudden gush, thereby drenching the unwary drinker. The trick to drinking out of a yard glass is actually pretty simple: Slowly rotate the glass as you drink, and the pressure won't build up in the bulb.

The supposed origin of the yard glass is interesting. The Napoleonic Code forbade aristocrats' coach drivers from descending from their coaches while passengers were seated inside, to avoid the risk of losing control of the horses. In order for the driver to get refreshment, a drink had to be handed up to him. An enterprising Belgian tavern keeper invented the yard glass to facilitate this transaction. The yard glass is still occasionally referred to as a *coachmen's horn.*

The plimsoll line

The interests of beer consumers are protected in many countries that require beer glasses to have a measure mark, called a *plimsoll line* (named for inventor Samuel Plimsoll, the brilliant guy who invented the way to mark hull-depth lines on the bows of ships). This line enables customers to see that they're getting full and proper servings. Drinkers in English pubs should be aware that the government long ago backed off from legal enforcement of this law.

Figure 11-4: A Kwak glass can stand only with the support of a wooden frame.

To keep customers from making the Kwak glass part of their personal collections, many Belgian bartenders require one of the customer's shoes as a security deposit on the glass.

Let's get practical: Determining the glasses you really need

Does every budding beer connoisseur have to run out and buy two dozen different sets of beer glassware in order to consume correctly? Not at all. Beer drinking is meant to be enjoyable, and a great part of that enjoyment is comfort. Choose a beer glass style that's pleasing to you, and enjoy using it — often.

At minimum, however, I recommend having a set of standard, 16-ounce pint glasses on hand, matched by a set of more elegant footed beer flutes. You can use brandy snifters for nightcap imbibing of Old Ales, Scotch Ales, Belgian Quadruples, Imperial Stouts, and barrel-aged Stouts.

Pouring It On

Although chugging beer from a can is a common occurrence, drinking beer straight out of the bottle is about as classy as hoisting a bottle of wine to your face (okay, okay, I confess that I've done it, too). Don't chug it — pour it!

Can you believe that you're reading about how to pour a beer? Don't laugh — you'll discover something new in the following sections, I promise. Life is full of surprises.

Knowing the right serving temperature before you pour

One of the finer points of beer enjoyment that's too often overlooked is proper serving temperature. Serving beers at their proper temperature may take a little extra effort or planning, but the rewards are significant. Drinking beer at the proper temperature allows you to really *taste* the beer.

Quality beers shouldn't be served colder than 44 degrees Fahrenheit. Here are some general temperature guidelines for different beers:

Lemon-aid: Beer garnishing

Beer garnishing — adding something to a beer both for taste and for ornamentation — is becoming more common but isn't without its traditions.

One of the few examples that people may recall goes back to the mid-1980s, when Corona beer first became popular, served with a wedge of lime crammed down the neck of the bottle. Though that may have seemed a purely U.S.-based schtick, it was probably based on the habit of people from Mexico who routinely rubbed a lime wedge around the rims of their cans of Tecate beer before drinking. Far from being a stylish affectation, rubbing the lime

was a way of disinfecting the can tops and openings.

Another example of beer garnishing that's catching on quickly is the addition of a slice of lemon or orange to a towering, frothy glass of Weizen (Wheat Beer). Traditionally a summer thirst quencher, a slice of citrus adds a nice tang to the beer.

Note: Some establishments position the citrus slice over the rim of the glass, giving the customer the choice of removing it, while others toss the slice into the glass before the beer is poured. You may want to make your preference known when you order your Wheat Beer.

✔ Serve most premium lagers between 42 and 48 degrees Fahrenheit (6 to 9 degrees Celsius) and quality ales between 44 and 52 degrees Fahrenheit (7 to 11 degrees Celsius).

✔ Serve authentic Stouts as warm as 55 degrees Fahrenheit (13 degrees Celsius), which is *British cellar temperature.*

✔ Serve some high-gravity Barleywines, Old Ales, and barrel-aged Stouts only very lightly chilled or at room temperature, like a snifter of brandy.

In the United States, most beers are served much too cold for serious appreciation. In fact, ice-cold temperatures ruin the flavor of good beer. The average refrigerator is set to keep food and drinks chilled at around 38 to 40 degrees Fahrenheit (about 4 degrees Celsius), but serving beers at this temperature has several negatives, including the following:

✔ The colder the beer, the less carbonation is released; the less carbonation that's released, the less aroma the beer gives off.

✔ The palate is numbed to the point that it can't discern many of the beer's flavor nuances. (So this explains why some beers are best served just above the freezing mark!) Why bother drinking a beer if you can't taste it? May as well have a Slurpee.

Cold temperatures = less carbonation released = less aroma = less taste = why bother? Save the really cold temps for *lawnmower beer* — the kind you chug down after mowing the lawn (taste? who cares?).

Deciding whether to tilt or not to tilt

Before you pour, make sure you have a glass that can hold the contents of a whole bottle or can plus a head. That makes everything easier. How to best pour a beer depends on the type of beer. For most craft beers, the best way to pour is right down the middle of the glass — again, a glass big enough to hold the whole bottle of beer — and tilt it or slow the pouring only after a big head has formed (see Figure 11-5). Go ahead — be aggressive! Assertive! Macho! Macha!

Beer warms the soul

In centuries past, consuming ale very warm during cold weather wasn't at all unusual. Because all taverns had large fireplaces, small iron pokers were hung by the fire to be used for warming drinks. These red-hot pokers, called *loggerheads,* were sometimes brandished by inebriated patrons when tempers flared, giving rise to the phrase "to be at loggerheads."

Figure 11-5:
Pour craft-
brewed
beer to
create a
head; use a
straight shot
right down
the middle
of the glass.

Why pour so vigorously? To release the carbon dioxide. You want to do this for the following reasons:

- Unless it's released by pouring, the gas is trapped in the bottle or can and goes straight into your belly, where it struggles to release itself in an unwelcome burst. Ugh and urp.

- Unpoured beer has an unpleasant and unappealing, gassy bite on the palate.

- Releasing the gas by pouring into a glass forms a head and lets the beer's fragrance waft from the beer. (Sniff right after pouring because the aromas dissipate quickly.)

Some types of beer require special techniques. These techniques aren't rocket science, but they're worthy of attention.

- **Wheat Beers and corked-bottle beers:** Be a little less aggressive when pouring these types of beers because they tend to throw a larger-than-normal head. A proper head should be at least 1 inch thick, or two fingers deep. (These same two fingers also come in handy for measuring tequila shots, but that's another story for another time.)

✔ **Bottle-conditioned beers:** You may want to pour these beers so you leave the last ½ inch or so of dregs in the bottle. Absolutely nothing is wrong with drinking the settled yeast sediment, except that it may cause excess flatulence — the live yeast continue the fermentation process within your digestive tract! In addition, not everyone is fond of this concentrated yeast taste, though some beer aficionados swear by it. But then, some folks like anchovies, too.

✔ **American Pale Lagers:** Beers such as Budweiser and Miller are best poured slowly down the side of a tilted glass, or else they produce a glass full of head. Because these beers have little protein, a big head dissipates quickly. Creating a big head slows the pouring process needlessly (and risks having a mess on the table).

Neatness Counts: Cleaning and Storing Glassware

After you've made your choice in glassware (I describe different types earlier in this chapter), make the commitment to keep your glasses clean and to store them properly. No matter which beer you pour into which glass, one thing is for sure: Keeping your beer glassware completely free of dust, oily fingerprints, lipstick, and soapy residue is absolutely crucial. These kinds of dirtiness can have a detrimental effect on your enjoyment of the beer, not to mention that your glasses look crummy.

Understanding "beer clean"

A certain level of glassware cleanliness is known as *beer clean*. That's not just lip service — it's a reality. Beer glasses need to be spotlessly clean if they're to present the beer in its best light. The beer betrays any shortcomings in cleansing and rinsing practices.

In the following sections, I explain how to check whether your glasses are beer clean. If they're not, don't worry; I also explain how to get them beer clean.

Checking for beer clean

Even though a glass looks clean, it may not be beer clean. Rinse water sheets off a glass that's beer clean; on a dirty glass, water breaks up, streaks, or spots. Bubbles that appear on the bottom or sides of the glass below the head indicate invisible fats — like soap residue, food, or makeup grease — or dust. These contaminants can cause a beer to go flat quickly because the presence of fats (emulsifiers) breaks down the surface of the head and destroys it. Cracks, chips, and scrapes also attract bubbles.

Cracks, chips, and scrapes in beer glassware are called *nucleation sites* where CO_2 bubbles form. Some brewers have designed logo glassware with nucleation sites purposely etched into the bottom to keep a steady stream of bubbles rising in the glass.

The most reliable way to check that a glass is beer clean is to pour a craft-brewed beer into the glass, allowing a good head to form. After the beer stands for a few minutes, the head should remain firm and compact. If the glass wasn't correctly cleaned, the foam breaks up, leaving large, fish-eye bubbles. Then again, you may just be pouring a lousy beer.

Another way to test for beer clean glasses is to rinse them briefly in warm water. Immediately thereafter, lightly shake some table salt on the glass; if the glass is clean, the salt will stick, if it's not, the salt will just bounce off. (Um, it's also best to do this over the sink.)

Getting your glasses beer clean

Depending on your level of seriousness — and I sure hope you're not taking this *too* seriously — you have various ways to properly clean beer glassware, including the following:

- **Rinse glasses thoroughly right after using them.** This practice is a bit compulsive, maybe, but very effective at keeping your glasses from becoming fouled. For some people, a hot-water rinse is as far as they want to go, partially because of the belief that you shouldn't clean beer glasses in soapy water. This argument has two sides:

  - One camp says that household dishwashing detergents are scented and can be hard to rinse off.

  - The other camp (Camp Marty) says that if you use very small amounts of *unscented* dishwashing liquids and follow up immediately with a hot-water rinse, no damage is done.

- **Draw a sink full of hot water and add a couple of heaping tablespoons of baking soda.** Use a nylon bristle brush to scrub the deepest recesses of the glass. Pay particular attention to the rim, being sure to remove any lipstick or lip balm. Follow with a good hot rinse and air dry only in a dish drain or empty dishwasher (the dishwasher itself can't do a better job).

If you want to clean a yard glass, just use a long brush, which is usually sold with the glass (see the earlier section for details on this glass).

At the professional or commercial level, where government regulations apply, health departments require chemical sanitizers or sterilizers, including products made with trisodium phosphate. Commercial establishments generally use a glass-cleaning compound that's odorless, sudsless, of a nonfat base, and free-rinsing.

Never towel-dry beer glasses. The towel can leave traces of soap, body oil, and especially lint on the glasses.

Putting everything away

Storing your glassware is only slightly less critical than cleaning it. A poor storage location can make your cleaning efforts all for naught. Be sure to store air-dried glasses away from the unpleasant odors, grease, and smoke that kitchens, washrooms, and ashtrays emit. If possible, store the glasses upside down in a breakfront, credenza, or enclosed cabinet that's relatively dust free. Of course, if you're a real beer geek, you'll keep them in your safe.

Don't store glassware in the freezer or refrigerator. The glasses can pick up food odors, and frozen glasses are uncomfortable to hold (they also leave a nasty water ring wherever you set them). Some misguided bars serve beer in iced glassware, but these glasses are terrible to use. The primary effect that iced glasses have on beer is to water it down. If that's what you're looking for, just opt for a light beer. Or go ahead and stick your fingers directly in the freezer to duplicate the sensation of holding onto one of these aberrations. Yikes!

Chapter 12

Making Your Buds Wiser: Tasting and Evaluating Beer

In This Chapter
▶ Using your senses to evaluate beer
▶ Recording your beer observations

*Y*ou've tasted beer before. How complicated can formal beer tasting be? You open the beer, pour it into a glass (or not), lift it to your lips, sip, swallow, and you're done, right?

Not so fast, barley breath! What did you see? What did you smell? What did you taste? Can you still taste it? Was it good, bad, or neither? Was it what you expected or what it was advertised to be? Would you recommend it to friends or buy it again for yourself? Beer evaluation can go way beyond just plain saying, "Tastes great — less filling!"

You want to pay attention to how you taste beer for plenty of reasons. Here are just a few:

✔ Knowledge and familiarity increase your drinking pleasure.

✔ You gain a better understanding of your personal likes and dislikes in beer flavors and beer styles.

✔ You may be interested in homebrewing and its focus on beer styles. (Flip to Chapter 18 for an introduction to homebrewing.)

✔ Someone you're crazy about is crazier about beer than you (are), and knowledge is power.

Keep in mind that you're on your way to becoming a beer connoisseur of sorts. Your old style of beer tasting was undoubtedly to pop the tab, gulp the brew down, belch (well, some of you, perhaps), and maybe toss the beer can over your left shoulder (in that order). Your new, enlightened approach, however, involves a slightly different sequence to evaluating beer. Don't worry — the steps are completely natural and quite easy. If you can open a bottle of beer, you can evaluate the beer.

If you've tasted only megabrewed, U.S.-style Pale Lagers, your beer-evaluating tools have been mostly dormant. But now that you're giving beer the respect it deserves and sampling a wide range of beer styles, you want to get as many of your senses involved as possible. How? Fetch a beer, sit down, and read on.

In this chapter, you discover how to evaluate beer not only by taste but also by smell, look, and feel. I also show you how to journal your beer evaluations and give ratings to beer so you can remember what you liked (and didn't like) about the brews you've encountered.

If you don't want to formalize your beer tasting, that's cool, too. Beer is meant to be simply enjoyed! That's rule number one, and don't forget it.

Evaluating Beer 1-2-3 (Actually, 1-2-3-4-5)

Drinking beer is a sensual experience. Oh, all right, maybe it's not as exciting as going on a date, but it's got to be more fun than doing your taxes. Consuming beer (or any food, for that matter) should be a full sensory experience; the more senses involved, the more you'll remember about the experience — positive or not.

When barbecuing a steak, you don't just see the meat cooking on the grill; you hear the sizzle and pop of its juices and smell its tantalizing aromas wafting through the air. When you taste the steak, you not only savor the flavor but also describe it in a tactile manner — for example, you may say that it's moist and tender, or if you're eating at my house, probably that it's as dry and tough as shoe leather.

Transfer these mental notes to tasting beer. When pouring a beer into a (clean) glass, *listen* for the plop-plop of the liquid and the fizzing of the escaping carbonation. But wait — don't drink it yet! *See* the tiny bubbles race upward only to get lost in a layer of dense foam. *Watch* the head rise and swell up over the lip of the glass. *Breathe* in the full bouquet of aromas emanating from the beer. *Taste* the many flavors of the grains, hops, and other ingredients. *Feel* the viscosity of the beer and the prickly effervescence of the carbonation on your tongue and palate. *Savor* the lingering flavors of the aftertaste.

You don't want any distractions when you're seriously tasting beer. Use a glass large enough to hold a whole bottle, and follow the pouring and cleaning guidelines in Chapter 11. And no frosted glassware, please! Subtle and nuanced flavors are difficult to discern if the beer is too cold.

Beer tasting has a particular order. I suggest doing the following steps in the order shown. Note that Steps 1 and 2 happen separately, as does Step 5, but

Steps 3 and 4 really happen together. Some of the most important tasting work is done before you even drink!

1. **Smell: Check aroma and bouquet.**

2. **Look: Check appearance.**

3. **Taste: Check flavor.**

4. **Touch: Check body and mouthfeel.**

5. **Reflect: Check final judgment.**

Of course, you can just skip all these steps and go ahead and drink, noting only whether you like the beer. But if you ever want to tell someone about a beer you like, you'll find all this discussion helpful. As Mom says, it always helps to talk.

Although the eyes, nose, and mouth are the key players, the ears can give you some important information as well. *Hearing* beer is pretty much limited to its carbonation (fizzzt) upon opening the bottle or the sound of breaking glass when you drop one. If the beer doesn't fizz when you open it, be prepared for a flat beer. If it doesn't fizz when you drop it, no loss (though it's a mess to clean up and you have to grab another beer).

Following from the steps of the five senses, you can easily see that you evaluate beer in five corresponding areas. Each beer style (see Chapter 4 for a list of beer styles) should have certain characteristics in each area, and these characteristics are what beer judges look for in beer competitions; on the other hand, as a consumer, you need only note the characteristics for comparison, except, of course, for affection or rejection.

Smell: The Nose Knows

Beer aromas are fleeting, so start with a sniff even before you take a look. Also, flavor is partly based on aroma — a full ¼ to ⅓ of your ability to taste is directly related to smell, so don't skip this step.

Like wine and whisky critics, beer evaluators use the term *nose* in two ways: to describe aroma and bouquet (if *aroma* were a sound, *bouquet* would be the volume) as well as the action. You may say, "While nosing his Porter, he commented on its robust licorice nose." You may also say, "While nosing around the pub, he commented on its robust clientele," but that has nothing to do with this discussion.

The most prominent aromas associated with beer's nose usually come first from malt and second from hops:

"Its noble bouquet belies its plebeian origins"

The exchange of information on any specific subject generally requires a special language, and — just your luck — beer tasting has its own jargon as well. This little-known language is the basis for menu and label descriptions, as well as being absolutely necessary for professional brewers and homebrewers, judges, and critics as a quality-control vocabulary. More importantly, you'll hear these words bandied about at any popular beer bar. I intersperse good terms to know throughout this chapter.

But the existence of serious beer words brings up the issue of beer snobbery. Please, beer lovers, don't bring wine snobbery into the beer arena. If you can't fathom how someone else is able to drink a particular beer that tastes awful to you, go ahead and say, "This beer stinks!" If you can't figure out what to say about a brew, don't try to fake it with an "Ah, er, a very complex beer indeed — reminds me of my days abroad" or the artsy phrase in the title of this sidebar when all you really want to say is "Dang, this tastes good!"

It's just beer, after all. For pleasure, remember?

- **Malt:** *Malty* aromas can run from perfumy-sweet to rich and caramel-like and are fairly obvious. Depending on how dark the beer is, roasty, toasty, or chocolaty aromas may come from the specialty grains added to the beer.

- **Hops:** This aroma depends on the variety and amount of hops added to the boiling beer during the brewing process and on whether aromatic hops were added to the beer during the fermentation or aging phases (see the discussion of dry hopping in Chapter 3). Hop aromas may be described as *herbal, perfumy,* spicy, *grassy, earthy, floral, piney, citrusy,* and occasionally *cheesy* (and Sleepy, Sneezy, Dopey, Grumpy, and Doc, too, no?).

Other aromas, such as fruity esters and alcohol aromas, are created during fermentation and are referred to as *fermentation characteristics.* Some ales have a *buttery* or *butterscotch* smell *(diacetyl)* that's the result of warm fermentations and certain yeast strains. If you smell or taste creamed corn in your lager, it may be something called *DMS (di-methyl sulfide).* Plastic, cooked vegetable, rotten eggs, skunky (catty), and wet dog smells are common signs of — guess what — badly made or stored beer.

Look: You Can't Judge a Bock by Its Cover

What should you look for in a beer? Your eyes can discern color, clarity, and head retention (as well as price, of course, and maybe even the meaning of life). I describe all of these in the following sections — although the meaning of life is something you'll have to figure out on your own, maybe while sipping your favorite brew.

Every color in the rainbrew

The colors that make up the various beer styles run the earth tone spectrum from pale straw to golden, amber, copper, orange, russet, brown, black, and everything in between. One color isn't necessarily better than the others, and none indicates directly how the beer will taste — color is dictated by style (see Figure 12-1). Generally speaking, Berliner Weisse beers are the palest, and Stouts are the darkest. However, I recommend avoiding any beer that's blue! Okay, green beer is acceptable, but only on St. Patrick's Day. Colorless malt beverages don't count at all — clear malt beverages are *not* beer — and you get five minutes in the penalty box for being caught drinking one.

On a clear day

Many beer drinkers are obsessed with beer clarity. If their beer isn't crystal clear, they won't drink it. Fair enough, but beer is transparent only as a consequence of modern filtering techniques. Not all beers are intended to be clear. Most brews throughout history have been anywhere from hazy to murky (no, *hazy* and *murky* aren't two long-lost Disney dwarfs) due to the organic ingredients used in the beer-making process, mostly the yeast. These particles that clouded the beer were also what helped make the beer the nutritious drink it was. Today, a cloudy appearance is appropriate for at least a half-dozen beer styles, such as Witbier, Hefeweizen, and any other unfiltered beer styles.

Figure 12-1: Beer styles come in a full range of colors, regardless of taste and strength.

A head in the hand

Head retention can tell a short story about the beer at hand.

- ✔ When a beer is poured, a head of foam should both form and stay (with some styles more than others, of course); the latter quality is as important as the former.

- ✔ The bubbles should be small and should quickly form a tightly knit head.

- ✔ The beer's head may also take on a rocky appearance if sufficient proteins (from the grain) are present.

If a beer can't form a head, either it's improperly carbonated or the vessel into which it's poured is dirty.

If the beer bubbles form and stick to the sides of your beer glass and don't get to the top, your glass is probably dusty or dirty; you may want to check out the section in Chapter 11 on cleaning beer glasses.

If the head forms but dissipates into big, soapy-looking bubbles, chances are that the beer has been charged up with a foam stabilizer (some foam stabilizers are made from a seaweed derivative). Most of the large breweries use foam stabilizers — a necessary evil, thanks to the clarifying process. Microfilters also remove all the head-coagulating proteins. The finest, all-malt brews have small bubbles and dense, creamy heads.

Finally, at least some of the head should remain atop the beer until the glass is empty. Along the way, some of the head's residue should leave what's commonly called *Belgian lace* on the sides of the glass.

Taste: Nuts and Bolts, Malt and Hops

After the first two steps in the beer-tasting process (smelling and looking, which I discuss earlier in this chapter), you can at last get down to the nuts and bolts of beer. Regardless of how a beer smells and looks, if it doesn't taste good, it hasn't fulfilled its promise.

For true beer nuts, a beer's overall flavor intensity can be thought of as a pyramid of taste, with slight but notable fluctuations from level to level. Related terms run through the following range:

Lacking → faint → mild → slight → moderate → definite → strong → intense

Use all the taste surfaces on your tongue (front, back, and sides) as you evaluate beer. Try to distinguish between the first taste sensation experienced by

the tip of the tongue *(foretaste)* and the *mid-taste* or *true taste,* in which the beer displays its taste attractions completely. Swish the beer around gently. The foretaste and mid-taste should blend harmoniously and make you want more. Good beer is complex: You can sometimes find a wide range of flavors in a single taste.

As with aroma, flavor comes from malt, hops, and fermentation, all of which are balanced in a good beer. A related but more concentrated taste sensation is the *aftertaste,* where alcohol asserts its throat-warming ability in the strong, high-octane brews, much as it does in brandy. The following sections give you more information about these four components of flavor.

Marvelous malt taste

The foretaste you encounter is the *sweetness* of the malt. With most industrial brews, the sweetness is delicate and perfumy and only vaguely tastes of true malt flavor, due to the lightening effect of the adjunct grain used, usually corn or rice (see Chapter 2). The fewer adjuncts used, the more the rich, caramel maltiness of the barley comes through. *All-malt* beers (those made without adjuncts) are appropriately referred to as having a *malty* character.

The more specialty grains that are used, roasted (kilned) ones in particular, the more *layered* or complex the beer's flavor becomes. These specialty grains rarely add sweetness — only the flavors of the individual grain. Kilned malts create a mosaic of toasty, roasty, nutty, toffee-like, and coffee-like flavors that meld into the brew. A lot of these flavors are registered in the middle and at the back of the tongue. Some of the more highly roasted malts add a dry *astringent* taste that's perceived by the tongue as being bitter, much like strong coffee or tea. Misuse of the grain by the brewer can also lead to a grainy or husky astringent flavor in the beer. Certain beers may exhibit a slight tartness that's detectable at mid-taste.

Beer as nutrition? Who knew?

Beer used to be considered nutritious — a concept far removed from the well-worn stereotype of the beer drinker as a pot-bellied couch potato.

Stone Age beer, though probably crude, may have been an important source of nutrients in the diet. The same grain used in beer was also used in the baking of bread and probably became more nutritious after undergoing the beer-making process in which the starchy insides of the kernel were transformed into proteins and soluble sugars not otherwise available. And it surely kept longer.

And jumping forward in time a bit, Martin Luther, founder of the Lutheran church, reportedly preserved his health while he fasted by drinking copious amounts of strong beer.

In the days before filtering . . .

The early Egyptians, like many people of the time, chose to drink their beer through reeds or tubes so they wouldn't choke on the barley husks left in the unfiltered brew. The University of Pennsylvania Museum displays a golden straw used by Queen Shubad of Mesopotamia for sipping beer.

Normally, *sour* flavors are considered a flaw in beer, but for several well-known Belgian beers, sourness is actually a prerequisite, as it is for a few odd ales (see Chapter 6 and Appendix A for more on Sour Beers). Lagers definitely shouldn't be sour.

Heavenly hops taste

The primary purpose of hops is to offset the malt sweetness with a pleasant and refreshing bitterness. Hop flavors are described with pretty much the same terms used for aroma, but hop bitterness uses some new terms.

- ✓ **Hop flavor:** Distinctive, usually tasting much like its aroma: grassy, piney, floral, citrusy, herbal, spicy, earthy, and so on; normally experienced at mid-taste. Expressed as *mild, normal, definite, pronounced,* or *aggressive.* The latter terms describe a *hoppy* beer.

- ✓ **Hop bitterness:** Rather one-dimensional; experienced at the back of the tongue, as an aftertaste. Expressed as *delicate, fine, coarse,* or *clinging.*

Hopheads are passionate beer nuts who crave the hop aspect of beer over all other aspects. If you drink with such a person, be sure to refrain from making any inflammatory anti-hop statements. Just hunker down and share the experience. You've been warned.

Fabulous fermentation

The fermentation process is responsible for some of beer's more appealing tastes, like fruit, butter, butterscotch (diacetyl), and alcohol tastes. Ales have more of the fruity and buttery flavors due to their warm fermentation temperatures; lagers shouldn't have any of these tastes. Alcohol taste should be evident in only the strongest of beers — typically those with 9 percent or more alcohol by volume.

On the negative side of the ledger, fermentation can stimulate a long list of unpleasant flavors: the rubbery taste of autolyzed (deteriorated) yeast, cidery aldehydes, medicinal phenolics, bloody metallics, poopy enterics, and dozens of other equally unappetizing off tastes that brewers and beer drinkers alike need to be on the lookout for. Yuck!

Other flavors you may encounter are the yeasty or bready odors of bottle-conditioned beers (see Chapter 3) and the winey or alcoholic flavors of stronger beers.

After you've honed in on the various flavors, try to gauge their intensity. Most beer styles share common flavors, but the intensity of each is different for each beer style (see Chapter 4).

Aftertaste: Let it linger

Beer's aftertaste, also called the *finish,* is one of the most essential and enjoyable aspects of the total beer-drinking experience, one that chiefly affects the decision about whether to take another sip. Yet many corporate megabrewers, with their advocacy and marketing of beers with little or no aftertaste (as in *light, dry,* and *ice* beer), have made aftertaste a *perspectiva non grata.* They'd have you believe that beer isn't supposed to have an aftertaste and that those with an aftertaste are bad.

Why is aftertaste desirable? Imagine dining on succulent Maine lobster dipped in pure, drawn butter, only to have the flavor disappear from your mouth the second you swallow. That lingering flavor *memory* is what aftertaste is all about. Don't let advertising campaigns condemning bitter beer face deter you from expecting and enjoying the aftertaste of quality brews.

Oooh, Mommy!

Until fairly recently, the four primary flavors — sweet, sour, salty, and bitter — were believed to be the only tastes detectable by the human tongue, and none of these primary flavors can be replicated by mixing together any of the other primary flavors. However, it's now known that there's actually a fifth primary taste called *umami.*

When humans eat, whether they realize it or not, they use most of their senses (sight, smell, taste, and touch) to form judgments about their food. Of course, taste is the most influential of the senses when it comes to determining how delicious a food is.

Now, here comes the technical part: *Umami* is a Japanese word that refers to a pleasant savory taste that's imparted by *glutamate* (a type of amino acid) and *ribonucleotides,* which occur naturally in many foods, including vegetables, fish, meat, and dairy products.

The taste of umami is very subtle and blends well with other tastes to expand and round out flavors. Most people don't recognize umami when they encounter it, but it plays an important role in making food flavorful and enjoyable. That's why I keep a bottle of umami in my pantry right next to the olive oil and cooking sherry (just kidding, of course).

Many facets of a beer become more obvious in the aftertaste in a sort of harmonic convergence (of course, the beer's faults, if any, are also magnified there). Certain beer styles are designed to accentuate malt over hops and vice versa, but no one ingredient should be allowed to completely dominate the other. No room for a bully here.

Touch: Mouthfeel and Body

The tactile aspects of beer evaluation are *mouthfeel* and *body*. You can literally *feel* the beer in your mouth and describe it in familiar physical terms (such as *thick* and *thin*). I describe these aspects further in the following list:

- **Mouthfeel:** This aspect is the sensory experience of the whole inside of the mouth and throat. You don't taste cold; you *feel* it. Finely carbonated beers (with their small bubbles) tend to have a creamy mouthfeel. So a continental lager beer may be effervescent, while a Stout is soft and chewy, but none of these descriptions has anything to do with how the beer tastes. Mouthfeel is how the beer feels (to you — this isn't about the beer's self-esteem).

- **Body:** In beer competitions, judges use the term *body* to refer to the weight or thickness of a beer. A light beer is described as *light-bodied*, an India Pale Ale is considered *medium-bodied*, and a Doppelbock is *full-bodied*. Higher carbonation levels help clear the palate and create the impression of a lighter-bodied beer.

Gravity and Plato: Weighty, nonphilosophical issues

Some fairly technical terms, *gravity* (as in *original gravity* and *final* or *terminal gravity*) and *attenuation,* find their way into beer enthusiasts' evaluations and written reviews, but these terms aren't directly related to taste. These more technical terms are brewers' measurements of fermentation and aren't an indication of quality, even though some labels or ads may boast about a beer's gravity.

What does gravity mean to the beer drinker? A beer's gravity is used to calculate its volume of alcohol. The specific gravity scale is based on water at 60 degrees Fahrenheit (15 degrees Celsius). Some brewers prefer to note gravity on the Balling scale, measured in degrees Plato, which indicates the same information as the specific gravity scale, just on a different scale.

Higher original gravities of beer — about 1.060 to 1.100 — usually mean stronger and creamier beers (often called *big beers*). Above 1.090 is rare indeed. Lower original gravities — about 1.032 to 1.044 — mean lower alcohol contents and thinner, lighter-bodied beers. The vast majority of beers fall in the middle ground — about 1.044 to 1.060 or 11.5 to 15 degrees Plato.

More details on this kind of stuff are tucked safely in the chapter on homebrewing (Chapter 18).

Colorful descriptors, such as *wimpy, voluptuous, massive, robust,* and *chewy,* are effective at getting the point across. Obviously, just as with people, one body type isn't necessarily better than another — thin folks, heavy folks, and everyone in between make the world an interesting place.

Win friends and influence people by using some of the other mouthfeel terms that pros use, such as *astringent, crisp, flat, full, gassy, light, sharp, smooth, thin, thick, vinous (winey), viscous,* and *watery.* Phew!

Reflect: Is the Whole Beer Greater than the Sum of Its Parts?

Not to get too philosophical on you, but didn't someone say that the unexamined life is a life not worth living? Well, so it goes with beer. Reflection doesn't mean trying to see your image in a beer glass (though I imagine some of us have been amused by that); it's about your overall impression of the beer. The difference here is that all the previous assessments — smell, look, taste, touch — are, or should be, made as *objectively* as possible. Reflection is a time to take into account all those objective observations and then form a *subjective* opinion about the beer.

Reflection is also the time to evaluate the harmony and balance of the various taste components of the beer and to reach some sort of conclusion, like "Hey, I'll have another one of those!" Bottom line — would you like another one?

Because of the wide availability and reasonable pricing of beer, you may want to keep a record of the beers you taste and your reactions to them. Following the points explained earlier in this chapter, you can write down a full profile of a beer in only a few sentences (see the later section "Put Your Tongue to the Test: Recording Your Beer Ratings" for details on getting started). You can use the form prepared by the American Homebrewers Association (shown in Figure 12-2), or you can easily organize your own notes on plain paper.

Although all the details are interesting, it's the bottom line that counts. Is the beer good, or is it not?

EASY STEPS FOR EVALUATING BEER

FIRST: Smell the beer for hop and malt **aroma** characteristics.

SECOND: Look at the beer to determine its **color** and clarity.

THIRD: Taste the beer to determine its **flavors** and **mouthfeel**. (Is it light, medium or full bodied?)

LAST: Rate your **overall impression** based on these four characteristics: aroma, color, flavor and mouthfeel.

HAVE A GOOD TIME.

American Homebrewers Association
PO Box 1679 / 736 Pearl St., Boulder, CO 80306-1679
(303) 447-0816; FAX (303) 447-2825

BEER NAME/STYLE _____

hoppy		AROMA		malty
pale	golden	COLOR amber	brown	black
bitter		FLAVOR		sweet
light/thin		MOUTHFEEL		full/thick
can't stand it		OVERALL IMPRESSION		can't get enough

BEER NAME/STYLE _____

hoppy		AROMA		malty
pale	golden	COLOR amber	brown	black
bitter		FLAVOR		sweet
light/thin		MOUTHFEEL		full/thick
can't stand it		OVERALL IMPRESSION		can't get enough

Figure 12-2:
The American Homebrewers Association evaluation sheet provides a good format for beer tastings.

Courtesy of the American Homebrewers Association

Put Your Tongue to the Test: Recording Your Beer Ratings

You don't have to be a beer expert to do your own beer evaluations at home. As long as you have access to a decent variety of beer styles and beer brands, you can begin your novice beer judgeship in the comfort of your own abode.

I started evaluating beers in my home more than 27 years ago. Each weekend, I made a point of buying a six-pack of beer that I'd never tried before. I'd sit down with a notebook, a pen, and a clean beer glass and dutifully describe each beer to the best of my ability as I tasted it. I still have those notes today and occasionally review them just for laughs.

In the following sections, I introduce you to two methods for recording your beer ratings: visiting online forums and keeping a personal journal.

You don't need to know the specific beer jargon to be a good beer evaluator; just record your observations in honest, straightforward, everyday language. What's important is that you dissect each beer, using your senses as described earlier in this chapter. What's also important is that you try to set aside your personal biases and approach your task objectively. You may not like everything you smell or taste, but you'll learn to identify those aromas and flavors that you like and dislike. A little humility and respect for the brewer goes a long way, too. Just because you don't like a particular beer flavor or beer style doesn't mean the brewer failed to make good beer. It just means that you haven't acquired an appreciation for that flavor or style yet.

BTI's bottom line: Does this beer bring me pleasure?

Professionals have consultants analyze their brews all the time for consumer feedback. You hedonists out there will be happy to know that the Beverage Testing Institute (BTI), the largest and only full-time independent product testing service specializing in beverages in the United States, employs a *hedonic* scoring method, which addresses the simple question at the root of consumerism: "Does this bring me pleasure?" The hedonic method suggests that tasting good is more important than tasting correct

or typical. It allows for subjective observations in an objective environment.

The BTI hands out the annual World Beer Championship awards to winners from hundreds of breweries around the world. Results are posted on BTI's searchable database (www.tastings.com), published in *All About Beer* magazine (www.allaboutbeer.com), and in the winners' press releases and advertisements, you can be sure.

Whether your goal is to become a beer judge, a beer writer, or a beer blogger, without established credentials as a beer evaluator, achieving credibility is tough. My best advice is to learn as much as you can as quickly as you can — and never stop learning. Read about beer, taste beer, visit breweries, discuss beer with others in the know. For a real education in this field of study, take up homebrewing (see Chapter 18 for details). You don't have to be a great brewer to learn a lot about the art and science of brewing. The beauty of all of this is that no matter which paths you take, you're going to have fun!

Rating beer in online forums

To get you started on beer evaluations, you may want to peruse some of the many websites on the Internet that give the general public access to the site and allow for public postings of beer ratings and evaluations (most require you to join the site or sign up for a free membership before posting). These rating sites have gotten quite popular in the past couple of years and are often considered *the* source of up-to-date information on all kinds of beers.

Because these beer-rating sites are online, they can be accessed and used by people around the world. Reading beer reviews from beer lovers in other countries and continents is always interesting. Similarly, these sites aren't limited to reviews of, say, just American microbrews; beers produced halfway around the world often get reviewed, too.

Here's a short list of some of the more popular beer review sites to get you started:

✔ **BeerAdvocate** (www.beeradvocate.com): This beer community is dedicated to supporting and promoting beer through education and appreciation.

✔ **RateBeer** (www.ratebeer.com): This site brings you the craft beer movement as it happens.

✔ **PhillyCraft** (www.phillycraft.com): This site is a network for everything craft beer.

Be aware that many more beer review sites are out there that don't invite the site visitor to participate in beer reviews or add content of any kind. Also, a lot of self-styled beer experts like to keep all the fun and opinionated reviews to themselves, so take them at face value.

Maintaining a personal journal

If you'd rather not have your beer ratings and evaluations posted in a public online forum (see the preceding section), keeping a personal beer journal at home is even easier. All you really need is a binder or notebook. If you should happen to go on an extended trip to far flung locations (like those in Part IV), you may want to make this journal packable so you can bring it with you as you taste excellent brews in exotic lands. Having a camera or similar means of capturing visual records of your beer-tasting exploits adds to the value and usefulness of your journal.

If you have a knack for writing and don't mind public exposure, another means of recording your beer evaluations and experiences is via a personal beer blog (you can set one up at popular sites like www.blogger.com and www.wordpress.com, just to name two). It's amazing how many beer blogs are on the Internet — and that can be a bit of a problem in itself. Unfortunately, it seems like everybody with a computer and Internet access is writing beer blogs these days, so it's difficult to be heard above the din of the crowd. For help in getting started, check out the latest edition of *Blogging For Dummies* by Susannah Gardner and Shane Birley (Wiley).

Chapter 13

Dining with Beer

In This Chapter

▶ Matching up food with the right beer style

▶ Timing your tippling based on mealtime and the seasons

Certain beers fit certain foods like hands fit in gloves — they're made to go together. Unlike hands, however, beer is made to be consumed. (On second thought, what about finger sandwiches?) This chapter is all about embarking on a new culinary course that aims to pair beer with food, so let the journey begin.

What a Pair! Making a Match with Beer and Food

A world of possibilities exists beyond pretzels and beer, even more than nachos and popcorn and beer, even more than barbecue and beer, even more than. . . . You get the idea. Lots of possibilities.

Unsophisticated is one of the more polite adjectives that elitists use to describe beer. Unfortunately, some folks see the average beer drinker as unsophisticated, too, which helps explain the prolonged absence of beer from the typical fine-dining experience.

Until more recently, restaurants that did stock beer often did so with an after-the-fact attitude; for as much attention as it was given, beer may as well have been served in water pitchers. It seemed unfair — while some upper-crust clientele yapped on about their brochette of lamb au chanterelles pairing wondrously with an early vintage Chateau Feux-Feux, beer drinkers were expected to wash down blue-plate specials with mugs full of cold and homogeneous light beer. Although vintage wines and aged spirits can boast of a long companionship with haute cuisine, beer — until recently in some places — is often relegated to the backyard barbecue.

European models (the best and the wurst)

Europeans seem to have no qualms about drinking beer with their meals, including an occasional breakfast nip. This fact is particularly true of those nations with dynamic brewing industries — Great Britain, Germany, and Belgium — which I outline in the following list:

✔ **Great Britain:** Although the island countries of Ireland and Britain may not be renowned for their highbrow culinary traditions, their everyday national cuisines are great in the pubs. *Pub grub,* as the food is modestly referred to, is hearty (though maybe uninspired), well portioned, and, best of all, inexpensive.

✔ **Germany:** In Germany and most of the other northern European countries, the national cuisines were built around beer. With this stick-to-your-ribs food, you can always find beer within reach in case you want to unstick it. Just about anything that these folks throw on a plate begs for a beer. Here, *wine* is the afterthought, not beer.

✔ **Belgium:** In Belgium, which is known for its gastronomic gusto as well as for its diverse beers, restaurants regularly feature *Cuisine à la bière.* It's not at all unusual for chefs to prepare dishes with beer and serve each course with yet another beer in accompaniment.

Well, that's wrong. Beer is only for thirst quenching as much as computers are only for number crunching and sports are only for boys. Get with it, folks! Beer is for dining, too.

Although it may have taken restaurateurs, gourmands, and culinary artistes forever to catch on to the concept of beer and food pairings, now that they have, it's a hot ticket. And why not — beer is considered the world's most popular beverage, with craft beer increasing in popularity every day. After far too many years, I'm happy to say that the outlook for beer drinkers is rosé — I mean, rosy. Thanks to the enthusiasm of brewers, restaurateurs, and consumers of flavorful craft-brewed beer, beer has reclaimed its rightful place on our dinner tables.

In the following sections, I provide some general tips on substituting beer for wine, pairing beer with different foods, and balancing the number of beers you serve at a meal.

Good craft-brewed beer can be much more interesting than wine — it's cool and refreshing and, depending on the style, can be much richer, more complex, and more flavorful than wine. Plus, if you have an average person's budget and capacity, you'll find that tasting several different beers during a meal is preferable to tasting several different wines.

Guessing at general guidelines

Within the sometimes intimidating world of wine and food, even the neophytes can lean on the old *red meat–red wine* axiom in a pinch. But beer drinkers have no such axiomatic, general guideline to fall back on, because none exists. And few people have a good enough grasp on the various beer styles and flavor profiles to easily make choices.

Actually, you'll find it hard to go wrong when matching beer and food. What's fun is trying to do better than not going wrong.

Every kind of food conceivably has an appropriate beer to accompany it. The beauty of beer is in its versatility. You can usually find a beer style that's a natural match for a given food. Beer even works better than wine with some dishes, such as especially spicy or sour ones. And slightly acidic beers are great foils for rich foods.

 People like general guidelines, so I list the main beer-related ones in the following sections. But please don't follow them slavishly. For simplicity's sake, I borrowed from wine's example to describe the two major beer categories and how to match them with particular foods.

Substituting beer for wine

The lager beer category is the white wine equivalent. When compared to ales, lagers have the following characteristics:

- ✓ Generally lighter in body and color
- ✓ Narrower flavor profile and a high degree of drinkability (that is, tend to appeal to a wider audience)

The ale category is the red wine equivalent. When compared to lagers, ales have these qualities:

Go ahead — Pour that beer into a wine glass!

The idea isn't to do a straightforward substitution of beer for wine, but when you do replace your wine with beer, you get some intriguing side effects, such as the following:

- ✓ You tend to need less beer than wine with a meal, so split a bottle with friends and use tulip-shaped wine glasses.

- ✓ One 12-ounce bottle usually suffices when dining alone (try to justify having a full bottle of wine just for yourself).

- ✓ You imbibe less alcohol and fewer calories. Always a plus!

- ✓ Ultimately, you save money because gourmet beer is cheaper than wine.

Neat, huh? A four-way winner.

✔ Typically darker

✔ Rounder, more robust and expressive

✔ Wider flavor profile and thus a lower drinkability (that is, tend to appeal to those with a more experienced beer palate)

Just to keep you on your toes, keep in mind that these guidelines are really general — dark and full-bodied lagers exist just as surely as do light and mild ales.

Next time you're about to go grape out of habit, consider a brew instead. Table 13-1 offers a few good ideas (flip to Chapter 4 for an introduction to the beer types listed).

Table 13-1	Beer Substitutions for Wine
Wine	*Suggested Beer Substitute*
Dry white wine	Blonde Ale, Kölsch, or German Pils
Dry red wine	Fruit Lambic or Flanders Red Beer
Champagne	Light and spritzy Witbier, Lambic, or Berliner Weisse
Brandy	Spirituous Barleywine or Old Ale
Port wine	Intensely flavored Russian Imperial Stout

Keep in mind that these suggested substitutions aren't trading taste for taste but style for style. In other words, don't expect the Imperial Stout to taste like a port wine; it's simply serving the same enjoyable purpose as a rich and spirited after-dinner libation.

Choosing beers for different cuisines

The general guideline for matching beers and foods is to save the heartier beers, such as characterful ales, for the heartier dishes and try the lighter-bodied, mildly malty lagers with more subtly flavored dishes. Table 13-2 offers just a few examples of matching beer with various styles of cuisine.

Table 13-2	Suggestions for Matching Beer and Cuisine Styles	
Cuisine	*Dish*	*Beer*
Mediterranean	Pasta dishes with red or white sauces	Dortmunder or Munich Helles
	Pork or lamb	Hoppy Pale Ale

Cuisine	Dish	Beer
Seafood	Fresh fish	Crisp Pilsner or Wheat Beer
	Shellfish	Porter, India Pale Ale
	Salt-cured fish	Porter
	Oysters	Dry Stout (a classic pairing)
Indian	Curry dishes	Premium Pale Lager, Golden Ale
Asian	Vegetable dishes (with fish sauce)	Premium Pale Lager
French	Aged, herbed cheeses	Bière de Garde, Saison
	Rich sauces	Spicy, sharply refreshing Saison
	Red meats	Earthy Belgian Trappist Ales
Continental	Cheeses	Altbier or Rauchbier (Smoked Beer)
	Steak	Schwarzbier or Porter (especially with Porterhouse steaks)
	Pork and chicken	Maibock or Munich Helles
	Pumpernickel or rye bread and butter	Munich Dunkel or Schwarzbier
	Sausages	Bock or Märzenbier/Oktoberfest
	Pizza	Vienna/Amber Lager
	Asparagus	Pale Lager or Trappist Tripel
Spicy hot foods	Buffalo wings	Märzenbier/Oktoberfest
	Five-alarm chili	Bock
	Mexican hot sauces	Vienna/Amber Lager
	Thai cuisine	Dark Wheat, Blonde Ale
Desserts	Heavy desserts	Doppelbock or Imperial Stout

Table 13-2 is only meant to give you some ideas of beer and food match-ups. The range of styles from light to dark, dry to sweet, and mild to robust presents an unlimited number of culinary combinations and lots of room for experimentation.

As for specific dishes that go well with beer, or better with beer than wine, check out *The Beerbistro Cookbook,* coauthored by Stephen Beaumont and Brian Morin (Key Porter Books), which is a book devoted to this delightful subject.

Cutting, contrasting, and complementing different flavors

Complementary flavors between beer and food are good, but contrasting tastes aren't necessarily bad. Serving an acidic beer, such as Berliner Weisse, with a vinegar and oil topped salad is complementary; serving a fruity Belgian Witbier instead is contrasting. Both options can work equally well; it just comes down to a matter of preference. Experimentation is half the fun!

Beer also serves to cut flavors. For example, highly hopped beers help to cut through the oiliness of meats, like duck or lamb, while pale and spritzy beers are effective at cutting through heat (such as hot peppers) and excessive spiciness.

With spicy food, rather than trying to extinguish the flames by rinsing the mouth with anything that's cold and wet, coat the mouth with a creamy, malty, medium-bodied lager and don't serve it ice-cold. You want sweeter, not drier, beers to cut through the heat; the extra alcohol in stronger beers also knocks out the heat. Water stinks at putting out fires on your tongue.

When preparing meals, chefs try to involve as many of the four flavor receptors of the human tongue — sweet, salty, sour, and bitter — as possible. This effort rounds out the meal and makes it more complete and interesting. On the other hand, if one of these flavors completely dominates or is missing altogether, the meal's balance suffers. What beer brings to the dinner table is mostly sweet and bitter, so you can make choices accordingly.

Paring down your pairing list

One of the best and most amazing ways to experience beer as a dinner beverage is to attend a *beer dinner,* where the chef has teamed up with a brewmaster or a beer importer to develop and pair food and beer recipes that call for the perfect beer as either an ingredient or a beverage. If you're even moderately intrigued by the concept, go for it. You'll find it unlike anything you've ever experienced. To find one near you, start by checking out the local brewpub, gastropub, or beer bar (see Chapter 15 to find out more about gastropubs).

You can make the idea of a beer dinner work for you at home, too. The ideal beer dinner pairs a different beer with each course being served. Depending on how many courses you plan to serve, this may mean too few beers are tasted, which can lead to disappointment, or too many, which can lead to palate fatigue and intoxication.

If you're serving only three or four courses, you may want to consider offering a second beer choice for some or all the courses. If you're serving seven or more courses, you may want to reduce the beer serving portion at each course to around 4 ounces. Serving more than eight different beers at a single beer dinner event is overkill (it's supposed to be a repast, not a debauch). Check out Figure 13-1 for a sample beer dinner menu.

Ideally, you should be able to serve two to three people from a single 12-ounce bottle, which reduces both the cost and that bloated feeling.

Vie Beer Dinner
April 20, 2011

Reception
fried burgundy snails, preserved garlic aioli
house-smoked Crawford farm ham, grapefruit marmalade, pickled artichokes
Werp farm ramp fritter, shunkyo radish, herb oil
Pale Ale

First
fried west coast oysters, sautéed farmer's daughter shrimp,
manila clam vinaigrette, slow cooked kale, wood-grilled ramps
Saison

Second
lobster bisque, poached lobster, maple crème fraiche,
pickled M&M Ranch kumquats
Imperial IPA

Third
Gunthorp farm duck confit, braised local cranberry beans,
cippolini aigre-doux, parsley, watercress
Sticke altbier

Fourth
roasted chicken livers, sorghum, peas, pickled onions, ginger snap
Brown porter

Fifth
wood-grilled Dietzler farm strip loin, beef fat poached and fried fingerlings,
roasted french horns, pickled green beans, wilted spinach
Brown ale

Sixth
Pleasant Ridge reserve, sour cherry almond jam, honey wheat
Dunkelweizen

Dessert
spiced waffle, butterscotch, barley malt ice cream, caramelized banana
Sahti

Figure 13-1:
An actual beer dinner menu from the Michelin-starred Vie restaurant in Western Springs, Illinois.

Timing Is Everything: Serving Beer for Different Occasions

In my line of work, I'm often asked what my favorite beer is. My honest but evasive-sounding response is always the same: It depends on where I am and what I'm doing. Seriously, my favorite beer(s) all depends on time and place.

Whatever beer satisfies on a hot summer's afternoon hardly suffices on a cold winter's night. A beer I choose to be the last one of the evening certainly isn't the one I start the evening with.

As you find out in the following sections, different beers are best enjoyed according to the time of day or the season (that's why breweries produce seasonal beers). Sometimes the best occasion for having a beer is nothing more than just enjoying a great beer.

Selecting beers for before and after dinner

Stretching out the party? Try the following ideas for the beginning and end of dinner.

Aperitifs

Light- to medium-bodied, tart, and well-hopped (bitter) beers make good before-dinner drinks with their appetite-whetting capabilities. Here are some examples:

- A dry, well-hopped Pilsner (the beer equivalent to the ubiquitous dry white wine, Chardonnay)
- Berliner Weisse
- California Common Beer (Steam Beer)
- India Pale Ale
- American Pale Ales
- Belgian Gueuze or Lambic (fruited beers, such as Kriek or Framboise, are only for those who like cranberry juice or other fruit juices as an aperitif)
- Flanders Red Ale

After-dinner drinks

Postprandial, or after-dinner, beers should be lightly carbonated and light- to medium-bodied. Here are some examples:

- Brown Ale/English Mild Ale
- British Bitters
- Kölsch
- Flanders Oud Bruin/Brown Ale

Nightcaps

Nightcap beers are generally big bodied and robust, with fairly high alcohol contents — hence their suggested use with late-night samplings on full stomachs. You can try these with dessert (or even in place of it):

- Barleywine
- Old Ale
- Doppelbock
- Eisbock
- Belgian Strong Ale
- Russian Imperial Stout
- Scotch Ale
- Trappist/Abbey Ales
- Any beer aged in a bourbon barrel

These sweet, dark, strong beers are often what go best with chocolate. I highly, highly recommend them, though not nightly, of course. Every other night, maybe — in small glasses.

Serving beer according to the season

One of the best things about craft breweries is that they like to produce different beers throughout the year, according to the season. Some beers are made only at certain times of the year, while others, available year-round, just have a natural taste link to a particular season.

Just as you wouldn't want to drink a rich, heavy beer with a high alcohol content on a hot summer afternoon, you may not enjoy a light, spritzy beer on a winter's evening. Here are some suggestions for beers to try as the calendar pages turn:

- **Winter:** These beers tend to be darker and medium- to full-bodied, and they tend to contain higher levels of alcohol. Often brewed with spices, fruits, and herbs, they add to the celebratory spirit of this time of year. They also make good gifts. Try Barleywine, Belgian Strong Ale, Eisbock, Imperial Stout, Old Ale, Scotch Ale, Spiced beers, and Wassail.

✔ **Spring:** The brewing industry has traditionally created its maltier beers for this season. Try Belgian Dubbel, Belgian Tripel, Bière de Garde, Bock, Doppelbock, Maibock, Porter, and Stout.

✔ **Summer:** Summer beers should be light-colored, light- to medium-bodied, and spritzy. These beers can be served cold but not cold enough to numb the palate. Try Berliner Weisse, Blonde Ales, Cream Ale, Fruit Beer, Kölsch, Pale Ale, Pilsner, Saison, Weizenbier, and Witbier.

✔ **Fall:** These beers are good midrange ones, neither light nor especially dark, neither light-bodied nor heavy-duty. Alcohol content is only a percent or two higher than in the summer beers. Try Amber Ale, Brown Ale, India Pale Ale, Oktoberfest/Märzenbier, Porter, Rauchbier, and Schwarzbier.

Chasing the heat

Beer is a terrific complementary beverage to other beverages. Unfortunately, acting as a chaser for vodka, gin, tequila, and various liqueurs, beer is demoted to the position of rinsing or flushing the mouth and throat of the heat of distilled alcohol. The most popular combination is the boilermaker: a shot of whisky with a beer chaser.

In the case of single-malt Scotch, however, quality beer is more of a companion beverage than a subservient wash. With good reason: Scotch whisky starts out as a beer, without hop bittering; the difference is that Scotch is distilled to its present form. The designation *single malt* refers to the fact that Scotch whisky is made from 100 percent barley malt and is unblended, unlike U.S.-made whiskies that are made from grains considered inferior for beer-making purposes, such as corn and rye (ever heard of corn squeezin's?).

Chapter 14

Cooking with Beer

*B*eer is not only a great beverage at mealtime, but it's also a terrific, low-cost, low-fat, versatile, easy-to-use ingredient in the cooking process. Compared to wine, beer comes out ahead (and *with* a head) in many different ways. Beer is easy and fun and has no fat or cholesterol. Most of its calories come from the alcohol, which is often cooked off when you use it in a recipe — something that doesn't happen with most other foods.

In fact, wine no longer holds the patent as the alcoholic beverage of choice as an ingredient in food. Beer is the perfect food partner in many instances. You can even say that beer is inherently superior, but there's no need to be judgmental. Thanks to the wide availability of high-quality, additive- and preservative-free, flavorful hand-crafted beers, a new gustatory door has opened.

In this chapter, I explain when you can use beer in a recipe and what kinds of beer you can use. I also provide several delicious recipes featuring beer — enjoy!

Using Beer as an Ingredient in Any Dish

Cooking with beer is nothing new. Beer has been used in the kitchen almost as long as food has — not surprising, given that beer was probably one of the first elements of civilization. Back when beer was first discovered, it was more often the base material to which other things were added than the other way around. Beer back then was also more food-like, with much of the ingredient solids suspended within the liquid.

Nowadays, brewpub and gastropub chefs are taking the lead in developing new and unusual recipes to incorporate brews into the food menu. Beer brings a whole new palette of flavors to the cooking pot or skillet. Chefs are even using it in the three *C*s of good nutrition: cakes, candy, and caramel sauce!

Beer cheese dips and soups, chili with beer, baked beans with beer, beer bread, beer gravy, anything with beer batter, and bratwurst boiled in beer and onions (a Legion Hall favorite) are the traditional beer food recipes. Classic cuisine has often included beery Belgian dishes, such as *carbonnade flamande* (beef stew). With some imagination, you have thousands of other possibilities.

In the following sections, I explain when you can (and can't) substitute beer in a recipe, and I provide some pointers on selecting a beer to use when cooking.

When cooking with beer, don't worry about your kids and nondrinking friends — alcohol has a lower boiling point than water (173 degrees Fahrenheit or 79 degrees Celsius) and evaporates quickly in the presence of heat. Unless beer goes unheated or is added to a dish just before serving, none of the alcohol ever gets to the table.

Knowing when you can (and can't) use beer in a recipe

Anywhere wine, broth, or water is called for in a recipe, beer usually offers a unique, and often improved, alternative. Imaginative cooks can have a field day experimenting with beer as a substitute for at least part of the other common cooking liquids.

The easiest place to start fooling around (with cooking and beer, that is) is with steamed food, soups, stews, marinades, glazes, and bastes. Just pour it on or in. On the other extreme, you can try chocolate stout ice cream, definitely an exercise in open-mindedness: Try it as a float (with stout, not root beer). What's next — beer mustard? Oh, wait — it's been done!

If you're new to beer and want to experiment with it in your own recipes, try using the following:

- Pale Lager for thinning a batter; you can also use Pale Lager for half the liquid in any bread recipe and a fifth to a quarter of the liquid in a soup recipe

- A lighter ale or lager (and some water) for steaming mussels

- Pale Lager mixed with water (and spices) for steaming shrimp

✔ Light- to medium-bodied lagers for lighter marinades

✔ Full-bodied lagers or ales for stronger marinades (such as Chinese-inspired ones)

Good news for vegetarians: Flavorful beer, such as Scottish Ale, is a terrific substitute for chicken or beef stock. Beer is made from grain, so it has a natural affinity for grain-based dishes.

Anytime you use beer in a recipe, cook it long enough for it to impart its flavor, which depends greatly on the beer you're using and what you're cooking.

One of the simplest ways to start cooking with beer is with a roast chicken: Simply pour one bottle of a flavorful beer, such as Märzen or Brown Ale, under the baking rack and let it mix with the pan drippings; add corn starch or flour and fresh beer when done, for a wonderful, lumpless gravy (the rest is up to you).

Don't automatically assume that beer is a complementary ingredient in every recipe. After all, of the four basic flavors (sweet, sour, salty, bitter), most beer contributes only sweet and bitter. Sometimes beer just won't work, usually because its natural bitterness or sweetness gets concentrated by cooking. (Wine isn't normally bitter, and sweet wines aren't commonly used for cooking.) Consider whether beer's concentrated sweetness or bitterness may detract from the dish you're cooking.

Choosing the right beer for a recipe

With the wide array of styles available, you need to make a choice about which beer to use in a recipe. Although the everyday, light-bodied, commercial lagers generally do fine, they obviously don't add as much flavor as other styles. Consider the following factors when choosing a cooking beer:

✔ **Color:** Beers brewed with a large percentage of dark grain, such as Stout and Porter, are likely to transpose their color to your meal — not an appetizing hue for fettuccine Alfredo or scrambled eggs.

✔ **Level of sweetness (maltiness) versus level of bitterness (hoppiness and grain astringency):** Malt is by far the predominant beer taste in a recipe, but bitterness can take over easily because beer's bitterness increases with *reduction* (that is, the decrease in volume caused by boiling). Add bitter beer later in a recipe, or if a beer is being cooked for a while, choose a maltier beer style. In general, go with a mild beer rather than a bold one and avoid highly hopped beers, such as some Pale Ales. Sweeter, heavier beers should be reserved for dessert mixes and glazes.

Note: As the water and alcohol boil off, both the sweet and bitter flavors of the beer intensify.

Grilling a chicken with beer

When cooking with beer, don't ignore the ridiculous. Just for fun: The recipe for Dancing Chicken in *John Willingham's World Champion Bar-B-Q* (William Morrow) calls for grilling a whole chicken with a half-full can of beer jammed into the cavity. Now that's different. I wonder: Does the delicate hop aroma come through intact?

> ✓ **Unusual flavors:** Keep in mind that beers are now available in a wide variety of styles, many with flavors that aren't traditionally associated with beer. You may encounter fruited beers, chocolate beers, sour beers, and smoked beers. It's not that these flavored beers don't present lots of culinary possibilities in their own right; they're just not meant for use in the average recipe.

Unless you're well versed in beer styles and know what to expect from each, you'll find the pale but tasty Munich Helles (pale Munich-style lager) well suited to cross-culinary usage.

Beware of the many recipes floating around out there that call for just plain beer as an ingredient, without specifying a particular brand or style (see Chapter 4 for info about beer styles). This generalization is evidence of the simplistic and uninformed mentality that a beer is a beer is a beer. I mean, come on, would any writer call for just plain vegetable or meat? Given the great diversity in beer today, using the wrong style can be a recipe for a disastrous meal. On the other hand, if the errant recipe author is from the United States, you can probably assume that a pale, commercial lager is the intended style.

Checking Out Great Recipes Featuring Beer as an Ingredient

The following recipes are relatively easy, and (hopefully) they'll inspire you to experiment with beer as an ingredient in other recipes. Candy Lesher, author of *The Great American Beer Cookbook* (Brewers Publications), created these recipes especially for this book. Passionate about food, Ms. Lesher is a veteran chef, culinary instructor (the featured culinary personality at the Great American Beer Festival for many years), writer, consultant, television personality, Arizona Culinary Hall of Fame inductee, and member of Les Dames d'Escoffier (a worldwide philanthropic society of professional women leaders in the fields of food, fine beverage, and hospitality).

If you want to go further in cooking with beer, many dedicated beer magazines usually have a recipe or two in each issue, and many beer books in publication list even more.

Using leftover malt and wort in recipes

If you're a homebrewer or have access to homebrew supplies, you may want to throw some steeped (spent) malt into bread dough along with some beer. The malt gives the bread an interesting sweetness and coarseness and increases the dietary fiber.

You can also try using malt extract or wort (the unfermented, unhopped syrupy stuff that's produced in the middle of the brewing process — see Chapter 18) as a base for sauces and baked confections. Brewpubs and serious restaurants connected to breweries have gone this route with intriguing results.

Here are some common U.S. measures and approximate metric conversions:

Liquid Conversions	*Temperature Equivalents*	*Mass Conversions*
1 teaspoon = 5 milliliters	110°F = 43°C	1 ounce = 30 grams
1 tablespoon = 15 milliliters	350°F = 180°C	1 pound = 0.45 kilogram
1 ounce = 29.6 milliliters	365°F = 185°C	
1 cup = 250 milliliters	375°F = 190°C	
	450°F = 230°C	

Roasted Garlic and Onion Soup

Prep time: About 10 min • **Cook time:** About 1¼ hr • **Yield:** 4–5 servings

Ingredients	*Directions*
3 large heads garlic	**1** Strip off the majority of the papery skin on the outside of the garlic heads; cut the tip end off each head of garlic to expose cloves. Place the garlic heads on a square of foil, and drizzle each cut end with ½ teaspoon olive oil; seal the foil.
1½ teaspoons olive oil	
4 tablespoons butter	
4 large yellow onions, thinly sliced	**2** Place the garlic heads on a baking dish and bake in a 375-degree oven for 35 minutes or until the packet feels very soft when squeezed lightly. Cool and then pop cloves out of their papery skins; set aside.
2 large shallots, thinly sliced (optional)	
1 tablespoon sugar	**3** While the garlic is baking, heat butter in a large saucepan over medium heat. Add onions and shallots, cooking until translucent, about 5 minutes.
1 teaspoon salt	
5 cups beef or vegetable stock (preferably homemade)	**4** Add sugar and salt to the onion mixture, continuing to cook until mixture is caramel-gold, about 4 minutes.
1½ teaspoons thyme or your favorite herb	**5** While the onion mixture cooks to caramel-gold, heat stock in a separate saucepan over medium-high heat until liquid is simmering; lower heat to maintain simmer.
2 tablespoons unbleached all-purpose flour	
1 12-ounce bottle English Brown Ale	**6** Sprinkle herbs and flour over the onion mixture, stirring well. Cook 3 minutes, and then pour the hot broth over the onion mixture, stirring constantly.
1 cup croutons and 1½ cup fresh grated cheese (Gruyère, Kaseri, or smoked provolone)	
	7 Mash roasted garlic with a fork. Add garlic and ale to soup and simmer for 30 minutes.
	8 Preheat broiler. Ladle soup into heat-proof bowls and top each one with enough croutons to just cover (amount will vary, depending on how wide your bowl is) and a generous sprinkling of cheese (3 to 4 tablespoons per serving). Run under a hot broiler briefly to melt and bubble cheese.

Per serving: Calories 349 (From Fat 174); Fat 19g (Saturated 10g); Cholesterol 46mg; Sodium 1,948mg; Carbohydrate 31g (Dietary Fiber 3g); Protein 14g.

Beer Batter Extraordinaire

Prep time: About 10 min • **Cook time:** Depends on ingredients being fried, about 3–4 min • **Yield:** Depends on ingredients being fried

Ingredients	Directions
Oil for frying (preferably corn oil), enough to cover the food by at least 1 inch (2.5 centimeters), about 24–32 ounces	*1* Heat the oil to 365 degrees in a deep frying pan over medium-high to high heat.
¾ cup unbleached cake flour, plus additional flour for dusting	*2* In a large bowl, stir together flour, cornmeal, baking powder, salt, and pepper.
¼ cup cornmeal	*3* In a separate, smaller bowl, stir together egg, liquid smoke, and beer. Stir the egg mixture into the flour mixture and whisk briefly, but don't over mix.
2 teaspoons baking powder	
1 teaspoon salt	
¼ teaspoon finely ground black pepper	*4* Pat dry the ingredients to be fried and dust them lightly with flour immediately before dipping into the batter.
1 large egg, beaten	
2 to 3 drops liquid smoke	*5* Using a long-handled slotted spoon or long tongs, fry until a uniform golden brown in color, turning if necessary — usually about 3 to 4 minutes, depending on thickness. Remove from the pan and place on paper towels. Cool just enough to be able to eat, about 90 seconds.
1 cup Kölsch or American Wheat Beer, ice cold	
Suggestions for food to fry: 6 cups sliced onion rings; 8 cups whole cleaned mushroom caps; 6 cups sliced zucchini; 4 cups sliced sweet potato; or a combination of your favorites!	

Per serving: Calories 272 (From Fat 134); Fat 15g (Saturated 0g); Cholesterol 35mg; Sodium 531mg; Carbohydrate 29g (Dietary Fiber 3g); Protein 4g.

Note: This batter is best used immediately after being prepared, so be sure to have the food being battered fully assembled before you begin to heat the oil.

Note: Always heat oil from 350 to 375 degrees Fahrenheit, and always use fresh oil — no exceptions!

Vary It! This batter works best on firm foods: shrimp, onion rings, mushrooms, firm fish, and thin slices of firm veggies, such as sweet potato, eggplant, and zucchini. Also, if you can't find unbleached cake flour, you can substitute unbleached all-purpose flour.

Beer-Glazed Focaccia

Prep time: About 2 hr (includes 90 min for rising) • **Cook time:** About 20 min • **Yield:** One 14- to 16-inch focaccia (4 servings)

Ingredients	Directions
⅔ cup water	**1** Heat the water to 110 degrees.
3½ to 4 cups bread flour, divided	
1 tablespoon yeast	**2** In a large mixing bowl, combine ½ cup bread flour with the yeast and sugar. Pour in water and whisk thoroughly. Let set for at least 15 minutes; it should become foamy and form a head to prove your yeast is alive.
1 tablespoon sugar	
⅔ cup Hefeweizen (room temperature)	
1 tablespoon dried basil	**3** Stir in the Hefeweizen, ½ tablespoon of the basil, salt, cheese, 2 tablespoons of the oil, black pepper, and cornmeal; beat thoroughly. Stir in more flour, 1 cup at a time, until the dough is too stiff to stir.
½ tablespoon kosher salt	
¼ cup grated Romano or Parmesan cheese	
6 tablespoons olive oil	**4** Turn dough onto counter and knead for 8 to 10 minutes, adding just enough flour to keep dough from sticking to the counter and your hands. The dough should be smooth and elastic after kneading.
½ teaspoon freshly ground black pepper	
½ cup cornmeal	
2 large yellow onions, sliced thin	**5** Place the dough in a lightly oiled bowl and cover with plastic wrap. Let rise until doubled — approximately 1 hour.
¼ teaspoon salt	
¼ teaspoon freshly ground black pepper	**6** While dough is rising, heat 1½ tablespoons of the olive oil in a heavy skillet over medium heat. When hot, add onions and cook, stirring frequently until translucent, about 3 to 4 minutes. Add salt, black pepper, remaining basil, and marjoram and cook until mixture is golden, about 4 to 5 more minutes.
½ tablespoon dried marjoram	
⅓ cup Scottish Ale	
Suggested toppings: ½ cup roasted red pepper strips, ½ cup minced Canadian bacon, ⅓ cup crumbled feta cheese, and 2 slices smoked provolone cheese cut into strips.	**7** Add Scottish Ale to the onion mixture and raise the heat to medium-high. Continue to stir and cook until liquid is evaporated, about 2 minutes.

8 Preheat the oven to 450 degrees; if you're using a pizza stone, place it on the bottom rack for preheating. While the oven is heating, punch dough down and let rest, covered, for 15 minutes.

9 Using fingertips and a lightly oiled surface, stretch and pat the dough into a 10-inch circle for a thick-crusted focaccia or a 14-inch circle for a thinner-crusted version. Place on a cornmeal dusted pizza peel if using a pizza stone; if you're not using a stone, use a cornmeal-dusted baking sheet.

10 Rub dough with enough olive oil to coat (about 1 tablespoon) and spread with glazed onions. Top with peppers, bacon, feta, and provolone, or toppings of your choice. Slide the dough onto the hot stone or place baking sheet in the oven on lowest shelf; bake until top is bubbly and bottom is golden — check after 15 minutes.

Per serving: Calories 736 (From Fat 221); Fat 25g (Saturated 4g); Cholesterol 4mg; Sodium 666mg; Carbohydrate 109g (Dietary Fiber 7g); Protein 20g.

Tip: This recipe makes the chewiest, fullest-flavored focaccia around, made just for beer lovers. Use the preceding dough recipe or buy frozen bread dough, thaw it, pat it into a ½-inch-thick circle, and start with Step 6.

Chile con Carne For Dummies

Prep time: About 20 min • **Cook time:** About 1 hr • **Yield:** 10–12 servings

Ingredients	*Directions*
2½ to 3 pounds super-lean ground pork, beef, or combination	*1* In a large skillet, cook the meat over medium heat just until all traces of pink are gone (don't cook until browned). Remove from heat, drain off the excess fat, and set aside.
2 tablespoons olive oil	
2 large onions, chopped	*2* Heat oil in a large Dutch oven over medium heat. Add onions and cook until translucent, about 2 minutes.
6 large cloves garlic, minced	
2 teaspoons ground cumin	*3* Lower heat to medium-low and add garlic, cumin, coriander, and oregano. Continue cooking for 4 minutes.
1½ teaspoons ground coriander	
2 teaspoons dried oregano, crushed	*4* Sprinkle in chile powder and cayenne (if using) and continue cooking for 1 minute.
⅓ to ½ cup mild, red chile powder (ancho if you can get it)	
1–2 teaspoons cayenne (optional)	*5* Add beer, broth, cooked meat, and beans. Simmer slowly, stirring frequently, for 40 minutes. Salt and pepper to taste.
2 cups Vienna/Märzen/ Oktoberfest style beer mixed with ⅓ cup masa harina (or fine-ground cornmeal)	
3 cups canned broth (chicken, vegetable, or beef) or water	
1 16-ounce can kidney beans, drained	
1 16-ounce can black beans, drained	
2 16-ounce cans pinto beans, drained	
salt and freshly ground black pepper to taste	

Per serving: Calories 302 (From Fat 82); Fat 9g (Saturated 2g); Cholesterol 65mg; Sodium 761mg; Carbohydrate 23g (Dietary Fiber 8g); Protein 30g.

Vary It! For a marvelous Southwestern twist, stir in 1 large can of drained hominy during the last 10 minutes of cooking. For a heartier chili, cook ½ pound chopped bacon and add it along with the meat and beans.

Brewers Pulled Beef

Prep time: About 35 min • **Cook time:** About 3½ hr • **Yield:** 8–10 servings

Ingredients	Directions
1 12-ounce bottle Cream Ale	**1** In a large saucepan, heat Cream Ale, salted water, oregano, 5 cloves of the garlic, 1 teaspoon of the pepper, and chili flakes (if using) to a rolling boil over high heat. Add meat to the boiling liquid to seal in juices, turning if necessary, and cook for about 8 minutes.
3 cups water mixed with 1 tablespoon kosher salt	
2 tablespoons dried oregano	
8 large cloves garlic, peeled and mashed	**2** Lower heat to very low, cover, and slowly simmer the meat an additional 2 to 3 hours or until meat pulls apart easily. Cool and pull into shreds.
2 teaspoons freshly ground black pepper (red chili flakes optional)	
4 pounds boneless beef chuck (or lean pork)	**3** In a heavy pan over medium heat, sauté the onion in a tablespoon of oil until golden, about 3 minutes.
1 small onion, chopped	
1 tablespoon olive oil	**4** Add the remaining 3 cloves of garlic, cayenne, salt, and 1 teaspoon pepper to the onions, and cook 2 minutes.
1–2 teaspoons ground cayenne (or to taste)	
1 teaspoon salt (or to taste)	**5** Pour in the Dortmunder and stir in the tomato paste, vinegar, brown sugar, steak sauce, and liquid smoke and gently simmer 10 minutes.
1 12-ounce bottle Dortmunder Dark	
⅓ cup tomato paste	**6** Add the pulled meat to the sauce, and simmer an additional 15 minutes so the meat can absorb the flavor of the sauce.
⅓ cup cider vinegar	
⅓ cup brown sugar	
⅓ cup steak sauce	
1–2 teaspoons liquid smoke (or to taste)	

Per serving: Calories 641 (From Fat 359); Fat 40g (Saturated 17g); Cholesterol 146mg; Sodium 869mg; Carbohydrate 28g (Dietary Fiber 1g); Protein 41g.

Tip: This simple-to-prepare barbecue of succulent shredded beef steeped in a deep, beer-enhanced barbecue sauce should be piled high on big sourdough buns and served with your best coleslaw.

Arizona Quiche

Prep: About 15 min • **Cook/cool time:** About 1 hr • **Yield:** 6 servings

Ingredients	*Directions*
½ cup sour cream	**1** Preheat oven to 375 degrees.
4 extra large eggs	
⅔ cup half-and-half	**2** In a blender or food processor, process the sour cream, eggs, half-and-half, and pepper just until smooth; stir in the beer.
½ teaspoon freshly ground black pepper	
⅓ cup Chili Beer (or American Pale Lager plus — optional — ½ seeded, chopped jalapeño)	**3** Heat the butter in a sauté pan over medium heat; add the onion and sauté until golden, about 5 to 6 minutes.
1 tablespoon butter	**4** Spread sautéed onions over the bottom of the pie crust. Sprinkle diced chilies (if using), red pepper, grated cheese, and bacon over the top.
1 small onion, sliced thin	
1 10-inch frozen pie crust	
⅓ cup diced green chilies (optional)	**5** Slowly pour egg mixture over the onion mixture. Do not stir. Place on the lower shelf of oven. Bake approximately 40 minutes or until a knife inserted into the center comes out clean. Cool 5 to 10 minutes before serving.
⅓ cup diced red bell pepper	
½ cup grated Monterey Jack cheese	
4 ounces (or about 8 strips) bacon, cooked until crisp and crumbled	

Per serving: Calories 499 (From Fat 345); Fat 38g (Saturated 15g); Cholesterol 212mg; Sodium 609mg; Carbohydrate 22g (Dietary Fiber 0g); Protein 16g.

Vary It! If the jalapeño and green chilies aren't for you, replace them with roasted red peppers or other veggies, like mushrooms or broccoli.

Vary It! For a lighter version of this recipe, use ⅔ cup light sour cream, 1¼ cups egg substitute, ½ cup skim milk, and pepper along with the beer. Sauté onion in nonstick pan with butter-flavored spray, use light cheese, and replace the bacon with low-fat chopped ham. For a beer-imbued rendition of the classic French quiche, substitute Swiss cheese and ham for the Monterey Jack cheese and bacon.

Publicans Hot-n-Spicy Chicken with E-Z Garlic Sauce

Prep time: About 25 min • **Cook time:** About 4–8 hr plus marinating time • **Yield:** 6–7 servings

Ingredients	*Directions*
1 teaspoon whole black peppercorns	*1* Heat a heavy skillet over medium heat until very hot. Remove from heat and toss in peppercorns and coriander seed, stirring for 1 minute. Add the cumin and continue stirring for an additional 30 seconds or until very fragrant. (Skip this step if you're in a rush.) Cool; then crush the spices.
1 teaspoon coriander seed	
1 teaspoon cumin seed	
⅔ cup **Munich Dunkel or Bock Beer**	
2 tablespoons olive oil	*2* In a small bowl, combine the beer and the olive oil with the crushed spices and the ginger, garlic, chili, paprika, honey, and salt. Let set 10 minutes.
2 teaspoons fresh grated ginger	
4 large cloves garlic, mashed in a garlic press	*3* While marinade is resting, slash the chicken pieces diagonally with ¼-inch-deep cuts, about 4 per piece.
1 serrano chili pepper or jalapeño, seeded and finely minced (optional, for chili-heads)	*4* Rub chicken thoroughly with the marinade. Marinate, covered, in the refrigerator for 4 to 8 hours.
2 tablespoons smoked paprika	
2 tablespoons honey	*5* Grill over medium heat until no sign of pink appears when meat is pierced with a sharp knife and meat reaches an internal temperature of 165 degrees. Serve with E-Z Garlic Sauce (see the next recipe); either drape the sauce over the grilled chicken for a dramatic effect or serve it pooled underneath or on the side for dipping.
1½ teaspoons salt (or to taste)	
3 to 4 pounds chicken, cut in pieces and washed (or boneless chicken breasts)	
About 4 cups E-Z Garlic Sauce (see the following recipe)	

E-Z Garlic Sauce

2 cups water

5 cups torn French or Italian bread, crusts removed

7 to 8 large cloves garlic, peeled

¼ cup lemon-enhanced summer beer (or lightly hopped Pale Ale with dash of lemon juice)

¼ cup buttermilk (or sour cream)

¼ cup olive oil

½–1 teaspoon salt (or to taste)

1 Pour water over bread and let soak 1 minute. Gently squeeze water out of bread with your hands.

2 Place bread and remaining ingredients in a blender or food processor and process until silky smooth.

Per serving: Calories 508 (From Fat 279); Fat 31g (Saturated 7g); Cholesterol 90mg; Sodium 1,058mg; Carbohydrate 25g (Dietary Fiber 2g); Protein 32g.

Bayou Shrimp

Prep time: About 15 min • **Cook time:** About 45 min • **Yield:** 6 servings

Ingredients	*Directions*
4 tablespoons olive or canola oil	**1** Heat oil in a large, heavy skillet over medium-low heat. Sprinkle in flour and cook until browned, stirring constantly, about 10 to 15 minutes.
4 tablespoons flour	
1 cup chopped onions	
1 cup chopped scallions	**2** Add onions, scallions, and celery to the flour, cooking an additional 5 minutes. Add parsley and garlic, cooking an additional 2 minutes.
1 cup chopped celery	
1 cup fresh Italian flat-leaf parsley, chopped	
3 cloves garlic, mashed	**3** Slowly stir in hot broth and then beer and tomatoes, stirring constantly. Add shrimp boil, paprika, and pepper. Cover and simmer slowly for 30 minutes.
1 cup hot chicken broth	
1 cup Stout or roasty-tasting Porter	
8 fresh Roma or whole canned tomatoes, chopped	**4** Add salt or cayenne to taste. Toss in shrimp and cook just until shrimp turn pink (about 2 minutes). Remove from heat and serve immediately over rice.
½ tablespoon shrimp/crab boil (a commercial spice mixture for shellfish), finely ground	
1 tablespoon smoked paprika	
½ teaspoon crushed black pepper	
½ teaspoon salt or ¼ teaspoon cayenne	
2½ pounds raw, peeled, deveined large shrimp	
4 cups cooked rice for serving	

Per serving: Calories 425 (From Fat 108); Fat 12g (Saturated 2g); Cholesterol 281mg; Sodium 832mg; Carbohydrate 43g (Dietary Fiber 3g); Protein 35g.

Tip: Serve this shrimp with lots of chilled brew (a malty beer, like Oktoberfest or a Brown Ale) and crusty French bread.

Vary It! Of course, fresh crawfish are also wonderful served in this sauce. If you enjoy mussels, nestle scrubbed mussels into the sauce 15 minutes into the simmer time. Cover and continue cooking an additional 20 minutes or until mussels have opened and are fully cooked.

Chocolate Stout Silk Pie

Prep time: About 10 min • **Chill time:** About 4–6 hr • **Yield:** 8–10 servings

Ingredients	*Directions*
12 ounces semi-sweet chocolate chips (or chopped bitter chocolate)	**1** Place chocolate chips, marshmallows, and salt in a medium bowl.
24 large marshmallows **pinch of salt** **⅔ cup Stout (or Porter)**	**2** In two separate saucepans, heat Stout and heavy cream until very hot but not boiling. (Don't heat them together in one container, or the cream will curdle.)
⅓ cup heavy cream or evaporated or condensed skim milk **1 teaspoon vanilla** **1 tablespoon quality bourbon or crème de cacao (optional)**	**3** Pour the Stout and cream over the chocolate and marshmallows and let sit for 5 minutes. Gently whisk together to thoroughly blend. Add the vanilla and bourbon (if using), continuing to whisk until very smooth.
1 ready-made butter-cookie-crumb or graham-cracker pie crust **Whipped cream and shaved chocolate and/or toasted crushed nuts for garnish**	**4** Pour the mixture into the crust and refrigerate 4 to 6 hours or until firm. Garnish with whipped cream and shaved chocolate or toasted nuts.

Per serving: Calories 444 (From Fat 195); Fat 22g (Saturated 10g); Cholesterol 13mg; Sodium 204mg; Carbohydrate 65g (Dietary Fiber 4g); Protein 5g.

Part IV
Exploring Beer around the World and at Home

The 5th Wave   By Rich Tennant

"I'm sure 'Vikings Pillage' is a very good beer, but do you have anything with a less violent label?"

In this part . . .

This part of the book is mostly about getting out and about to taste beer — often where it's made (which is the best way to taste beer, by the way). I keep it closer to home (namely, in North America) in Chapter 15, and then I move farther afield to Europe, Asia, and beyond in Chapter 16.

Chapter 17 is also about travel in search of good beer, but specifically the kind of travel that focuses strictly on beer. Yes, some companies design entire vacations around beer, and they're spotlighted here.

And then there's Chapter 18, which approaches beer exploration in a rather novel way: brewing it yourself. Don't overlook this possibility; millions of people around the world have been brewing their own beer at home (I'm one of them), and many more are joining them every day.

Chapter 15

Sampling Beer in North America

. . . .

In This Chapter

▶ Revisiting North America's brewing traditions

▶ Sampling beer at North American bars, brewpubs, and beyond

▶ Checking out beer festivals and museums in North America

. . . .

Despite beer's decidedly European roots, North American beer explorers needn't travel too far to satisfy their curiosity. People can find lots to celebrate and explore in North American breweries, beer festivals, and even brewery museums. And because most microbrewed or brewpub beer isn't distributed nationally, beer exploration in the United States, Canada, and even Mexico can provide great rewards at every turn, as you find out in this chapter. Talk about instant gratification!

With more than 2,000 craft brewers or brewpubs now plying their trade in the United States and Canada, you can find good beer just about everywhere, though it's concentrated in the big urban areas. Although beer generally isn't as regional as it is in Germany or Belgium (see Chapter 16 for details), at least one region merits special mention: the Pacific Northwest — beer nirvana, the Promised Land for North American beer explorers — with its great pubs, publicans, microbreweries, and innovative brewers. Some 30 percent of the world's hops are grown there, along with 30,000 tons of barley each year.

Looking to Beer's Past in the United States

Before jumping in to the steak and potatoes of this chapter — namely, where to find great beer to enjoy with your steak and potatoes in North America — you may want to reflect a little bit on the history and events that got brewing in the United States to where it is today. Check out the following sections for a little U.S. brewing history.

Respecting the elders: Tracing back great U.S. brewing traditions

Even though the New World was discovered a mere 500 years ago, brewing beer on the North American continent has been an ongoing trade for about 400 of those years. Granted, the earliest concoctions produced by European explorers were rather crude, having to be made from available ingredients, such as tree sap, molasses, and maize; those beers showed the colonists' dedication and tenacity (and intestinal fortitude?).

The oldest brewing company in North America is the Molson Brewery in Montreal, Quebec, Canada, founded in 1786. (It also happens to be the second oldest company in Canada, after the Hudson Bay Company.)

After building personal dwellings, a colonial order of priority was to build a church, followed by an alehouse. Both were great meeting places: one for religious purposes, the other for social and political purposes.

Eventually, among the droves of immigrants from Europe came those whose trade was making beer — genuine beer with genuine beer-making ingredients. Commercial brewing enterprises were quickly established in most urban centers to slake the thirsts of the burgeoning populations.

As U.S. state boundaries pushed ever westward, so did the need for new breweries at every outpost. By the mid-1870s, an all-time high of more than 4,000 breweries existed in the United States alone. Following are the still-recognizable names of brewers from that general era:

- Anheuser (Eberhard) and Busch (Adolphus)
- Coors (Adolph)
- Hamm (Theodore)
- Leinenkugel (Jacob)
- Matt (Francis Xavier)
- Miller (Frederick)
- Pabst (Frederick)
- Schlitz (Joseph)
- Spoetzl (Kosmas)

The following are other brewer names that are fading into history or are no longer recognized:

- Blatz (Valentin)
- Heileman (Gottlieb)
- Huber (Joseph)
- Ortlieb (Henry)
- Schaefer (Frederick and Maximilian)
- Schmidt (Christian)
- Stegmaier (Charles)
- Stroh (Bernard)
- Weinhard (Henry)

The oldest continuously operating brewery in the United States is the D. G. Yuengling & Son Brewery in Pottsville, Pennsylvania, which opened in 1829. The Yuengling brewery managed to survive 13 years of prohibition by producing *near beer* (non-alcoholic beer) and dairy products.

Though none of the aforementioned brewers — and they're just a fraction of those who came before — were known for producing spectacularly unique beer styles or flavors, all were part of a rapidly expanding industry that set the bar much higher in terms of production. Quality and consistency became the new standards — not that quality was ever *not* part of the industry standard, but the commitment to consistency was rather impressive.

Annual barrelage in the U.S. brewing industry also began to soar around this time. The Pabst Brewing Company of Milwaukee, Wisconsin, became the first to produce more than 1 million barrels of beer per year in the 1890s. The Anheuser-Busch Brewing Company of St. Louis, Missouri, and the Joseph Schlitz Brewing Company of Milwaukee, Wisconsin, closely followed. These breweries represented the three largest breweries in the United States at the turn of the century (the 20th century). The beer itself may not have been very notable, but the sheer volume being produced certainly was.

Moving on up: The boom in U.S. brewing during the 20th century

Since 1933, when the 21st Amendment brought an end to prohibition, beer production in the United States has steadily increased (despite the fact that there were fewer operating breweries in the U.S. following prohibition). Canada had its own prohibition that started and ended earlier, but it had little overall effect on brewing in that country. Beer production in Mexico, which never had any period of prohibition, continued unabated.

During prohibition, Southern Californians did their boozing across the Mexican border in Tijuana. To address the daily swell of thirsty tourists, ever more bars and cantinas sprung up in Tijuana, giving the dusty little cattle town the notorious claim to "most bars per capita (in the world)."

In the 1940s and 1950s, when smaller American breweries continued to fail and close, annual barrelage still continued to rise. Not even in 1980, when the number of existing breweries in the United States hit an all-time low, did beer production numbers dip (an estimated 175 million barrels of beer were produced in 1980 by approximately 44 breweries). You can see the ups and downs of breweries in operation in the United States in Figure 15-1.

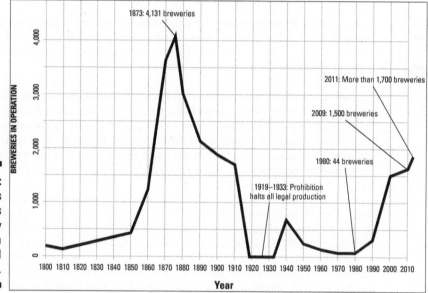

Figure 15-1: The highs and lows of brewery operation in the United States.

Teaching an old dog new tricks: The rise of small craft brewers

When craft brewers (also known as *microbrewers*) first came on the scene in the late 1970s and early 1980s, just about everyone ignored them. Consumers didn't take them very seriously, and as far as the big brewers were concerned, well, let's just say they weren't concerned. Early craft brewers were like a gnat on an elephant's backside; when the elephant swishes his tail, though, the gnat knows it has the elephant's attention.

Exactly when big brewers started taking microbrewers seriously is open to debate, but the contract brewing companies likely had something to do with it. A *contract brewer* is a company that doesn't own any brewing equipment of its own; it hires a real brewery to brew its beer for it on contract.

Contract brewers had their heyday in the mid-1980s (the Boston Beer Company is one of the few contract brewers to survive that era). Because beers that were brewed on contract looked, and (for the most part) tasted, like other non-contract microbrewed beer, consumers had a hard time telling the difference between them. A few contract brewers succeeded and eventually opened their own brewing facilities, but most of them failed and faded into oblivion. The one thing that contract brewers succeeded in doing was rapidly expanding the craft beer market, getting the attention of both the consumers and the big corporate brewers, like Miller, Coors, and Anheuser-Busch.

When microbrewing became a hot concept, just about everyone and his grandmother started a craft-brewing operation. Scores of new brands hit the market with regularity. That's about the time the elephant started noticing the gnat.

The Anheuser-Busch, Coors, and Miller Brewing companies sent a message industry-wide when they began introducing their own new specialty brands to the market (from the mid-1980s to the mid-1990s). The message was twofold:

✔ They weren't giving up shelf space to a bunch of snot-nosed upstarts.

✔ They could produce craft beers quicker and better than any small brewery. (At least they were right about the quicker part.)

Several national and regional breweries tried to get in on the craft beer movement by attempting to produce craft beers of their own. Some brewers genuinely understood the notion of artisanal beer and did their best to emulate it, while others missed the concept by a country mile. These guys did little more than put a mediocre-tasting beer in a brown bottle and dress it up with a cool label and a funky name. They thought it'd pass for a microbrew. It didn't.

When enough of these pretenders failed, the big boys decided to take a different tack. They set their sights on buying their way into the craft beer movement by purchasing smaller breweries — either whole or in part. Who says you can't teach an old dog new tricks? Some of the big brewers' more notable forays into craft beer ownership include the following:

✔ Anheuser-Busch got involved with Seattle's Redhook Ale Brewery, Portland's Widmer Brothers Brewing Company, Honolulu's Kona Brewing Company, and Chicago's Goose Island Beer Company (known collectively as the *Craft Brewers Alliance, Inc.*). Anheuser-Busch opened a brewery in Portsmouth, New Hampshire, in order to brew the Redhook, Widmer, Kona, and, more recently, Goose Island Beers there to more easily distribute those brands on the East Coast.

✔ Miller invested heavily in the former family-owned Wisconsin regional Jacob Leinenkugel Brewing Company and built that brand nationally.

✔ Coors was a little stealthier when it formed the surreptitious Blue Moon Brewing Company — a little-known Coors subsidiary that has fared quite well. (In 2010, Coors also announced the creation of Tenth and Blake Beer Company, a new company focused on craft and import beers.)

Even today, as production and sales numbers for the largest brewers in North America are either flat or declining, overall barrelage is still on the rise. Credit the craft brewers.

Renaissance or revolution? U.S. brewing today and tomorrow

Have we experienced a renaissance or a revolution in the brewing industry? The answer is yes. Beer pundits have used both terms with vacillating regularity and, honestly, both fit. We've experienced both a turning around and a great change in the way things are done in the brewing industry, including in the United States. We're also still in the midst of a revival or rebirth of old beer styles and methods of production. As long as nothing is violently overthrown and we don't return all the way to the 15th century, revolution and renaissance are good things.

Speaking of revolution: Just for grins, check out Chicago's Revolution Brewing Company (www.revbrew.com) if you're ever in the city. And while you're in the neighborhood, stop in Haymarket Pub & Brewery (www.haymarketbrewing.com) near the site of the Haymarket Square riots of 1886.

Although the revolution part of this new North American beer experience may be over, the renaissance part is still ongoing — about three decades and counting. (That's nothing; the European Renaissance lasted almost three centuries!) Even as the number of craft breweries continues to rise in North America, there's always room for more. As long as a town without its own alehouse exists and an unconverted beer drinker remains, there's room for more breweries and more beer. Bet the mortgage on it!

Howdy, Neighbors! Checking Out the Beer Scene in Canada and Mexico

As fun as watching and participating in the growth of the craft-brewing industry in the United States has been (as I describe earlier in this chapter), you can't forget that Americans aren't alone in this movement. For better or worse, our fellow North American neighbors to the north and south are often influenced by what U.S. brewers do. And sometimes they even beat them at their game, as you find out in the following sections.

Oh, Canada

Canada's brewing roots are just about as old and well established as those in the United States. Actually, much of Canada's history is intertwined with American history because the Great White North was discovered, pioneered, and settled by many of the same people at the same time. It stands to reason that Canadian brewing history follows a similar timeline as well.

Englishman John Molson was the first to set up a brewery in Canada in 1786, ironically, in the wine-drinking, French-dominated province of Quebec. Irishman Eugene O'Keefe followed him in 1862 and later merged his company with Thomas Carling's brewery. John LaBatt made his name by acquiring the brewery that was sold to his father in 1866. All these iconic names are revered by Canadian beer drinkers. (What was that Moosehead guy's first name, eh?)

Virtually unknown to Americans who've been fed a steady and limited diet of Canadian Golden Lagers and Pale Ales, the popular maple leaf megabrewers, such as Molson, O'Keefe, Carling, and Labatt, produce a fairly wide variety of brand names and beer styles that Canadians keep to themselves. In fact, Molson Porter was my epiphany beer, which kindled my interest in good beer, back in 1982.

Anyway, mirroring the craft beer movement in the United States, Canadian craft brewers have been producing the same high-quality brews in the same wide variety of styles. Some prominent packaged brands to look for while north of the border include the following:

- Amsterdam, Toronto, Ontario
- Brasserie McAuslan (St. Ambroise), Montreal, Quebec
- Brick Brewery, Waterloo, Ontario
- Granite Brewery, Halifax, Nova Scotia
- Granville Island Brewing, Vancouver, British Columbia
- Okanagan Spring, Vernon, British Columbia
- Sleeman Brewing & Malting, Guelph, Ontario
- Unibroue, Chambly, Quebec

Canada's larger cities are also home to many excellent brewpubs, renowned for their great beer. Among them are

---

LCBO and The Beer Store

Beer travelers accustomed to buying their beer at a variety of retail locations are in for a bit of a surprise when they get to Ontario. Stemming from Canadian prohibition, the Liquor Control Board of Ontario (LCBO) was instituted to ease the transition from being a temperance society. LCBO stores are, in effect, run by the provincial government, and they're one of only two places where packaged beer can be purchased. The other location is called *The Beer Store* (clever, huh?), which is jointly owned by Molson Coors, Anheuser-Busch InBev, and Sapporo Brewery (sounds like a monopoly to me). Oh, and one more thing — Canadian taxes on beer are painfully high!

- ✔ C'est What? Toronto, Ontario
- ✔ Dieu du Ceil, Montreal, Quebec
- ✔ Hart & Thistle, Halifax, Nova Scotia
- ✔ Bushwakker, Regina, Saskatchewan
- ✔ Spinnakers, Victoria, British Columbia
- ✔ Yaletown Brewery, Vancouver, British Columbia
- ✔ Whistler Brewhouse, Whistler, British Columbia
- ✔ The Grizzly Paw, Canmore, Alberta

Down Mexico way

Mexican beer is far from glamorous; it's never been considered much more than another thirst-quenching beverage in a hot and parched country. However, a number of major and craft beer brands are available, as you find out in the following sections.

Major beer brands in Mexico

Only two companies have had a stranglehold on the Mexican brewing industry for decades: Grupo Modelo and Cervecería Cuauhtémoc Moctezuma. Unfortunately, they produce a wide variety of brands without offering a wide variety of flavor.

Interestingly enough, about 30 years ago, the Mexican government mounted a public campaign to call beer *una bebida de moderación* — a beverage of moderation — in order to stem the rising incidence of public intoxication.

Still, if you want to try some authentic Mexican beer, you have a few mediocre options. The following are the top brands brewed by the Mexico City–based Grupo Modelo:

- ✔ Corona
- ✔ Estrella
- ✔ Modelo Especial
- ✔ Negra Modelo
- ✔ Pacifico Clara
- ✔ Victoria

The top brands brewed by the Monterrey-based Cervecería Cuauhtémoc Moctezuma are

- ✔ Bohemia
- ✔ Carta Blanca
- ✔ Dos Equis
- ✔ Indio
- ✔ Sol
- ✔ Tecate

The *Salón de la Fama del Béisbol* (Mexican Baseball Hall of Fame) is housed on the grounds of the huge Cuauhtémoc Moctezuma Brewery in Monterrey. Visitors can sample beer in its breezy beer garden.

The dozen or so major brands are mostly Pale Lagers, with two notable exceptions:

- ✔ The brewer of Corona (a minor brand in Mexico) also produces one of the country's few dark beers: Negra Modelo.
- ✔ The relatively malty Dos Equis is a small wonder: It's a rare descendant of the Vienna Lagers brewed in Mexico during the mid-19th-century occupation by Austrian Emperor Maximilian.

Craft beers in Mexico

For a while, it looked as though the craft beer movement was going to pass Mexico by. With the country's depressed economy and peasant traditions, whether artisanal beer would ever catch on there was a big question mark. But, alas, a new generation of beer drinkers — and social networkers — finally discovered what the rest of us had been enjoying for many years: *cerveza artesanal!* These new indigenous craft brewers have been in existence since about 2005, but they're finding favor among Mexico's young urban elite. Here are a few brands and styles worth seeking out:

✔ Cervecería Primus (Tlalnepantla de Baz — essentially a suburb north of Mexico City)

- Tempus Alt (Altbier)
- Tempus Doble Malta (Imperial Altbier)
- Tempus Dorada (Golden Ale)

Primus Brewery is helping lead the fight to introduce more artisanal Mexican beers into the marketplace, and many small local producers are banding together to share importing costs and encourage the growth of a craft beer culture in Mexico.

✔ Cervecería Minerva (Guadalajara)

- Minerva Colonial (Kölsch)
- Minerva Pale Ale (English Pale Mild Ale)
- Minerva Stout (Irish Dry Stout)
- Minerva Viena (Vienna Lager)

✔ Minerva Malverde (Pilsner)

✔ Cervecería Cucapá (Mexicali)

- Cucapá Barleywine (American Barleywine)
- Cucapá Chupacabras (English Pale Ale)
- Cucapá Clasica (Blonde Ale)
- Cucapá Honey (Blonde Ale)
- Cucapá Imperio (Belgian Strong Dark Ale)
- Cucapá Jefe (American Pale Wheat Ale)
- Cucapá La Migra (Imperial Stout)
- Cucapá Light (Light Lager)
- Cucapá Lowrider (Rye Beer)
- Cucapá Oscura (American Brown Ale)
- Cucapá Runaway (American India Pale Ale)
- Cucapá Trigueña (American Blonde Ale)

Going Where the Beer Is

Even as more beer choices become available to folks in North America, beer still doesn't just show up on your doorstep (unless you belong to a beer-of-the-month club, but that's another story). If you want to enjoy good beer, you've got to go out and find it (unless you're a homebrewer, but that's also another story).

The good news is that you don't have to wander far from home to find good beer. It's right down the block (for a growing number of people, anyway). In the following sections, you discover the most common beer destinations in North America.

Beer bars

In Ireland, the United Kingdom, and most of western and central Europe, the pub culture is still intact. Many pubs and taverns are quaint, quiet places where you can comfortably enjoy a drink with the local folk, who know just about everybody (Norm!). Women and children are traditionally part of the daytime crowd. More often than not, the beer on tap is a local delicacy that's served and drunk with pride and respect.

Despite the history of prohibition, the beer-can culture, and the lack of beer variety, some of that Old World–style pride and respect is returning to the United States in the form of dedicated *beer bars*. Beer bars, unlike the brewpubs and gastropubs that I describe later in this chapter, have reputations built on the quantity and quality of beers on their beer menu. Of course, this trend isn't without its extremes: Some U.S. beer bars endeavor to be grand Germanic beer halls, others strive to be old-fashioned Celtic pubs, and others aspire to the brewpub concept, going as far as installing fake or inoperable brewing equipment in order to affect the ambience of a pub-brewery.

The beer police have recently reported that beer snobbery is on the rise, so watch out for those people who've just discovered that good beer is cool and have become beer experts overnight. As more everyday bars with good beer selections enter this expanding and competitive market, beer is sometimes forced to take a back seat to live bands, the clang and crash of pinball machines, rowdy crowds, and beer ignoramuses. Choose your destinations carefully.

Many beer bars stake their reputation on the length and breadth of their bottled beer list. Offering three, four, and even five *hundred* different brands of beer isn't unusual for some of these places — and isn't necessarily a good thing. Why?

- ✔ First of all, stocking that many different brands in any quantity is a near physical impossibility, so your choice is likely to be sold out.

- ✔ Second, not only is stocking that much beer difficult, but storing it at the proper cool temperature is probably out of the question.

- ✔ Third, when a bar offers such a mind-boggling number of beers, stocks of particular beers can't possibly sell quickly.

Instead of stocking hundreds of aging and breakable bottles of beer, wise bar owners have invested in dozens of draught lines and tap handles and now offer as many beers on draught as space allows. You can find bars that offer 10, 20, or 50 different brews on tap, much of it as fresh as just-picked hops.

In the United States, craft-brewed beers occupy most of the tap space; a few bars have even made arrangements with local craft brewers to receive a regular supply of beer to be sold under the bar brand name.

To most beer drinkers, draught beer is better than bottled beer. Why? Because draught beer

- ✔ Is fresher (the beer is delivered quickly, sometimes directly from the brewery)

- ✔ Is usually unpasteurized (the taste hasn't been killed along with the microbes)

- ✔ Has probably been stored properly (people who order by the keg are typically more interested in beer quality than those who don't)

- ✔ Has smaller bubbles and a creamier texture than bottled beer, if poured right — especially with a handpull tap (see Chapter 5 for more info about handpulls)

Brewpubs

One of the best places to taste different beers in North America is at a *brewpub* — a pub, usually with a restaurant, that serves its own beer made in a small brewery on the premises, kind of like a restaurant with its own bakery.

By definition, a brewpub doesn't distribute more than 50 percent of its beer outside the pub — and most brewpubs don't distribute any — though you can usually get it to go in small kegs and growlers (see Chapter 9 for more about these containers). Brewpubs come in all sizes, from an innkeeper's hobby with an annual output of a couple hundred barrels to huge commercial operations that brew thousands of barrels a year.

Even with the 1,033 or so brewpubs now operating in the United States (as of 2010) and new ones opening elsewhere in North America and in Europe (especially the United Kingdom — see Chapter 16), brewpubs still aren't local to the majority of people. But brewpubs are opening with mushroom-like frequency in every kind of place — especially urban areas but also suburban and rural vacation areas. Even chains of brewpubs have appeared in the United States and United Kingdom, though not everyone is convinced artisanal brewing can be franchised.

The best and easiest way to find a local brewpub is to use your favorite Internet search engine. If that doesn't work, check the dedicated beer websites listed in Chapter 19.

Beer lovers treasure brewpubs for a number of good reasons, including the following:

✔ **Fresh beer:** Brewpub beer is about as fresh a product as you're going to find anywhere. (Brewpubs routinely boast that while commercial mega-brews may travel hundreds of miles before they get to your glass, their brewpub beer travels only a few yards from the serving tanks to the tap.) With beer, freshness is paramount for preserving flavor.

✔ **Variety:** Brewpubs offer beer in a variety of regular major styles, one or two seasonal specials, and a brew or two in exotic styles, normally for a limited run (keeps you coming back to see what's new). Brewers like to test the scope of their skills as much as they like to please your palate. Imported or guest beers are often featured alongside the house brews, just for fun. Many brewpubs illustrate some of their most popular brews on their placemats so customers see them as soon as they sit down (see Figure 15-2 for an example).

✔ **Serving know-how:** Brewpubs know how to serve beer. For example, no serious beer drinker wants a frosted mug, and I've yet to encounter one at a brewpub. Most brewpubs serve beer at proper temperatures and in the appropriate glasses (see Chapter 11 for the skinny on serving beer).

✔ **Elementary education:** The curious and the inquisitive can see the brewing equipment and get the chance to watch the brewmaster at work and ask questions. With luck, you may even be able to take a tour. What's really cool is when brewers offer a particularly intrigued customer the opportunity to spend a day working alongside them.

Figure 15-2: This beer placemat is a good example of what you can expect to find at many brewpubs.

Island Hopper Tasting Mat courtesy of Kona Brewing Company

- **Postgraduate work:** Brewpubs may sponsor weekend beer and brewing seminars or tasting clubs. The Goose Island Brewing Company in Chicago, Illinois, was among the first to do so. This company offers its Master of Beer Appreciation (MBA) program, which encourages customers to sample a curriculum of styles throughout the year and earn points toward premiums such as MBA T-shirts and free beer (you expected parchment?).

- **Camaraderie:** One thing you're sure to find at brewpubs is camaraderie — not the sporting, testosterone-laced kind, but the beer-aficionado kind, the beer-geek kind, the hophead kind, and the gourmet-beer-fan kind. Striking up conversations about the beer is pretty easy in these places. (And some brewpub owners are former homebrewers.) The weather and sports come up, too, of course, but beer-as-topic is special.

- **Food:** Oh, yes, the food. Good brewpub folks generally like to cook recipes that feature their beers, and they're glad to suggest beer and food matches. But food is secondary to good beer (pity the rare brewpub with bad brews). When the food is imaginative and excellent, the experience is blissful. (Flip to Chapter 13 for details on dining with beer and Chapter 14 for more about cooking with beer.)

A good brewpub is defined by good beer, of course, but also by evidence of the brewer's passion, even reverence and respect, for beer. These qualities are what make a brewer take the time to talk beer with you, to show you around the brewery, and to train the wait staff. Brewers have to have the passion to run a brewpub, or else it's just another bar.

Gastropubs

Gastropubs are the latest concept destination for beer lovers in North America (they differ from brewpubs in that they don't brew their own beer). These places, which are fashioned after the European model (pubs and cafes), are intended to introduce foodies and beer geeks to one another's passions. The beer menus, although not necessarily lengthy in terms of the number of beers offered, typically have depth with a wide variety of styles. The food menus are designed around beer or deliberately planned to be complemented by the beer, which makes gastropubs perfect locations for organized beer dinners (see the next section for more info).

Gastropubs are often in smaller, more intimate settings than brewpubs, but the fare and attendant bill can range from simple and affordable to extravagant and pricey. Either way, expect a truly gastronomic experience when you visit your next gastropub.

The best and easiest way to find a local gastropub is to use your preferred search engine. If you can't find one that way, check the dedicated beer websites listed in Chapter 19. It doesn't hurt to ask the locals, either.

Beer dinners

Usually, a restaurant is an unlikely place to find a good beer. Wine has always been, and still is, the conceptual favorite for food and drink pairing. But now there's hope. More and more often, you can expect to find an upscale eatery that's either decided to wake up and smell the barley or has received numerous requests for something other than Chateauneuf Dew Pop and Vin d'Pay d'ay. Such a restaurant has a beer list, or at least a few decent craft brews to offer. Some are also starting to have occasional beer dinners.

The *beer dinner* is a phenomenon inspired by the plethora of available gourmet brews. Beer dinners are hosted by restaurants, brewpubs, gastropubs, and beer bars across the country. These places may not necessarily be known for their lengthy beer menus, but their owners recognize the draw of good beer. Beer dinners are often a joint effort between the chef and a hired *beer celebrity* — a brewmaster, beer importer, or beer writer.

Beer dinners customarily feature several courses that spotlight certain beer and food combinations and often use beer as an ingredient in as many of the dishes as possible. A typical beer dinner menu lists the dishes along with the beer served with each course; menus may also have a few lines of background about each beer. These events are a real treat, but they don't come cheap. Look for special promotions and plan on making reservations way in advance.

Because beer dinners don't occur every night of the week, they are, more or less, hit-or-miss propositions. To make sure you don't miss any of these events, you may want to get on the mailing (and e-mail) list of establishments that are known to host beer dinners.

Some dinners may be themed. For example, one dinner may feature beers from only Germany or Belgium. Or at a banquet that features oyster dishes, Stout may be the only beer style served (oysters and Stout are a classic pairing). Themes can be food (such as game or fish), seasons, local specialties, or cooking styles. Check out Chapter 13 for additional details about beer dinners.

Celebrating at North American Beer Festivals

Beer lovers love to celebrate beer. Craft beer fests seem to be popping up wherever a small collection of brewpubs or microbreweries exists. Can it be that beer is a good social lubricant? Something to ponder.

Americans have discovered that the true meaning of *beer festival* goes far beyond the ubiquitous Oktoberfests that take place in practically every two-horse town in the country. You need a little more than grilled bratwurst and oom-pah music to please the beer crowd nowadays. In beer festival parlance, *quantity* means *variety*, as in number of brewers and styles — not a high rate of consumption. And you need good beer. Craft-brewed beer.

Beer festivals are becoming somewhat standardized, with the sponsors having learned from early mistakes.

- Attendees can expect to pay a healthy entrance fee, which is easily justified in order to cover high insurance premiums, rental of the hall or festival grounds, a mess of Porta-Potties, advertising, and festival glassware (the glasses may become collector's items, especially if they're dated).

- If the cost of the beer itself isn't included in the entrance fee, then serving tickets or tokens may be purchased for a little more than pocket change. Some festivals serve as little as 1 ounce per beer (usually the festivals with all-inclusive entrance fees, of course), while others allow as much as 10- or 12-ounce servings — but this amount is more of an exception than the rule.

Beer festivals aren't just places to taste-test beer nowadays. Many of these extravaganzas now feature homebrew demonstrations, cooking-with-beer seminars, book signings, and sponsored booths peddling all kinds of beer-related goods and paraphernalia. At the smaller festivals, one of the treats is to chat with the brewer and get the sense of passion and artistry that's so much a part of craft brewing. However, as festivals tend to grow (and grow in popularity), meeting with the brewer is, unfortunately, becoming rare. Staff or volunteers do the pouring and talking now.

In the following sections, I provide some handy pointers on enjoying yourself at a beer festival, and I list some of the best festivals in North America.

If you're really into beer and fun, you can ask to volunteer to be a server or guide at a festival — a good idea whose time has come and whose rewards (guess what) are simple.

Discovering beer festival do's and don'ts

As a slightly jaded veteran of many local, regional, and national beer festivals, I've come up with a list of do's and don'ts to maximize your enjoyment and learning at beer festivals — it's a rough job, but hey, somebody's gotta do it.

The do's

The do's of attending a beer festival include the following:

- Bring a designated nondrinking driver or scout out public transportation.

- Get there early to avoid a huge crowd. Crowds can hinder any conversation you may try to have with a brewer. And parking is usually less of a problem for early birds. You may also want to leave earlier if traffic and congestion are issues.

✔ Take, use, and keep your festival program. The large and well-established festivals hand out detailed programs loaded with fun and educational information that may be useful for months beyond the festival date. Plus, you need to keep on top of the schedule for demonstrations and classes if they're offered.

✔ Wear comfortable shoes; expect to walk and stand around a lot — and possibly get your toes stepped on. Beer festivals aren't known for lounge-chair seating accommodations.

✔ Dress appropriately. Protect yourself from the elements if the festival is outdoors.

✔ Bring along a small backpack or large fanny pack if they're allowed. Most large indoor festivals no longer allow backpacks.

✔ Bring a portable container of drinking water. Too often, the glass-rinsing stations are out of water, and drinking fountains are either hard to find or draw long lines. Heat, humidity, and beer drinking aren't the best partners. Dehydration is a problem worth avoiding. You also want to rinse your palate, don't you?

✔ Bring bread, pretzels, crackers, or some kind of munchies (avoid greasy or spicy items if you're taking your tasting seriously).

✔ Bring a pen or pencil and a small pad of paper and take (legible) notes of the beers you taste. You'd be surprised how valuable good notes can be the next time you visit your favorite beer store or festival. You'd also be surprised at how much you can forget after four hours of beer tasting!

✔ Accept anything handed out for free. You may not want all the buttons, pins, coasters, posters, and matchbooks, but someone you know may — and they're *free!*

The don'ts

The don'ts of attending a beer festival include the following:

✔ Don't let lousy weather keep you from going to an outdoor beer festival unless the weather is *seriously* bad. Most festivals are shielded from the elements under large tents. A little rain in your beer isn't a problem.

✔ Don't go to a beer festival on an empty stomach unless you're sure that food is being served there. Most beer festivals offer food, but quality and variety can vary greatly. Festival concessions can also be ridiculously expensive.

✔ Don't bring children. For the safety of your child as well as for your own enjoyment, find an alternative to dragging Junior along with you.

✔ Don't buy a book or any other heavy item until you're ready to leave, or else you'll have to lug it around with you. Of course, they may sell out by then, too!

✔ Don't stand around the pouring table after receiving your beer. Nothing is more irritating than having to fight through a crowd to get to the beer. Get outta da way, already!

✔ Don't hang out all day or night at the table that serves your favorite beer. Be bold, be experimental — try those beers that you can't get at the local Liquor Barn. Beer festivals are the best places to learn about a wide variety of unusual beers and beer styles. Don't make one place your corner tavern.

✔ Don't make tasting every single beer at the festival your goal. In some cases it can't be done; and in most cases, it shouldn't be.

✔ Don't drive after drinking beer all afternoon or evening.

Looking at notable beer festivals in the United States, Canada, and Mexico

The following list offers just a few of the better-known festivals in the United States, Canada, and Mexico. New ones are being organized faster than you can say, "Hoppapalooza." To find out about more festivals, keep up your contacts at brewpubs and homebrew-supply shops and check out websites that are dedicated to beer festivals, such as www.beerfestivals.org. Then again, you can always use Google.

✔ **Microbrew Festival (Eugene, Oregon), second week of February:** Estimated 100 brews are represented from 50 breweries. This festival's focus is on Pacific Northwest beers, but others are welcome. It also features live entertainment. For more information, contact microbrew festival@klcc.org.

✔ **American Craft Beer Fest (ACBF) (Boston, Massachusetts), first week of May:** The ACBF is East Coast's largest celebration of American beer, featuring more than 100 American brewers and more than 500 beers! For more information, check out www.beeradvocate.com/acbf.

✔ **Mondial de la bière (Montreal, Canada), second week of June:** A ten-day festival, billed as "the largest international beer festival in North America," attracts more than 50,000 attendees and features beers from five continents. The festival is held in the Old Port/Old Montreal area. Check out www.festivalmondialbiere.qc.ca for more information.

✔ **Colorado Brewers' Festival (Fort Collins, Colorado), June:** Nearly 60 Colorado beers and 30 Colorado breweries are represented at this festival, which includes great live music in historic downtown Fort Collins. For more information, check out www.downtownfortcollins.com/dba.php/brewfest.

✔ **Nando's Canada Cup of Beer (Vancouver, Canada), second week of July:** Vancouver's largest beer festival features more than 200 different beers. For more information, check out www.canadacupofbeer.com.

- ✔ **Great Taste of the Midwest (Madison, Wisconsin), second week of August:** This festival is hosted by the Madison Homebrewers & Tasters Guild and is the oldest and best one-day event in the Midwest — always a sellout. More than 119 breweries participated in 2011. Contact greattaste@mhtg.org and/or check out www.mhtg.org/great-taste-of-the-midwest for more info.

- ✔ **Great American Beer Festival (Denver, Colorado), late September or early October:** The granddaddy of American beer festivals celebrated its 30th year in 2011. The GABF hosts the single largest conglomeration of beers and brewers in America, with more than 3,500 beers from more than 450 breweries across the nation. This festival is always the biggest and the best. For details, check out www.gabf.org.

- ✔ **Congreso Cerveza Mexico: Por la Cerveza Libre (Mexico City, Mexico), early September:** Because craft brewing is new to Mexico, so are beer-centered festivals. This beer festival, which happens to be the largest of its kind in Mexico, is actually part of a national Gourmet Show. Check out: www.cervezamexico.mx/.

Exploring North American Beer Museums

Beer enthusiasts often can't stop at the direct experience. Craving ever-more sudsy stimulation, they veer off the beaten track to the more contemplative scene of brewing museums. The few U.S. museums aren't known for their completeness or their scholarly approach to the topic, but they come in enough variations to warrant exploration. Here are a few you may want to check out:

- ✔ **August Schell Brewing Company (New Ulm, Minnesota):** An operating brewery since 1860, this museum's tours include the brewery, the Schell family mansion, a deer park, and an on-site museum. Phone 507-354-5528; website www.schellsbrewery.com/home.php.

- ✔ **F. X. Matt Brewery, formerly the West End Brewery (Utica, New York):** This museum is a veritable repository of antique brewery advertising; memorabilia is showcased on every wall of the brewery hospitality center. Phone 315-732-3181; website www.saranac.com.

Like the F. X. Matt Brewery, most of the oldest and largest breweries in the United States display a wealth of brewery antiques and advertising memorabilia. Check out the D. G. Yuengling & Son Brewery in Pottsville, Pennsylvania (www.yuengling.com), and the Jacob Leinenkugel Brewery in Chippewa Falls, Wisconsin (www.leinie.com).

- ✔ **Joseph Wolf Brewery Caves (Stillwater, Minnesota):** These caves are part of a museum of an 1870 brewery. If you check this place out, you may just find out why a good brewmaster has bad teeth. Phone 651-430-0560; website www.lunarossawinebar.com/cavetour.html.

- **Les Brasseurs Du Temps (Gatineau, Quebec):** This brewing heritage museum, located within the Brasseurs Du Temps brewery, exhibits more than 160 years of brewing artifacts and history. The tour is self-guided and free. Website www.brasseursdutemps.com/museum.

- **100 Center (Mishawaka, Indiana):** A shopping, dining, and entertaining experience, this museum is listed on the National Register of Historic Places and occupies the buildings that once housed the Kamm & Schellinger Brewing Company in 1853. Plenty of relics are left from the old brewery. Website www.centerforhistory.org/learn-history/business-history/mishawaka-kamm-and-schellinger-brewery.

- **The Pabst Mansion (Milwaukee, Wisconsin):** Captain Frederick Pabst, founder of the Pabst Brewery, built this mansion in 1893. It's considered the finest Flemish Renaissance Revival mansion in the United States and a testament to Pabst's success, his love of life, and his German heritage. Phone 414-931-0808; website www.pabstmansion.com.

- **Potosi Brewing Company (Potosi, Wisconsin):** The National Brewing Museum's mission is to present the history of America's breweries by preserving and exhibiting brewery memorabilia. Phone 608-763-4002; website www.potosibrewery.com.

- **Seattle Microbrewery Museum (Seattle, Washington):** Part of Pike Brewing Company in the Pike Place Historical District, this museum hosts a collection about the history of brewing in the northwest United States. Phone 206-622-6044; website www.pikebrewing.com.

Where does a 2,000-pound horse sleep?

The Budweiser Clydesdales weigh up to 2,300 pounds and stand nearly 6 feet tall at the shoulder. Each horse may consume as much as 30 quarts of feed, 50 pounds of hay, and 30 gallons of water every day (no figures are available for beer consumption).

The ornate Clydesdale stables at the Anheuser-Busch brewing facility in St. Louis, Missouri, have been designated a National Historic Landmark and are a top tourist attraction. Check out www.budweisertours.com/toursSTL.htm for more information.

Chapter 16

Trying Beer in Europe, Asia, and Elsewhere

*O*kay, beer fans: If you've got the beer bug bad, you're going to want to experience firsthand the thrill of drinking fresh beer where it's always been loved most, made best, and served just right. Yes, I'm talking about Europe (though the United States isn't exactly dry — see Chapter 15). Although beer wasn't born in Europe, it grew up there and became the world's most popular beverage because of European brewers; commercial brewing has been serious business in Europe since the 12th century. So now's the time to do some serious beer touring. After all, don't you want to someday be able to say, "Ah, yes — been there, drank that!"

Outside Europe — with the possible exception of Australia — probably only the United States and Canada have created a beer culture you can actually visit. No other countries offer a beer enthusiast much to explore. The major breweries established outside Europe and North America have generally been created by German or British brewers (the home of Tsingtao beer in China looks like a Bavarian village) and aren't distinctly local; the recipes and the styles are European (mostly light lagers, although Stouts are brewed in Ghana, Nigeria, South Africa, Sri Lanka, Barbados, Jamaica, and Singapore, among other places). So let's face it: World beer travel — just like world beer styles — is mostly European beer travel.

You can drink well or revel in beer stuff in almost all European countries, but the crown jewels of beerdom for beer tourists are, hands down, Germany, the United Kingdom, Ireland, Belgium, and the Czech Republic. I explore these locations and more in this chapter. Certified beer nuts, your pilgrimage awaits, complete with beer shrines (biggest, oldest, original, and so on). For the more sane among you, a little bit of beer trekking can provide a really great accent to a more normal trip, say a business trip or a family vacation. (Flip to Chapter 17 for general information on beer travel and tours.)

Building Your Own Beer Adventure

The pub culture in most of the major brewing nations is mostly intact, and a visit to practically any local bar is likely to yield a good beer discovery. In Germany, the sheer number of breweries may overwhelm you (Bavaria alone has more than 600), while beer trekkers in Belgium may get thoroughly bewildered by the variety of unusual beer styles served at any given bar.

The best way to get over being confused and overwhelmed is to get a little serious. Start tasting the beers deliberately and without apprehension. As you would at a beer tasting or festival, take good notes — preferably on paper, but coasters and bar napkins will do in a pinch. Anywhere you land in these countries, be an intrepid beer explorer: Ask for something local, something full of flavor. By keeping a record, your experience is transformed into a keepsake (and also may make more sense). A record also helps when you get back home and want to buy bottled versions of what you tasted on your trek.

Some of the best beer parties anywhere in the world are European festivals. Quite often rooted in religious or obscure historical contexts, they now usually serve only as modern-day justifications for fun. Joyous celebration is the purpose of these festivities; beer is an integral means to that end. And joining the party is easy!

The Campaign For Real Ale (CAMRA) is *the* source for information on good beer in the United Kingdom and on the continent. In addition to reeducating their countrymen about traditional, cask-conditioned real ale (see Chapter 5 for more information), the folks at CAMRA publish the best, most incredibly detailed guides for the beer-oriented tourist (notes include "real fire in fireplace," "family room," and "traditional pub games played"). *The Good Beer Guide* lists more than 5,000 pubs in Great Britain (England, Wales, Scotland, Northern Ireland, and the Channel Islands, all listed by county) that serve good cask-conditioned ale; nothing but the real thing makes it into this passionate beer guide. Another CAMRA book *Good Pub Food* helps with notes on a lesser form of nourishment. CAMRA also has similar guides to Bavaria, Belgium, and Holland. (Check out www.camra.org.uk for details on how to pick up these guides.)

Exploring Beer in Germany

You've no doubt heard that Germans like beer and that they kind of wrote the book on brewing. Despite the fact that the number of breweries in the United States (1,700 as of this writing) has eclipsed the number of breweries in Germany (holding strong at 1,200), nowhere is the beer culture more established and ingrained (pun intended) than in Germany.

Few people are aware that beer in Germany is very localized. Because of the number of breweries, and in particular the number of breweries per capita,

Germany is pretty well saturated with beer on a local level. Due to this circumstance, there's never been any need or motivation for German brewers to market or ship their beers very far from the brewery. Hence, high-profile export brands that have come to represent German beer in other countries, such as Becks or St. Pauli Girl, are virtually unknown outside their own region in Germany.

I've heard similar complaints all too often: Disgruntled beer travelers bemoan the fact that they can't get a Kolschbier in Hamburg or a Rauchbier in Heidelberg. These beers, like most in Germany, are local products rarely found outside their towns of origin. The well-prepared beer trekker in Germany knows this and plans accordingly.

About the only style of beer you can expect to find in virtually any location throughout Germany is the ubiquitous German Pils, a paler, hoppier version of the venerable Bohemian Pilsner.

German brewers shortened the name from Pilsner to Pils when the Czech brewers from Pilsen threatened to take legal action against them.

In the following sections, you discover all you've ever wanted to know about beer in Germany, including the beer regions, the biggest beer towns, and the best festivals and museums that are just begging for a visit.

Discovering regional tastes: The north, west, and east

One generalization about beer in Germany that seems to hold up is that drier, hoppier beers can be found in the north, while maltier, sweeter beers are found in the south. That leaves midrange beers in the middle. Good examples of this generalization are the bracingly bitter and dry Jever Pils, brewed in the northern province of Friesland, and the mouthfillingly malty Augustiner Edelstoff, brewed in the southern state of Bavaria (see the next section for more about this state). The well-balanced and flavorful Dortmunder-style lager can be found in central Germany — look for the brand DAB (Dortmunder Actien Brauerei).

Two other beer styles of notable exception in west central Germany are Kolschbier and Altbier. First, these two hybrid brews are about as close as German brewers get to producing ales (see Chapter 4 for details on different beer styles). Second, you're unlikely to find Altbier very far outside the region near Düsseldorf, and good luck trying to find Kolschbier outside Koln's (Cologne) city limits. Popular brands to search for are Zum Uerige Altbier and P.J. Früh Kolschbier.

Kölsch is a protected appellation in Koln. Only the 20 or so brewers in and around Koln may use this word *Kölsch* to advertise their product.

While most breweries in the former East Germany plodded along brewing unremarkable lagers for 40 years under communist rule, one beer style in particular remained popular in Berlin: *Berliner Weisse* is singularly unique among German beers; it's not a lager, and it's not a Weizenbier (or Weissbier). Weisse — purposely spelled with a final *e* — is a pale and tart refreshing beer. Look for the Schultheiss or Berliner Kindl brands.

Consider it a feather in your cap or a notch in your belt (and a beer in your belly) if you happen to find another unusual beer style in the Eastern German states called *Gose,* or *Leipziger Gose.* This light and highly carbonated tart beer shares much in common with Berliner Weisse but is a bit harder to find.

Gose takes its name from the town of Goslar. It became very popular in the nearby town of Leipzig but almost vanished in the early to mid-20th century. Thankfully, due to the determination of a few brewers, the Gose style hasn't been lost forever and is undergoing something of a revival. Now a handful of breweries are producing it after an absence of more than 30 years.

Gose is a spontaneously fermented beer — similar to Belgian Lambic — and is sometimes given a dose of coriander and salt for flavoring.

Heading south to Bavaria

Of the estimated 1,200 breweries in Germany, most are in the southern state of Bavaria and the region of Franconia, centered near Munich and Bamberg.

Munich alone is home to a dozen brewers of various sizes, some of whose brands are easily found in the United States: Spaten, Augustiner, Hacker-Pschorr, Löwenbräu, Paulaner, and Hofbräu. Each of these six breweries also operates beer halls in Munich; all are outstanding places to sample the local fare (Muncheners consume more beer than just about any other group of people). During the hot summer months, entire families flock to the many refreshing beer gardens; and at some, you bring your own food. Even better are the local, small breweries scattered mostly throughout Bavaria. The entire experience is much better than you can ever find back home (wherever that is), just in case you need another excuse to go.

Even though Munich is the romanticized center of beer in Germany, the actual beer center is the northern Bavarian region of Franconia and the town of Bamberg. More than 300 breweries are in Franconia, and around nine or so are in the town of Bamberg alone. Bamberg's breweries don't have the same level of name recognition as those in Munich, but they're every bit as worthy of your attention (and your taste buds). Look for the Kaiserdom, Fässla, and Schlenkerla brands.

Bamberg is considered the Rauchbier (smoked beer) capital of the world. Several of the brewers there use malt smoked over beechwood fires to give their beer its unusual and esoteric flavor — that to some folks smells and tastes like liquid ham or even bacon. Admittedly, Rauchbier isn't for everyone, but everyone who visits Bamberg should at least try it once; it helps to have a plate of cheddar cheese or smoked sausage within arm's reach.

Elsewhere in Bavaria, finding a brewery worth visiting and a beer worth drinking is easy. I recommend the following, not only for their locations but also for their ties to their religious past:

✔ The baroque Kloster Ettal in the quaint southern Bavarian town of Ettal produces wonderful beer, and a visit to the basilica offers a glimpse of the impressive murals that grace the interior of the huge dome.

✔ The monastery of Andechs, southwest of Munich, is accessible by car or train. Situated at the top of a hill, it affords a nice view of the countryside. What better place to sit out in the Biergarten and quaff a few steins of some of the best dark lager made in all of Germany!

✔ The Weihenstephan Brewery in the northern Munich suburb of Freising is a former Benedictine Brewery that's been in operation for nearly a thousand years. Weihenstephan is the oldest operating brewery in the world, dating back to 1040. Okay, the brewery did burn down four times in its history, but with typical Bavarian tenacity, it was always rebuilt. Smoked beer, anyone?

Weihenstephan Hefeweizen is one of the best Bavarian-style Wheat Beers in the world — so much so that its yeast is even considered a proprietary ingredient.

The seven-minute pour

In Germany, you're likely to encounter something virtually unknown in the United States, or anywhere else for that matter: the *seven-minute pour*. This pour is a way of serving a beer with a firm, rocky head that can rise up and over the rim of the glass without spilling.

This method requires the bartender to draw beer into the same glass three or four times, each time allowing a couple of minutes for the head to properly condense and strengthen. So customers aren't waiting a full seven minutes for their beer, a good bartender has several glasses waiting at various stages of readiness.

One Chicago-area brewer of a high-quality Pilsner beer (Baderbrau) once asked all his draught outlets to serve his beer this way but was scoffed at: They all said that no American would ever wait that long for a beer. That brewer is no longer in business.

Tapping German shrines, festivals, and museums

The following sections list notable shrines, festivals, and museums in Germany. *Tip:* Although you can find many well-known brands of German beer within Germany, try the local brewers' products wherever you go, regardless of the name. You can be sure liquid treasure is just waiting to be found.

Shrines

Here are some beer shrines to visit in Germany. Note that you can't taste all Munich's beers at one place: Each place either has its few favorites or is a *tied house,* which is owned by one of the breweries and features only that brewer's brand. Good guides list the beers served at each location.

- **The Hofbräuhaus (court brewhouse), Munich:** This is the oldest and most famous beer hall in all of Germany (and thus, probably, the world). Because of its enormity (it can seat more than 4,000 people on three levels), its antiquity (it was commissioned in 1589 by Duke Wilhelm V), and political history (both Adolf Hitler and Vladimir Lenin plotted here), the beer may seem secondary, but it's not! Standards plus seasonals, such as Delicator in March, Maibock in May, and Märzen from September to October, are all wonderful.

- **Zum Uerige, Düsseldorf:** This brewpub of local renown is said to brew the finest Altbier in all of Germany.

- **Köln:** Any one of the dozens of small local brewhouses (P.J. Früh is a tourist favorite) serve the local delicacy, Kölsch beer.

- **Villages:** Some small villages boast their own breweries, each with a distinctive recipe. Try the local stuff: The perfect liter may await you (and modern ways make these small-fries somewhat endangered).

Festivals

Germany has no shortage of festivals at which you can enjoy the local brews. To attend one is to experience what Germans call *gemütlichkeit,* a distinctly German easy-going, genial good time. At the top of the heap is the revered and sometimes reviled Oktoberfest. Many others occur throughout the year and throughout Bavaria.

- **Fasching (Bavaria), February:** The German equivalent of Mardi Gras, a raucous pre-Lenten celebration, Fasching (fasting) is celebrated primarily throughout Bavaria, which has Germany's greatest concentration of Catholics.

- ✔ **Starkbierfest (Munich), March:** Referred to as Munich's secret beer festival, the Starkbierfest is every bit as big and rowdy as the Oktoberfest, but it's devoid of stark commercialism and drunken tourists (but not necessarily drunken Muncheners). The Starkbierfest (strong beer fest) is held when the city is still shaking off the winter chill. The Starkbierfest is a celebration of the annual release of the Doppelbocks (*Doppelbock,* locally called a *spring beer cure,* usually sets the alcohol meter off at 7.5 percent alcohol by volume).

- ✔ **Schützenfeste (Hanover), July:** This beer festival is held throughout Germany, but the most notable one is held each July in Hanover. Originally a sharpshooter's competition, this gathering of civil vigilante groups has been diluted over the centuries to become just another good excuse to have a beer party.

- ✔ **Oktoberfest (Munich), September to October:** Ironically, this most famous fest *ends* on the first Sunday in October, having begun the second-to-last Saturday in September. All Oktoberfests began as harvest-time country fairs, but Munich's Oktoberfest bears little resemblance to a country fair today. More than 6 million people attend the event every year, the majority of whom don't live in Munich — or Germany, for that matter! Reservations are essential (full meals are served, and you can drink only when sitting down). Many travel agents sponsor all-inclusive tours. Some *country fair* — it even has its own website (www.munich-tourist.de)!

- ✔ **Cannstatter Volksfest (Stuttgart), October:** This autumn festival, considerably smaller than Munich's Oktoberfest, harkens back to the days of the simple country fairs. Noticeably missing are the tourists, but the beer is every bit as good and plentiful. Bavarian locals are more likely to do their celebrating here. The Volksfest begins just about the time Munich's debauch comes to a close.

Museums

Because beer is so much a part of German history and culture (and because museums are great places to learn more about local history and culture), you can't be a true beer trekker in Germany without visiting a few beer museums:

- ✔ **Brauerei Museum (Dortmund):** This beer museum is located in what used to be part of Kronen Beer Works. Check out its website at www. brauereimuseum.dortmund.de/en.

- ✔ **Brauereimuseum (Lüneburg):** Located in a building that served as a brewery for more than 500 years, the centerpiece of this museum is a large stein collection.

- ✔ **Schwaebisches Brauereimuseum (Stuttgart):** If you're in the area, be sure to check out this museum of brewing history as well as current brewing techniques.

German mixed beer drinks

In June 1922, when Franz Kugler, an enterprising young Munich tavern owner, blazed a bicycle path through the woods that skirted his Gasthaus property, more than 13,000 cyclists tried it out. Realizing an impending shortage of blond beer, Kugler quickly decided to mix the more plentiful dark beer with bottles of clear lemon soda, which he happened to have in abundance. Not one to miss a promotional opportunity, Kugler told the cyclists that this concoction was something he invented especially for them so they wouldn't get too tired or inebriated for their ride home. The *Radlermass* (bicyclist's mug), as he named it, became a hit, and mixed beer drinks were born.

Here's a rundown of other mixed beer drinks you may encounter in Germany:

- **Altbierbowle:** Altbier poured over a goblet or small bowl of fresh fruit — popular in the region near Düsseldorf, long associated with Altbier.

- **Alt Schuss (alt shot):** Equal parts Altbier and cola.

- **Alsterwasser (Alster water):** Equal parts light lager (the Munich Helles type, not light beer) and lemonade or lemon soda.

- **Bierbowle:** Like the Altbierbowle, but for half a dozen people: six 12-ounce bottles of light lager, 8 ounces strained sour cherries, the ground pulp of 1 whole lemon, 2½ tablespoons sugar, and 12 ounces whisky, served cold.

- **Biergrog:** A heated mixture of dark beer (12 ounces), 3 tablespoons sugar, and grated lemon peel to taste.

- **Bismarck:** Dark beer mixed with Champagne — a favorite of Prussian Chancellor Otto von Bismarck.

- **Heller Moritz:** Equal parts Wheat Beer and Champagne or sparkling wine.

- **Honigbier (honey beer):** A heated mixture of light lager, 1½ tablespoons honey, ¼ cup oatmeal, and shot of whisky (optional).

- **Lüttje Lage:** More of an exercise in manual dexterity than a drink: In northern Germany, the *tricky devil* is performed by hoisting two small glasses held between the digits of the same hand. One glass, held above the other, contains whisky or schnapps that pours into the lower glass (filled with beer) as it is poured into the mouth.

- **Russ:** Wheat Beer and lemon soda.

- **Schaumbier (foam beer):** A heated mixture of light lager with 2 eggs, ½ cup sugar, and grated lemon peel beaten together.

Looking at Beer in the United Kingdom

The United Kingdom may lack the number of brewers that Germany has, but it makes up for it in the variety of beers offered and the sheer number of pubs — an estimated 55,000. This beer-trekking stuff is hard work if you want to visit even a small percentage of pubs.

The United Kingdom is the ale stronghold of the world. Similar to the U.S. brewing industry, a handful of large, national breweries dominate the market, but several hundred brewpubs, micros, and regional brewers produce the more interesting and more flavorful interpretations of traditional styles for impassioned consumers, especially cask-conditioned ale (unpasteurized, unfiltered, naturally carbonated, handpumped beer; also called *real ale* — see Chapter 5).

These delicate brews are treated locally like estate-bottled wines are in France, and with reason: They don't travel — further justification to go there yourself. Ironically, even the beer made by the British national brewers (such as Bass) is considered good stuff in the United States. In short, one drinks well in Great Britain. So whether you're trekking to England, Wales, or Scotland — or all three — in the following sections, I provide a little background for the beer you'll find in these places and point out the best pubs and festivals the United Kingdom has to offer.

Biting the bitters in England and Wales

Almost any pub in England or Wales offers the British standard, *Bitter,* but the Bitter style isn't so bitter — it's fairly light-bodied, softly carbonated, and light in alcohol (*bitter* is an ancient tag dating from when hops were first used). Bitters can be found on draught as Ordinary Bitter, Best Bitter, and Extra Special Bitter (also known as ESB). This lineup of beers isn't simply in ascending order of quality; these designations also refer to the body and strength of these beers relative to each other. In truth, the differences are rather miniscule and barely perceptible to the untrained palate — just something you should know.

Not all pubs offer a wide array of styles, but many do feature big, bold, and brawny beers, such as Old Ales and Barleywines (see Chapter 4 and Appendix A), so strong (8 to 12 percent alcohol) that they may well put you under the table quicker than you can say, "Llanfairpwllgwyngyllgogerychwyrndrobwllllantysiliogogogoch" (which happens to be the town in Wales with the longest name in the world).

Many of the pubs in the United Kingdom are *tied houses* — they're at least partly owned by a brewery and, therefore, can serve the beers only of that particular brewery. You can usually spot a tied house by the mention of the brewery, or the beer served within, on the pub sign. If you want to try a variety of lesser-known beers, avoid the tied houses.

Pub games

Regardless of a pub's ownership or the beers served, pub games are popular throughout the United Kingdom. Some beer nuts consider pub games to be central to British culture, if not the embodiment of it. They aren't, but they are fun.

Darts, of course, are commonplace, but other lesser-known games — cribbage, dominoes, and the British pub favorite *skittles* (a table-top version of nine-pin bowling that uses finger-sized skittles, or pins) — can often be seen in play.

Great Britain's great pub grub

The old pub grub standbys include plough-man's lunch (cheese and bread plate), steak and kidney pie, shepherd's pie (beef, potatoes, and veggies), bangers and mash (sausage and mashed potatoes), pasties (a northern variation on shepherd's pie), and the ever-present fish and chips (the British version of a burger and fries). Other gustatory treats may include upside-down pie (stilton cheese and bacon), jacket spud (baked potato), curries, vegetable hot-pot, and Yorkshire pudding. In Scotland, you can investigate gammon steak (ham), neeps and tatties (turnips and potatoes), and haggis (you don't want to know).

Beer drinkers new to the United Kingdom may be taken aback by the odd, humorous, and sometimes vulgar names given to British beers by their brewers: Baz's Bonce Blower, Bishop's Tipple, Blackout, Croaker, Double Dagger, Enoch's Hammer, Head Cracker, Once a Knight, Roger & Out, Tanglefoot, Topsy-Turvy, Willie Warmer, and Wobbly Bob can all be ordered without putting your tongue in your cheeks; others may put a little blush in them.

Holding strong with Scotland

Scotland accounts for only about 10 percent of all the pubs in the United Kingdom, but that's understandable considering that Scotland is a much less populous country. Heck, the Scottish people are even outnumbered by sheep in their own land by a margin of 5 to 1!

Due to its more northerly climes, Scotland has a tradition of producing fuller-bodied, dark, malty ales. And they're no strangers to stronger libations, either — whisky notwithstanding. Their strong Scotch Ale is well respected in other countries, most notably Belgium.

That said, Scottish brewers also produce lighter-bodied beers. In fact, for every style of Bitter British brewers make, there's a Scottish equivalent — though they're still darker and maltier than Bitter. The beers I speak of are called Scottish Ales (duh!), and they're identified by an antiquated shilling designation.

At the lightest end of the beer spectrum is 60 shilling (which is lighter bodied than anything brewed by a corporate brewer in the United States), followed by a 70 shilling, the equivalent to an ordinary Bitter. The 80 shilling — also called Export — is the equivalent of a Best Bitter.

The aforementioned Scotch Ale weighs in at about 120 shilling, but it's not referred to as such. Scotch Ales are known locally as *Wee Heavy* and are the Caledonian equivalent of Old Ale or Barleywine (8 to 12 percent) in terms of alcoholic strength.

Exploring shrines, festivals, and museums in the United Kingdom

Britain has a long and illustrious past, much of which is infused with beer. What better way to acquaint yourself with British history than experiencing it through beer-related events and locations? Here are some highlights to check out:

- **U.K. breweries and brewpubs:** The United Kingdom has too many good breweries to put on the A list — you'll never see them all. Your best bet is to check out the local pubs in each town (some tours make a point of this). Most pubs offer good food and even better beer, not to mention an excellent opportunity to mix with the locals and hear interesting stories about past customers. Plenty of guidebooks and tours in the bigger cities exist for this purpose. (If you're a Charles Dickens fan, you'll feel quite at home at the Saracen's Head, in Bath, where Dickens wrote *The Pickwick Papers*.)

- **The Traquair House, Innerleithen, Scotland:** A four-story manor house (now a museum) has not only a small working brewery but also an abundance of history dating back to the 1500s. (Bonnie Prince Charlie, leader of the Jacobite rebellion against the English Monarchy, supped here.) You won't want to miss the Traquair House Ale.

- **Edinburgh, Scotland:** A great town for walking, Edinburgh's numerous pubs also make it perfect for *pub crawls* (walking tours of local public houses at which the "wares" are tasted). Rose Street in the New Town section has Britain's highest density of pubs per square foot. Many serve cask-conditioned ale. Ales are usually labeled by strength, as in Light, Heavy, Export, and Wee Heavy (so strong it must be served in wee servings). Alternative units are expressed as 60 to 90 shillings.

- **Southeastern England:** In addition to visiting the breweries and pubs, if you're here in the late summer or early autumn, check out the famous hop farms that dot the countryside in Kent County, "the Garden of England" and home of the famed East Kent Golding variety. The high trellises are amazing.

CAMRA's *Good Beer Guide* lists more than 100 festivals by date and location, complete with local phone numbers. Its local branches also organize regional beer festivals throughout the country and throughout the year. Consult CAMRA's monthly newsletter, *What's Brewing* (check out www.camra.org. uk for details).

One festival I recommend is the Great British Beer Festival in London, England. Held each year in August, in the Grand Hall at Olympia, the CAMRA is responsible for putting together this largest beer festival on British soil, said to rival the Great American Beer Festival in Denver, Colorado (see Chapter 15). In addition to hundreds of varieties of beer and cider, the festival offers pub games, collectibles, publications, and contact with various beer-related organizations.

English mixed beer drinks

Germans aren't the only ones who like to make mixed drinks with beer. The Brits are also quite fond of the practice. Here are some British favorites:

- **Black Velvet:** Stout and Champagne: According to pub lore, the Stout represents the common folk, and the Champagne represents nobility (what a tired old stereotype). This drink goes great with oysters.

- **Brown Betty:** Ale and brandy served warm. In Old England, this drink was served with spiced toast intended for dipping.

- **Brown Velvet:** Stout and port wine.

 The best way to experience U.K. beers and culture is to visit the local pubs. No matter where you are, you're likely to see many of the same beer styles featured on tap; what's most likely to change is the brand names. Also be on the lookout for anything on handpump; real ales are the real way to enjoy British beer (see Chapter 5).

When it comes to brewing museums in the United Kingdom, the National Brewery Centre in Burton upon Trent, Staffsordshire, is my top pick. This museum celebrates Burton upon Trent's renowned brewing heritage and its influence on brewing techniques used around the world. Check it out at www. nationalbrewerycentre.co.uk.

Getting a Taste of Ireland

Ironically, though well known for both its wonderful pub culture (the tales! the music!) and internationally successful brewers Guinness, Murphy, and Beamish, Ireland doesn't have many breweries, museums, or festivals, but it does have plenty of pubs — wonderful pubs. Dry Stout is the national brew, and the major brands display a range of dryness. However, don't think you can't find other tasty ales and lagers or that Ireland isn't worth the trip, because you can and it is. I show you how and where in the following sections.

Brewing Guinness for the nation

When Arthur Guinness started his brewery in 1759, he could never have foreseen the results of his efforts. His beer, the venerable Guinness Stout, would become the national drink of Ireland (though some may argue in favor of Jameson's Whiskey).

The Guinness Brewery celebrated its 250th anniversary in 2009. In addition to being the national drink of Ireland, Guinness is also brewed in more than 40 countries around the world. An estimated 10 million pints of Guinness Stout are consumed every day.

While Guinness may very well be good for you (according to a popular Guinness slogan, anyway), it's not inherently better than the other Dry Stouts found on the Emerald Isle. Both Murphy's (established in 1792) and Beamish (established in 1883) hail from County Cork and can accompany corned beef and cabbage equally well.

Going beyond traditional Dry Stout

Another style of beer is attributed to Ireland, though it's actually fading in popularity. *Red Ales,* as they came to be known, are malt-driven brews that were typically deep copper in color. Ireland's most famous exported brand — George Killian Lett — is credited with popularizing the wave of red beers in the United States back in the 1980s and 1990s.

The Coors Brewing Company acquired the rights to George Killian's Ruby Ale and marketed it in the United States as Killian's Red Ale — though that it was ever brewed by Coors as an ale is doubtful. Eventually, Coors simply shortened the name to Killian's Red, and no one ever questioned its stylistic authenticity.

Two other national brands you're likely to encounter in Ireland are Smithwicks (pronounced *smitticks*) Ale and Harp Lager. A subsidiary of Guinness produces Harp, which is one of the few domestically produced lagers.

Unfortunately, much of Ireland's brewing heritage is giving way to the increasingly popular lagers, mostly big-name brands imported from Europe and America. Irish youth seem to care little for Guinness Stout and its stodgy ilk.

Checking in to Irish breweries and pubs

Ireland is similar to England in its pub culture; in fact, Ireland's pub culture may even be more deeply rooted. Before trekking beyond the Wicklow Mountains, be sure to linger a bit longer in Dublin and savor its beery delights.

A trip to Dublin (and frankly, a trip to Ireland) isn't complete without a stop at the Guinness Brewery. Established in 1759, the Guinness St. James Gate Brewery produces the world's finest Dry Stout. Check out the Guinness Museum for the history of brewing in Ireland, beer advertising, brewing equipment, cooper's tools, and free samples of Guinness Stout.

Pub crawls are done with great flair in Dublin. With advice from the locals, you can improvise a traditional Irish music crawl; actors performing O'Casey, Beckett, Yeats, Joyce, Behand, and other Irish luminaries, with a little bit of local lore thrown in for good measure, lead the Literary Pub Crawl.

Sipping Beer in Belgium

Belgium is heaven for beer explorers. Beer is Belgium's claim to fame (in beer lovers' eyes), much as wine is to France. With more than 100 breweries (and almost ten times that a few generations ago) in a country of 10 million, you can see why. And the brewers produce more than 50 definitive styles, in more than ten times as many brands, including more famous specialty beers than any other nation.

Belgian gastronomy, unlike its history or sociology, is legendary among European countries, perhaps ranking a close second behind French *haute cuisine*. Featuring dishes made with beer or matched to beers, *cuisine à la bière* is a Belgian specialty not to be missed. Definitely seek it out.

Belgian brewers continue to produce beer styles developed over centuries — some still using yeast strains that are direct descendants of the originals. Some of these beer styles are indigenous to Belgium and made nowhere else in the world; others are emulated elsewhere, often with surprisingly good results. Either way, that necessitates a trip to sample the local beer, freshly made and freshly drawn, whether you visit a century-old brewhouse, a Trappist abbey, or one of the beer cafes, which I discuss in the following sections. The beer is often served in proprietary glassware, an interesting and amusing attraction in itself.

Trekking for secular brews

Like the beers they produce, many Belgian breweries are antiquated. The century-old brewhouses are like working museums. Some brewers even refuse to brush away the cobwebs, claiming that they don't want to disturb the spiders and the very essence of the brewery.

Having much in common with French wine regions, Belgium has its own beer regions. What you're likely to find locally depends greatly on where in Belgium you happen to be. Of course, if you're in Brussels or any metropolitan area, you shouldn't have trouble finding most of the Belgian specialty beers, but if you're travelling the countryside, then it becomes a regional thing. Fortunately, for fans of Trappist beers, the Trappist monasteries are fairly evenly spaced in the north and south of the country (see the next section).

If you're big on sour Red Ales, head west into Flanders; if Oud Bruin is your thing, aim for Oudenaarde. Lambic beers can be found southwest of Brussels, and fans of Witbier should experience it at its source in Hoegaarden (east of Brussels). (For more on these beer styles, see Chapter 4.)

Marketing Trappist beers and Abbeys

Six legitimate Trappist breweries — meaning that the beer is actually brewed in a brewery within a Trappist monastery and/or brewed by Trappist monks — exist in Belgium. Only beers brewed at one of these six locations can be legally marketed as Trappist beer. (There is a seventh Trappist brewery in Europe — Konigshoeven — but it's located across Belgium's border in The Netherlands.)

However, several secular breweries brew beers that are similar to Trappist beers, or they brew beers under license of monasteries that have no brewing facilities. These beers are limited to marketing their brews as *Abby, Abbey, Abbaye, Abdij,* or similar spellings. Don't be fooled by names like St. Feullien (note that the pronunciation of the first syllable is *fool*).

Finding the best Belgian shrines, festivals, and museums

Belgians are acutely aware that beer is a huge part of their national heritage, and they don't miss many opportunities to celebrate that fact. Hence, the beer trekker can always find something to visit or experience in Belgium.

Shrines

Though the Belgians are much more nonchalant about their incredible beer experiences, beer geeks consider tours of certain Belgian breweries, cities, or regions nothing less than pilgrimages to beer shrines. Here's a glance at some possibilities:

- ✔ **Abbey Road:** Trappist Ale fans should prearrange a visit to some of the six beer-producing Trappist abbeys in Belgium (you may want to include a seventh one across the border in The Netherlands, too): Rochefort, Scourmont (Chimay), and Orval in the south and southeast, Westmalle and Achel in the north, and Westvleteren (St. Bernardus) in the west. Not only do these abbeys produce beer for secular consumption, but some of them, such as Chimay and Orval, also produce abundant amounts of cheese and bread.

✔ **Lambic Lane:** Lovers of Lambic beer will want to take a spin on the Bruegel route, south and west of Brussels. Named for the famed Flemish painter, the route takes you through the villages that inspired his landscapes. In many of these villages, the unique Lambic Beer is either brewed or blended (blended Lambic Beer is called *Gueuze*).

✔ **Cafes:** All the larger cities (and many of the quainter towns) have at least one outstanding beer bar or cafe (cafes in Belgium are as widespread as pubs in England). Some cafes are known to stock as many as 500 different Belgian beers. Outside of Brussels, the medieval town of Bruges has more cafes than any other town of its size. Again, a location call is the only way to appreciate these cafes, so go! And see whether you can resist *pomme frites* (Belgian-style French fries) served with mayonnaise.

Festivals

Just like other countries with dynamic brewing industries, Belgium makes a point of celebrating beer in big and sometimes ostentatious ways. Here's a brief look at a few of Belgium's most popular festivals:

✔ **Poperinge Hopfeesten (Poperinge), every third September:** Poperinge is located in the middle of Belgium's small hop-growing region. This festival features a folkloric procession of townspeople, a hop-picking contest, and a lot of beer drinking. Unfortunately, the Hopfeesten is held only every three years — 2005, 2008, 2011, and so on. At other times, you can drive the 36-mile hop route around the region's hop farms.

✔ **Zythos Bier Fest (Leuven), April:** This festival, which moved to its new location of Leuven in 2011, is the closest thing to a national beer festival that Belgium has.

✔ **Adriaan Brouwer Bierfeesten (Oudenaarde), June:** This beer festival is an annual commemorative festival held yearly in honor of the famous painter (Adriaan Brouwer) born there in 1605.

The best and easiest way to enjoy the sometimes odd and unusual Belgian beers is to approach them with a completely open mind. Don't think of them as beer but rather a local delicacy. And sipping some of the Belgian brews with the delicious and often beer-inspired Belgian cuisine certainly wouldn't hurt either.

If you're looking for a break from Belgian specialty beers, you should have no trouble finding the best-selling Belgian Pilsner beer, Stella Artois, or one of equal quality, Maes. Even Belgium's least exciting beers are still pretty tasty.

Museums

Belgium also has its share of museums that are dedicated to beer and brewing. Some are big and grandiose, some are small and intimate, but all celebrate the mutual love of Belgian beer.

- **Het Brouwershuis or La Maison des Brasseurs (Brussels):** Though not a brewery, this palatial museum (headquarters of the Knights of the Mashing Fork and translated as Brewer's Guildhouse and Confederation of Belgian Brewers Museum) is one of the biggest beer shrines in all of Europe, appropriately located on Brouwersstraat (Brewer's Street) on the Grand-Place. In one of the city's greatest ironies, the famous fountain known as the Mannekin Pis (a cherubic child unburdening his bladder) is located right there, too.

- **De Geuzen Van Oud Beersel (Beersel):** Brewing artifacts in this small museum form an extension of the brewery tour. To arrange a brewery tour, go to www.degeuzenvanoudbeersel.be/en/home-en.

- **Brugse Brouwerij Mouterijmuseum (Bruges):** This site shows the history of brewing in the city of Bruges. The museum is located in a basement brewery, De Halve Maan.

- **Musée Bruxelloise de la Gueuze (Brussels):** This living museum-brewery of the Cantillon brewery, with displays of brewing history, holds public brewing sessions twice yearly. A tour fee of 6 Euros includes a free beer sample.

Checking Out Beer in the Czech Republic

The Czechs drink about as much beer per capita as any population does. And like Germany, locally produced beers can be found in almost every Czech town. Be aware that the Czech Republic is a lager-producing country (after all, it's the birthplace of Pilsner), so anyone thirsting for ales is going to be parched. But if you happen to love lagers, this country's brews, from light to dark to black (which I expand on in the sections that follow) will certainly pique your taste buds.

Visiting the birthplace of Pilsner

Prior to 1842, Pilsner beers didn't exist. The Urquell Brewery in Plzen introduced the first golden-colored lager to the world — and the world hasn't been the same since. It's believed that 80 percent of all the beer made in the world today is a derivative of the Pilsner style.

The brand name *Pilsner Urquell* literally means "the original source of Pilsner."

Trying other Czech beers

Though the Czech Republic — and especially the region of Bohemia — is forever linked to Pilsner beer, this country has a long and storied history of brewing before the first Pilsner was produced. Long and storied, but not necessarily varied.

What you can expect to find is a progression of pale *(světlé)* and dark *(tmavé)* lagers of varying strengths. Not unlike the British Bitters or Scottish Ales, Czech beers are often ordered by their alcoholic strength, as denoted by their degrees Balling (which is a measure of gravity or density on the day the beer was brewed). A beer with a gravity of 11 to 12 degrees Balling has an alcohol content of 4.5 to 5.0 percent; a beer with a gravity of 13 to 20 degrees Balling has an alcohol content between 5.5 to 7.5 percent.

Around the winter holidays, brewers may introduce a special black *(černé)* beer that's marginally darker that its regular dark beer. And, yes, it's a lager.

Exploring historical Czech beer establishments

Like their Western European brethren, Czechs love their beer, and they love to preserve their brewing history and culture. Here are some locations throughout the Czech Republic where you can enjoy and celebrate beer:

- **Pivovarské Museum (Plzen):** This brewery museum is set up in a Gothic malt house in the historically significant town of Plzen. Hundreds of unique exhibits testify to the history of brewing and the culture of drinking beer, from the earliest times to the present day.

- **Pilsner Urquell Brewery (Plzen):** The Pilsner Urquell Brewery introduced the world to the golden, clear Pilsner beer, granddaddy of all commercial lagers. This area was the medieval kingdom of the good King Wenceslas. Devotees say that the beer doesn't travel well, so you need to try it on site — need I say more?

- **U Fleků Brewery and Restaurant (Prague):** This brewpub is one of the largest and oldest (started in 1499) brewpubs in the world. Only one beer is served here — oddly enough, a dark lager.

- **Budweis:** Any beer from this town, once the location of the royal brewery, is called *Budweiser* (note the relationship to kings). Anheuser-Busch modeled its flagship brew on this local brew long ago. Michelob is also based on a nearby town name.

Finding Noteworthy Beers in Other Corners of the World

A serious beer trekker need not stop with the major brewing countries; other countries hold plenty of discoveries, although because of locals' loyalties to their favorite brews, finding unusual beers may be more difficult. As you (physically) check out the countries' breweries and beer museums in the following sections, be sure to ask about any beer-lovers' groups as a lead to specialty bars or beer festivals.

Austria

An entire beer style — Vienna Lager — is attributed to old Vienna, which has about a dozen wonderful brewpubs but only one production brewery — Ottakringer. Throughout the country, breweries are known to operate very good restaurants, too. The cuisine is typically Tyrolean (very similar to Bavarian), heavy in meats and starches — in other words, great beer food!

As in Germany, Belgium, and Britain, many of Austria's smaller towns have their own local breweries (not quite as numerous as in Germany, though).

Denmark

Denmark isn't often noted as a producer or exporter of any beers of renown, but that doesn't mean there aren't any beer experiences to savor there. Denmark simply has the misfortune of being in the shadow of its neighbor to the south (Germany).

The Carlsberg Brewery (located in Copenhagen is the largest in Denmark and is the site of much study and development of the lager beer style. A century of Danish brewing history is on display here; the self-guided tour concludes with a couple of free samples.

The Netherlands

Dutch beer is popularized by perhaps its least interesting brand, Heineken. That's too bad considering everything the brewers in The Netherlands have to offer. The Dutch people are also very fond of beer and import a wide variety from around the world. Here are just some of the beer-related sites you need to see if you're ever in The Netherlands:

✔ **Amsterdam:** Heineken is one of the world's biggest brewers and a tour of its brewery in Amsterdam is great fun (the main facility, outside of Amsterdam, is the largest brewery in Europe).

✔ **Biermuseum de Boom (Alkmar):** This museum consists of displays of brewing, malting, and cooperage set up in an old brewhouse.

✔ **Brewery De Konigshoeven (Berkel-Enschot):** The only Trappist beer produced outside of Belgium is made at the Koningshoeven Abbey (*Abdij* in Dutch) and sold under the name La Trappe in Europe. In the United States and Canada, these beers are marketed as Konigshoeven Trappist Ales.

✔ **Bokbier Festival (Amsterdam):** In the Fall, the Dutch group PINT (Promotie Informatie Traditioneel Bier) celebrates Dutch beers in the Netherlands' largest beer festival. Established in 1980, PINT is one of the oldest beer consumer organizations in the world.

Norway

Beer brewing in Norway is more than 1,000 years old, and, until a couple of centuries ago, a farmhouse-brewing tradition persisted. Unfortunately, most of the traditional Norwegian brews have passed into history. Today, big brewers Carlsberg-Ringnes and Hansa-Borg dominate the market.

On the plus side, craft brewing has arrived in this frigid country, with microbrewers well established in Oslo (Oslo Mikrobryggeri) and Grimstad (Nogne O).

The Aass (pronounced *ohss*) Bryggeri (brewery) in Drammen, Norway, has outstanding quality beers in a variety of styles. Check out www.aass.no/ for more info.

Australia and New Zealand

The Australians are notorious for their high per-capita consumption, which is on par with the Germans and the Czechs. This fact should come as no surprise for a hot, arid country with a wild frontier past. The Aussies prefer their beer ice cold (they probably don't get many complaints from visiting Yanks), which is one of the reasons that Australian bars serve beer in small glasses: It can be drunk more quickly without suffering any loss of coldness.

Despite the deep Anglo influence on the Australian brewing industry and an occasional well-made ale, Australia is a lager beer country-continent. Some of the standout ales include Coopers Real Ale and Stout, Tooth's Sheaf Stout, and a down-under favorite, Castlemaine XXXX (known affectionately as *fourex*).

Aussies can be a bit provincial about their beer. You drink XXXX if you're from Queensland, but you'd prefer a Victoria Bitter if you're from Victoria. Swan is enjoyed in Western Australia, while Tooheys is quaffed in New South Wales. And don't forget Boag's in Tasmania; the brewery gives a great tour and tasting!

Locations of note in Australia include numerous brewpubs. As you'd expect, these brewpubs tend to be concentrated in and around the metropolitan centers of Sydney, Melbourne, and Perth.

New Zealand is a beer lover's paradise. Not only is beer New Zealand's most popular drink, but it's produced in a wide variety of styles. Even though the market is dominated by the country's two largest breweries (Lion Nathan and DB Breweries), New Zealand has its share of microbreweries (15) and brewpubs (18) as well, mostly centered around Auckland, Christchurch, Nelson, and Wellington.

If you should happen to be in Auckland, New Zealand, in late March, buy a ticket to the New Zealand Beer Festival. This kiwi celebration features more than 70 beers from a couple dozen breweries.

Japan

Throughout Asia, the German influence on brewing is unmistakable, and light lagers predominate. The internationally famous Japanese megabrewers have some beer gardens (Sapporo has the most famous one) and theme pubs, and more and more bars are opening with large international beer selections, featuring Belgian and American microbrewed beers. Homebrewing has caught on, as have microbreweries and brewpubs. And don't forget that the Japanese have been brewing for a long time: *Sake* is actually beer, made entirely from rice.

Thailand

Thailand has some well-established megabrewers, such as Boon Rawd Brewery, which produces the popular Singha and Leo brands. Another company, Thai Beverages, makes the competing Chang brand that has a slightly elevated alcohol content (locals warn of "changovers"). Also, the celebrated German brewer Paulaner operates a beer hall in Bangkok.

A beer is a bier is a pivo

Here's how to ask for a beer in various countries:

Country	"Beer"
China	mai chiu
Czechoslovakia	pivo
Denmark	ol
Finland	olut
France/Belgium	bière
Germany	bier
Italy	birra
Japan	biru
Latvia	alus
Netherlands	bier
Poland	piwo
Spain/Mexico	cerveza

Chapter 17

Embarking on Beer Travel and Tours

*N*ot all beer is consumed at home or at your local pub or bar. Sometimes you've got to get out and go find new and exciting beers, whether you join a group tour or trek on your own. The good news is that doing so is getting easier, especially if you're taking a vacation. Throughout this chapter, I highlight some of the best and easiest ways to plan your beer travels.

Keeping a Few Beer-Trekking Tips in Mind before You Leave Home

These days, beer lovers don't have to go very far to find good beer — at least not as far as they had to go just a couple decades ago. This easy access to good beer has always been the case in Europe and is now true for North America, Australia, and New Zealand. (In other parts of the world, however, finding good beer may still take a bit of effort, but the liquid rewards, as always, are worth it.)

If you're new to the craft beer experience, you may not be aware of great beer-tasting opportunities right in your neck of the woods. But simply checking with your local business directory or Chamber of Commerce can easily set you on the right path; Chapter 15 notes some spots you can try in North America, such as beer bars, brewpubs, and the like. Of course, nothing works as well as good old-fashioned word-of-mouth, too.

Chasing after beer experiences farther from home involves considerably more effort and investigation. Thankfully, because people now live in a more global community and have all-hours access to reliable and up-to-date information, making plans for beer trekking many miles from home is pretty easy.

Here are some general ideas and suggestions you may want to consider if you intend to do any serious beer trekking — particularly out of the country:

✔ **Do as much planning as possible.** After you decide where you're going, find out what beery opportunities exist in or around that destination. Consider what breweries are there and whether tours are given or need to be scheduled. Learn about the local pub or tavern culture, and find out where you can taste a variety of beers — and catch a good meal, too. Consider buying one (or more) of the many beer guides in publication.

✔ **Learn about local laws and customs:**

• Alcohol may be forbidden in certain countries, or even counties (in the United States).

• Beer may not be available for retail purchase during certain hours of the day or on certain days of the week.

• Pubs and taverns may keep unusual and inconvenient hours on certain days of the week.

• The drinking age may be lower than you expect, allowing a younger friend or family member to join in your trek.

• Be aware that penalties for public intoxication or driving under the influence can be especially severe in some countries, including incarceration.

✔ **Before leaving home, make contact (at least via e-mail) with those breweries or beer-related locations on your agenda.** You want to make sure they'll be open at the date and time of your visit.

✔ **Bring a camera to record your tour or visit.** Depending on where you are, you may need to ask whether taking pictures is okay.

✔ **Bring writing implements and something to write on.** Taking notes, especially of beer tasting, is helpful. The more beers you sample, the less you tend to remember.

✔ **By all means, collect and keep business cards, coasters, and other free mementos of your trip.** They'll help you remember where you've been and what you've tasted.

Working Beer into Your Vacation Adventures

Naturally, people plan vacations around their personal interests, whether that includes snorkeling in the Caribbean, hiking in the Cotswolds, or bird watching in Costa Rica. So what about Uncle Fred who likes to try different beers? Well, there's a place just for him, too.

As it turns out, many important beer destinations just happen to be in or near popular and desirable tourist destinations around the world, making these treks all the more interesting and inviting for everybody involved. (My wife and now college-aged children have been dragged through more brewery tours than they care to remember, but these tours were always on the way to a national park or a theme park; I swear!)

In the following sections, I note a number of planned vacations that focus on beer and discuss the advantages of an unplanned beer adventure.

All together now: Going with tour groups

Planning beer-specific vacations is becoming easier — and more commonplace — thanks to the proliferation of vacation companies that specialize in this sort of thing. The beauty is in not having to make all the arrangements yourself. Furthermore, these vacations are led by experts (in the vacation industry, if not the brewing industry) that see that every detail of the trip is worked out.

The following sections offer a listing of some of the beercation choices out there, and this list is by no means exhaustive. Even the most jaded beer trekker in the world should be able to find a vacation of interest here.

Traveling around Europe

BeerTrips.com (www.beertrips.com) features relaxed itineraries that allow plenty of time for exploration on your own. Following are some of the tours BeerTrips.com organizes in Europe:

- Farmhouse Ales of Belgium and France
- The Czech Republic: Independent Breweries and World Heritage Sites
- Beer & Cuisine of Northern Italy!

- ✔ Prague, Munich, & Bamberg
- ✔ The Great Beers of Belgium
- ✔ Winter Warmer: Brugge & London
- ✔ Zythos Belgian Beer Binge
- ✔ Germany: Cologne, Bamberg & Fruehlingsfest in Munich

Belgian Beer Me! (www.belgianbeerme.com) tours only one country (guess which one), but tours it extensively (this company also teaches Belgian beer classes in the United States). Here are four of the annual tours led by Belgian Beer Me!

- ✔ The Best Damn Farmhouse Ale Tour of Belgium & France
- ✔ The Lonely Monks Trappist Beer Tour of Belgium & the Netherlands
- ✔ The Essen Christmas Beer Festival Tour of Belgium
- ✔ The Great Zythos Beer Festival Tour of Belgium

Bier-Mania! Cultural Beer Tours (www.bier-mania.com) offers this fun and funky variety of European excursions:

- ✔ Great European Beer Tour (Europe-wide tours, 10 days)
- ✔ Great Belgium Beer Tour (Belgium and France, 10 days)
- ✔ Franconia and Bamberg Special (Franconia, Annafest, Bamberg, and Pilsen, 10 days)
- ✔ Bohemia Czech Special (Bohemia, Zoigl Land, and Franconia, 10 days)
- ✔ Bavaria and Tyrol Alps Special (Oktoberfest and Alps, 4 or 10 days)
- ✔ Go East Berlin Special (Eastern Germany and Berlin, 10 days)
- ✔ Lower Rhine Classic Tour (weekend or midweek in the Lower Rhine)
- ✔ Ardennes Special (Ardennes region of Belgium, 3 days)
- ✔ Bière de Garde Special (Verdun and Pays de Meuse in France, 3 days)
- ✔ Bruges and Flanders Special (Belgium and French Flanders, 3 days)
- ✔ Combination Tours and Events (mixed tours and beer festivals)

Note: Bier-Mania! Cultural Beer Tours also offers a Colorado Wild West Special (Rocky Mountains, 8 days) for folks who want to remain in the United States; see the next section for more U.S. options.

Knickerbocker's Bier Tours (www.knickerbockersbiertours.de/) hosts a beer tour of Germany that includes the following:

✔ A visit to six different German breweries

✔ Two beer and brewing seminars

✔ A Dutch pub that features 130 different beers

✔ A Bierboerse (beer exchange) with 900 beers

NovoGuide Tours offers The Great Brewery Tour (www.novoguide.com/brewery) that lasts nine days and eight nights and visits five European countries, including

✔ The Czech Republic (Prague and Pilzen)

✔ Germany (Munich)

✔ Belgium (Leuven)

✔ England (London)

✔ Ireland (Dublin)

Hiking and biking in the United States

For U.S. beer trekkers who would rather stay stateside, Zephyr Adventures (www.zephyradventures.com) has just the thing for you. The Yellowstone Hike, Bike, & Beer Adventure activities consist of hiking and biking in and around Yellowstone National Park in Wyoming, near Bozeman, Montana, and Harriman State Park in Idaho. Mountain biking is also done on lower slopes of Big Sky ski resort, Grand Teton National Park, and a downhill cruise on a National Scenic Byway from the top of the Beartooth Pass at 10,947 feet in Wyoming down to Red Lodge, Montana, at 5,555 feet. Each day, you're given easy and hard options, making the tour suitable for everyone.

As far as the beer portion of the adventure goes, you tour the following six breweries in six days in Montana, Idaho, and Wyoming:

✔ Bozeman Brewing Company in Bozeman, Montana

✔ Lone Peak Brewery in Big Sky, Montana

✔ Grand Teton Brewing in Victor, Idaho

✔ Snake River Brewing in Jackson, Wyoming

✔ Red Lodge Ales in Red Lodge, Montana

✔ Yellowstone Valley Brewing Company in Billings, Montana

Sailing away

Not all beer adventures are completely land based. Now you can find several opportunities to enjoy beer cruises. Some are large, some are small; some are luxurious, some, um, not so much. All the following beer cruises allow you to enjoy great beer without going overboard!

✔ Magic Happens (www.alaskabrewcruise.com/Home.html), in conjunction with Celebrator Beer News, presents an annual Ultimate Beer Experience cruise. This seven-night Alaskan cruise via the inside passage, takes place on Celebrity Cruise Line's Infinity ship. In addition to the phenomenal cruise itinerary and its regular ports of call, you take two brewery tour excursions (Juneau and Skagway/Haines) and six different beer-tasting events while onboard — the perfect antidote for seasickness.

✔ The Northwest Rafting Company (www.nwrafting.com) has added Brews with Views rafting itineraries on the Rogue River in Oregon. Brews with Views trips mirror the regular rafting trips, but when you arrive at your campsite, a variety of microbrews on draft are just waiting for you to enjoy. Each trip also has a brewer or brewery representative present to provide tastings of special beers. The Northwest Rafting Company guides also prepare a special meal to complement the evening's offerings. The summer 2012 itinerary includes trips with Deschutes Brewery, Double Mountain Brewery, and Sierra Nevada Brewing Company.

✔ In Milwaukee, Wisconsin, you can take a short tour of that city's breweries along the Milwaukee River on Riverwalk Boat Tours (www.riverwalk boats.com). The Sunday Brewery Tour stops in at Lakefront Brewing Company, Milwaukee Ale House, and Rock Bottom Restaurant & Brewery. You can start your cruise at any one of these three locations.

✔ Rogue Wilderness Adventures (www.wildrogue.com) again launches its Paddles and Pints rafting trip on the Rogue River in Oregon. This four-day whitewater adventure partners with an acclaimed brewmaster to pair two of Oregon's prized offerings. During the day, the staff of Rogue Wilderness Adventures takes paddlers down one of the most beautiful whitewater rivers in the country. Evenings are spent camping on sandy beaches as guides serve riverside fare that perfectly complements the beer tasting.

Malty meandering: Unplanned beer adventures

Although I recommend planning time around your destinations as much as possible (see the earlier section "Keeping a Few Beer Trekking Tips in Mind before You Leave Home"), one of the more rewarding aspects of open-ended — and open-minded — travel is being flexible enough to take that last-minute detour to something unplanned and unexpected. Spontaneity is valuable in these situations and can lead to some memorable beer experiences. This type of adventure is more of a do-it-yourself, spur-of-the-moment beer vacation. Drink where the locals drink rather than where the tourists drink. Always keep your eyes and mind open when trekking; your tongue and tummy will thank you.

Here are just a few of the unplanned beer adventures that your humble author has embarked on:

✔ Visiting a cosmopolitan city like Venice, where gondola rides and Italian wine are the order of the day, affords you the opportunity to discover that Venice actually has a brewpub! (For the record, it's BEFeD Brew Pub Mestre.)

✔ Most tourists who visit Salzburg, Austria, eventually make their way to the Hohensalzburg fortress that overlooks the city. And most visitors to the Hohensalzburg choose to get up there by taking the convenient funicular (inclined railcar). By walking the steep and narrow street that wends its way up the hillside instead, my wife and I tripped over the entrance to the Stiegl Bierkeller along the way. (Okay, so we didn't have time to stop in, but that's beside the point.)

✔ Casually strolling the pedestrian mall in Heidelberg, Germany, one afternoon brought my wife and I to the doorstep of a bierstube that boasted more than 100 different bottled beers — many of which I'd never seen before at home. It's no wonder I can't remember the name of that place.

✔ Ducking into a tiny, non-descript grocery store in London for a late evening snack afforded me an opportunity to buy several bottles of ale I hadn't seen in any of the pubs I visited. They were promptly enjoyed in my hotel room that night.

Hop Pillows for Everyone! Lodging Near and in Breweries

For centuries, some folks have believed that hops can help bring on restful sleep, and thus, hop pillows were used as a remedy against insomnia and anxiety. The pungent, spicy aroma of hops is considered a gentle and effective method of inducing sleep. True or not, the belief in hops' ability as a sleep aid dates back to hop pickers continually getting sleepy on the job.

Even if you choose not to take an organized group vacation that focuses on beer (see the earlier section "All together now: Going with tour groups"), numerous opportunities exist to sleep at a bed and breakfast that makes local beer a part of the experience — or you may find lodging in or near a working brewery. I discuss both types of opportunities and give suggestions for places to stay in the following sections. My guess is that your drowsiness will be more greatly affected by the ingestion of alcohol than the breathing in of hop aromas but perhaps intensified by both.

Beer, bed, and breakfast

Though bed and breakfast (B&B) locations are quite plentiful in many countries, they aren't nearly as numerous as they seem to be in Britain. To add to their intrigue, however, some of these B&Bs have added a third *B* to their title (for *beer*) — and now the game has changed.

The countrysides of England, Scotland, and Wales are strewn with B&B locations that cater to beer lovers. Literally hundreds of quaint, old country inns, city taverns, and simple alehouses are waiting to be explored. If you're considering beer trekking through Britain, seriously consider the B,B,&B option.

Anyone planning a trip to any of the U.K. countries would be well served by obtaining a copy of *Beer, Bed & Breakfast,* a guide to pubs with good value accommodation and excellent food and beer. This comprehensive 200-plus page book breaks the countries down by county and even tells you which beers to expect to see on tap at each location. All entries include contact details, type and extent of accommodation, list of beers served, meal types and times, and an easy-to-understand price guide to help you plan your budget. This guide is available through CAMRA (Campaign for Real Ale) at www.camra.org.uk.

Meanwhile, here's a brief list of U.S. B&B locations that have joined the beer revolution:

✔ The Black Friar Inn and Pub in Bar Harbor, Maine (www.blackfriarinn. com), is described as "a gentleman's retreat" by the innkeepers. It's home to the Friar's Pub, which serves a full line of spirits, wines, and Gritty McDuff's microbrews (which is brewed in Portland, Maine). Drink in the pub itself or on the roof deck.

✔ Forty Putney Road Bed & Breakfast in Brattleboro, Vermont (www.forty putneyroad.com), overlooks the water and has several peaceful waterfront trails and gardens, but it's just a short walk to vibrant downtown Brattleboro. The innkeepers are self-proclaimed beer geeks and have a small pub on-site with more than 30 local craft beers. Every Saturday night, they host a craft beer tasting, and they often have other beer-related events.

✔ The Inn at Ellis River in Jackson, New Hampshire (www.innatellis river.com), offers a two-night beercation package. Start your stay by sampling a glass of the local ale and cheese and crackers in its game room/pub. The next day, check out the microbrews in nearby North Conway's shops and then tour Tuckerman's Brewery. Your three-course dinner that evening at White Mountain Cider Company includes your choice of one of its five regional beers on tap.

Steep 'n' sleep, mash 'n' crash: Spending the night at a brewery

A limited number of locations exist where guests can overnight at a brewery or on the brewery grounds, such as the following. Sleepwalking is acceptable, sleep drinking is frowned upon!

- Brewery Creek Bed and Breakfast Inn in Mineral Point, Wisconsin (www.brewerycreek.com), is actually three businesses in one. The lodging business includes five rooms at the Inn and two cottages on Shake Rag Street. The other two businesses include the brewpub restaurant at the Inn and the Brewery Creek Brewing Company adjacent to the restaurant. The Brewery Creek Inn is legally a hotel, but because a breakfast is served, it went with bed and breakfast inn. Good thing it's not located on Dairy Creek.

- Calistoga Inn Restaurant & Brewery (www.calistogainn.com) is a charming turn-of-the-century European-style hotel with a full-service restaurant and craft brewery right in the heart of California wine country. With a hundred-year history of serving visitors to Napa Valley, in 1987, the Calistoga Inn added the brewery, formally known as Napa Valley Brewing Company. All the beer brewed there is also served there. After long hours of wine tasting, there's nothing like a cold beer on the patio of the Calistoga Inn. Brewery tours are available Monday through Friday.

- The Fredericksburg Brewing Company (www.yourbrewery.com) is the oldest and most respected brewpub in the state of Texas. It began operation in 1994, shortly after legislation was passed that allowed brewpubs in the Lone Star State. Located on Main Street in the heart of the downtown shopping district, Fredericksburg Brewing Company set up shop in a two-story building that was restored according to historical standards. The second floor provides space for its unique Bed & Brew facilities, which include 12 private rooms with baths. Each guest is entitled to a free four sampler of beer for each night's stay.

- The House of Rogue (www.rogue.com/locations/bb.php) offers a unique way to enjoy Newport, Oregon. The cozy apartments are located above the Rogue Ales Public House on Newport's historic working waterfront. You can enjoy a beautiful view of the town's bayfront where one of Oregon's largest fishing fleets coexists with a thriving tourism industry. Among the many activities are watching the sea lions down at the wharf and stopping in the Public House and sampling several of its award-winning ales.

- For those of you looking for something a bit more upscale, check out Swans Hotel and Public House in Victoria, British Columbia (www.swanshotel.com). Located in the heart of historic Old Towne Victoria, Swans is just minutes to Victoria's famous Inner Harbour where you can enjoy local attractions, events and entertainment, shopping and more. Of course, you can choose to stay put and just enjoy the house beers brewed at Swans Buckerfield Brewery at street level. This pub won National Brewpub of the Year in 2006.

- In the early 1940s, after having fled the Nazi regime in Europe, the von Trapp family settled in Stowe, Vermont, on an enchanting farm with sweeping mountain vistas reminiscent of their beloved Austria. (Yes, this is the famous von Trapp family depicted in the movie *The Sound of Music*.) The Trapp family first began welcoming guests to its rustic 27-room lodge in Stowe, Vermont, in the summer of 1950. After a devastating fire in 1980, the original structure was replaced by a new 96-room alpine lodge.

A bona fide beer, bed, and breakfast bonanza

I think it's safe to say that no other company in the world offers the beer trekker such an incredible number of choices of places to stay than McMenamins. Founded by brothers Mike and Brian McMenamin in 1985, their empire includes a chain of nearly 60 brewpubs, microbreweries, movie theaters, music venues, and historic hotels, most of which are located in the Portland, Oregon, metro area, with additional sites elsewhere in Oregon and Washington.

What makes the various locations so interesting is where they've been situated, nine of which are on the National Register of Historic Places. Here's just a partial list:

✔ A building that was originally part of the Lewis and Clark Centennial Exposition

✔ A former brothel

✔ A former Church of Sweden

✔ A former elementary school

✔ A former funeral home

✔ A movie theater built by Universal Studios

McMenamins currently operates 24 breweries. Collectively, it's produced 54,000 batches of beer since 1985. In 2010 alone, it produced 47,700 kegs of beer, or an astounding 5.9 million pints.

Be aware that not every McMenamin property operates a brewery and not every property offers overnight accommodations. To choose your beer-friendliest location, go to www.mcmenamins.com.

Johannes von Trapp then started thinking about brewing his own beer for guests of the resort. His dream was to produce an American version of the tasty lager he'd enjoyed on his trips to his ancestral Austrian home. Johannes's dream became reality in the spring of 2010, with the opening of the Trapp Family Brewery. The modest facility (60,000 or so gallons a year) is located in the lower level of the lodge's DeliBakery, where draughts of the local brew are available year round. The three flagship beers are a Golden Helles, Vienna Amber, and Dunkel Lager. (For more info, check out www.trappfamily.com.)

Taking a Look at Brewery Tours

Brewery tours are one of the few ways people can taste beer for free (or almost free) and get a brief education in brewing processes all in the same afternoon. What's more, brewery tours are nothing new — major breweries have been hosting them for years as part of their ongoing public-relations programs (Anheuser-Busch even possesses a national landmark, the Clydesdale stables), and the passion of microbrewery and brewpub owners and brewers is such that a tour is usually a sure bet for a fun thing.

Each of the big, nationally known brewhouses has regularly scheduled, multimedia tours that eventually lead to a spacious and comfortable tasting room, sure to include a gift shop in the hopes that you'll feel compelled to buy something in return for the hospitality. Some regional brewers also have tours of various types, while others can't be bothered (or can't host tours for insurance reasons).

Things are more casual on the microbrewery level. An advance phone call is usually enough to get you in the door. Brewpubs require only a gift for gab on the brewer's and customer's parts (and a moment when the brewer isn't super-busy). In some cases, all you have to do to see the brewing operation is to rotate a bit on your bar stool (my kind of exercise).

At these smaller places, given the nature of the industry, you'll probably be able to meet the brewmaster, the maintenance crew, the owner, and the president all with the shake of one hand. You won't find a better opportunity to learn the intimate side of brewing, and the enthusiasm for the craft at this level can be infectious. Watch out, though — you may find yourself helping clean up!

In the following sections, I provide pointers on touring breweries on your own, and I describe tours that go by bus and by bicycle.

Touring breweries on your own

Touring breweries has become one of the easiest beer geek things to do these days. Almost all breweries — especially craft breweries — host tours of their facilities, but it often comes down to convenience. Having people traipse through the brewhouse on brewing or bottling day can be bothersome and even a bit risky for the guests.

Nevertheless, don't let that stop you from pursuing your hobby. Simply calling ahead or checking the brewery's website for information can alleviate a lot of hassle for everyone involved. Most breweries have posted days and times for scheduled tours; others are limited to one tour a week. It depends on how busy they are and what personnel are available to lead tours.

To pique your interest in taking brewery tours, here's a list of some unique opportunities to be found at breweries around the world:

- The Buller Pub & Brewery in Buenos Aires, Argentina (www.bullerpub.com), is modeled after American brewpubs. This rollicking bar has extensive food, beer, and liqueur menus. Groups of eight can tour the brewery and learn about the brewing methods and materials. Visitors have a chance to sample one of the pub's six beers: a lager, Cream Pale Ale, Oktoberfest, India Pale Ale, Dry Stout, and Honey Beer.

- The Chimay Brewery in Belgium (www.chimay.com) is considered by many to be a beer mecca. Unfortunately, fans of this famous beer-making Trappist monastery aren't allowed inside the brewery. But tourists can still visit the abbey's gardens, cemetery, and church. And afterward, they can head to L'Auberge de Poteaupre, an old school turned restaurant-brasserie, where Chimay beers and other Belgian brews are on tap.

✔ The Kiuchi Brewery in Ibaraki, Japan (www.kodawari.cc/?en_home.html), brewers of Hitachino Birds Nest Beer, caters to budding beer makers with a personal lesson in devising a recipe, measuring malts, mashing grain, and other brewing techniques. The final product takes three weeks to ferment and can be shipped to you when it's done. The catch? It can only be shipped to an address in Japan.

✔ High in the Swiss Alps, the Monsteiner Bier Brewery (www.biervision-monstein.ch/) offers no fewer than nine unique beer-tasting opportunities, including a train ride and Nordic walking. These excursions end with a tour of the brewery, a tasting, or both. The brewery also produces homemade specialties like brewer's bacon and cheese and spare grain bread.

✔ For about $25, visitors to the Wells & Young's Brewery in the United Kingdom (www.wellsandyoungs.co.uk) get a glimpse of the English beer tradition. In 1876, Young's brewery opened its doors; in 2006, it merged with another local beer company called Wells. Together they make lagers and traditional ales. The tour includes drinks, a dinner like steak and bombardier pie, and three free bottles of your choice.

Trying group bus tours

If you're travelling to a location that's fortunate enough to support many breweries in a relatively small geographical area, you may want to investigate the possibility of group bus tours. These tours make it convenient and easy to tour a handful of breweries in a single afternoon, and you don't have to drive from one brewery location to the next — especially if you're unfamiliar with the surroundings. Taking one of these bus tours also means that you won't be behind the wheel after consuming several beers. Lastly, being on a bus full of fellow beer geeks pursuing their passion is always a lot of fun. *"Ninety-nine bottles of beer on the wall, ninety-nine bottles of beer . . ."*

Here are some places where beer tours by bus are available in the United States:

✔ Brewery Tours of San Diego, California (www.brewerytoursofsandiego.com), offers scheduled public brewery tours seven days a week — both day and night tours are available. Its Monday-through-Thursday tours visit two breweries, and its Friday-to-Sunday tours visit three breweries. Bus tours include transportation, brewery tours, beer tasting, one meal, and a souvenir beer glass.

✔ Burlington Brew Tours (BBT) (www.burlingtonbrewtours.com) represents the state of Vermont in the beer-touring world. BBT offers an opportunity to see first-hand the inner workings of various breweries in that state as well as taste their potables. Tours include round-trip transportation, a sampling of at least 18 different microbrews, a sumptuous lunch, and two private brewery tours. Choose between the Classic Burlington Brew

Tour (Magic Hat Brewery, Switchback Brewery, Zero Gravity Brewery, and Vermont Pub and Brewery) and the Stowe Tour (Rock Art Brewery, the Shed Restaurant and Brewery, and the Alchemist Pub and Brewery, and a beer dinner at Stowe Mountain Lodge).

✔ Hop Head Beer Tour Company (www.hopheadbeertours.com), which is based in Wisconsin, specializes in arranging brewery tours in the Badger State and surrounding region, including Chicago. Tours include motor coach transportation, brewery tours, beer samples, beer glasses, meals, and a lively discussion with the onboard beer expert.

✔ Using limousines and party buses, Long Island Brewery Tours (www.longislandbrewerytours.com) offers beer lovers the opportunity to go brewery touring in style. All tours visit a minimum of three brewpubs on Long Island, New York. You can spend a leisurely afternoon tasting beer samples and chatting with the brewer, or you can choose to schedule your visit to coincide with brewing sessions where you can learn about brewing beer in detail.

✔ Motor City Brew Tours (www.motorcitybrewtours.com) is located near Detroit, Michigan. A typical bus tour is a five-hour guided tour to three breweries, where you spend an hour at each brewery and taste three beers at each one; a light lunch is served at the first stop. Growlers and bottles of beer are available for purchase at each stop and may be consumed on the bus. Plenty of water and snacks are available on the bus.

✔ The Portland Brew Bus (www.brewbus.com) in Portland, Oregon, leads beer lovers and curious tourists on a four-hour tour of the Rose City's breweries to sample their beers. Scheduled public tours typically depart downtown Portland at 1:30 p.m.; some Saturday tours start in the morning. Tours visit three or four breweries and sample between 15 and 25 different beers. Your onboard guide provides a fun and educational tour of Portland and the history of craft brewing.

Pedaling your way to Pilsners and Porters: Bike tours

Because of the sheer number of small breweries springing up everywhere, fewer miles are between them — mostly in more urban areas, anyway. With this increasing population density, touring several breweries in a day or even an afternoon — on a bicycle! — is conceivable.

How can anyone not like the idea of touring breweries by bike? It's healthy; it's aerobic; it burns calories and exercises various muscle groups. Still not convinced? How about the fact that it has minimal-to-nil carbon footprint? Hard to argue with that, huh?

In the following sections, I list a variety of bike tour companies around the world and describe a special type of vehicle called the *PedalPub*.

The New Belgium Brewing Company in Fort Collins, Colorado (one of the greenest breweries in the world), encourages its employees to ride bikes to work. How serious is it? On the occasion of an employee's first anniversary, he's given a brand new bike as a gift.

Bike and brew companies around the world

Anyone can take the initiative to ride her bike from brewery to brewery — it wouldn't be hard to do — but not everyone has the initiative, and not everyone has a bike.

With this in mind, a new business model was born. A whole slew of eco-friendly bike and brew touring companies are now in operation in many countries. Here's a smattering of examples:

- ✔ Adventura Bike Holidays visits many central European countries and cities but has only one tour dedicated strictly to beer (as if you couldn't improvise in central Europe!). This four-day trek in the Czech Republic takes you from Prague down to the spa town of Trebon, with stops in Cesky Krumlov and Ceske Budejovice (the birthplace of Budweiser). Tours of trademark beer houses and plenty of great Czech beer are included. Go to www.bikeholidays.eu/ to find out more.

- ✔ Should you find yourself in Munich with a couple hours to kill, try taking a Bicycle Tour of Munich (www.getyourguide.com/en/tours/germany-munich/munich-beer-tour-on-bicycle/?id=1615). Limited to eight people, this three-hour tour includes information about beer barons, famous beer battles, and the German Beer Purity Law; it also includes a tour of one of Munich's famed breweries complete with beer tasting.

- ✔ ExperiencePlus! Bicycle Tours (www.experienceplus.com) offers a biking tour of Belgium for anyone who loves to drink beer. The tour begins and ends in Brussels after cycling 30 to 55 miles a day, for a total of up to 173 miles over 8 days and 277 miles over 11 days. World War I battle and historical sites, the UNESCO World Heritage sites of Brugge and Tournai, and Trappist breweries and Lambic beer are included on the tour. The rates include use of a quality 27- to 30-speed bicycle, accommodations, breakfasts, some dinners, guided brewery visits and beer tastings with dinner, transfers to and from Brussels, and more. Take me with you — please!

- ✔ As you may expect, the craft brewery–filled city of Portland, Oregon, offers an excellent way to tour those breweries on bike (www.portlandbicycle tours.com). The Pub Peddler Brewery Tour provides an opportunity to learn about the brewing processes and the beer culture as well as to taste a variety of local beer. Note that beverages aren't included in the price so there's no pressure to "drink your money's worth."

- Santa Cruz Bike Tours (www.santacruzbiketours.com) in California offers a brewery tour that includes stops at Seabright Brewery, Santa Cruz Aleworks, and Santa Cruz Mountain Brewing. The tour is approximately 3.5 hours, and the tour price doesn't include the cost of beer sampling.

- Okay, so this bike tour may not be entirely focused on beer, but Shuttle Guy Tours (www.shuttleguytours.com) sure makes everything that's not about beer sound pretty good. And who doesn't like cheese? The Bike Ride Exploring Wisconsin (great acronym: BREW) offers you tours and samples of Wisconsin craft beer, artist gallery and cheese factory visits, small towns, and beautiful scenery. What more can you want? Okay, more beer.

- Urban AdvenTours (www.urbanadventours.com) is a unique, eco-friendly bicycle tour company in Boston, Massachusetts, that provides original bicycle tours and bike rentals from downtown Boston. Urban AdvenTours has teamed up with the Harpoon Brewery for a fantastic ride through Boston's Fort Point and Seaport Districts, culminating in a tour of the Harpoon brewing facilities and a complimentary tasting. Thar she brews!

A bicycle built for brew: The PedalPub

A new concept sweeping the streets of several international cities is a bicycle built for drinking and enjoying beer while riding. In Holland it's known as a *Fietscafe,* in Germany it's a *Bierbike,* and in the United States, it goes by *PedalPub* or *Pedal Party.*

The original vehicle (Fietscafe) is a pedal-powered bar, invented in the Netherlands by brothers Henk and Zwier van Laar in 1997. The 17-person vehicle has 10 seats for pedalers, 2 non-pedaling seats, 1 driver's seat, a bench that seats 3, and space for a bartender in the middle. Obviously, the passengers provide the power for the vehicle by pedaling while the sober person steers. The rest are just along for the ride — to wherever that may be.

Since 2005, Bierbikes can be seen all around Germany. Starting in Köln (Cologne), a network of dealers has more than 50 Bierbikes on the streets of 35 cities in Germany.

In 2007, two friends from Minnesota, Eric Olson and Al Boyce, saw the Fietscafe while visiting Amsterdam and decided to import the vehicle to the United States. The first PedalPub was launched in Minneapolis and has since expanded to Houston, Denver, and Chicago (check one out in Figure 17-1). For more information, go to www.pedalpub.com. (For the record, accidents are extremely rare; the Fietscafe can go only 5 miles per hour, unless it's downhill, and the wind is at your back.)

Figure 17-1:
The PedalPub is a pedal-powered bar that can seat 17 people.

Chapter 18

Brewing Beer at Home

- -

In This Chapter

▶ Getting your hands on the right equipment

▶ Sanitizing your gear

▶ Brewing, fermenting, bottling, and record keeping

▶ Taking your brewing to the next level

- -

*O*ne of the recurring questions about homebrewing is, "Why should I go through the trouble of brewing beer if I can just buy my favorite beer at the store?" After homebrewing for 25 years, writing several articles on the topic, teaching an occasional homebrew class, and making two videos on the subject, I can offer you several good answers to that question.

✔ First, homebrewed beer may be every bit as good as some commercial beer or even better, with as much flavor and character as most craft beers. Although avoiding mass-marketed beer was the original inspiration for homebrewing, emulating your favorite craft brew is now a primary inspiration for taking up the hobby.

✔ Second, if you can cook, you can make beer (with store-bought malt extract). It's easy!

✔ Third, with practice and experience, you can make any style of beer you want.

Here are some other reasons people make stove-top beer:

✔ Participating in the current do-it-yourself homebrewing trend — what other hobby allows you to drink the fruits of your labor? (Okay, perhaps growing apples for cider or grapes for wine.)

✔ Making beers comparable to hard-to-find microbrews and expensive imported beers from around the world.

✔ Winning awards in homebrewing competitions.

✔ Sharing homebrewing as an entertaining pastime with friends and family members.

✔ Practicing for when you start your own microbrewery.

I wrote this chapter for those of you who've never brewed beer and want to know about the essential tools and procedures needed to produce a simple, no-frills, malt-extract beer.

Before you go on, I suggest you read the later sidebar "The legalities of U.S. homebrewing" to determine whether or how you can proceed, legally speaking.

Getting Started with Homebrewing

New homebrewers are no different from other hobbyists; they're champing at the bit (foaming at the mouth?) to get started with their hobby. Although this enthusiasm is good, jumping headlong into the unknown isn't. In the following sections, I explain where you can shop for supplies; I also list the gear and ingredients you need to begin brewing.

If you want to try your hand at brewing without the commitment — what, me, afraid of commitment? — you may want to visit a Brew On Premise (BOP) where you can use the facility's equipment, recipes, and ingredients. BOPs aren't as prevalent as they used to be, so the likelihood that you have one in your neighborhood is small; an Internet search can confirm that reality.

The legalities of U.S. homebrewing

With the repeal of the 18th Amendment in 1933, homebrewing should have been made legal right along with home winemaking. Unfortunately, the phrase *and/or beer* never made it into the Federal Register, ostensibly through a stenographer's error.

This situation remained unchanged until 1979, when a bill was signed into law by President Jimmy Carter, and after almost 40 years, homebrewing was legal again, as far as the Feds were concerned. Because the right to brew beer at home opened the door to abuses of the privilege, some safeguards were built in to the law. Following are the two most important federal laws for homebrewers to abide by:

✔ Homebrewers are limited to 100 gallons of homebrew per person, per year (or 200 gallons per year per household).

✔ Homebrew is not, *under any circumstances,* to be sold.

Despite the federal government's recognition of the right to brew at home, individual state laws may supersede the federal statute. Only 48 of 50 states have "statutorily recognized" homebrewing, Alabama and Mississippi being the last two holdouts. The American Homebrewers Association (AHA) is currently lobbying to get all 50 states in step with one another.

Meanwhile, check with your state and local governments regarding the legalities of homebrewing before starting. You can call the AHA toll free at 888-822-6273 or visit its website at www.homebrewersassociaton.org to check on the homebrewing status within your state.

Something's brewing here

According to 2010 estimates, the United States has more than 750,000 homebrewers and more than 900 homebrewing clubs. The clubs are mostly small, but the national group, the American Homebrewers Association (AHA), boasts 24,000 members. Homebrew associations around the world are growing, too — on all continents. Because of Internet sales, brick-and-mortar homebrew shops aren't as common as they used to be, but homebrew equipment and supplies are now plentiful and easy to obtain.

Supply shopping

Before you start shopping for homebrewing supplies, locate a local homebrew-supply store. Start with an Internet search of "Beer Homebrewing Equipment and Supplies." Call or stop in a store and ask for a catalog and price list if the store offers one. Look at the equipment and supplies and ask questions about the stock, especially the ingredients.

If you're not fortunate enough to have a local homebrew-supply store, you can just order what you need over the Internet. A simple search on "Homebrewing supplies" nets you a wide range of sources.

Pots, buckets, brushes, and such

What you need to get going isn't exotic. The following sections list (and Figure 18-1 shows) what you need at a minimum and recommends nonessential time- and effort-saving tools. Forget any preconceived notions about shiny copper kettles and coils taking up the entire kitchen or huge wooden vats bubbling and churning in the cellar — such are the product of a vivid imagination. This whole process is much more like baking bread.

Starter equipment kits, found at your local (or online) homebrew shops, can range from bare-bones to top-of-the-line quality; you can find good ones for less than $200. Before buying a kit, consider your needs and what you're willing and able to spend. The following sections list the necessary items with descriptions and approximate costs.

Airlock

An airlock is an inexpensive but simple, efficient way to allow carbon dioxide to escape from the fermenter without letting any air in and compromising the hermetic seal of the lid. This three-piece gizmo has a cylindrical outside piece with a tubelike stem, an internal float piece that resembles an inverted cup, and a cap to fit over the cylindrical part. A similar contraption, called a *bubbler,* is a two-chamber device that works on the same principle. The difference is that an airlock can be easily cleaned and sanitized on the inside, whereas the totally enclosed bubbler can't. *Cost:* $2 or less.

Bottle brush

A bottle brush is an important piece of equipment. You need a soft-bristle brush to properly clean inside the bottles before you fill them. *Cost:* $4.

Bottle capper

A bottle capper affixes the fresh caps to the just-filled bottles. Cappers come in all shapes, sizes, and costs. Most work equally well, but I suggest you choose a *bench capper* over the *two-handed* style, even though bench cappers cost more than two-handed cappers. A bench capper is free-standing and can be attached to a work surface, leaving one hand free to hold the bottle steady. The two-handed cappers can be tricky to use if nothing is holding the bottle steady. *Cost:* $12 (two-handed) to $35 (bench-type).

Bottle washer

A bottle washer is a curved copper apparatus that threads onto a faucet. It works as a spraying device for the insides of bottles — an added convenience for cleaning bottles. Not a necessity, but for the money, you may as well take advantage of it. *Cost:* $15.

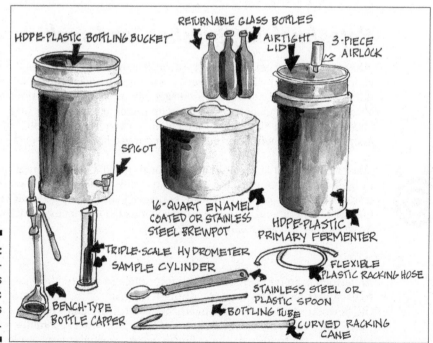

Figure 18-1:
Many home-
brew shops
sell basic
equipment as
a startup kit.

If you buy a bottle washer, take note of which faucet in your home you'll be using. Utility faucets usually have larger hose threads; other types, such as bathroom and kitchen faucets, have fine threads and require an adapter. Make sure the bottle washer and any adapters you buy have a rubber washer (gasket) in place.

Bottles

Look for heavy, returnable bottles, without a threaded opening (a bottle crown can't seal properly across the threads). You need enough to hold 5 gallons of beer: 54 12-ounce bottles, or 40 16-ounce bottles, or any combination that adds up to 640 ounces. *Bombers* (22-ounce bottles) are popular with homebrewers. *Cost:* Cost of retailer deposit, or up to $28 per case if purchased, depending on the style.

You can buy new bottles from a homebrew supplier, but used bottles from commercial breweries are much cheaper — though they're becoming much rarer. Find out whether a local liquor store sells any beer in returnable bottles (not the cheap, recyclable kind). If so, buy a couple cases, drink the beer, and voilà — you have 48 bottles (not to mention a swollen bladder) right off the bat for the cost of a deposit.

An (expensive) alternative is to get self-sealing swing-top bottles (also called *Grolsch bottles,* after the Dutch beer that popularized them). The upside of swing-top bottles is that you don't need to buy bottle caps or cappers; the downside (besides the initial expense) is that the rubber gaskets eventually wear out. Swing-top bottles also require closer attention at cleaning time than regular bottles do, and they're not allowed in most homebrew competitions.

Bottling bucket

You need an HDPE (high-density polyethylene — food-grade plastic) plastic vessel on bottling day. It doesn't require a lid but is considerably more efficient if it has a removable spigot at the bottom. This plastic vessel is also called a *priming vessel* because your fermented beer is primed with corn sugar (dextrose) just before bottling (a process discussed in detail later in this chapter). *Cost:* $14.

Bottling tube

A bottling tube is a long, hard plastic tube with a spring-loaded valve at the tip. It attaches to the plastic hose (which attaches to the spigot on the bottling bucket or the *racking cane,* or tube); the bottling tube is inserted into the bottles for filling. *Cost:* $3.

Brew spoon

A brew spoon is a stainless steel or plastic spoon with a long handle — 18 inches or longer. Never use wooden spoons for brewing: They can be difficult to clean properly. Use your brew spoon only for brewing beer. *Cost:* $4 (plastic) to $8 (stainless steel).

Brew pot

A brew pot is a stainless steel, aluminum, or enamel-coated metal pot. Your brew pot should have a 16-quart minimum capacity because the more *wort* (unfermented beer) you boil, the better your finished beer. A big, old, inexpensive enamel lobster pot is perfect, as long as the enamel isn't chipped. *Cost:* $25 and up.

Flexible plastic hose

A flexible plastic hose is an important, multifunctional piece of equipment used to transfer beer from bucket to bucket or from bucket to bottle. Be sure to keep it clean and undamaged. You need at least 3 feet of hosing; any more than 4 feet can be a nuisance. *Cost:* $0.50 to $0.75 a foot.

Primary fermentation vessel

A primary fermentation vessel is a plastic bucket in which to pour cooled wort shortly after the brewing process. It must be sealed airtight for the duration of the fermentation. It must have a 7-gallon capacity to accommodate a 5-gallon batch of beer and still have room for all the vigorous bubbling action and yeast build-up *(barm)* of the fermenting beer. *Cost:* $18 with lid.

I recommend plastic over glass for the fermenter because plastic is so much easier to clean and won't break. The plastics used in homebrewing are of the same quality and standards as the plastics used in the food industry (HDPE plastics). These plastics, unlike lesser grades of plastic, restrict — sufficiently, although not completely — gaseous transfer through the plastic.

For ease of use, you can buy specially made plastic fermenters with removable plastic spigots. If your fermenter has no spigot, you need a *racking cane* to siphon the beer out of the primary fermenter. Make sure your plastic hosing fits the racking cane.

Rubber stopper

A rubber stopper fits over the stem of the airlock or bubbler to act as a sealed wedge when the airlock is inserted into the hole in the fermenter lid. These so-called drilled stoppers are sized by number (for example, #3 stoppers). Buy a stopper that fits the opening in the fermenter lid; your equipment supplier will know what you need. *Cost:* $2 or less.

Triple-scale hydrometer

A triple-scale hydrometer is a device used to determine the gravity of your brew, which, in turn, allows you to calculate the alcohol content (see Figure 18-2 later in this chapter). It's easy to use and not very expensive. I suggest learning to use one if you want to progress in homebrewing. Also be sure to buy a plastic *cylinder* to hold the test sample. *Cost:* about $15 for both.

Conversion equations for homebrewing

Here are some approximate metric conversions for the liquid and length measurements used in this chapter:

¾ cup = 177.75 milliliters

1 cup = 237 milliliters

1 ounce = 29.6 milliliters

12 ounces = 355 milliliters

16 ounces (U.S. pint) = 473 milliliters

20 ounces (imperial pint) = 592 milliliters

22 ounces = 651 milliliters

1 gallon = 3.8 liters

5 gallons = 19 liters

1 inch = 25 millimeters

1 foot = 30 centimeters

A *hydrometer* — be it triple scale or not — is a fragile measuring device, used solely to determine the density of liquids. When the weighted end is submerged in liquid, the calibrated stem projects out of the liquid at a height determined by the density of the liquid; that height gives you the reading. For more information on hydrometer reading, see the later section "Ready, set, brew!"

Brew ingredients

Okay, you've got your pots, buckets, tubes, spoon, and whatnot. Moving on to buying the ingredients for your first batch of beer is easy, almost a no-brainer. You go into a homebrew-supply shop or fill out an online order form and buy an extract kit (a can or bag of malt extract), hops, a packet of yeast, corn sugar (*dextrose* — ⅔ cup minimum), and enough caps (*crowns*) for 50 to 60 bottles. Done. That's it! (Don't worry about a recipe, all kit beers come with recipes included.)

Extract kit (malt extract and yeast)

The beer you're about to make is *kit* beer — no grains, no muss, no fuss. A kit brew comes complete with its own packet of dried yeast and is sold by beer style. When making beer from a kit, your only decision is what style of beer you want to make. Liquid malt extract (syrup) comes in a variety of colors and flavors, clearly labeled according to the style of beer that it's meant to produce.

The typical can of liquid malt extract is 3.3 pounds. For full body and taste, buy two 3.3-pound cans to make one full batch of beer (5 gallons). Liquid malt extract is also occasionally packaged in bags, which are simply sold by the pound.

Dry malt extract versus liquid malt syrup

Dry malt extract, also called *powdered extract* or *DME,* is just a dehydrated version of the liquid malt syrup found in most kits. Dry extract is made the same way as malt extract syrups but with the added process of being spray-dried completely (which, by the way, makes it more expensive). Dry extract is usually sold generically; it's not pre-packaged according to any style, though you can still get it in light (pale), amber, and dark variations.

The best thing about dry extract in comparison to syrup is its convenience. Retailers usually sell it by the pound in any quantity you want. If it comes in a resealable bag, you can use a portion of it and put the rest back in the refrigerator

for later use, whereas unused portions of sticky malt syrup are difficult to store.

Using dry malt extract in place of malt syrup extract affects your original gravities slightly in a pound-for-pound comparison. Syrups contain approximately 20 percent water content, whereas the dry extract has almost none. The difference adds up to about 1 specific gravity degree per pound, the dry extract having a greater yield than the syrup. That is, 6 pounds of syrup achieve a specific gravity of 1.048, while 6 pounds of dry extract achieve a specific gravity 6 degrees higher, or 1.054 — not a major difference, but something you should know.

The rather odd — by U.S. standards — measure of 3.3 pounds is due to the fact that the British pioneered the malt-extract–producing industry. The majority of kits on the market are from the United Kingdom, where, translated to 1.5 kilograms, a 3.3-pound can is the standard size.

When buying homebrewing kits, you aren't given any choices regarding the way the malt extract is packaged; just so you're not caught off guard, you should be aware that malt extract is also sold in dry form (see the nearby sidebar "Dry malt extract versus liquid malt syrup" for details). As you progress in the hobby, chances are you'll come to prefer dry malt extract.

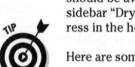

Here are some things to keep in mind when buying your kit:

- ✔ For the sake of reality and authenticity, stick with an ale kit. Quality lager beers are impossible to make at the beginner level.

- ✔ Just for laughs, read the directions included with the kit. If these directions call for large additions of white (cane) sugar (much like Prohibition-era homebrew), then ignore them. Follow my instructions, and you'll do fine. Trust me! (By the way, did I mention that I have a bridge to sell?)

Hops

Hops are available in many different varieties; they're chosen according to the beer style the kit is designed to brew. Hops are typically packaged in 1-ounce increments and, depending on the beer style, your kit may include a few different varieties of hops.

Yeast

Yeast is also available in a number of different types; they're also chosen according to the beer style the kit is designed to brew. Yeast found in beer kits is dry and packaged in small packets. Be aware that liquid yeast products are also available, but they're not typically found in kits because liquid yeast products needs to be kept refrigerated.

Sugar

At bottling time, you need a type of sugar called *dextrose,* or *corn sugar.* This highly refined sugar is used to prime the beer just before it's bottled. *Priming* is the procedure in which a measured amount of corn sugar is mixed with the already fermented beer in order to create carbonation in the bottle (see the later section "Bottle it up!"). Dextrose is inexpensive and can be purchased in any volume, although many homebrew suppliers sell it in prepackaged amounts. For one 5-gallon batch, you need ¾ cup of corn sugar for priming — no more.

Water

Water is the ingredient that makes up the bulk of your homebrew, but it's too often taken for granted. I recommend bottled water over tap water — only if you're unsure of the quality of your tap water. Tap water can present various problems, including the following:

- ✔ If the water you're using for brewing is from an underground well, chances are that it's high in iron and other tastable minerals.
- ✔ If your water is softened, it's probably high in sodium.
- ✔ If your water is supplied by a public works department, it may have a high chlorine content. Chlorine is volatile and can easily be boiled off, but you'd have to boil all 5 gallons — a daunting task. Chlorine can also be filtered out, or if left sitting out in an open container for about 24 hours, the chlorine will eventually degas itself from the water.

Crowns

Bottle crowns are sometimes sold by the batch (60 crowns, which is enough for 54 bottles, with a few extras) but more typically by the gross (144 crowns). Although bottle crowns may seem to be equipment rather than ingredients, they're consumable objects because you can use them only one time; so I call them ingredients (just not very tasty ones).

Department of Sanitation: Keeping Clean During the Brewing Process

Before moving on to the actual process of homebrewing later in this chapter, I need to discuss one *major* factor in making good beer: If you want your beer to taste fresh and be drinkable and enjoyable, you need to protect it from the millions of hungry microbes that are waiting to ambush your brew. Germs are everywhere; they live with us and even on us. Look out! There's one now!

In the following sections, I describe the importance of keeping your home-brewing gear clean, the types of cleaners available, and some general guidelines to follow.

The importance of sterilizing and sanitizing

I don't know who first said that cleanliness is next to godliness, but I'd be willing to bet that he or she brewed beer. Scrupulously clean equipment and a pristine brewing environment are the keys to making good beer. *Clean* doesn't mean just soap-and-water clean; when it comes to beer, serious sanitation is a necessity. Why?

Fungi and bacteria, the two bad guys of the germ world that you need to worry about with beer, are opportunistic; if you give them half a chance at a free meal, they take it without reservation. (Wouldn't you, if it were your wonderful beer being offered?) Here's who you're battling:

- Fungi consist of mold spores and wild yeast. Beer yeast fall into the fungus category, but they're the friendly variety.

- Only a couple of strains of bacteria show up in beer — usually in spontaneously fermented Belgian beers.

Fungi and bacteria thrive in very warm temperatures — often up to 120 degrees Fahrenheit (49 degrees Celsius). Microbial activity tends to decrease as the temperature drops, so cooling down the hot wort as quickly as possible is imperative. (See the later section "Ready, set, brew!" for more info about this task.)

You can't possibly kill *all* the fungi and bacteria in your home. The idea is to keep the germs from enjoying your beer before you have a chance to; if they get to the beer first, you may not want it.

I can't make this point too often: Anything and everything that comes into contact with your beer *at any time* must be either sterilized or sanitized.

✔ _Sterilizing_ refers to disinfecting items (such as the brew pot and the brew's ingredients) by boiling.

✔ _Sanitizing_ refers to cleaning and disinfecting all the rest of the equipment by using chemicals (and isn't to be confused with _sanity,_ which you can lose during all the cleaning you have to do).

Note: Because unfermented beer is warm and sweet, it's the perfect breeding ground for all the microbiological bad boys. However, none of the bacteria that grow in beer are remotely as dangerous as the _E. coli_ or _Salmonella_ bacteria that occur in uncooked meat, fish, and eggs. The germs that breed in beer are just freeloading little buggers that make the beer taste bad. Beer germs won't kill you (although having to throw out an entire batch of brew may). You certainly don't have to attain the same level of sterility in your home brewery that you expect in an operating room.

Soaps for suds

The chemicals used to clean homebrewing equipment include iodine-based products, ammonia, chlorine-based products, lye, and at least one environmentally safe cleanser that uses percarbonates. Following are the pros and cons of various chemicals:

✔ _Iodine_ is widely used in the medical field and the restaurant industry as a disinfectant. The disinfectant properties of iodine can be applied to homebrewing, but unless the iodine solution is well diluted, it stains plastics as well as human skin. (Dilute the iodine according to package directions.)

✔ _Ammonia_ is best used for cleaning bottles in a dilution of 1 cup ammonia to 5 gallons of water — if you can stand the pungent odor. Ammonia requires a thorough hot-water rinse.

✔ _Chlorine_ is in simple household bleach, which is very effective and cost-efficient for cleaning homebrewing equipment. A 1-ounce-per-gallon dilution ratio is sufficient, making a gallon of generic bleach an incredibly good deal. Be sure to buy _unscented_ bleach and to rinse all equipment thoroughly. Good old plain bleach is best.

Just so you don't try to double up on your sanitizing procedures, _never_ mix ammonia with chlorine. This combination releases toxic chlorine gas.

✔ _Lye_ should be used only to remove the most stubborn stains and obstinate organic material from bottles or glass carboys. Always wear protective gear, such as goggles and rubber gloves, when you work with lye. Also, be sure to always use lye according to package directions.

✔ _Percarbonates_ supposedly accomplish their cleaning activity with oxygen molecules — exactly how is beyond me. Sanitizers that contain percarbonates don't require rinsing. (Always use percarbonates according to package directions.)

Several brand-name sanitizers — including Iodophor, One Step, and B-Bright — are available through homebrew suppliers. The capacity of these products to sanitize homebrewing equipment is in direct proportion to the way in which they're used, meaning if you don't follow instructions, don't blame the manufacturer for a blown batch of beer.

General cleaning practices

Sterilizing and sanitizing your equipment is the sixth step in the brewing process (see the later section "Ready, set, brew!" for full details). The best place to handle sanitizing procedures is a utility basin or a large-capacity sink. (A bathtub will do in a pinch, but remember that bathrooms harbor tons of bacteria and also, on occasion, small children. Remove both prior to use.) The most effective methods of sanitizing involve soaking rather than intensive scrubbing. The length of soaking time depends completely on the sanitizer you're using, so be sure to refer to package directions.

Never use any abrasives or materials that can scratch your plastic equipment, because pits and scratches are excellent hiding places for those wily bacteria. A soft sponge, used only for cleaning homebrew equipment, is the way to go.

Following Step-by-Step Homebrewing Instructions

Making and bottling a batch of beer, like building Rome, can't be done in a day. On the other hand, it doesn't take a heck of a lot longer than a day, either. Because the raw, sweet wort must undergo fermentation before it officially becomes beer, bottling can't take place until fermentation is complete. Fermentation of a 5-gallon batch usually takes a minimum of seven days, depending on the yeast. So you need to set aside two days, about a week apart, for the job. Allow three hours each day to set up, brew (or bottle), and clean up. Patience is a virtue; good homebrew is its own reward.

In the following sections, I describe each stage of the beginner homebrewing process, from the initial brew and fermentation to bottling and record keeping.

Everything that comes in contact with the beer can potentially contaminate it. Keep your equipment clean, keep your brewery clean, keep your hands clean, and practice good hygiene; every cough or sneeze is a threat to your beer. You may even want to consider banishing Spot and Sylvester from your brewing area until cleanup time. Beer isn't serious, but sanitation is.

Ready, set, brew!

Okay, now it's time to make beer. Be sure to have all your equipment and ingredients on hand before starting. Without further abrew, here are the steps for making a simple extract beer:

1. **Fill your brew pot two-thirds full of cool water and place it on the stove, with the burner set on medium-high.**

   Use the largest burner available.

   The quantity of water used in this step isn't important, but you should boil as much as possible. Don't worry — you'll make up the difference to 5 gallons by adding more water to the fermenter later (in Step 12).

2. **Heat the thick, syrupy malt extract to make it less viscous and easier to scoop out of the can (or squeeze out of the bag).**

   You can heat it by immersing it in hot water for about 5 minutes.

3. **Open the can or bag, scrape all the extract into the brew pot, and use your virgin brew spoon to give the mix a vigorous stir.**

4. **Set a timer or note the time when you poured extract into the brew pot. Boil *uncovered* for 1 hour, stirring regularly and keeping the brew pot at a slow, rolling boil.**

   The universally suggested minimum boil is 1 hour — the amount of time required to mix and boil the ingredients properly.

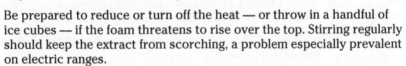

   Be prepared to reduce or turn off the heat — or throw in a handful of ice cubes — if the foam threatens to rise over the top. Stirring regularly should keep the extract from scorching, a problem especially prevalent on electric ranges.

   Sticky, sweet stuff all over your stove isn't a good thing — not to mention a waste of potential beer. So remember, to prevent boilovers, *don't* cover the brew pot.

5. **Add your hops to the brew pot according to your recipe.**

   Hops are typically added to the brew pot in small increments like an ounce or a half an ounce at a time. They're also typically added at quarter-hour increments of time like 15 minutes or 30 minutes. The timing affects the aroma and the flavor of the beer; hops added early in the boiling process add more bitterness to the beer, while hops added late in the boiling process add more aroma. Hops added in the last half of a 1-hour boil contribute to hop flavor in the beer.

6. **While the extract is boiling, sanitize the equipment you need for fermentation.**

The items you need to sanitize are

- Primary fermenter and lid

- Disassembled airlock or bubbler

- Rubber stopper

- Clean coffee cup or small bowl (for the yeast)

- Triple-scale hydrometer (not the cylinder)

Place the fermenter in the utility tub (or large sink) and begin drawing cold water into the fermenter. Add cleansing/sanitizing chemicals, according to package directions, or 1 ounce of unscented household bleach per gallon of water. Allow water to fill the fermenter; then shut off the water. Immerse the remaining equipment in the fermenter, including the fermenter lid (you'll have to force it in a bit).

Then crack open a beer; you've got time to kill. While you're at it, stir the brew pot (with the spoon, not the beer bottle!).

7. **After half an hour has elapsed, remove and rinse the various pieces of sanitized equipment.**

If your fermenter has a spigot, drain the water through it to sanitize it, too. Rinse everything in hot water and place the items on a *clean* surface. Allow them to air-dry.

The fermenter lid, placed upside-down on a clean surface, is a good place to put the smaller items.

8. **When 1 hour has elapsed since you poured in the extract, turn off the burner and *now* place the lid on the brew pot.**

9. **Cool the wort (after it's mixed with water, the boiled extract is transformed into *wort*).**

Put a stopper in the sink drain and carefully place the covered brew pot in the sink. Run cold tap water until the sink is full, making sure you keep the water from seeping into the brew pot and the boiled wort. Heat from the brew pot will be drawn away by the cold water, which won't stay cold for long.

Drain the water and repeat this procedure two or three times, or as often as necessary. When the water surrounding the brew pot no longer gets noticeably warm in the first couple of minutes, you can stop.

Adding ice to the water speeds the cooling process. If you live in a cold climate, snow banks work well for cooling wort. *Don't* add ice directly into the brew pot, or you may contaminate the wort.

You need to cool the wort as quickly as possible at this point because cooling inhibits the growth of bacteria and readies the wort for the addition of the yeast. Anything that decreases the time it takes to cool down your wort is a positive step toward making better beer, which is why you may want to consider making or buying an immersion wort chiller (see the "New toys: Equipment upgrades" section later in this chapter).

10. **While the wort is cooling, fill your sanitized cup or bowl with lukewarm water (approximately 80 degrees Fahrenheit, 27 degrees Celsius), tear open the yeast packet, and sprinkle the yeast into the water.**

    To avoid contamination, don't stir. Allow the mixture to stand for at least 10 minutes, covered with plastic wrap to ensure against airborne contamination. This process, called *proofing,* is a gentle wake-up call for the dormant yeast and prepares it for fermentation.

11. **When the brew pot is cool to the touch, carefully pour the cooled wort into the sanitized fermenter.**

    Make sure the spigot is in the closed position (you don't even want to *think* about the consequences of leaving it open).

12. **Top up the fermenter to the 5-gallon line with cold bottled water (or tap water, if yours is of acceptable quality).**

    Yeast needs oxygen to begin the respiration phase of the fermentation cycle. Vigorously pouring and splashing cold water into the fermenter is an effective way to mix the water and the wort, as well as to aerate the wort for the yeast.

13. **Take a hydrometer reading (optional).**

    As you immerse the sanitized hydrometer (see Figure 18-2) into the now-diluted wort, give the hydrometer a quick spin with your thumb and index finger. This action keeps tiny bubbles from clinging to the side of the hydrometer, which can cause you to get an incorrect reading.

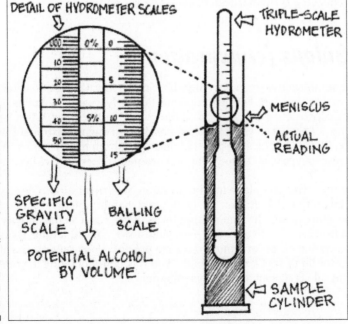

Figure 18-2: Be sure to read your triple-scale hydrometer carefully, sighting only the actual surface of the wort, not the ridges of the meniscus.

Record the numbers on the scales (see the nearby sidebar "Hydrometers made simple" for more info about using a hydrometer) and remove.

14. **Pour the yeast into the cooled wort to start the fermentation process.**

    Brewers call this step *pitching* the yeast. So as not to destroy the living yeast, the wort must be cooled to approximately 80 degrees Fahrenheit (27 degrees Celsius); 70 degrees Fahrenheit (21 degrees Celsius) is ideal. Gently pour the yeast in a wide circle to disperse it well.

15. **Close the fermenter with its lid, leaving the airlock or bubbler out, and place the fermenter in a cool, dark location, such as a basement, crawl space, or closet.**

    Don't put the fermenter in direct sunlight or someplace where the daily temperature fluctuates (such as your garage). These fluctuating temperatures mess with the natural fermentation process, which isn't good for your beer.

16. **When the fermenter is in place, attach the rubber stopper to the air-lock, fill it halfway with water, and snap on the airlock cap; then position the airlock (bubbler) securely into the hole in the fermenter lid.**

    To make sure the fermenter lid and airlock are sealed properly, gently push down on the lid. This push should cause the inner float piece to rise. If the float piece doesn't move, the seal has a breach; check the lid and the airlock.

17. **Wait seven or eight days.**

    This step is the hardest, especially for first-timers.

Fabulous fermentation

Fermentation activity can start anywhere in the first 12 to 24 hours after you add the yeast to the wort. Fermentation starts slowly, gradually builds in intensity, and usually reaches a crescendo on the second or third day. When fermentation reaches its peak, the airlock may sound like an engine piston at low rev, with carbon dioxide bubbles making their hasty exit from the fermenter. A quick whiff of the escaping gas gives you your first aromatic experience of beer making.

Leave the fermenter alone for the duration of fermentation. The exact length of fermentation depends on the health and viability of the yeast and on the temperature at which fermentation takes place. Even as the activity slows and the bubbles in the airlock start emerging slowly, one at a time, fermentation may continue for several more days. Be patient. *Don't* remove the airlock or fermenter lid to sneak a peek inside; you risk contaminating the beer. The general rule is to wait seven days minimum.

Hydrometers made simple

Reading the triple-scale hydrometer at the beginner level is an option, not a necessity, but performing this simple task helps you better understand and appreciate the magic of fermentation. First, you measure the density of your brew with a hydrometer. Knowing the beer's density enables you to calculate the volume of alcohol in your brew. More importantly, you can find out with certainty whether your brew is done fermenting (your bottles may explode if it isn't!).

Hydrometers are like thermometers — really simple. But they can be daunting if you're unfamiliar with them. Here's how it all works: The specific gravity scale compares all liquids to ordinary water at 60 degrees Fahrenheit (15 degrees Celsius), which has a specific gravity of 1.000.

✔ Taking a hydrometer reading after the wort is cooled gives you the original gravity (OG), which gives you an idea of how much fermentable sugar is in your brew before fermentation (that's the potential alcohol).

✔ Taking a second hydrometer reading after fermentation is over (just prior to bottling), you get a final gravity (FG, also called *terminal gravity*).

Subtracting the FG from the OG tells you, by way of conversion, how much of the sugar was eaten by the yeast. How? When yeast eat sugar, they produce alcohol, so each decrease in gravity results in an increase in alcohol. On the triple-scale hydrometer, the alcohol-potential scale is right next to the specific gravity scale. (If you're ready to call for pizza, you've got company. But it's easier the second time around, believe me.)

The main reason you need a hydrometer is to avoid exploding bottles. Bottles explode when, due to fermentation problems, a lot of sugars remain in the beer when it's bottled. Average healthy yeast consume at least 70 percent of available sugars; if the final gravity reading on your fermented beer isn't 30 percent or less of the original gravity, too much sugar may still be left in your beer. If the beer is bottled with priming sugar to boot, you're headed for the homebrew version of fireworks. Allow the beer a couple more days to ferment and check again.

Here's a sample equation: If your beer has an original gravity of 1.048, subtract 1 so you have 0.048; then multiply 0.048 by 0.30, which results in 0.014. If the final gravity of your beer is higher than 1.014, you should delay bottling a few more days.

Note: A couple of things to remember when using a hydrometer:

✔ If your liquid's temperature at reading time isn't near 60 degrees Fahrenheit (15 degrees Celsius), the numbers will be skewed. Hot wort readings (OG) will be lower than they should be, and cold bottling readings (FG) will be higher than they should be.

✔ Be sure to sight your reading at the lowest point of the *meniscus* (the concave shape of the surface in the sampling cylinder).

Optional reading: Just in case you're curious, the third scale on the triple-scale hydrometer is the *Balling scale*. Its gradations are called *degrees Plato*. On this scale, water at 60 degrees Fahrenheit (15 degrees Celsius) is 0 degrees Plato. You can use it in exactly the same way that you use the specific gravity scale. In fact, many megabrewers, most European brewers, and a majority of microbrewers use the Balling scale. The same homebrew with an OG of 1.048 will have a density of 12.5 degrees Plato. Most homebrewers and some microbrewers prefer to work with the specific gravity scale.

On the seventh day of fermentation, start paying close attention to the brew (no, it's not the day to rest). With the aid of a wristwatch or a clock that has a second hand, count the amount of time between bubbles emerging from the airlock. When a minute or more elapses between bubbles, plan to bottle the next day or very soon thereafter. If after seven days, the float piece in the airlock isn't even floating, you should start bottling.

If you have a hydrometer, fill the hydrometer cylinder with a sample of beer through the spigot of the fermenter and take a hydrometer reading to verify that fermentation is complete. (See the nearby sidebar "Hydrometers made simple" for the numbers you're looking for.)

After you take your hydrometer reading, don't pour the sample from the cylinder back in with the rest of the beer; doing so risks contaminating it. More important, don't throw the sample down the sink; it may be uncarbonated, but it's still good beer, so drink it. You may be surprised by how good it already tastes. Ah!

Bottle it up!

After you've made certain that the beer is fully fermented, retrieved the bottling equipment, and quarantined the family pets, you're ready to start the bottling procedures.

As always, setup starts with sanitizing all the necessary equipment, which includes the following:

- Bottles
- Bottling bucket
- Bottling tube
- Plastic hose

In addition to the items to be sanitized and a sanitizing agent, you need the following equipment:

- Bottle brush
- Bottle capper
- Bottle caps
- Bottle washer
- ¾ cup dextrose
- Two small saucepans

You'll also need your hydrometer and cylinder to measure your beer's gravity, but those items don't need to be sanitized.

Follow these steps to bottle your beer:

1. **Fill your utility tub or other designated sanitizing basin about three-quarters full of cold water. Add bleach or another sanitizing agent, as directed on the package, and submerge all the bottles needed to contain the full 5-gallon batch of beer.**

   Allow the bottles to soak for at least half an hour (or according to package directions).

2. **While the bottles are soaking, put ¾ cup dextrose into one of the saucepans, dissolve the dextrose in a pint or so of water, cover, and place the pan on the stove over low heat.**

3. **Into the other saucepan, put enough bottle caps for the number of bottles you have soaking plus a few extra. Fill the pan with enough water to cover all the caps, and place the pan on the stove over low heat.**

   Having too many bottle caps sterilized and ready for bottling is better than not enough.

4. **Allow the contents of both saucepans to come to a boil. Then turn off the heat and allow both to cool.**

5. **When half an hour has passed, clean the bottles.**

   Connect the bottle washer to the faucet over the tub in which the bottles have been soaking and turn on the hot water (the bottle washer holds back the water pressure until a bottle is lowered over the stem and pushed down). Then, clean the bottles one by one with the bottle brush, drain the sanitizer, rinse the bottles with the bottle washer, and allow to air-dry. Continue until all bottles are cleaned. Visually check each bottle for cleanliness instead of just assuming that all the bottles are sanitized.

   Four dozen free-standing bottles can make for one heck of a domino effect. Always put cleaned bottles back into six-pack holders or cardboard cases to prevent an aggravating, easily avoidable accident.

6. **Drain the bottle-cleaning water out of the utility tub and place the bottling bucket in the tub. Fill the bucket with water and the sanitizing agent of your choice. Then place the bottling hose and bottling tube in the bottling bucket and allow them to soak.**

7. **While the bottling equipment is soaking, retrieve the still-covered fermenter from its resting place and put it on a sturdy table, countertop, or work surface about 3 or 4 feet off the ground.**

8. **Set up your bottling station, making sure you have the priming sugar (dextrose) and bottle caps — still in their respective saucepans — as well as the bottle capper and bottles.**

If you're taking gravity readings, have your hydrometer and cylinder ready to use, too.

9. **After half an hour, drain the sanitizing solution from the bottling bucket through the spigot on the bottom. Then thoroughly rinse the remaining pieces of equipment, along with the bottles, and bring them to your bottling station.**

Whistle while you work.

10. **Place the bottling bucket on the floor directly below the fermenter and connect the plastic hose to the spigot on the fermenter, allowing the other end of the hose to hang inside the bottling bucket. Pour the dextrose-and-water mixture from one saucepan into the bottling bucket.**

The dissolved corn sugar mixes with the beer as it drains from the fermenter into the bottling bucket; this procedure is called *priming*. After all the beer is bottled, this sugar becomes another source of food for the few yeast cells that remain in the liquid. As the yeast consume the sugar, they produce the beer's carbonation within the bottle. Eventually, the yeast again fall dormant and create a thin layer of sediment on the bottom of each bottle.

If by chance your beer isn't fully fermented or if you somehow added too much dextrose at bottling time, you may find out firsthand what a mess exploding bottles can make. Excess sugar — whether leftover maltose from an unfinished fermentation or added corn sugar — overfeeds the yeast in an enclosed bottle. With nowhere for the pressure to go, the glass will give before the bottle cap will. Kaboom! Big mess! Don't over prime! (Remember, the recommended amount of sugar to add is 34 cup.)

11. **Open the spigot on the fermenter and allow all the beer to run into the bottling bucket.**

Don't try to salvage every last drop from the fermenter by tilting it as the beer drains down the spigot. The spigot is purposely positioned about ¾ inch above the bottom of the fermenter to allow all the spent yeast and miscellaneous organic fallout to remain behind.

12. **Prepare to take a gravity reading.**

While the beer is draining from the fermenter to the bottling bucket, carefully fill the hydrometer cylinder from the hose (fill it to within 1 inch from the top). Place the cylinder on a flat surface and take a gravity reading with your hydrometer. Drink the flat beer from the cylinder.

Avoid splashing or aerating your beer while you're bottling. You'll later be able to taste any oxidation that the beer picks up now. Yuck.

13. **After the last of the beer is drained, close the spigot, remove the hose, and put all the equipment aside to be cleaned after you're done bottling.**

14. **Carefully place the bottling bucket up where the fermenter was. Connect the rinsed hose to the spigot on the bottling bucket and attach the bottling tube to the other end. Arrange all your bottles on the floor directly below the bottling bucket.**

Keeping all your bottles in cardboard six-pack carriers or cases prevents potential breakage and spillage.

15. **Open the spigot on the bottling bucket and fill the bottles.**

Gently push the bottling tube down to the bottom of each bottle to start the flow of beer. The bottle may take a short while to fill, but the flow always seems to accelerate as the beer nears the top. Usually, a bit of foam rushes to the top of the bottle — don't worry! As soon as you withdraw the bottling tube, the liquid level in the bottle falls. Remove the tube from each bottle when foam or liquid reaches the top of the bottle.

When you remove the bottling tube from the bottle, the level of the beer falls to about an inch or so below the opening. This airspace is called the *ullage*. Homebrewers have differing opinions as to how much airspace there should be. Some people say that the smaller the airspace, the less that oxidation will occur; others say that without proper ullage, the beer won't carbonate properly. Rather than jump into the fray, I say that if the airspace looks like the space in bottles of beer from commercial breweries, go with it.

16. **After draining the bottling bucket, close the spigot, remove the hose, toss the hose inside the bottling bucket, and set everything aside to be cleaned later.**

17. **Place all the bottles on your table top or work surface, place a cap on each bottle (as insurance against everything that can go wrong), and cap one bottle at a time. Pull down on the capper lever slowly and evenly.**

Both bench and two-handle cappers come with a small magnet in the capper head, which is designed to hold and align the cap as you start crimping. (I've learned not to trust the magnet to hold the caps in alignment; I prefer to seat them on the bottles by hand.)

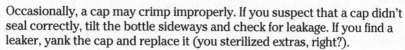

Occasionally, a cap may crimp improperly. If you suspect that a cap didn't seal correctly, tilt the bottle sideways and check for leakage. If you find a leaker, yank the cap and replace it (you sterilized extras, right?).

18. **Store your liquid lucre in a cool, dark location (such as the place where you kept the fermenter) for two weeks.**

Your homebrew needs to undergo a two-week conditioning phase, during which the remaining yeast cells chow down on the dextrose and carbonate your beer.

Putting your brew in the fridge isn't a good idea (at least for the first two weeks) because overly cold temperatures stunt the yeast's activity.

19. **Thoroughly rinse your brewing equipment in hot water and store it in a place that's relatively free of dust and mildew.**

This step may be the most important one of all, not so much for your new brew but for the next one. Consider this procedure to be an insurance policy on your next batch of beer — boring but worthwhile, like most insurance policies.

After two weeks have passed, check to see whether the bottles have clarified; the yeasty cloudiness should have settled out. Chill a bottle or two for taste-testing.

Homebrew, like any commercial beer, should be decanted (poured into a glass) before you drink it. Decanting not only releases the carbonation and the beer's aromatics but also enables you to pour a clear beer; drinking it out of the bottle stirs up the sediment, creating a hazy beer.

Congratulations! Your first batch of beer is ready to enjoy. As you can see in this section and the preceding sections, homebrewing at this level is easy. You're creating beer strictly from a kit: You just add a beer concentrate to water and then heat, ferment, and bottle it. If you can make basic breads, you can make tasty beer.

Keeping records

The primary goal of every homebrewer is to create a drinkable, enjoyable beer. Although quality is a noble objective, *consistency* is the mark of an accomplished homebrewer.

You can achieve both quality and consistency in a shorter period of time with the help of accurate records. Pedantic though it seems, keeping track of times, temperatures, weights, and measures establishes a pattern for the homebrewer. These records tell you not only what went right but also — and more important — what may have gone wrong. You can catalog and file successes and failures for future consideration.

A few published guidebooks and workbooks for homebrewers are available, but an old-fashioned spiral-bound notebook is as good as anything. Exactly how useful a notebook is depends on how accurate and timely your entries are; they have to be good to be useful. The data that you should track at the beginner level include

- ✔ Brand names of malts
- ✔ Varieties of hops
- ✔ Quantities of ingredients
- ✔ Length of boil
- ✔ Types of yeast
- ✔ Hydrometer readings (if you take gravity readings)
- ✔ Approximate fermentation times and temperatures

If you start this good habit early, record keeping at the intermediate and advanced levels — when record keeping is much more important — should come much easier and will be worth the effort.

The most common mistakes made by beginning homebrewers

"Nobody's perfect," as the saying goes. Chances are, your first efforts at making beer won't be, either, if you make any of these common mistakes:

- Infecting a batch of beer because of improperly sanitizing equipment.

- Infecting a batch of beer because of improperly handling or transferring the wort or beer.

- Causing a stove-top boil over by keeping the brew pot lid on during boiling.

- Starting the brewing or bottling procedures without having all the necessary equipment or ingredients on hand.

- Interrupting a fermentation (or allowing one to go on too long).

- Over priming the beer at bottling time, resulting in over-carbonated beer or exploding bottles.

- Attempting to cap twist-off bottles with threaded necks.

- Failing to learn and understand general brewing procedures before plowing ahead.

- Keeping poor records or none at all (to be good, you have to learn from your failures).

- Failing to adjust to the realities of home-brewing: What you *set out* to make doesn't matter; what you *make* is what counts. More often than not, your beer turns out to be something other than what you intended it to be. Relax and go with the flow (literally).

- Taking it all much too seriously: Homebrewing is supposed to be fun. It's just beer, after all.

Stepping Your Brewing Up a Notch

As homebrewers are wont to do, at some point you'll probably start thinking about how you can improve your homemade beer. While nothing is wrong with the beginner ingredients and processes explained and laid out earlier in this chapter, you can definitely make even better beer.

The suggestions I introduce in the following sections aren't difficult, but they add to the cost of your beer in terms of equipment and ingredients, and they add to the time it takes you to make your beer, but, most importantly, they add to your homebrew drinking enjoyment.

The way beer is made at commercial breweries and the way I instruct you to brew it in this chapter are considerably different. Commercial brewhouses don't use malt extract to make their beer, but for simplicity, beginner home-brewers do. And you can continue to brew this way for as long as you care to. However, I'd be remiss if I didn't mention that homebrewers can also gradu-ate to making beer the same way as commercial brewers do. Unfortunately, there's not enough page space in this book to cover the equipment and techniques needed to do that. Lucky for you, I also wrote *Homebrewing For Dummies,* 2nd Edition (Wiley). You need this book to progress to making beer directly from grain at home. And I've included plenty of recipes in that book to help you along.

New toys: Equipment upgrades

A more hands-on approach to anything calls for more-specialized equipment. Sophomore-level homebrewing requires a little more equipment than beginning homebrewing:

- ✔ **Carboy cleaning brush:** For proper cleaning of your secondary fermenter, or *carboy,* you need a carboy cleaning brush. This heavy-duty, soft-bristle brush is similar to a large toilet scrubber (please don't confuse the two types at home!) and is specially made to reach every curve and corner of the carboy. *Cost:* $5.

- ✔ **Curved racking tube (or cane):** Because glass carboys aren't made with a spigot, you need a hard plastic, curved racking tube to siphon the beer. *Cost:* $4.

- ✔ **Drilled rubber stopper (for carboy):** You need a drilled rubber stopper to fit the carboy's neck (usually a #6 or #7 stopper) — in addition to the rubber stopper that you use for beginning homebrewing. *Cost:* $2 or less.

- ✔ **Glass carboy:** Primarily used as a secondary fermenter (see Figure 18-3), the glass carboy can be a water jug that bottled-water companies deliver only to businesses, or it can be a jug purchased from homebrew-supply shops — with or without water! (*Note:* Avoid using plastic carboys unless specifically designed for homebrewing.) The carboy represents one of the biggest differences in equipment from the beginning stages. *Cost:* $28 for a 5-gallon glass carboy.

- ✔ **Grain mill:** You use a grain mill to crack grain prior to mashing or steeping it. You can buy grain precracked, but many homebrew stores or store personnel don't crack it properly, and precracked grain can also go stale more quickly. Cracking your own grain is a terrific advantage. *Cost:* $45 and up (see Figure 18-3).

The mill-less homebrewer can find inventive ways to crack the grain, such as putting it in a large, sealable bag and rolling it with a rolling pin or baseball bat, but a mill is really the way to go.

Whatever you do, don't use a coffee grinder to do your grain milling: Your grain will end up looking like sawdust (and how it looks is just the beginning of your problems; finely ground grain can lead to harsh and unpleasant tastes in your beer).

Figure 18-3:
A glass carboy and a hand-cranked grain mill are among the more important additions you may want to make to your home brewery.

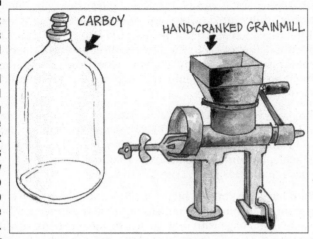

✓ **Immersion wort chiller:** An *immersion wort chiller* is a highly effective piece of equipment that's used to chill down your hot wort immediately following the boil so you can pitch your yeast quicker and get fermentation started sooner. It's not too terribly expensive, either — typically $50 and up. You can even save money and make one yourself. An immersion wort chiller is basically a long coil of copper tubing (½ to ¾ inches in diameter, 25 to 40 feet long), two short pieces of garden hose, a couple of hose clamps, and a threaded faucet attachment. (See Figure 18-4.)

Figure 18-4:
An immersion wort chiller, shown in a homebrewing brew pot, is easy to make. Cold water enters at one end and exits at the other as warm water, like a radiator in reverse.

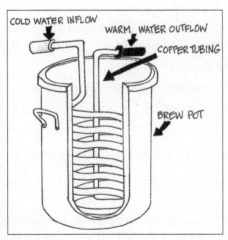

After your 1-hour boil is complete, carefully transfer your filled brew pot near a sink or utility tub. Lower your clean wort chiller into the hot wort. Connect the threaded end of the hose to the faucet and direct the open end of the opposite hose into the sink (or directly down the drain). Turn on the cold water and voilà! Chilling your wort down to pitching temperature (about 80 degrees Fahrenheit, 27 degrees Celsius) shouldn't take more than 5 minutes.

✔ **Scale:** After you start brewing beer according to homebrew recipes, you'll find that many ingredients (like hops and specialty grains) are called for in small quantities, often less than an ounce. A good kitchen or postal scale, because it can measure fractions of ounces, is vital to getting these quantities right. *Cost:* $20 to $30.

✔ **Sparge/hop bags:** Essentially, huge tea bags. Sparge bags are effective for steeping grain or keeping hops under control in the brew pot. You can buy reusable nylon bags with drawstrings or the inexpensive, throwaway cheesecloth kind. *Cost:* $5 (reusable nylon), $0.50 (muslin throwaway).

Specialty grains

If all the beer-making grain in the world was exactly the same, very few unique beer styles would exist. Because grain (mostly barley) is responsible for providing beer with much of its color, flavor, and texture, adding specialty grains to your beer recipe goes a long way toward changing your beer's character. *Specialty grains* — barley, wheat, oats, rye, and so on — are grains added in order to get special characteristic. They're not used as a substitute for malt extract but rather as an enhancement.

Specialty grains are

✔ *Kilned* (roasted) to various degrees of roastedness after they've been malted (in some cases, unmalted and still-wet malted grain are kilned as well)

✔ Added to give the malt extract the following:

  • A variety of visual, aromatic, and taste enhancements

  • Head-retaining and body-building (the beer's body, not yours) proteins and dextrins

In the following sections, I provide a few tips for using specialty grains and list some popular types.

A few steeping pointers

In a 5-gallon batch, you don't need much grain to create a noticeable effect. Depending on the grain, quantities of as little as a quarter pound are detectable. For measurement conversions, 1 cup of *cracked* grain equals approximately ¼ pound; hence, 1 pound of grain fills 4 cups.

Note: Specialty grains aren't normally added directly to the brew pot. And like all other grains in the brewing business, they should never be boiled; they're meant to be steeped in hot water just long enough for them to yield their goods — 20 to 30 minutes should be enough.

Steeping can be done in the brew pot with the rest of the brew, but two reasons for not using this method include

- ✔ If you don't use a sparge bag, you need to strain all the grain out before you can bring the wort to a boil.

- ✔ If the grain is in the brew pot at the same time as the extract, the grain's yield may not be maximized due to the viscosity of the wort.

Steeping in clear water captures all that the grain has to offer. Try steeping the specialty grain in a separate pot and then adding it to the extract, or steep it in the brew pot before you add the extract. After the grain is properly steeped, pour the now-flavored water into the brew pot through a strainer, keeping all the grain out of the brew pot.

In order to capture as much of the grain flavor as possible, be sure to *sparge* the grain — sparging is pouring hot water through the grain in the strainer (and into the brew pot) until the water runs clear. About a half gallon of water should do the trick.

Types of specialty grains

Here are the most common specialty grains and their typical uses:

- ✔ **Black malt:** Black malt is malt that's been roasted to such a high degree that all malt flavor and aroma have been burned off. Because of its charred aroma and flavor, use this malt sparingly; overgenerous use creates an unpleasant harshness in flavor and mouthfeel. Black malt is typically used in Schwarzbier, Porter, and Stout.

- ✔ **Chocolate malt:** Chocolate malt is malt that's been roasted to a dark brown color, retaining a hint of its malt character. Used in conservative amounts, chocolate malt actually imbues beers with a distinct chocolate aroma and taste. This malt is used in Brown Ales and Bock Beers, among others.

- ✔ **Crystal malt:** Crystal malt is named for the kilning procedure that crystallizes the caramel-like sugars inside the still-moist grain. It adds a caramel-like sweetness to the beer, along with some color and an improvement in head retention (it's sometimes called *caramel malt* for obvious reasons). It isn't the cure-all for bad extract beers that some homebrewers think it is, but it's a step in that direction.

- ✔ **Roasted barley:** Because this barley isn't malted before it's kilned, it isn't called a malt. The kilning procedure calls for gradual increases in temperature so the grain isn't charred like black malt. This dark brown grain gives a rich, roasted, coffee-like aroma and flavor and is used primarily in Stouts.

✔ **Biscuit malt:** Biscuit malt is a lightly kilned grain that's primarily used in Pale Ales and several brands of red beer. It smells and tastes a bit like toasted bread; it can also give a beer a nutty quality.

You shouldn't mill highly roasted grains. Because they're somewhat brittle, they have a tendency to crumble during the milling procedure, and that fine, dark grain powder should be avoided because it creates a harsh flavor in the beer.

With the ability to add color and flavor to your beer by using specialty grains, you no longer need to buy amber or dark extracts to make amber or dark beers; you can make them all with light malt extract. In fact, after you're comfortable using specialty grains, you're better off deriving these colors and flavors from grain anyway; the taste difference is appreciable, and it's more authentic-tasting. You have more control over the taste and color by using real grain any day than by using premade extract.

Secondary fermentation and the art of siphoning

Secondary fermentation is about transferring your beer from the primary fermentation vessel to a secondary vessel. In doing this, you're leaving most of the yeast dregs and organic sludge behind, thus allowing your beer to clarify, age, and mellow in a fresh and clean vessel.

The term *secondary fermentation* is really a misnomer as most or all the fermentation process takes place in the primary fermenter. I guess no one has come up with a better descriptor for this phase of brewing.

The only new equipment you need for this process is a *carboy* (see the earlier section "New toys: Equipment upgrades") and a couple of related items. A carboy is the large glass jug that bottled water companies used to use before replacing them with plastic jugs — and before you ask, those replacement plastic jugs aren't recommended for use in brewing.

Not to confuse you, but some carboys are made of plastic specifically designed to be used for brewing; they're made of HDPE (food-grade) plastic and, like glass carboys, they're also available through homebrew retailers.

To complete the carboy set up, you need another airlock as well as an appropriately sized drilled rubber stopper. You also need a curved racking cane in order to siphon the beer. Though it's not absolutely necessary, buying a special heavy-duty curved cleaning brush for the carboy is a good idea as well.

Transferring your beer from the primary fermenter to the carboy is no different than the method described earlier in the "Bottle it up!" section, where you transfer your beer to the bottling bucket. The only thing that's different is the vessel into which the beer is flowing.

The typical period of time a beer should be in a secondary fermenter is two weeks, which is usually plenty of time for the beer to clarify; however, if you've brewed a high-gravity, high-alcohol beer, it may not age and mellow in that span of time. Allowing a Barleywine or similar style of beer to sit in a carboy for a month or more before bottling it isn't unusual.

After your beer is done clarifying and mellowing (depending on the beer style), it's time to bottle it up, just like you did before using secondary fermentation. The only difference is that now you need to transfer your beer from the carboy into the bottling bucket.

No phase of homebrewing is exempt from cleaning and sanitizing. Adding another fermentation phase means disinfecting all the equipment that goes along with it. You may as well get used to it and stop complaining.

The use of a carboy in homebrewing requires the brewer to practice siphoning techniques because carboys don't come equipped with spigots. With the tubing connected to the racking cane, the opening of the siphon hose must be lower than the bottom of the vessel from which the beer is being siphoned to be effective (the lower the better). Keeping large air bubbles or voids out of the siphon hose increases siphoning efficiency; air bubbles and voids can slow or stop liquid flow and can also oxidize the beer. (See Figure 18-5.)

You can start a siphon in a handful of ways, but not all of them are acceptable for homebrewing. For speed and simplicity, sucking on one end of the siphon hose surely gets a flow going, but this opens the door to all kinds of contamination possibilities. Some brewers feel that a good gargle and rinse with whiskey or vodka is a good way to prevent this problem. (Just limit yourself to rinsing so you don't mess up the rest of the job.)

Another, more widely accepted practice is to fill the plastic hosing with water just prior to fitting the hosing onto the racking tube. After the racking cane and hose are connected (with the cane resting in the carboy), just dropping the open end of the hose into the bottling bucket automatically starts the flow of beer. This method may take a few tries before you get the system down.

What's the driving force behind the principle of siphoning? This force is gravitational acceleration × mass ($F = mg$). The beer (or any liquid) is pulled by gravity and pushed by the weight of its own mass. As its own mass decreases, so does the pushing pressure; gravitational pull remains constant.

After your beer has been transferred from the carboy into your bottling bucket, simply follow the bottling instructions from the "Bottle it up!" section earlier in this chapter.

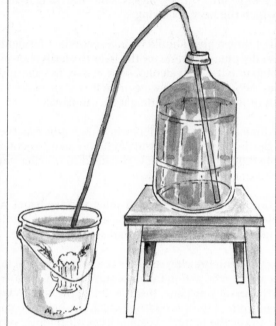

Figure 18-5:
You transfer
beer from
the carboy
to the
bottling
bucket,
using
siphoning
equipment.

Part V
The Part of Tens

The 5th Wave   By Rich Tennant

In this part . . .

*T*he chapters in this part are designed to entice you to continue your beer education, both at home and away — and each chapter does so with a short list of ten items. Chapter 19 shows you various ways to gain a greater appreciation of beer, many of which are right at your fingertips . . . via your computer keyboard.

The plan for Chapters 20 and 21 is to draw a hypothetical map you can use to follow your fancy to great beer cities and festivals around the world. They're all out there just waiting for you to visit and enjoy.

Chapter 19

Ten Ways to Grow Your Appreciation of Beer

In This Chapter

▶ Drinking, evaluating, and writing about beer

▶ Brewing beer and receiving different certifications

▶ Collecting beer memorabilia and meeting up with other beer enthusiasts

▶ Becoming a professional brewer

You can immerse yourself in beer in a lot of ways these days — figuratively speaking, of course. Whether you're consuming, brewing, collecting, or just associating with beer, there's no shortage of opportunities to get involved. This chapter has a few ideas to get you started.

Drink Beer with a Purpose

You won't find a better way to appreciate beer than to drink it (no earth-shattering revelation here!). But when you begin evaluating beer as you drink it, rather than just chugging it down with little to no thought, you start to hone in on the complexities of the product, and you develop a keen palate and appreciation of the beers you drink. Even when you drink beers you don't particularly enjoy, you get more in tune with whatever it is about the beer that doesn't turn you on. All these factors make you a better consumer. (You can start with the evaluation guidelines I provide in Chapter 12.)

For those of you who want to drink and evaluate beer on a more serious level, I strongly recommend making a point of trying beer brands and beer styles that you haven't experienced before. You may not be a fan of every single brand and style (few people are), but you'll gain a much greater insight as an objective evaluator. I also strongly endorse the habit of committing your impressions of the beers you try to paper. Writing down your thoughts and observations will serve you well as your list of beer evaluations grows into the dozens and hundreds. I still occasionally review beer-tasting notes I scribbled almost 25 years ago. Some are slightly illegible but helpful nonetheless. (Who knows, some day you may want to start publicly sharing your observations with others. Read on.)

Post Beer Reviews Online

When you feel you've gained enough knowledge and familiarity with beer brands and beer styles, you may want to share your opinions and observations with others of like mind. Thanks to the Internet, many different sites provide opportunities to post beer evaluations in a public forum. Some of them require that you join the community (almost universally for free), and some of them don't. Here are three of the most popular sites that provide online beer evaluations:

- BeerAdvocate (`www.beeradvocate.com`)
- RateBeer (`www.ratebeer.com`)
- PhillyCraft (`www.phillycraft.com`)

Note: Even if you have no intention of posting material to these sites, they're still good sources of beer reviews that can help you make informed beer-buying decisions. All three sites also offer other goodies, such as print magazines, beer resources, beer event calendars, and the obligatory beer merchandise.

Maintain a Beer Blog

Okay, suppose you've been doing beer evaluations in your kitchen for a while, and you've been lurking on several of the online beer evaluation sites. Your confidence is up, and your inner Michael Jackson (the famed beer expert and writer from London) can no longer be contained. You've just got to start sharing your beer knowledge with the world — what do you do? You blog.

Be aware that the blogosphere is littered with the blatherings of hundreds of overnight experts in the new and dynamic field of craft beer. Go ahead and write your fool head off, but if you want to stand out in the crowd you've got to, well, stand out in the crowd. Allow me to offer some helpful suggestions (see Chapter 12 for more tips):

- **Be literate, first and foremost.** People who can't cobble together simple and coherent sentences are hard to take seriously. And for beer's sake, know the difference between *palate, pallet,* and *palette* — only one of these words refers to beverage tasting.

- ✔ **Establish credibility.** Nothing kills credibility quicker than not knowing your subject matter. So be sure to know your beer stuff before you start writing. One way to establish credibility is to earn a certification (see the later section "Become Beer Educated and Beer Certified" for details).

- ✔ **Stay current.** Fresh information is of utmost importance. Plenty of sites online manage to remain relevant and in touch on a daily basis, that even week-old information can render your blog hopelessly out of date.

- ✔ **Immerse yourself in beer culture.** Being a part of the craft beer movement means being present to document events. Attend as many beer tappings, brewery openings, and beer festivals as you can. Get to know the big names in the industry and get your name known as you go. (See the later section "Associate with Others Who Share Your Passion for Beer" for more information.)

- ✔ **Promote yourself.** Your blog, no matter how well written, won't find readers by accident. You need to put yourself out there, and social media is the best way to do that. Use Facebook, Google +, Twitter, Tumblr, and other sites to your best advantage. Photos and videos are often worth a thousand words.

Write a Great Book about Beer

Just kidding, I've got that covered.

Okay, if you're really intent on writing a beer book, you'd better bone up on your beer education. You absolutely must be plugged in to the industry (by attending festivals and brewery openings) and know the ins and outs of beer styles and so on. Writing a good beer blog could even act as a good springboard (see the preceding section).

Become Beer Educated and Beer Certified

With the explosion in craft breweries in the United States and the proliferation of imported beers from near and far, beer has rather suddenly catapulted into renewed international stardom. With the newfound interest following this upward trend, people have realized the need for serious beer education. Here are two of the biggest certification programs out there:

✔ **Cicerone® Certification Program (**www.cicerone.org**):** Just as wine sommeliers help the average person find his way through often daunting restaurant wine lists, Ray Daniels of the Craft Beer Institute recognized that the time had come for a beer equivalent to the sommelier. In 2008, Daniels devised and instituted a program that tests would-be beer sommeliers and dubbed it *Cicerone.* To date, more than 7,000 people have passed the initial online Beer Server portion of the program ($69), only 200 or so have passed the three-to-four hour, in-person second phase of the certification exam ($345), and only 3 people have reached the ultimate two-day Master Cicerone grail ($595). Obviously, this serious program is targeted at those who work within the beer industry.

✔ **Ale-Conner Beer Certification Program (**www.beerexam.com**):** Aiming to reach a much broader audience with a somewhat less rigorous approach than the Cicerone Certification Program, the Ale-Conner Beer Certification program (see Figure 19-1) offers casual beer enthusiasts as well as industry-leading professionals an opportunity to prove their knowledge, passion, and appreciation of beer. Two separate online exams — Beer Authority ($20) and Beer Expert ($30) — offer separate levels of difficulty, covering topics such as beer evaluation, beer styles, brewing ingredients and processes, as well as general beer questions. Upon successful completion of the exams, you'll be able to print your personalized certificate, accompanied by a wallet card that attests to your new status as an Ale-Conner Certified Beer Authority/Expert. (Um, in the interest of full disclosure, that's my signature on the bottom of the certificate.)

Figure 19-1: The Ale-Conner Beer Certification Program is for casual beer enthusiasts.

Brew Beer at Home

The best way to really understand and appreciate beer — and those who brew it — is to brew your own beer at home. Even if you have no intentions of excelling at the craft, the education you gain from brewing beer with your own two hands is immeasurable. (Brewing bad beer doesn't count, though. You have to be at least reasonably successful in the venture to earn the respect of others and to develop the respect deserved by those who brew on a commercial scale.)

Should you be game enough to try your hand at homebrewing, you'll find all the information you need to get started in Chapter 18. (You can also check out the latest edition of my book *Homebrewing For Dummies,* published by Wiley.) And should you become a regular homebrewer (homebrewing has a way of sucking you in and not letting you go), you'll likely be tempted to do what thousands of homebrewers do with regularity: enter your beer into competitions. In addition to the glory and validation that come with receiving high scores, several competitions also offer very nice and sometimes valuable prizes for winning entrants. The American Homebrewers Association (www.homebrewersassociation.org) maintains the most comprehensive list of competitions in the United States.

Become a Certified Beer Judge

If and when you become a successful homebrewer (see the preceding section), you're in a good position to become a Certified Beer Judge. The Beer Judge Certification Program (BJCP; www.bjcp.org) was established in 1985 as a means of standardizing how homebrewed beers are judged at competitions. (I certified in the first year of the program and continue to be involved in it.)

The purpose of the BJCP today is to promote beer literacy and the appreciation of real beer and to recognize beer tasting and evaluation skills. The BJCP certifies and ranks beer judges through an examination and monitoring process. Currently, more than 6,000 BJCP judges are walking the globe.

You don't need to be a homebrewer to become a BJCP judge, but being one is extremely helpful. Brewing beer gives you many of the skills and experiences needed to pass the BJCP exam and to be an effective judge. You can also gain much of the skill and knowledge through book study, but nothing is better or more effective than hands-on brewing.

Note: For the record, BJCP judging isn't a viable career track. Judges aren't paid for their services or their travel; I guess you can say they work for beer.

Collect Beer-Related Stuff

For some beer geeks, savoring a brew just isn't enough. They need something to hold on to, something to keep. Preferably something cheap or free. These beer nuts are called *breweriana collectors.* Anything and everything that's either used at a brewery or bar or bears the name of a brewery or a brand name is of value to these enthusiasts. Coasters, openers, labels, signs — anything goes. Or more correctly, anything stays. Not every collector is a complete maniac, though; casual collecting is just as much fun as compulsive collecting.

The range of collectible items, both antique and new, is astounding. Serious collectors get into more obscure promotional items, such as foam skimmers, ashtrays, brewing company letterheads, and *shelf talkers* (small signs placed on store shelves to call customers' attention to a product). These types of folks spend a lot of time and money tracking down those prized items that'll make their collections *complete,* although they'll never be completely satisfied. For them, breweriana collecting is somewhere between a hobby and a lifestyle. Maybe a mania.

What drives this urge? Nostalgia — lots of regional breweries are gone, but their names evoke places and times of the recent past — and the sheer fun of collecting. Collecting is also a great link to other beer enthusiasts. Like drinking beer, collecting beer-related things acts as a great social lubricant. Collectors love to meet, organize, and swap. (See the next section for more about hanging out with other folks passionate about beer.) And the craft-brewing movement we're experiencing today is providing lots of collectable stuff for tomorrow. Stake your claims now.

Collectors of breweriana have no shortage of clubs to associate with. Here's just a sampling:

- American Breweriana Association (www.americanbreweriana.org)
- Brewery Collectibles Club of America (www.bcca.com)
- National Association Breweriana Advertising (www.nababrew.com)

Associate with Others Who Share Your Passion for Beer

One thing about us beer folks, we like to get together. Forming clubs and associations seems to come as naturally to beer people as forming a head does to good beer. Whether you wish to further the cause of drinking, brewing, or collecting, you can always find like-minded beer enthusiasts to help you.

As you may assume, groups of people dedicated to the consumption of beer have proliferated greatly over the past two decades. As you may also assume, brewpubs and beer bars can take much of the credit because many of them have formed *mug clubs* — customers who belong to these mug clubs get regular deals on beer, food, and events — within their establishments. Check with your local craft beer purveyor to see whether it has such a gathering — if not, start one!

Many of today's beer-consumer clubs are either conglomerations or offshoots of already-established homebrewing clubs. Homebrewers, naturally, are beer lovers; it stands to reason that anyone who loves good beer makes a good candidate for club membership. To find your local homebrew club, check out www.homebrewersassociation.org/pages/directories/find-a-club.

One of the oldest beer appreciation groups in the United States is the Chicago Beer Society (CBS). When it was established in 1977, it had a membership in the dozens and gathered only for quarterly events each year. When homebrewing started gaining traction in the early to mid-1980s, though, the CBS roster populated with a growing number of people who brewed their beer at home, and it began hosting beer events on a bimonthly schedule. Today, the CBS is one of the largest and most vibrant beer clubs in the United States, with a membership that exceeds 500 members. It also hosts close to a dozen highly anticipated beer events throughout the year. The CBS can also lay claim to being the home club of beer writers Ray Daniels and Randy Mosher. (Though I'm no longer an active member, I was for several years back in the 1980s and 1990s.)

In the United Kingdom and Canada, beer lovers can look forward to getting involved with one of the largest and most active beer organizations in the world. CAMRA (Campaign for Real Ale) has been defending beer for several decades. To find out more about CAMRA, check out Chapter 5 (you can also go to www.camra.org.uk). Elsewhere in Europe, two of the more active beer consumer groups are Zythos (formerly Objectiv Bierprovers) in Belgium (www.zythos.be) and PINT in the Netherlands (www.pint.nl).

Go Pro — Brewer, That Is

If you've been fantasizing about starting your own brewery — or even just brewing in someone else's brewery — you can find plenty of educational opportunities out there, especially in today's market. For a small-time brewer, getting in on the ground floor isn't a bad way to go. Become an assistant brewer and work your way up to bigger and better. Quite a few homebrewers have trodden that path. If you're thinking career, however, you need disciplined education. Brewing beer at the corporate level (and even the artisanal level) is more about chemistry than it is about passion.

Some schools whose entire curriculum encompasses brewing beer include:

✔ American Brewers Guild (www.abgbrew.com)

✔ Siebel Institute of Technology and World Brewing Academy in Chicago (www.siebelinstitute.com)

✔ UCDavis Extension (University of California at Davis; www.extension. ucdavis.edu/unit/brewing)

✔ Doemens Academy in Munich, Germany (partnered with Siebel Institute; www.doemens.org, www.siebelinstitute.com/munich)

✔ Wissenschaftszentrum Weihenstephan in Freising, Germany (www. wzw.tum.de)

✔ Heriot-Watt University in Edinburgh, Scotland (postgraduate studies only; www.hw.ac.uk)

Chapter 20

The Ten Best Beer Cities in the World (And a Few Extras)

In This Chapter

▶ Honoring a few great beer cities in Europe

▶ Checking out some super beer cities in the United States

▶ Recognizing a handful of honorable mentions around the world

As it was developing into the fan favorite it is today, beer gained a regionality that's still mostly intact in various cities around the world. This chapter focuses on those cities that best represent the traditions of beer and brewing.

The cities that appear in this chapter have been chosen for a handful of reasons. Number one: They *have* to offer the beer lover a lot of great beer — and preferably in a variety of styles. But beyond consumption, these cities also have to have a *beer culture* (meaning that beer is integral to everyday life and that the city's history has been shaped in part by beer or brewing) and/or offer a unique beer experience.

Here, then, are the ten best beer cities in the world in no particular order (other than the fact that they're grouped by continent).

Munich, Germany

You had to see this one coming. When the topic of conversation has to do with beer in Germany, Bavaria (of which Munich is the capital) and Bavarians seem to get most of the world's attention. It could be that the state of Bavaria has an inordinate number of Germany's breweries — estimated to be around 1,200 well into the 20th century and estimated to still be around 800 today.

It could also have something to do with the number of beer festivals held in and around Munich, not the least of which is Munich's Oktoberfest, which attracts an estimated 6 million attendees every year (see Chapters 16 and 21 for more info).

Not to be overlooked are the world-famous brands that emanate from Munich and its environs, including:

- ✔ Augustiner Bräu
- ✔ Hacker-Pschorr
- ✔ HofBräu
- ✔ Löwenbräu
- ✔ Paulaner
- ✔ Spaten
- ✔ Weihenstephan

Of course, I can't forget to mention the plentiful beer halls — the Hofbräuhaus being the city's most famous, dating back to the 1500s — that render some of Munich's best victuals, such as wienerschnitzel, sauerbraten, pork knuckle, and the best of the wursts (bratwursts, that is). These halls range in size and scope from huge and raucous to not-so-huge and not-so-raucous. Great beer, accompanied by great beer food and great beer music, makes these locations must-sees in Munich.

All of this together adds up to give Muncheners a pride in their history and tradition that's extended to one another and visitors in the form of *gemütlichkeit,* which is variously described as coziness, cheerfulness, and friendliness. That alone makes Munich a great beer city.

Bamberg, Germany

The Franconian town of Bamberg, Germany, is only three hours away from Munich (see the preceding section). Although Bamberg is considerably smaller and quainter, it offers the beer tourist everything that Munich does in spirit and tradition, but the actual beer experiences are quite different, which is why Bamberg deserves its own distinction.

Franconia is in the northern part of Bavaria and lays claim to having the greatest density of breweries in all of Germany. Bamberg, itself, claims to have more breweries than any other German town of its size (approximately 70,000 inhabitants). Current brewery population in town is eight breweries and one brewpub (Ambrausianum), with many more breweries dotting the local countryside.

Bamberg is renowned for its esoteric smoked beer and is considered the Rauchbier capital of the world. Several local brewers make this burnished copper brew, using malt smoked over beechwood fires to give their beer its unusual flavor. Rauchbier is said to be an acquired taste, and I agree. I acquired a taste for it with my first sip!

Bruges, Belgium

Great beer cities don't need to have a profusion of breweries to make such a list. The medieval town of Bruges in Belgium's northwest is a prime example. Though at one time more than 30 breweries existed in and around Bruges, only one is currently in operation: Brouwerij Straffe Hendrik/De Halve Maan (Brewery Strong Henry/The Half Moon).

What mostly captures the beer lover's imagination in Bruges now is the town's many popular cafes, bars, and bottle shops — and the occasional beer festival. More than 400 different brands of beer can be found in Bruges, and you can spend days (or more likely, weeks) searching them all out.

While you're out and about looking for beer, you may want to check out the Gruuthuse Museum. This diverse museum is situated in the House of Gruuthuse, which belonged to the family Van Brugghe-van der Aa in the late Middle Ages. This family owned the monopoly of *gruut* selling (gruut was a medieval mixture of spices used to make beer). The Archeological Society of Bruges started the present antiques and art collections in 1865. In 1955, the city of Bruges acquired and expanded the collection and the museum.

Prague, Czech Republic

The history of beer in Bohemia, a region located in the Czech Republic, is long and storied, dating back to the 12th century. Bohemian taverns became very popular in the 17th century and at least 30 were set up in Prague's New Town on Charles Square. About half a dozen of these taverns brewed beer on the premises. In the late 1800s, Czech brewers were among the first to produce beers in the relatively new bottom-fermentation (lager) style.

Hops are also a big deal in northern Bohemia. One of the world's most popular hop varieties is the *Saaz* hop from the region of Zatec. The spicy Saaz hop is strongly associated with the Pilsner style, which was born in the nearby town of Plzen. Similarly, some of the finest pale malts (another important ingredient in brewing classic Pilsner beer) are grown in Moravia.

The Czech beer culture is alive and well and continuing to thrive in the many taverns throughout Prague. The Czech people consume beer with regularity; it's considered a customary beverage in daily life (the Czech Republic consistently leads the word in per capita consumption of beer).

You won't find a huge variety of beer styles in Prague — or all of the Czech Republic, for that matter. What you will find are a few very well-made lager beers that fluctuate modestly in terms of color and alcohol levels and only minimally between brewers and brand names. They're very generously malted but always finished with an appropriate balance of hop bitterness. A famous saying in Bohemia goes, "A second glass of beer praises the first and calls for a third." Hard to argue with that.

London, England

As it regards beer, London has been and will forever be associated with its pubs, and rightly so. The ubiquitous neighborhood *pub* — short for Public House — has been inextricably linked to everyday life throughout Great Britain.

As for the beer itself, non-Brits often see it as somewhat of a singular product: warm and flat beer. Comparatively speaking, beer in London isn't as cold or as carbonated as most beer drinkers are accustomed to, but that's also an integral part of the beer-drinking experience in the United Kingdom (see Chapter 16 for details).

Expect to see a lot of variations on Bitters and Mild Ales in London, with the occasional Porter or Stout thrown in for good measure. Also, be on the lookout for anything on handpull or beer engine (see Chapter 5 for more about these items) and give it a go for "research purposes."

On its own, London has had its share of breweries and brewing history. Following are some of the more famous names associated with London:

- Bass
- Courage
- Fuller's
- Watney's
- Whitbread
- Young's

Brewing companies aside, taste-testing is at its best at the pubs. Be aware that most pubs in London are *tied houses,* which means that the products served on tap are those from the brewery whose name or logo is on the entrance to the pub. Having a good guide to London's pubs is highly recommended for serious beer trekking in this city. You can find many good pub guides, but the best can be obtained from CAMRA (Campaign for Real Ale; www.camra.org.uk/).

Portland, Oregon, United States

Portland, Oregon, is one of two American cities that quickly rose to prominence during the microbrewery revolution/renaissance (the other being Seattle, Washington; see the next section). And 25 years later, Portland is still considered America's favorite beer city.

For its size (population of less than 600,000), Portland can boast of having not only 28 breweries within city limits but also many more just beyond its fringe. Beer bard Michael Jackson (the respected beer writer) called Portland the "beer capital of the world." The Portland Oregon Visitors Association suggests *Beervana* and *Brewtopia* as nicknames for the city. In January 2006, Mayor Tom Potter gave the city a new unofficial nickname: Beertown.

Though it has little significant brewing history beyond the old brewery established by Henry Weinhard in Portland in 1862, Portland has made its mark in history for its role in the craft beer movement. Visitors to Portland can experience an incredibly wide range of beer styles, from the traditional (simple ales) to cutting edge (robust barrel-aged beers).

Aside from the vast number of craft breweries, Portland also has a dynamic beer scene in its many beer bars and gastropubs (see Chapter 15 for details about these types of establishments). The craft brewers of Portland, with the help of the Oregon Brewers Guild, also host some of the oldest, best, and most popular beer festivals in the United States, such as Oregon Brewers Festival (see Chapter 21 for more festival info).

A leisurely drive south toward Corvallis, Oregon, also affords beer geeks the opportunity to see some of the largest and most productive hop farms in North America.

Seattle, Washington, United States

Even though Seattle is more closely associated with a famous worldwide coffee shop chain, another brew makes it a destination for beer lovers. Like Portland, Oregon (see the preceding section), Seattle was also on the leading edge of the craft beer revolution back in the early 1980s.

Seattle was responsible for producing Redhook, one of the earliest and most successful microbreweries in the United States. Redhook was one of the first brands of craft beer to be widely distributed back in the 1980s before it became part of the Anheuser-Busch beer empire in the 1990s.

Seattle is also home to the Pike Brewing Company, also one of the early and successful craft brewers in the Pacific Northwest. Pike Brewing is owned by the Finkel family who also founded Merchant du Vin, importer of dozens of tasty and interesting never-before-seen European beers to the United States.

And like Portland, Seattle is home to many well-established brewpubs and gastropubs, making the beer scene there vibrant and dynamic. And the scenery is tough to beat, too.

Denver, Colorado, United States

Which came first: the chicken or the egg? The relevance of that question is in trying to determine whether Denver became a fanatical craft beer city because of the Great American Beer Festival (GABF), or if the GABF settled in Denver because of its craft beer fanaticism.

I think it's the former. The GABF was initially held a few miles up the pike from Denver in the beer-forward burg of Boulder. Only after the GABF outgrew its Boulder digs did it finally move southward to take advantage of the convention facilities in the Mile High City.

Nevertheless, Denver has responded to the honor of being GABF host by becoming one of the best beer cities in the United States. The issue of brewery density aside (that's a given), Denver has also stood up to the challenge of hosting the GABF each fall by hosting even more one-off beer festivals in conjunction with the GABF. Beer dinners, special tappings, you name it — for one week each September/October, Denver becomes *the* best place on earth for beer geeks, hands down.

Even for the other 51 weeks in the year, Denver is a phenomenal place for beer lovers to visit and see what's on the cutting edge of the industry. Denver has a legit beer culture. Not only are there a multitude of breweries, brewpubs, and beer bars in town, its residents have a high intelligence quotient when it comes to knowing a lot about good beer.

It bears noting that quite a profusion of craft breweries are within a rather small radius north and west of Denver. Known collectively as the *Front Range Breweries,* this scattered bunch of artisans makes for one big beer trek. Comprising more than 30 different brewing facilities, the Front Range Breweries are located in the following Colorado cities, with the number of breweries in parentheses — not including the big beer factories in Fort Collins (Anheuser-Busch) and Golden (Coors):

- Boulder (9)
- Central City (1)
- Estes Park (1)
- Fort Collins (8)
- Golden (2)
- Greeley (2)
- Longmont (4)
- Loveland (3)

San Francisco, California, United States

Compiling a list of great beer cities without including San Francisco would be just as difficult as putting together a list of uniquely American beer styles without including Steam Beer. The two are forever entwined.

When California experienced a gold rush in the late 1880s, San Francisco was a boom town. The gold rush brought people, and people brought money and thirst. Breweries were quickly established to slake the thirsts of prospectors and would-be millionaires. At about that time, lager was also overtaking ale as the beer of preference in the United States, but the equipment necessary to cold-ferment beer was hard to come by — especially in a West Coast outpost. The resulting beer fermented with lager yeast at warm temperatures spawned what came to be known as *Steam Beer* but is now referred to more generically as *California Common Beer,* thanks to a trademark on the Steam Beer name.

The Anchor Brewing Company in San Francisco, responsible for reviving and trademarking the old Steam Beer recipe, is also credited with fostering the American craft beer revolution. Since then, scores of highly regarded craft breweries have opened in San Fran as well as in the greater bay region in central California, from Santa Rosa down to San Jose and beyond. Even in tony wine country, a thirst for good beer exists; both Napa and Sonoma Valleys boast of craft breweries.

Go ahead and leave your heart in San Francisco, but I suggest holding on to your liver.

Philadelphia, Pennsylvania, United States

Based on this city's impressive brewing heritage alone, it'd be hard not to recommend Philadelphia for this list. Unfortunately, you can't drink memories.

Since its founding in the late 1600s, Philadelphia has been home to more breweries (estimated to be around 200) than any other city in America. And don't forget that John Wagner was the first brewer to make lager beer in the United States back in 1840.

Philly's brewers suffered much the same fate as in the rest of the country; only 33 breweries were operating in town at the outset of Prohibition and only 17 managed to reopen when Prohibition ended in 1933. Currently, the City of Brotherly Love is proud of its two packaging breweries and its five brewpubs.

What really puts Philly on the beer map, though, is the staggering (pun intended) number of beer bars and gastropubs in town. This city is a pub crawler's fantasy.

A Few More Great Beer Cities to Consider

No short list of great beer cities will ever be sufficient to cover them all, so here are a few more for you to think about:

- **Amsterdam, the Netherlands:** This city has lots of good beer bars. The Dutch are not only good at making rich lager beers, but they're also into international beer styles (especially from neighboring Belgium).

- **Brussels, Belgium:** Brussels is the center of brewing in Belgium with a profusion of excellent beer bars. It's also home to the opulent Brewers Guild House in the Grand-Place (town square).

- **Toronto, Ontario, Canada:** In this easy-to-navigate city, you can find excellent brewpubs, gastropubs, and beer.

- **Vancouver, British Columbia, Canada:** Aside from its scenic location, Vancouver also boasts of a dynamic brewing scene.

- **San Diego, California, United States:** One of the late bloomers in the American craft-brewing movement, San Diego now has one of the greatest densities of breweries in the United States.

- **Chicago, Illinois, United States:** Chicago has had more breweries than any other American city, except Philadelphia. Also a late bloomer, the greater Chicago area is home to more than 30 breweries and brewpubs.

- **Milwaukee, Wisconsin, United States:** Great brewing history exists in Milwaukee (Pabst, Schlitz, Miller) with many of the old brewery buildings intact. Dynamic new craft breweries are producing excellent beers.

- **Asheville, North Carolina, United States:** This city isn't only one of the smallest cities on this list but also the only one in the American South, where craft brewing has been slow to catch on. Asheville was recently named one of the top ten up-and-coming cities for craft beer.

Chapter 21

The Ten Best Beer Festivals in the World

In This Chapter

▶ Checking out beer festivals in the United States

▶ Visiting beer festivals around the world

*O*f all the ways to enjoy drinking beer, perhaps none is as fun as attending a festival that's all about beer. Nothing else is as important. Okay, sure, noshing on tasty food and listening to enjoyable music is nice, too, but they just serve as sideshows for the main event.

Here are some reasons I love beer festivals:

✔ Few other opportunities allow you to enjoy such a wide variety of beer styles and beer brands under one roof or one tent — or even under a bright blue sky!

✔ Even fewer opportunities allow you to meet and greet the people responsible for making the wonderful elixir in your glass, drooling superlatives and overwhelming them with adulation.

✔ Most festivals are set up so you can try many different beers without spending a fortune or losing consciousness. All-inclusive fees that allow for endless samples — in small amounts — are the best way to go.

✔ Sharing the wonderfulness of good beer with fellow enthusiasts is great. In my experience, people who love good beer are good people. And besides, beer is a great social lubricant.

So, with all that in mind, this chapter features my top-ten picks for great beer festivals in the United States and elsewhere in the world. Bear in mind that this list is by no means complete — scores of beer festivals occur around the world every year — and this list is likely to stir controversy, primarily among those who are disappointed to see their favorite events missing. I know I'm just scratching the surface here; I could write a whole 'nother book on beer festivals alone.

Great American Beer Festival, Denver, Colorado, United States

Starting out big, the Great American Beer Festival (GABF) is the granddaddy of them all. If such a thing as a beer festival bucket list exists, this one should be at the top. The GABF is one of the oldest beer festivals in the United States and certainly one of the biggest. Close to 50,000 people attended the 2011 GABF over 3 days.

Taking place every year in late September/early October, the 2011 edition was the 30th annual festival, and it sold out in one week! More than 2,400 beers were served — all of them American made — and 465 breweries were in attendance, pouring more than 36,000 gallons of beer.

The cool thing about the GABF is the way the festival hall is divided into eight U.S. regions: mid-Atlantic, Midwest, Rocky Mountain, New England, Pacific, Pacific Northwest, Southeast, and Southwest. This organization not only makes it so much easier to navigate and find your favorite breweries, but it also helps to locate breweries in your own neck of the woods. For more info, check out www.greatamericanbeerfestival.com/.

Great Taste of the Midwest, Madison, Wisconsin, United States

The Great Taste of the Midwest is one of the premier beer festivals in the United States. Started in 1987 by the local homebrew club (Madison Homebrewers and Tasters Guild), this event has grown to include more than 120 brewers serving more than 900 beers.

The stature of this event has grown commensurately; the festival sells out quickly (only 6,000 people are admitted) and tickets are hard to come by. The Great Taste of the Midwest is always held on the second Saturday in August, so plan accordingly. Go to www.mhtg.org/great-taste-of-the-midwest for more info.

Part of what makes this festival such a destination festival is its outdoor venue. Beautiful Olin-Turville Park overlooks Lake Monona in Madison; it's one of the most scenic and serene places to gather in celebration of good beer.

Oregon Brewers Festival, Portland, Oregon, United States

The Oregon Brewers Festival is one of the longest-running craft-beer festivals in the United States, dating back to 1988. It's the brainchild of Art Larrance, who cofounded the Portland Brewing Company.

OBF, as it's known locally, takes place at Tom McCall Waterfront Park, situated on the west bank of the Willamette River, with Mt. Hood as a backdrop. This four-day event typically features more than 80 brewers, serving the estimated 80,000 people who turn out for this event every July (always on the last full weekend of July). Check out www.oregonbrewfest.com/ to plan your trip.

OBF has a special feature called Buzz Tent where you can find a collection of experimental beers and beers that are "well off the beaten path." Needless to say, these beers are highly prized, very expensive, and limited in quantity.

SAVOR, Washington, D.C., United States

The full and correct name of this festival, which takes place each June, is *SAVOR: An American Craft Beer and Food Experience,* which neatly sums up what this festival is all about — experiencing the best of the craft-beer world, paired with the best of the artisanal food world. As you can imagine, SAVOR sells out very quickly.

The 2011 edition of SAVOR (www.savorcraftbeer.com/) was only the fourth in its history, but expectations continue to soar. This soiree excited and amused attendees with more than 140 craft beers from 72 small and independent brewers. Forty-two different foods allowed for diverse pairings that included artisanal cheeses, sushi, oysters, and chocolate truffles. Attendees are always encouraged to create their own favorite pairings.

A new component was added to the 2011 event that's sure to become a mainstay: Attendees had the opportunity to bring a little bit of SAVOR home with them. Each attendee received a bottle of *SAVOR Flowers,* the first annual SAVOR collaboration beer, brewed by Boston Beer Company and Dogfish Head Craft Brewery in Delaware. SAVOR Flowers was served during the event and distributed as a parting gift. Organizers hope that many collaboration beers celebrating SAVOR are to come.

American Craft Beer Fest, Boston, Massachusetts, United States

The American Craft Beer Fest (ACBF) is relatively new (2011 was the fourth annual), but it's an up-and-comer. ACBF has rapidly become the largest beer festival on the East Coast. Taking place in June, its two-day, three-session format allows a maximum of 5,000 people per session (a *session* at a beer festival is a block of time — typically 3 to 4 hours). Located at the Seaport World Trade Center, this event features more than 100 American brewers, serving more than 500 different brews. Check out www.beeradvocate.com/acbf/ for more info.

One especially great feature of ACBF is the Beer Forum Series in which guest speakers and brewers give presentations on various beer-related themes.

Celebrating American Craft Beer Week

American Craft Beer Week (ACBW) isn't a festival in the strictest sense of the word. Although it certainly is a grand celebration of beer, it doesn't take place in one location or at one time. Beer Weeks take place in various cities at various slots on the calendar. Some run concurrently, some run apart from all others. Most of them take place in the late spring or early summer.

ACBW also isn't a festival in the sense that it takes place in one location within each city, but it's celebrated at any venue that wants to get in on the action — breweries, brewpubs, beer bars, gastropubs, restaurants, and so forth. Depending on how well organized the beer week is, you can celebrate at a different location each night of the week. Some cities boast 50 or more events in a seven-day period!

Here are just some of the major cities that participated in ACBW in 2011:

- ✔ Chicago
- ✔ Cleveland
- ✔ Denver
- ✔ Los Angeles
- ✔ Philadelphia
- ✔ San Diego
- ✔ San Francisco
- ✔ Seattle
- ✔ St. Louis
- ✔ Washington, D.C.

To monitor American Craft Beer Week events in your area or across the country, go to: www.craftbeer.com/pages/news-and-events/american-craft-beer-week.

Mondial de la Bière, Montreal, Quebec, Canada

Begun in 1994, this unique and convivial festival of beer tasting is considered to be a gateway to Quebec and the international beer industry. Mondial de la Bière (www.festivalmondialbiere.qc.ca) is the largest and most important beer festival in North America, serving 600 imported and domestic beers to more than 96,000 people over its four-day run in June.

Mondial de la Bière also has a sister celebration in Strasbourg, France, that takes place in October.

Oktoberfest, Munich, Germany

Munich's Oktoberfest (www.oktoberfest.de/en/) is unquestionably the world's biggest and most famous beer festival but not necessarily the world's best. To understand what I mean, you need to understand Oktoberfest's history.

European fall festivals always coincided with the annual harvest, a time of abundance and celebration. In Germany, as in most of northern Europe, beer was integral to that celebration. In Bavaria, the typical autumn fest took on a whole new meaning in 1810, when the prince married the daughter of a wealthy aristocrat. The nuptial celebration went on for two weeks, including parades and carnival rides and all the attendant regalia — and lots of Märzenbier supplied by Munich's brewers. Muncheners enjoyed the celebration so much, it was decreed that the improved and extended Oktoberfest would start anew every year.

More than 200 years later, Munich's Oktoberfest is much less about a nuptial celebration and lots more about tourism and over-consumption. Anyone who wants to visit Munich and experience true *gemütlichkeit* (cheerfulness) should attend Oktoberfest at least once in their lives — but don't spend all your time at the *Theresienwiese* (fest grounds); be sure to stop in at the various beer halls and biergartens to get a more complete picture of beer enjoyment in Munich. After all, it'll be just you and 6 million other tourists.

If you're looking for beer variety at the Oktoberfest, you're out of luck; Märzenbier, otherwise known as Oktoberfest beer, is all that's served on the fest grounds.

Great British Beer Festival, London, England

The Great British Beer Festival (GBBF) takes place every August at Earls Court in London and is Britain's biggest beer festival. This impressive event brings together more than a thousand real ales, ciders, *perries* (ciders that are made with pear juice instead of apple juice), and international beers from around the world.

The GBBF has plenty to occupy you (besides just drinking beer): You can play traditional pub games, enjoy live music, sample food, including good traditional pub snacks, and also attend tutored beer tastings. To find out more about this festival, check out `gbbf.camra.org.uk/home`.

Zythos Bier Festival, Belgium

The Zythos Bier Festival (ZBF), which takes place every April, is the largest beer fest in Belgium. It's noted for being one of the few beer festivals where you get to try Belgium's diverse, unique, and intensely flavored beers all in one place.

Each year's event features 50 to 60 beer stands run by brewers or brewing company employees, serving about 250 different beers. The ZBF moves to a new city every year; it'll celebrate its ninth anniversary in 2012 at the Brabanthal in Louvain. For more info, go to `www.zbf.be`.

Poperinge Hop and Beer Festival, Poperinge, Belgium

Did you notice that this festival's title has the word *hop* in it? Poperinge is the charming hop metropolis in the southwest of West Flanders and has celebrated the hop harvest for centuries — which, of course, always includes the consumption of beer. This three-day festival culminates with a parade that features 1,300 people, dozens of horsemen, and many beautiful hop-themed floats. You can also vote for the festival's Hop Queen. Visit `www.hoppefeesten.be/` to find out more.

Unlike most other festivals, Poperinge celebrates only every third year (2011, 2014, 2017, and so on) and always takes place in September (the hop-harvesting season). But if you should find yourself in Poperinge on an off year, you can always visit the Hop Museum in town.

Part VI
Appendixes

The 5th Wave   By Rich Tennant

TRUTH IN ADVERTISING

"I'll have one Long Belch ale, an Old Makesmepee, and two Dumb Flirt Lights on tap."

In this part . . .

This is the part that can convert you from a casual, everyday beer lover to a full-blown beer geek. Appendix A supplies you with all the technical minutiae about beer styles that you won't find in the early parts of this book. This information is what separates the pretenders and wannabes from genuine beer experts.

Appendix B is also pretty handy when it comes to impressing friends, family, and strangers with your incredible grasp of beer history. The narrative in this appendix goes a long way toward instilling a deep appreciation for beer and brewing history.

Appendix A

A Quick Guide to Beer Styles and Stats

• •

After you've digested all the information in this book — heck, after you've glanced at it for a few minutes — you're going to want to start trying different beers. And one of the great delights of being a beer drinker today is that a tremendous choice of beers is available. In this appendix, I list a number of beers by style, gravity, and alcohol content.

A Sampling of Beer Styles

The following tables include some suggested beers for you to try, by style. The last column in each of these tables lists (whenever possible) a European or Canadian brand name (an import in the United States) and/or a U.S. brand name (a U.S. domestic), with the country or state of origin.

The really driven among you may even want to photocopy these tables and work your way through them, one beer at a time. You'll be the darling of the beer store if you do. Don't worry if you can't get the specific brand noted here — each one is just one of many suggestions that could have been made. Happy beer exploring!

Table A-1		Ales
Style	*Substyle*	*Brand Names*
Barleywine		Young's Old Nick (England); Sierra Nevada Bigfoot Barleywine (California)
Belgian Beer	Belgian Pale Ale	Chimay (Belgium); Ommegang Rare Vos (New York)
	Belgian Strong Ale	Duvel (Belgium); Great Divide Hades Ale (Colorado)
	Bière de Garde	Jenlain (France); Lost Abbey Avant Garde (California)
	Faro	Lindemans (Belgium)
	Flanders Brown Ale	Corsendonk (Belgium)
	Flanders Red Ale	Rodenbach (Belgium); New Belgium La Folie (Colorado)
	Gueuze	Lindeman's Gueuze Cuvée René (Belgium)
	Lambic (fruited)	Boon Kriek/Framboise (Belgium)
	Saison	DuPont (Belgium); Funkwerks Belgian Resistance (Colorado)
	Trappist Dubbel	Affligem (Belgium); Lost Abbey Lost & Found (California)
	Trappist Tripel	La Trappe (Belgium); Victory Golden Monkey (Pennsylvania)
	Trappist Quadrupel	St. Bernardus Abt 12 (Belgium); Russian River Salvation (California)
	Witbier	Hoegaarden (Belgium); Allagash White (Maine)
Bitter	Ordinary Bitter	Tetley's (England)
	Special Bitter	Fuller's London Pride (England); Hale's Special Bitter (Washington)
	Extra Special Bitter (ESB)	Fuller's ESB (England); Anderson Valley Boont ESB (California)
Brown Ale	English Brown Ale	Samuel Smith Nut Brown Ale (England); Lost Coast Downtown Brown (California)
	American Brown Ale	Brooklyn Brown Ale (New York)
Pale Ale	Classic Pale Ale	Bass (England); D.L. Geary's (Maine)
	American Pale Ale	Sierra Nevada Pale Ale (California)

Style	Substyle	Brand Names
	India Pale Ale (IPA)	Eldridge Pope Royal Oak (England); Stone IPA (California)
	Double/Imperial IPA	Russian River Pliny the Elder (California)
Porter	Brown Porter	Samuel Smith's Taddy Porter (England); Wasatch Polygamy Porter (Utah)
	Robust Porter	Meantime London Porter (England); Great Lakes Edmund Fitzgerald Porter (Ohio)
	Baltic Porter	Sinebrychoff Porter (Finland); Southampton Imperial Baltic Porter (New York)
Stout	Dry (Irish style)	Guinness Extra Stout (Ireland); Rogue Shakespeare Stout (Oregon)
	Sweet (London style)	Mackeson XXX (England); Left Hand Milk Stout (Colorado)
	Oatmeal	McAuslan St. Ambroise Oatmeal Stout (Canada); New Holland The Poet Oatmeal Stout (Michigan)
	Russian Imperial	Samuel Smith's Imperial Stout (England); North Coast Old Rasputin Russian Imperial Stout (California)
	Foreign	Dragon Stout (Jamaica, England); Elysian Dragonstooth Stout (Washington)
Strong Ale	English Old Ale	Old Peculier (England); Geary'Hampshire Special Ale (Maine)
	Scotch Ale	MacAndrew's Scotch Ale (Scotland); Samuel Adams Wee Heavy (Massachusetts)
Wheat Beer	American Wheat	Bell's Oberon (Michigan)
	Berliner Weisse	Berliner Kindl Weisse (Germany)
	Dunkelweizen	Hopf. Dunkel Weisse (Germany); Sprecher Dunkel Weizen (Wisconsin)
	Hefeweizen	Franziskaner (Germany); Odell Easy Street Wheat (Colorado)
	Weizenbock	Schneider Aventinus (Germany); Capitol Weizen Doppelbock (Wisconsin)

Table A-2	Lagers	
Style	*Substyle*	*Brand Names*
American Lager	American Pale Lager	Leinenkugel's (Wisconsin)
	American Dark Lager	Spoetzl Shiner Bock (Texas)
Bock	Traditional Bock	Spaten (Germany); Tröegs Troegenator (Pennsylvania)
	Doppelbock	Paulaner Salvator (Germany); Sun King Dominator (Indiana)
	Helles Bock	Scheidmantel Silber (Germany); Gordon Biersch Blonde Bock (California)
	Maibock	Ayinger Maibock (Germany); Sprecher Maibock (Wisconsin)
	Eisbock	E.K.U. Kulminator Urtyp Hell 28 (Germany); Capital Eisphyre (Wisconsin)
German Dark Lager	Munich Dunkel	Altbayerische Dunkles (Germany); Triumph Dark Lager (Pennsylvania)
	Schwarzbier	Köstritzer (Germany); Sprecher Black Bavarian (Wisconsin)
German Pale Lager	Dortmunder	DAB (Germany); Berghoff (Wisconsin)
	Munich Helles	Spaten (Germany); Capital Garten Brau Lager (Wisconsin)
Märzenbier/Oktoberfest		Paulaner Oktoberfest Märzen (Germany); Victory Festbier (Pennsylvania)
Pilsner	Bohemian Pilsner	Pilsner Urquell (Czechoslovakia); Hübsch Pilsner (California)

Style	Substyle	Brand Names
	German Pils	Bitburger Pils (Germany); Victory Prima Pils (Pennsylvania)
Rauchbier (German Smoked Lager Beer)		Aecht Schlenkerla (Germany)
Vienna Lager		Gösser (Austria); Great Lakes Eliot Ness (Ohio)

Table A-3	Hybrid Beers
Style	**Brand Names**
Altbier	Pinkus Alt (Germany); Alaskan Amber (Alaska)
California Common Beer (Steam Beer)	Maisel's Dampfbier (Germany); Anchor Steam (California)
Cream Ale	New Glarus Spotted Cow (Wisconsin)
Kölsch	Küppers Kölsch (Germany); St. Arnold Fancy Lawnmower Beer (Texas)

Table A-4	Specialty Beers
Style	**Brand Names**
Fruit	Wells Banana Bread Beer (England); New Glarus Belgian Red (Wisconsin)
Herb and Spice	Hoegaarden Wit (Belgium); Good JuJu Ginger Beer (Colorado)
Oak-Aged Beer	Samuel Smith's Stingo (England); Goose Island Bourbon County Stout (Illinois)
Roggenbier (Rye Beer)	Paulaner Roggen (Germany); Bear Republic Roggenbier (California)
Smoked	Adelscott (France); Alaskan Smoked Porter (Alaska)
Wassail	Anchor Our Special Ale (California)

Gravity and Alcohol Content of Various Beer Styles

Until 1994, brewers in the United States were prevented by law from showing the alcohol content of their beer on labels, leaving consumers in the dark. But *strength* — as indicated by percentage of alcohol by volume, as well as the original gravity — is largely dictated by the recipe for each style of beer, so the figures can be made available to you even if they're not found on labels. The following tables show general parameters for both gravity and strength; keep in mind that these figures may vary from brewer to brewer even for the same style. Only some of the more common styles are listed.

Although this information may not be essential, as you become more interested in beer, you'll find yourself needing more information, if not out of curiosity, then out of need for means of comparison and description. Many reviewers cite these figures, and some labels list the gravity (sometimes it acts as a code where *high gravity* translates as strong). So having these numbers helps.

Beer *gravity* is basically the density of the brew, as measured by a hydrometer. Specific gravity figures are based on ordinary water at 60 degrees Fahrenheit (15 degrees Celsius), which has a specific gravity of 1.000.

The tables also indicate *degrees Plato* (the parenthetic number in the second column), which is another way of measuring gravity. The Balling scale on triple-scale hydrometers measures in degrees Plato. A beer with an original gravity of 1.048, for example, has a density of 12.5 degrees Plato.

Alcohol content is indicated both by volume and by weight (weight is the number in parentheses).

Source: *American Homebrewers Association and Beer Judge Certification Program (BJCP) 2008 Style Guidelines*

Ales

Table A-5	American-Style Ale	
Style	*Original Gravity (Degrees Plato)*	*Alcohol Content by Volume (Weight)*
American Pale Ale	1.044–1.056 (11–14)	4.5–5.5 (3.5–4.2)
Barleywine	1.090–1.120 (22.5–29)	8.5–12 (6.7–9.6)

Table A-6	Belgian and French Ales	
Style	*Original Gravity (Degrees Plato)*	*Alcohol Content by Volume (Weight)*
Belgian Ale	1.044–1.054 (11–14)	4–6.2 (3.2–4.9)
Belgian Strong Ale	1.064–1.096 (16.5–24)	7–11 (5.5–8.6)
Bière de Garde	1.060–1.080 (16–20)	4.5–8 (3.5–6.3)
Flanders Brown/Red	1.044–1.056 (11–14.5)	4.8–5.2 (3.8–4.1)
Saison	1.044–1.080 (13–20)	4–7.5 (3.2–6)
Trappist Dubbel	1.050–1.070 (12.5–17.5)	6–7.5 (4.7–5.9)
Trappist Quadrupel	1.075–1.110 (19–27.5)	8–11 (6.5–9.0)
Trappist Tripel	1.060–1.096 (16–24)	7–10 (5.5–7.9)
Witbier	1.044–1.050 (11–13)	4.8–5.2 (3.8–4.1)

Table A-7	Belgian-Style Lambic	
Style	*Original Gravity (Degrees Plato)*	*Alcohol Content by Volume (Weight)*
Belgian Faro	1.044–1.056 (10–14.5)	5–6 (4–5)
Belgian Fruit Lambic	1.040–1.072 (10–18.5)	5–7 (4–6)
Belgian Gueuze	1.044–1.056 (11–14)	5–6 (4–5)

Table A-8	Brown Ale	
Style	*Original Gravity (Degrees Plato)*	*Alcohol Content by Volume (Weight)*
American Brown	1.040–1.055 (10–14)	4–5.9 (3.3–4.9)
English Brown	1.040–1.050 (10–13)	4–5.5 (3.3–4.7)
Mild	1.030–1.038 (7.5–9.5)	3.2–4 (2.7–3.2)

Table A-9	English-Style Pale Ale	
Style	*Original Gravity (Degrees Plato)*	*Alcohol Content by Volume (Weight)*
Classic English Pale Ale	1.044–1.056 (11–14)	4.5–5.5 (3.5–4.2)
Double/Imperial IPA	1.070–1.090 (17.5–22.5)	7.5–10 (5.9–7.9)
India Pale Ale (IPA)	1.050–1.070 (12.5–17.5)	5–7.5 (4–6)

Table A-10	English Bitter	
Style	*Original Gravity (Degrees Plato)*	*Alcohol Content by Volume (Weight)*
Extra Special Bitter (ESB)	1.046–1.060 (11.5–15)	4.5–5.8 (3.8–4.6)
Ordinary Bitter	1.033–1.038 (8–9.5)	3–3.7 (2.4–3)
Special Bitter	1.038–1.045 (9.5–11)	4–4.8 (3.3–3.8)

Table A-11	Porter	
Style	*Original Gravity (Degrees Plato)*	*Alcohol Content by Volume (Weight)*
Baltic Porter	1.060–1.090 (16–22)	5.5–9.5 (4.4–7.6)
Brown Porter	1.044–1.050 (11.5–13)	4–4.5 (3.2–3.6)
Robust Porter	1.050–1.060 (13–15.5)	4.8–5.8 (3.8–4.6)

Table A-12	English and Scottish Strong Ales	
Style	*Original Gravity (Degrees Plato)*	*Alcohol Content by Volume (Weight)*
Barleywine	1.080–1.120 (21–29)	8–12 (6.4–9.6)
Old Ale	1.055–1.075 (14–19)	6–8 (4.8–6.4)
Scotch Ale	1.072–1.085 (18–21.5)	6.2–8 (5.2–6.7)

Table A-13	Stout	
Style	*Original Gravity (Degrees Plato)*	*Alcohol Content by Volume (Weight)*
Dry (Irish)	1.038–1.048 (9.5–12)	3.8–5 (3.2–4.2)
Foreign style	1.052–1.072 (13–18)	6–7.5 (4–8.6)
Oatmeal	1.052–1.072 (13–18)	6–7.5 (4–8.6)
Russian Imperial	1.075–1.090 (19–22.5)	7–9 (5–7.2)
Sweet (London)	1.044–1.056 (11–14)	3–6 (2.5–5)

Table A-14	German Wheat Beer	
Style	*Original Gravity (Degrees Plato)*	*Alcohol Content by Volume (Weight)*
American Wheat Beer	1.030–1.050 (9.5–12.5)	3.5–4.5 (2.8–3.6)
Berliner Weisse	1.028–1.032 (7–8)	2.8–3.4 (2.2–2.7)
Dunkelweizen	1.046–1.056 (11.5–14)	4.8–5.4 (3.8–4.3)
Weizen (includes Hefeweizen)	1.046–1.056 (11.5–14)	4.9–5.5 (3.9–4.4)
Weizenbock	1.066–1.080 (16–20)	6.9–9.3 (5.5–7.5)

Lagers

Table A-15	Bock	
Style	*Original Gravity (Degrees Plato)*	*Alcohol Content by Volume (Weight)*
Doppelbock	1.074–1.080 (18.5–20)	6.5–8 (5.2–6.2)
Eisbock	1.092–1.116 (23–29)	8.6–14.4 (6.8–11.3)
Helles Bock	1.066–1.068 (17–17.5)	6–7 (5–5.8)
Maibock	1.066–1.068 (17–17.5)	6–7 (5–5.8)
Traditional Bock	1.066–1.074 (17–19)	6–7.5 (5–6)

Table A-16	German Dark Lager	
Style	*Original Gravity (Degrees Plato)*	*Alcohol Content by Volume (Weight)*
Munich Dunkel	1.052–1.056 (13–14)	4.5–5 (3.8–4.2)
Schwarzbier	1.044–1.052 (11–13)	3.8–5 (3–3.9)

Table A-17	German Pale Lager	
Style	*Original Gravity (Degrees Plato)*	*Alcohol Content by Volume (Weight)*
Dortmunder	1.048–1.056 (12–14)	5–6 (4–4.8)
Munich Helles	1.044–1.050 (11–13)	4.5–5 (3.8–4.4)

Table A-18	Classic Pilsner	
Style	*Original Gravity (Degrees Plato)*	*Alcohol Content by Volume (Weight)*
Bohemian Pilsner	1.044–1.056 (11–14)	4–5 (3.6–4.2)
German Pils	1.044–1.050 (11–12.5)	4–5 (3.6–4.2)

Table A-19	American Lager	
Style	*Original Gravity (Degrees Plato)*	*Alcohol Content by Volume (Weight)*
Light (diet) Lager	1.024–1.040 (6–10)	3.5–4.4 (2.8–3.5)
Dark Lager	1.040–1.050 (10–13)	4–5.5 (3.2–4.5)
Premium Lager	1.046–1.050 (11.5–13)	4.3–5 (3.6–4)
Standard Lager	1.040–1.046 (10–11.5)	3.8–4.5 (3.2–3.8)

Table A-20	Märzenbier/Oktoberfest, Rauchbier, Vienna Lager	
Style	*Original Gravity (Degrees Plato)*	*Alcohol Content by Volume (Weight)*
Märzenbier/Oktoberfest	1.050–1.056 (13–14.5)	5.3–5.9 (4–4.7)
Rauchbier	1.048–1.052 (12–13)	4.3–4.8 (3.6–4)
Vienna Lager	1.048–1.056 (12–14)	4.8–5.4 (3.8–4.3)

Hybrid beers and specialty beers

Table A-21	Hybrid Beers	
Style	*Original Gravity (Degrees Plato)*	*Alcohol Content by Volume (Weight)*
Altbier	1.044–1.048 (11–12)	4.3–5 (3.6–4)
California Common Beer	1.040–1.055 (10–14)	3.6–5 (2.8–3.9)
Cream Ale	1.044–1.056 (11–14)	4.2–5.6 (3.4–4.5)
Kölsch	1.042–1.046 (10.5–11.5)	4.4–5 (3.8–4.1)

Table A-22	Specialty Beers	
Style	*Original Gravity (Degrees Plato)*	*Alcohol Content by Volume (Weight)*
Fruit/Vegetable Beer	1.030–1.110 (7.5–27.5)	2.5–12 (2–9.5)
Herb and Spice Beer	1.030–1.110 (7.5–27.5)	2.5–12 (2–9.5)
Smoked Beer	Refer to individual classic styles	
Wassail	No standard	No standard

Appendix B

A Short History of Beer (For the True Beer Nut)

· ·

*B*eer history goes back beyond recorded history. Beer has been speculated to be the oldest alcoholic beverage known. It's been through many, many incarnations and has been both revered and reviled. (Fortunately, a craft beer renaissance is currently going on, meaning that now is one of the revering times.)

Some significant events throughout the course of history have been inspired by (or at least have involved) this magical, fabulous brew. This little review of beer through the millennia is dedicated to all you beer nuts who never liked history in grammar school.

Beer at the Dawn of Civilization and throughout World History

According to Dr. Solomon Katz, a professor of anthropology at the University of Pennsylvania, the realization that grain could be used to make beer (and bread) was what provided the motivation for the major transition from hunting and gathering to agriculture.

As hunter-gatherers, these Neolithic tribes were very nomadic, always in search of their daily sustenance. In order to grow crops, however, they had to give up their nomadic ways and remain in one place.

In becoming stationary, primitive people established communes. Eventually, commerce took place between these communes. The communes prospered and attracted more inhabitants to become towns, and the paths that linked these towns became roads, leading to more inhabitants.

Crude though it may have been, beer was an important source of nutrients in the diet of early hominids. This same grain that was used in the baking of bread was made more nutritious after undergoing the beer-making process, in which the starchy insides of the kernel were transformed into proteins and soluble sugars not otherwise available. Smart folks, those cave people!

Ancient races — Africans, Assyrians, Babylonians, Chinese, Egyptians, Hebrews, Incas, Saxons, Teutons, and various wandering tribes throughout Eurasia — all made a rough form of beer. Wherever cereal grains could be grown, beer could be made. In Africa, beer was made with millet and sorghum; in the Middle East, with wheat and barley; in Asia, with rice; and in the Americas, with corn.

From its discovery to the present, beer has been used in religious rituals, depicted on coins, and honored in epic sagas. Here are some interesting tidbits about global beer history through the ages:

- Babylonian clay tablets more than 6,000 years old depict the brewing of beer and give detailed recipes.

- A 3,000-year-old Egyptian clay tablet shows that beer was believed to have been invented by the gods. Beer gods and goddesses, deities of high rank and honor, received regular praise and offerings in ancient Babylon, Sumeria, and Mesopotamia. These spiritual beings wielded power and authority over the sun, the rain, and the soil — all things necessary to provide a bountiful harvest of grain.

- The world's oldest narrative tale, the 5,000-year-old Epic of Gilgamesh, tells us that "he drank seven goblets of beer and his spirit loosened. He became hilarious. His heart gladdened and his face shone." Those ancient Mesopotamians really knew how to party, man.

- A 4,500-year-old tablet covered with hieroglyphics that was discovered in Egypt contains a beer recipe in the form of a love poem to the Sumerian beer goddess, Ninkasi. (A few California brewers attempted to brew from it, with some interpretation, but the word is that recipes and techniques have improved somewhat since ancient times.)

- Archaeological excavations at Ninevah (the ancient capital of Assyria, in modern-day Iraq) uncovered clay tablets that listed beer among the food items taken aboard the ark by Noah. (This begs the question: Did he bring *two* six-packs?)

- In Pharaoh's Egypt, beer was often used as a form of liquid currency. Tax debts were paid with jugs of beer; the king's laborers were paid with daily stipends of beer. According to an Egyptian saying in the time of the Pharaohs, "Happy is the man whose mouth is filled with beer."

- An Egyptian papyrus from the third century BC describes the making of a strong beer called *Zythum,* which was flavored with juniper berries, ginger, cumin, saffron, and other herbs. Additionally, directions were included for making a stronger Dizythum, a palace variety called Carmi, and a mild family beer called Busa.

✔ Beer was believed to have medicinal properties. One Sumerian clay tablet contains a prescription that specifically calls for beer in the healing process, and in a medicinal text from 1600 BC, 100 of the 700 prescriptions contain beer. These medicinal applications run the gamut from a laxative to a cure for scorpion stings. Placing half an onion in beer froth was considered a remedy against death (but consuming the two together is tantamount to death).

✔ Venetian traveler Marco Polo wrote about Chinese beer, and an ancient Chinese manuscript states that beer, or *Kiu,* was known to the Chinese as early as the second or third century BC.

✔ So highly did early Europeans regard beer that Norse legends promised outstanding warriors the ultimate reward in the afterlife: a brimming ale horn. The typical Norse ale horns bore *ale runes,* inscriptions to ward against poisons. Norse ales were often served with garlic in them to ward off all evils (thus creating a new one, no?).

✔ Hops have been used in beer making since the eighth century, in central Europe, replacing other flowers, leaves, berries, spices, and odd items used to bitter the beer. Hops weren't widely accepted, though, until the 1500s.

In 15th-century England, ale brewers were just beginning to use hops in the beer-making process. Ale drinkers made a clear distinction between brewers who steadfastly refused to use hops and those who used them, and so fervently opposed to hop usage were many ale drinkers that in 1436, the king had to issue a writ to the sheriffs of London, ordering them to protect the brewers of hopping beer against acts of violence.

✔ With the rise of commerce and the growth of cities during the Middle Ages, brewing became more than a household activity. Municipal brew-houses were established, which eventually led to the formation of the brewing guilds. Commercial brewing on a significantly larger scale began around the 12th century in Germany. By the late 1300s, beer was well established as the national drink of England. Its refreshing qualities were enjoyed by both common folk and nobility.

✔ According to city records, commercial brewing in Plzen and Budweis dates back to the 1200s. By the 1500s, the Budweis brewery was sup-plying beer to the Royal Bohemian Court, thus giving foundation to its motto *Beer of Kings*.

✔ In 1502, Christopher Columbus discovered something more important than America: Native American beer, made from corn and tree sap. He's said to have hoisted a few with the locals.

✔ Lager beer swept Europe like a plague in the mid-1800s, albeit a welcome one. This new style of beer was lighter in color and body than ale and, thanks to the aging process, mellower. Eons of ale-drinking traditions gave way to the new and improved beer with the smooth, drinkable nature. Only the British Isles and Belgium resisted, though their resis-tance has softened in recent years.

Beer History in the United States

Beer has been a part of North American history since before its "discovery" by Christopher Columbus or Leif Ericson. Native peoples made a crude form of beer by using corn, which was already a staple in their diet. But along with the ensuing hordes of European explorers and colonists came the knowledge and ability to brew real beer — as well as thirsts equal to the task.

Colonial times through the 1800s

The first beer brewed by American colonists was at Sir Walter Raleigh's Roanoke colony in 1587. The beer must not have been very good, though, because Colonists continued to request shipments of beer from England. (Unfortunately, most of the ships' consignments of beer were drunk on the transatlantic crossing by thirsty sailors.) And in 1609, colonists placed America's first help-wanted ad in a London paper, asking for brewers to come to America.

Rather than continue on to their destination in Virginia, the pilgrims on the *Mayflower* made their landing at Plymouth Rock for lack of beer. A December 19, 1620, entry in the diary of a *Mayflower* passenger tells the story: "We could not now take time for further search or consideration, our victuals being much spent, especially our beere."

Beer was far more healthful than the impure water sources available to American colonists. Dr. Benjamin Rush, a noted physician and a signer of the Declaration of Independence, wrote, "Beer is a wholesome liquor compared with spirits. It abounds with nourishment. . . . While I wish to see a law imposing the heaviest taxes on whiskey distilleries, I should be glad to see breweries wholly exempt from taxation." (Amen!)

Breweries in the New World were among the first businesses established. American breweries preexisted American government; some of the breweries' staunchest supporters were also the leaders of the new nation.

In colonial America, the alehouse was second only to the church in importance. (As Martin Luther once said, "'Tis better to think of church in the alehouse than to think of the alehouse in church.") Aside from being where the brewer plied his trade, the tavern also served as the unofficial town hall and the social and political focal point of every town. It was here that the townsfolk gathered to deliberate and debate, to socialize and share news and information with the community. To the colonists, the alehouses were cradles of liberty; while to the British, the alehouses were hotbeds of sedition. As early as 1768, the Sons of Liberty were holding meetings at the Liberty Tree Tavern in Providence; the Green Dragon Inn in Boston was called the headquarters for the revolution. George Washington made his headquarters at Fraunces

Tavern in New York, where it still stands and serves beer, now in the heart of the financial district.

Most of the early breweries were small, house-based operations. Traditional ingredients, hard to come by in the New World, were often replaced with maize, molasses, bran, persimmons, potatoes, spruce twigs, birch bark, ginger, and allspice.

The first real brewery in the New World was founded in New Amsterdam (New York) in 1633. Boston's first brewery debuted in 1637 and was a favorite among colonial leaders, who believed that beer was a moderate alternative to distilled spirits. The city of Philadelphia got its first brewery in 1685 (but made up for lost time, as Philadelphia has had more breweries in its history than any other U.S. city). This date is confirmed by an entry in the diary of William Penn, who was a brewer himself. Historians have studied Penn's ledgers and concluded that he ran malt and brewhouses at his Pennsbury mansion in Pennsylvania's Bucks County.

Other early politicos liked to brew, too:

- George Washington had his own brewhouse on the grounds of Mount Vernon. His handwritten recipe for beer, dated 1757 in a diary he kept during his days as a Virginia colonel, is still preserved.
- Thomas Jefferson was another homebrewer, at Monticello. He collected all the books he could find on the subject and added them to his extensive library.
- Benjamin Franklin proposed the idea of a national brewery (talk about bloated government!).
- James Madison expressed hope that the brewing industry would "strike deep root in every state in the union."

Early colonists stayed true to the belief that beer was of great importance and an integral part of everyday life. This influence is witnessed in some of the colonial laws:

- Beer, beer bottles, brewers, and beer properties were exempt from taxation.
- Only voters and church members could brew and dispense beer.
- No tapping of beer was allowed during divine services.
- No person without skill and mastery of brewing was allowed to brew beer.
- Beer debts were excluded from court.
- Beer had to be served in standard half-pint, pint, and quart vessels.

> ✔ In 1789, the Massachusetts Legislature passed an act to encourage the manufacture of "strong beer, ale, and other malt liquors. . . . The wholesome qualities of malt liquors greatly recommend them to general use as an important means of preserving health of the citizens of the commonwealth."

> ✔ The price of beer was fixed to be "not more than one penny a quart at most" by the Massachusetts Bay Colony legislature in 1637.

As the United States became an instant magnet for people looking to start a new life, breweries opened as quickly as each ethnic enclave settled. Throughout the 1800s, most of the arrivals came from the *beer belt* countries of northern Europe (Ireland, Germany, Poland, Czechoslovakia, the Netherlands — the majority of brewers were of Irish and German origin), and with them came the knowledge of brewing and an appreciation for the craft.

In 1840, about 140 breweries were operating in the United States, at least 1 in each of the 13 original colonies. Annual output totaled about 200,000 barrels. The American brewing industry boasted as many as 1,400 breweries by 1914 and employed more than 75,000 people.

The Volstead Act

When the United States celebrated its 50th birthday in July 1826, hundreds of breweries were in operation. By the turn of the century, more than a thousand existed. By 1920, though, none produced beer — legally, that is. An industry that was more than two centuries in the making was decimated in less than a decade and a half, thanks to the efforts of the prohibitionist Carry Nation and her like-minded friends in Washington.

The single most destructive force in U.S. brewing history was the Volstead Act — Prohibition — which completely shut down the industry for 13 long years (January 18, 1920, to December 5, 1933). Imagine having to endure the stock market crash of 1929 without a beer to cry in. No wonder they called it a depression!

Prohibition not only ruined a legitimate and successful American industry and put thousands of workers out on the street, but it also gave rise to underworld figures who capitalized on the situation to brew and sell bootleg beer for millions of dollars in ill-gotten profits. In Chicago, more than 700 deaths during Prohibition were attributed to mob-related business.

Another side effect was American Prohibition's transformation of the Mexican siesta town of Tijuana into a beer boom town — a dubious distinction. More than 75 storefront bars operated on a main street only 600 feet in length.

Prohibition was the great experiment that went terribly wrong. According to government statistics, it cost the country more than $34.5 billion in lost tax revenue and enforcement costs. And it didn't work.

Of the breweries that narrowly survived Prohibition to reopen in 1933, most got by on meager income from producing ice, soda pop, near beer, and malt syrups (ostensibly used for baking but often used by clandestine homebrewers) or from brewing illegal beer for the thousands of speakeasies operated by the mob.

Post-Prohibition blues

When brewing beer again became legal, the laws governing its sale and distribution had changed drastically. Prior to Prohibition, the *tied house system,* under which a brewery also owned the local taverns and served its own brands exclusively, provided the larger breweries with an unfair advantage over the smaller ones. Lawmakers sought to break up the tied house system by instituting a *three-tier system,* in which the brewer, the distributor, and the retailer had to be independently owned; not even family members were allowed to own another tier in the system. This change was effective in opening the market to small brewers but later proved to be a major obstacle for the brewpub industry.

Of the 400 or so breweries that reopened following Prohibition, about half never regained the financial ground that had been lost; they eventually shut their doors. Even as new breweries continued to open, most found that the market had changed considerably. Several factors came into play: the introduction of the beer can, World War II, improved shipping methods, television, industry mergers and buyouts, and consumer preferences.

The can comes around

The introduction of the beer can to the consumer market in 1935 helped change the way Americans drank their beer — or at least *where* they drank their beer. Previously, most of the beer consumed in the United States was drunk in draught form, usually at a neighborhood tavern or saloon or carried home in a bucket. It was always fresh. With the convenience of the beer can, Americans began to buy it in stores and in bulk and to drink it at home. Breweries that couldn't afford the expensive equipment necessary to can their beer lost a piece of the pie.

The effects of World War II

World War II had a major impact on the brewing industry for a number of reasons. For starters, a huge chunk of the beer-drinking demographic was off to war. Replacing the young men down at the munitions plant were young women, many of whom didn't drink beer or only drank the lightest stuff available — which was just as well, as a general conservation effort was going on and brewing ingredients were in short supply. The men stationed at U.S. military bases were all drinking the only beer available down at the PX, one that was contract-brewed for the government. Ironically, while stateside military personnel were all forced to drink the government-issue beer, troops stationed in Europe brought home a taste for western European brews.

Gravy train: Improved shipping methods

Immediately following World War II, and for many years beyond, over-the-road and rail transportation systems were greatly improved. In addition to greater access and higher speeds, refrigerated trucks and rail cars were a boon to the industry. Big breweries could ship their beer much farther, much faster, with limited adverse effect on the beer. The new interstate highway system introduced in the 1950s only made things better for the big guys.

Boob tube: The impact of television

Television, believed to be a vast wasteland when it was first introduced, is at least partly to blame for creating a wasteland in the American brewing industry. TV proved to be an invaluable medium for large, high-resource breweries looking to capture a greater share of the marketing pie. In raising advertising competition to a new level, TV helped create the concept of national-brand beers and galvanize the concept of beer product recognition and brand loyalty.

Lords of the ring (of foam): Brewery mergers and acquisitions

Following the four-hit combination of beer cans, World War II, better shipping methods, and TV, all landed over a 20-year period, many welterweight breweries were either KO'd or were hanging on the ropes and given a standing 8-count. This is when the heavyweights took off the gloves for the finishing blow. Most of the remaining small breweries in the 1960s and 1970s were beaten to a pulp by the brewing titans and became pawns in a high-stake game of mergers and acquisitions. Brewing plants were shut down, and brand names and labels became movable property.

Consumer preferences

Not long after the beer wars of the 1960s and 1970s, the United States was swept into a health and fitness craze. Beer never did rank high on any fitness buff's list of desired foods, so it had to gain acceptance or fall by the wayside. Along came light beer, perhaps the least beer-like product ever made at a brewery, in this author's opinion.

By around 1980, beer drinkers were left with a half-dozen major brewing companies and a couple dozen regionals, producing millions of barrels of very light, very stable, very consistent beer. Interestingly, this style of beer making became a double-edged sword for the industry. Despite megabrewed beer's popularity, beer drinkers began to complain that this level of lightness, stability, and consistency had turned much of the world's beer into a very dull and lifeless product. This pallid mediocrity in the beer marketplace eventually led to the demand for tastier beer and the U.S. beer renaissance.

The Contemporary Beer Renaissance in the United States

Demand for a well-made, interesting, classic product is always high. Americans not only expect choices but demand them. In the world of cars, for example, many people began choosing Toyotas, Volvos, and BMWs, even with their inflated sticker prices, over bland American-made cars, and this clamoring for better quality and selection was noticed by some American entrepreneurial spirits, who then created American-made cars that met the standards of cars made elsewhere. Similar circumstances precipitated the birth of micro and craft breweries. Consumer backlash against light beer, the dull product of the late 1970s and early 1980s, fueled the current U.S. beer renaissance (other factors also contributed, of course).

Throughout the course of events in the U.S. brewing saga, the phenomenon of *mystique beers* — however few there were, coming from a small number of regional breweries — has held strong. Mystique beers are those with a limited distribution area and are often believed to be better than they really are by those who can't get them. Some beer lovers have gone as far as bootlegging these beers across state lines to share with family or friends (or to hoard for themselves). I remember how friends were willing to drive all the way to Iowa to buy Coors or into Wisconsin's hinterlands to get their hands on some Point Beer (the gas to get there cost more than the beer).

The notion that these beers were somehow better than the products on the shelves of the local liquor store helped pave the way for the great influx of imported beer. Foreign brewers anxious to cash in on America's beer-drinking habits managed to stoke the fires of consumer backlash in the late 1970s. The effects were almost immediate and eventually profound. Several high-profile brands, such as Heineken, Beck's, and Corona, experienced a meteoric rise in popularity that prompted a quick reaction by foreign brewers and importers everywhere. Soon, the market was flooded with foreign beer. The belief was that any beer in a green bottle with a foreign label on it would sell. Later on, clear bottles with silk-screened labels were all the rage.

At about the same time, many disillusioned beer lovers took to brewing their favorite beers right in their own kitchens. Brewing beer at home, though it became quasi legal in 1979, was still considered a clandestine hobby. In time, though, the craft grew, clubs and associations formed, information was shared, and homebrewing came out of the closet. So far out of the closet, in fact, that many novice brewers made the leap to professional brewing.

The people who made the leap from brewing in their homes to brewing professionally became the pioneers of the microbrewing industry. Like trails in the Old West, the road to small-brewing success was rough and rocky. Two major pitfalls stunted the early growth:

- **The three-tier system of distribution:** Laws dating back to the end of Prohibition stipulated that the brewer, the distributor, and the retailer had to be independently owned. Opening a small brewery or brewpub in most states guaranteed a fair amount of legal jousting.

- **The average beer drinker's lack of understanding and appreciation of craft brewing:** Without the consumer's elementary understanding of beer and its many examples of style, the small brewer couldn't profitably produce a wide range of flavorful lagers and ales.

Most of the earliest microbrewers hailed from the West Coast, already noted for its trend-setting ideas. Northern California, Oregon, and Washington — especially Portland and Seattle — have been on the cutting edge of this movement since its inception.

In 1977, the first of what later came to be known as microbreweries opened in Sonoma, California. Though the New Albion Brewing Company managed to survive for only five years, it fired the first salvo in the war against mass-marketed beer. Following closely on New Albion's heels were the DeBakker Brewing Company (1979) in California and the Boulder Brewery (1980) in Colorado. Later in 1980, Cartwright Brewing opened in Oregon. In 1981, the Sierra Nevada Brewing Company in California began brewing high-quality ales and hasn't looked back since; along with Boulder, Sierra Nevada is the only one of these pioneering brewers still operating.

Soon thereafter, the idea caught on in the East and, finally, in the Midwest. With the notable exceptions of Florida and Texas, the southern states had been slow to jump on the beerwagon and are still playing catch-up. In the beginning, for obvious reasons, the movement gravitated toward the larger cities, but these days, microbrewers and pub brewers have found a home in rural America.

Today, many of the prohibitive distribution laws have been altered to allow for self-distribution, which can make for considerably easier startup. Where cash investment for such an undertaking was initially scarce, investors were practically tripping over each other trying to throw money at small brewers in need of capital. Many microbrewers have even gone public, offering shares of stock in the company in exchange for investment money, and are doing very nicely, thank you.

Even the well-established brewing industries in western European countries have begun to sit up and take notice of the beer revolution taking place in the United States. The tail is wagging the dog, for sure, as the big commercial brewers are beginning to bring more flavorful beers to market, beer brewed with a nod to tradition.

Index

• C •

• K •

• N •

• O •

Oregon Brewers Festival, 297
organic beer
  celebrating, 97
  certifications, 94–95
  GMOs (genetically modified organisms), 94
  levels of, 94–95
  organic hops, 98
  origins of, 93–94
  sampling of, 96–97
  USDA standards, 94–96
Oud Bruin/Flanders Brown Ale, described, 50
ounce, measures and conversions, 175
oxidation
  avoiding, 118
  checking, 76–77
  detecting, 118
  occurrence of, 109

• P •

Pabst Brewing Company, 191
The Pabst Mansion beer museum, 208
packaging process, 32
Pale Ale, described, 49, 52, 151
Pale Lager
  color, 151
  cooking with, 172
  varieties, 56
pasteurization
  flash, 32
  tunnel, 32
pectinase fining, described, 65
The PedalPub, bike tours, 245–246
pediococcus microbe, use in Sour Beers, 79
percarbonates, using to clean equipment, 257
Philadelphia, Pennsylvania, 293–294
PhillyCraft
  beer ratings, 280
  online forum, 160
Pilsner beer, 23
  color, 151
  described, 55
  glass, 137
  source of, 225
pin cask, described, 63
PINT beer consumer group, 285
pint beer glass, drinking from, 137
plastic hose, using, 252
plimsoll line, explained, 140
Poland, requesting beer in, 230
pony beer glass, drinking from, 137
Porter Ale, 43, 49, 52
  alcohol content, 310
  color, 151

gravity, 310
  naming of, 53
Portland, Oregon, 291
Portland Brew Bus, 243
Potosi Brewing Company beer museum, 208
pound, equivalent for kilogram, 175
pouring
  American Pale Lager, 144
  beer, 142–144
  bottle-conditioned beer, 144
  breathing, 148
  corked-bottle beer, 143
  listening to, 148
  Wheat Beer, 143
Prague, Czech Republic, 289–290
preservatives, including on labels, 122–123
Prohibition, period of, 120, 320–321
Pub Heritage Group, 70
Pub Peddler Brewery Tour, 244
Publicans Chicken, 183–184
pubs, obtaining listing of, 210
pumps and hoses, using for brewing, 27
puncheon cask, described, 63
PVPP (polyvinylpolypyrrolidone) fining, described, 65

• Q •

Quadrupels, origins of, 85
quality-control analysis
  ale-conner, 125
  bierkiesers, 125
  Chief Beer Inspector, 125

• R •

RateBeer
  beer ratings, 280
  online forum, 160
Rauchbier Lager, described, 55–56, 213
real ale. See also ale
  adding finings to, 64–65
  allowing to breathe, 65–66
  CAMRA (Campaign for Real Ale), 69–70
  Cask Marque, 60
  casks, 61–62
  consuming, 66, 68
  defining, 59–60
  dispensing, 66–68
  head pressure, 59–60
  packaging, 60
  putting through beer engines, 66
  using tap for gravity dispense, 68

Apple & Macs

iPad For Dummies
978-0-470-58027-1

iPhone For Dummies,
4th Edition
978-0-470-87870-5

MacBook For Dummies, 3rd
Edition
978-0-470-76918-8

Mac OS X Snow Leopard For
Dummies
978-0-470-43543-4

Business

Bookkeeping For Dummies
978-0-7645-9848-7

Job Interviews
For Dummies,
3rd Edition
978-0-470-17748-8

Resumes For Dummies,
5th Edition
978-0-470-08037-5

Starting an
Online Business
For Dummies,
6th Edition
978-0-470-60210-2

Stock Investing
For Dummies,
3rd Edition
978-0-470-40114-9

Successful
Time Management
For Dummies
978-0-470-29034-7

Computer Hardware

BlackBerry
For Dummies,
4th Edition
978-0-470-60700-8

Computers For Seniors
For Dummies,
2nd Edition
978-0-470-53483-0

PCs For Dummies,
Windows
7 Edition
978-0-470-46542-4

Laptops For Dummies,
4th Edition
978-0-470-57829-2

Cooking & Entertaining

Cooking Basics
For Dummies,
3rd Edition
978-0-7645-7206-7

Wine For Dummies,
4th Edition
978-0-470-04579-4

Diet & Nutrition

Dieting For Dummies,
2nd Edition
978-0-7645-4149-0

Nutrition For Dummies,
4th Edition
978-0-471-79868-2

Weight Training
For Dummies,
3rd Edition
978-0-471-76845-6

Digital Photography

Digital SLR Cameras &
Photography For Dummies,
3rd Edition
978-0-470-46606-3

Photoshop Elements 8
For Dummies
978-0-470-52967-6

Gardening

Gardening Basics
For Dummies
978-0-470-03749-2

Organic Gardening
For Dummies,
2nd Edition
978-0-470-43067-5

Green/Sustainable

Raising Chickens
For Dummies
978-0-470-46544-8

Green Cleaning
For Dummies
978-0-470-39106-8

Health

Diabetes For Dummies,
3rd Edition
978-0-470-27086-8

Food Allergies
For Dummies
978-0-470-09584-3

Living Gluten-Free
For Dummies,
2nd Edition
978-0-470-58589-4

Hobbies/General

Chess For Dummies,
2nd Edition
978-0-7645-8404-6

Drawing
Cartoons & Comics
For Dummies
978-0-470-42683-8

Knitting For Dummies,
2nd Edition
978-0-470-28747-7

Organizing
For Dummies
978-0-7645-5300-4

Su Doku For Dummies
978-0-470-01892-7

Home Improvement

Home Maintenance
For Dummies,
2nd Edition
978-0-470-43063-7

Home Theater
For Dummies,
3rd Edition
978-0-470-41189-6

Living the
Country Lifestyle
All-in-One
For Dummies
978-0-470-43061-3

Solar Power Your Home
For Dummies,
2nd Edition
978-0-470-59678-4

Internet

Blogging For Dummies,
3rd Edition
978-0-470-61996-4

eBay For Dummies,
6th Edition
978-0-470-49741-8

Facebook For Dummies,
3rd Edition
978-0-470-87804-0

Web Marketing
For Dummies,
2nd Edition
978-0-470-37181-7

WordPress
For Dummies,
3rd Edition
978-0-470-59274-8

Language & Foreign Language

French For Dummies
978-0-7645-5193-2

Italian Phrases
For Dummies
978-0-7645-7203-6

Spanish For Dummies,
2nd Edition
978-0-470-87855-2

Spanish
For Dummies,
Audio Set
978-0-470-09585-0

Math & Science

Algebra I
For Dummies,
2nd Edition
978-0-470-55964-2

Biology For Dummies,
2nd Edition
978-0-470-59875-7

Calculus For Dummies
978-0-7645-2498-1

Chemistry For Dummies
978-0-7645-5430-8

Microsoft Office

Excel 2010 For Dummies
978-0-470-48953-6

Office 2010 All-in-One
For Dummies
978-0-470-49748-7

Office 2010 For Dummies,
Book + DVD Bundle
978-0-470-62698-6

Word 2010 For Dummies
978-0-470-48772-3

Music

Guitar For Dummies,
2nd Edition
978-0-7645-9904-0

iPod & iTunes For
Dummies, 8th Edition
978-0-470-87871-2

Piano Exercises
For Dummies
978-0-470-38765-8

Parenting & Education

Parenting For Dummies,
2nd Edition
978-0-7645-5418-6

Type 1 Diabetes
For Dummies
978-0-470-17811-9

Pets

Cats For Dummies,
2nd Edition
978-0-7645-5275-5

Dog Training For Dummies,
3rd Edition
978-0-470-60029-0

Puppies For Dummies,
2nd Edition
978-0-470-03717-1

Religion & Inspiration

The Bible For Dummies
978-0-7645-5296-0

Catholicism For Dummies
978-0-7645-5391-2

Women in the Bible
For Dummies
978-0-7645-8475-6

Self-Help & Relationship

Anger Management
For Dummies
978-0-470-03715-7

Overcoming Anxiety
For Dummies,
2nd Edition
978-0-470-57441-6

Sports

Baseball
For Dummies,
3rd Edition
978-0-7645-7537-2

Basketball
For Dummies,
2nd Edition
978-0-7645-5248-9

Golf For Dummies,
3rd Edition
978-0-471-76871-5

Web Development

Web Design
All-in-One
For Dummies
978-0-470-41796-6

Web Sites
Do-It-Yourself
For Dummies,
2nd Edition
978-0-470-56520-9

Windows 7

Windows 7
For Dummies
978-0-470-49743-2

Windows 7
For Dummies,
Book + DVD Bundle
978-0-470-52398-8

Windows 7 All-in-One
For Dummies
978-0-470-48763-1

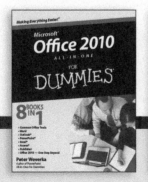

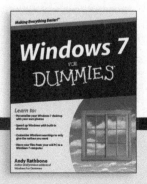

Available wherever books are sold. For more information or to order direct U.S. customers visit www.dummies.com or call 1-877-762-2974
U.K. customers visit www.wileyeurope.com or call (0) 1243 843291. Canad   w.wiley.ca or call 1-800-567-4797.